THE TEMPLE *of* TONE

THE TEMPLE *of* TONE

A DISQUISITION ON THE SCIENTIFIC AND
ARTISTIC TONAL APPOINTMENT AND
CONTROL OF CONCERT-ROOM, CHURCH,
AND THEATER ORGANS,
ACCORDING TO THE ADVANCED SYSTEM OF COMPOUND
TONAL FLEXIBILITY AND EXPRESSION
WITH COMPLETE SPECIFICATIONS

BY

GEORGE ASHDOWN AUDSLEY

AMS PRESS
NEW YORK

Reprinted from the edition of 1925, New York
First AMS EDITION published 1969
Manufactured in the United States of America

Library of Congress Catalog Card Number: 79-108119
SBN: 404-00417-2

AMS PRESS, INC.
New York, N.Y. 10003

CONTENTS

THE TEMPLE *of* TONE

PART FIRST

INTRODUCTORY

EMPLE OF TONE! What better name could be given to the organ, in anticipation of the time when it will possess that perfection of tonal structure which we venture to believe it is destined to display, when old-time methods are swept away, to give place to those dictated by scientific knowledge and artistic ethos; and fostered by refined taste and common-sense? When will the organ appear to which these words can be addressed in very truth?

> Temple of Tone art thou! The shrine supreme
> Of Sound's mysterious powers and richest gifts,
> God-given thought alone could have inspired
> The human mind to frame so grand a work;
> Great Organ—Monarch of all Instruments!

There is much to unlearn, and much to be learnt; and much that has yet to be done, that must be done; before the organ can justly claim the expressive and dignified title we have given it: and it is with the earnest desire to help in the good work, in this direction, that this dissertation has been undertaken.

On matters or details strictly belonging to the formation and purely mechanical equipment of the organ, little shall be said, beyond such as properly belong to the complete command and the efficient control of all the tonal forces of the instrument, operated directly by the hands and feet of the performer, seated at the Console. Of these it is necessary and desirable that full particulars should be given; chiefly because the forces to be commanded and effectively controlled differ considerably in description and disposition from those obtaining in the old-fashioned and commonplace instruments, still considered adequate organs—an opinion we reject as unsupported by facts.

DIFFERENTIATION

Since the appearance of the great Work, "L'Art du Facteur d'Orgues," by François Bédos de Celles, O.S.B., in the years 1766–78, no writer on the Organ in France or Germany seems to have recognized, so far as our knowledge extends, the possibility or desirability of there being more than one system of organ tonal appointment and general treatment—that of the Church Organ. No writer in the English language, prior to the year 1886, has, in any printed form, attempted the Differentiation of the Organ along any systematic and art-directed lines. Even in the Work which, since its publication in 1855, has been considered the English Classic on the Organ; namely, "The Organ," by Edward J. Hopkins, no attempt is made to differentiate. A Church Organ is the only form contemplated—large or small.

Dom Bédos, in his important essay, goes far to describe and ably illustrate the construction and tonal appointment of small organs, so far suitable as he could imagine for French salons and music-rooms. These he treats of in the Fourth Part of his Work. In the stop-apportionments of these instruments he can hardly be said to have aimed at consistent tonal differentiation, for he simply followed the appointments of the small Church Organs of his time. He gives schemes for Concert Organs of twenty-three and forty-five stops; and for Salon Organs of twelve, sixteen, and twenty-three stops; none of which indicate any attempt at tonal differentiation. It is, perhaps, unnecessary to remark that nothing in the nature of a Swell Organ was known in France when Dom Bédos wrote, although it had made its appearance in England forty years before the conclusion of his great Work was published.

It may interest the student of organ-building to know that Dom Bédos describes and fully illustrates two extremely noteworthy instruments, to which he devotes two Chapters; respectively captioned, "Organisation d'un Pianoforté" and "Organisation du Clavecin Ordinaire." To the descriptions of these compound instruments the author devotes ten pages of his Work, and illustrates them in six beautiful Plates. The former instrument was designed and constructed by M. Lepine, of Paris, Organ-builder to the King. It consists of a quadrangular case, about 5 feet long, 2 feet wide, and 3 feet high, which is closed on all sides with paneled shutters. The piano sound-board and strings extend over the entire upper portion; the clavier and its action being located toward the left end, the compass of which is five octaves. Directly under this clavier is that of the organ, of the same compass. Underneath the claviers, and close to the floor, is the wind-chest of the organ, constructed for the reception of two lingual and two labial stops, the lower octaves of the latter, formed of stopped wood pipes, being compactly arranged in three horizontal tiers along the rear side of the case. The bellows, which is small, square, and of several folds, is located toward the right end of the case, and is operated by a foot-lever. The piano action is of the earliest form, the strings being struck by carton or stiff leather rings carried on wooden hammers. The entire arrangement is extremely clever, and was, doubtless, effective.

The "Clavecin" is still more interesting. Its case, in form, resembles that of the harpsichord, but is carried down to the floor, so as to completely inclose the pipe-work of the organ. The sound-board and strings occupy the upper portion of the case. The action comprises two claviers, operating a double set of harpsichord jacks; and under these is the clavier belonging to the organ. Directly under the claviers and close to the floor is placed the small wind-chest, constructed for two lingual and two labial stops, the former being planted thereon, along with the treble pipes of the labial stops; the lower octaves, comprising fifty-one stopped wood pipes, are arranged in four horizontal tiers extending from the wind-chest to the end of the case, the largest pipe being about six feet in length, and speaking the FFF note. The bellows of this instrument is located in a case which forms the player's seat. It is of several folds, and is operated by a lever upon which rests the right foot of the player. A flat wind-trunk extends, close to the floor, from the seat to the wind-chest of the organ. Supposing that the inclosed stops were very artistically voiced on wind of 1½ inches pressure, one can imagine this instrument to have been capable of producing very beautiful compound musical effects. Although the tonal schemes of these instruments are interesting, so far as their organ divisions are concerned, they cannot be well recognized as belonging to any system of differentiation. Four stops, whatever they may be, cannot be accepted to form an organ, in any modern sense of the term, unless, perhaps, as an Ancillary Organ.

In the time of Dom Bédos, Regals and Portatives, having a single lingual stop, were frequently made. He describes and illustrates an instrument of this sort in the form of a table. Instruments of this type cannot be considered organs in any proper signification of the term, and they cannot enter into any system of differentiation. It must be realized that the mere number of stops does not necessarily imply differentiation; for that, properly defined, embraces other equally important conditions, which may be correctly stated to be those which impart to an organ a special tonal structure or appointment, and proper means of tonal control, adapting it to the place it is to occupy, and the office it has to fulfil in the realm of music.

It seems strange that no writer on the organ, prior to the year 1886, attempted to institute a system of differentiation which would properly render Concert-room, Church, and Chamber Organs practically distinct and specially effective instruments of different tonal characters and powers, commensurate with the calls to which they must satisfactorily respond in their respective offices. All the writers on the organ and all organ-builders up to the date named seem to have held only one idea regarding differentiation and that an incorrect one. To them, it had no relation to the all-important matters of tonal character and scope, but solely to the mere matter of size or number of stops. Indeed, it may be correctly said that in all the organs designed and constructed by organ-builders to-day, whatever their class may be, the same blind clinging to the Church Organ type of tonal appointment is to be observed. Yet at no time, since the firm establishment of the art and industry of organ-building, is correct tonal differentiation, and the grasp of its true significance, more urgently called for than at the present day—the greatest period in the industry of organ-building the world has known: and, strange to say, the greatest period of ignorance and inartistic blundering in organ tonal appointment the history of the art can show. Fortunately, however, this blundering is at present confined to certain quarters, in which art is not, and trade considerations reign supreme. There is grave danger, however, that this art-cancer may eat further and deeper into the foundations of the Temple of Tone. The mild medicine of weak protest will fail to stamp out this growing disease. Surgeon organists, furnished with biting caustics, and the sharp knives of musical knowledge and firm assurance are required to root out this destructive complaint, deep seated in ignorance and unscrupulousness.

We may pass over all the French and German writings on the organ subsequent to those of Dom Bédos, for they are absolutely barren of any ideas regarding consistent tonal differentiation. The same may be said of all the books published in England. In the first of these, "The Organ," by Hopkins (Edition of 1870), a Chapter is given, captioned, "Plans for Organs of Various Sizes." This opens with the following seemingly promising words:—

"Some plans or Specifications for organs of various sizes will now be given, which will illustrate the several rules that have been explained in detail in preceding chapters of this book; and will also serve to show by what easy and successive steps an instrument may be gradually developed from a small Chancel or School-room organ into a Cathedral or Town Hall organ, without any of the primary laws of the science being overturned or modified in any way. In their preparation, the schemes of the best English and Foreign organs of old as well as of recent times have been consulted, and their best features embodied, so far as has been found practicable, or seemed to be in accordance with the requirements of a modern English organ. As, however, nearly every organ-builder and organist has his predilection in favour of particular Stops; some of the details of the following Specifications would of course be modified to adapt them to particular tastes."

Notwithstanding what these words seemed to promise, in the remainder of the Chapter of twenty-one closely printed pages, containing twenty lists of stops for instruments ranging from a useless toy of two stops, with a compass of thirty-nine notes, to an organ of ninety stops, with a manual compass of sixty-one and a pedal compass of thirty notes, classed as Positive, Chancel, and Church Organs; all having old-style and common-place schemes, in which size has alone been considered as instituting differentiation. Radical tonal differentiation, from an artistic point of view, adapting organs of different dimensions to the places they have to occupy and the special offices they have to fulfil, seems never to have entered the learned writer's mind; and even the stop-apportionments, given in the principal schemes, are so loose that they are practically left open to the caprice of the organ-builder or the organist. As the Work, in which this Chapter appears, was for many years accepted as the great English *Directorium* in the art of organ-building, it is not difficult to account for the evident ignorance and disregard of the essential principles of tonal differentiation, displayed by conservative organ-builders and careless organists, in scheming organs of different classes and for different uses and places.

The year 1886 has been specially mentioned, because on August 6th of that year was commenced, in the pages of "*The English Mechanic and World of Science*," the first essay, in the extensive literature of the organ, devoted to the true Differentiation of the Concert-room, Church, and Chamber Organs, along proper and clearly marked scientific and artistic tonal and structural lines. The first series, of eight Articles, treats of the tonal appointment and the general construction of the Chamber Organ, as the smallest type of instrument. To show the position taken in the matter of tonal differentiation, the following extract from the first Article may be given:—

"It does not appear to have struck those interested in Chamber Organ building that the church type is the very last one that should be taken as a starting point; and that, if they desire to produce instruments which shall prove thoroughly suitable and interesting for chamber use, they must adopt the model furnished by a properly appointed Concert-room Organ. A Chamber Organ, built on the former model, may be made to yield a few effective combinations of tone, and full effects of some dignity in what is commonly understood as *Organ-tone*, but it will certainly be deficient in solo and accompanimental effects. Such being the case, the instrument would be most unsatisfactory for true Chamber-organ music. On the other hand, if it is built from the Concert Organ point of view, replete with decided contrasts of tone, and capable of producing numerous pleasing combinations and *nuances*, it becomes a perpetual source of interest and enjoyment to every one brought within its influence.

"The true Chamber Organ must be on the Concert or Orchestral Organ model; it must, in fact, be the orchestra *da camera*—the center of the music of the household. Whatever instruments may otherwise be available, the piano, violin, violoncello, or flute, all should take their positions here in relation to the dominating instrument—the Organ. With one or more, or with all four combined, the properly constructed Chamber Organ leads to results of never-ending variety, beauty, and interest.

"Although we have pointed to the Concert-room Organ as the model to be taken as a starting point, we do not desire it to be understood that any direct copying is to be contemplated; for, between an instrument of one hundred stops and one of say fifteen or twenty, such a thing as direct copying is out of all reason. On the contrary, it must, once for all, be understood and accepted that the true Chamber Organ is an instrument distinct and peculiar; a work constructed on special lines, for a special purpose, perfect within its self-imposed limits; and aiming at nothing beyond its legitimate powers. Viewed in this light, the Chamber Organ assumes a dignity not hitherto accorded it, and becomes a study of great interest to the artist."

The second series, commenced December 3, 1886, comprising six Articles, treats of the tonal appointment and general construction of the true Church Organ, as a distinct type of instrument. Regarding its tonal differentiation, the following remarks may be quoted:—

"In approaching the subject of the Church Organ, one enters on the consideration of a problem widely different in its general bearings to that presented by the Chamber Organ. Between the Church Organ and the chamber instrument there are few points in common beyond those which are connected with general excellence of manufacture and purity of tone. As the two instruments are designed for entirely different spheres of usefulness, so must they, if properly schemed and appointed, be widely different in their tonal structures and musical resources. While the maximum powers of expression (even at the risk of some loss of brilliancy), and the greatest possible delicacy and variety of tone, are necessary for the Chamber Organ, less powers of expression and the greatest richness and dignity of tone are requisite in the true Church Organ. Excellence of workmanship, perfection of voicing, and general refinement of tone are required alike in both classes of instruments.

"A Church Organ should be designed throughout on the simplest and most thorough principles; there should be no ambition on the part of its founders to make a display in the shape of a great number of speaking stops; but, on the contrary, a determination to have, in every possible way, a work of art—true and perfect in materials and workmanship, and developed on the soundest lines of organ-building. The tonal structure of the instrument, be it small or large, should be characterized by gravity, dignity, and softness—gravity, secured by an adequate and properly balanced Pedal department; dignity, by volume of foundation tone; and softness, by skilful voicing, under a copious windage at a moderate pressure. . . . Dignity combined with softness cannot be secured by small-scaled foundation work, numerous incomplete stops, and many ranks of acute pipes, blown by high pressure wind until they literally scream a coarse apology for their short-comings. Gravity combined with softness cannot be arrived at by one master-of-all-work pedal stop—a 'deep booming' 16-ft. *Open Diapason;* and much less by an apology in the shape of a *Bourdon,* in which the fundamental and the second upper partial tone seem to be perpetually struggling for the mastery."

The third series, commenced August 5, 1887, comprising nine Articles, treats of the tonal appointment and general construction of the Concert-room

Organ as a complete and resourceful instrument. Regarding its tonal differentiation, the following extract from the second Article may be given:—

"Before going into details, scientific and practical, connected with the Concert-room Organ, it is desirable to briefly define the nature of such an instrument when it can be pronounced properly appointed. It is quite certain that no other class of organ is called upon to meet so many demands upon its resources as that designed for the concert-room. A Chamber Organ has, at the most, to meet very reasonable calls both in solo and accompanimental playing; while a Church Organ has, in its legitimate office, only to accompany the voices of the choir and congregation, and to lend itself to a limited range of dignified solo music. On the other hand, a Concert-room Organ has a threefold office to fulfill, and it must be able to meet any demand the musician may think proper to make. It must be capable of taking part, in conjunction with a full orchestra, in the accompaniment of the most complicated choral works; it should be equally capable, alone, of furnishing a substitute for the entire orchestra, in the accompaniment of the same choral works, when an orchestra is not forthcoming; and, lastly, it must furnish the musician (I do not mean the ordinary organist, for his demands are limited) with proper materials for the effective interpretation of the thoughts of his own or other minds; and for the rendition of the most complex compositions written either for the organ or orchestra. In short, the concert-room instrument should be a perfect organ and a full orchestra combined."

When we ventured to write the twenty-three Articles, from which the extracts given above are made, our knowledge and experience were not so full as they are to-day in the matter of organ tonal differentiation; yet even then we went far to fill a page in the literature of the organ, which had remained practically blank for more than two centuries and a half, or from the time Michael Praetorius wrote his work, "Die Organographia," in 1616.

THE CLAVIERS

The most important mechanical portions of the organ with which the organist is primarily concerned, are those by means of which he directly commands the tonal forces of the instrument, namely, the Pedal and Manual Claviers. Accordingly, these properly claim special attention here. Whatever the class and tonal resources of the organ may be, the claviers must be perfect in their forms, proportions, and dispositions; so as to be, in all respects, convenient to the feet and hands of the performer. A badly formed and necessarily awkward pedalier, and incorrectly proportioned and inconveniently adjusted manual claviers, are abominations, and should never be tolerated in any organ. The more manual claviers there are (never exceeding five), the more care must be taken in their relative adjustments, and in their position with regard to the correct position of the seated performer. Care must be taken to have them constructed of proper materials, as hereinafter described, for they are conducive to good results and physical comfort in playing. No imperfect workmanship must be tolerated in these all-important portions of the organ; and they must be fully and clearly specified, and critically examined before being accepted from the hands of the organ-builder.

THE PEDALIER—The evolution of the Pedal Clavier was, as might be expected, extremely slow, beginning with a few rudimentary keys or foot-touches, placed on or near the floor, and merely pulling down, by means of chords or wires, bass notes of a manual clavier. It is commonly held that the Pedal Organ was instituted some time toward the end of the fourteenth century. Praetorius, in his "Theatrum seu Sciagraphia," gives a drawing of the pedalier of the interesting Halberstadt Organ,[1] constructed in 1361 and renovated in 1495; but to which date the pedalier belongs is uncertain. This consisted of twelve keys, in the form of levers, projecting through openings in a vertical face-board. Other evolutionary forms doubtless appeared, of which no record exists: so one may pass on to what Dom Bédos shows us in "L'Art du Facteur d'Orgues." This pedalier has a compass of twenty-seven notes—CCC to D. The keys are very short, and are formed to pass through openings in a sloping board,[2] so as to be conveniently depressed by the toe of the foot. Turning now to the Plates of what appears to be the greatest authority on organ-building in the German language—"Die Theorie und Praxis des Orgelbaues" (1888)—we find prominence given to a pedalier which presents all the objectionable features which could well be brought together in so important an appliance. It clearly indicates that Bach must have found the pedal clavier of his day a sorry affair.

Although the Pedal Clavier was not invented in England, it was there that it attained a practical form far in advance of that it ever reached in Germany or France: yet to-day, we venture to assert that, in its most scientific and convenient form, it is unknown to the organists of Great Britain. This developed form was devised in the United States, and examples of it exists only in American organs at the present time. It must be acknowledged, however, that it was due to the common-sense and ingenuity of a German organ-builder that the first important impetus was given in England toward the radical alteration and improvement of the pedalier. Herr Schulze, of Paulinzelle, sent to the Great Exhibition, held in London (1851), an organ having a concave pedal clavier. This was the first example of the treatment seen in England; and its advantage was at once recognized. It is commonly held that the principle of key-radiation was first applied to the pedal clavier by Elliot, the English organ-builder, in 1834. But it was left to the late Henry Willis, England's most renowned organ-builder, to produce the most sensible and convenient pedal clavier that has been constructed in England up to the present time, by combining the radiating and concave principles of formation; giving to the organ-building world what is properly known as the "Willis pedal board." In this, the radius adopted, for both the radiation of the keys and the arc of their concavity, is

[1] Shown on page 176 of "The Organ of the Twentieth Century."

[2] Shown on page 177 of the same Work.

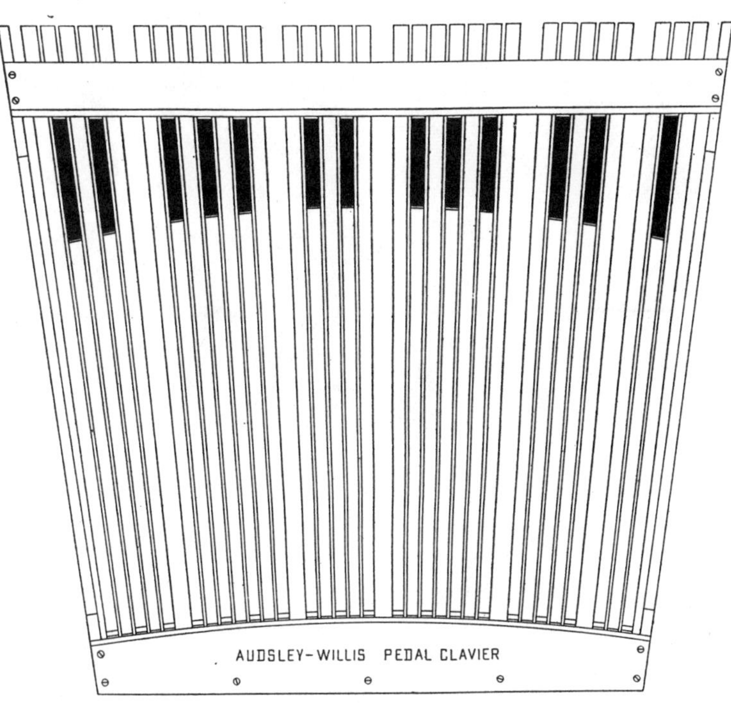

— PLAN-SHOWN FLAT —

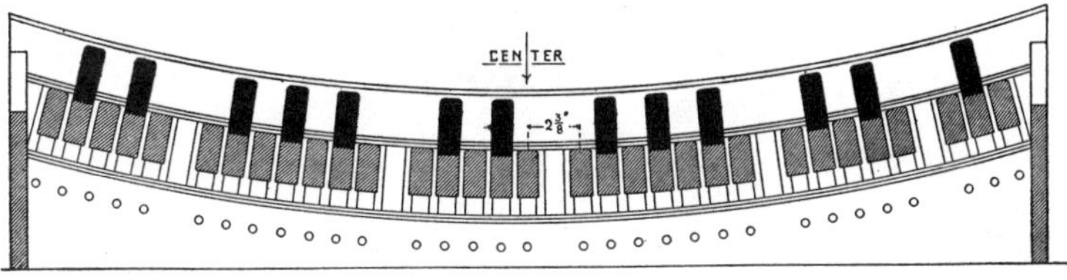

— SECTION AT TOE-BOARD —

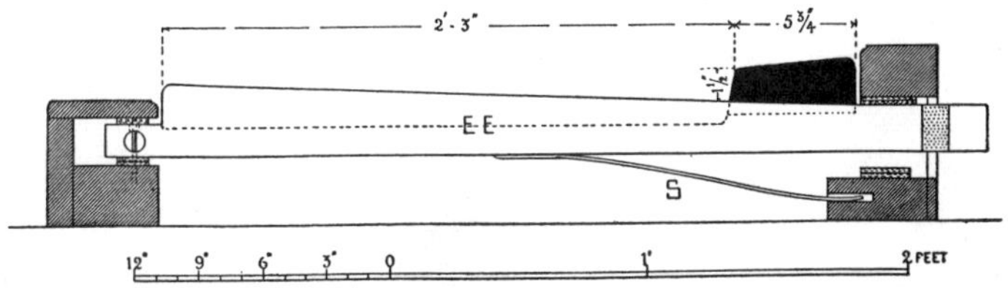

8 feet 6 inches. On what grounds this measurement for both radii was decided we fail to discover, for certainly it is not desirable.[3] We may pass over, without comment, the stupid "Resolutions" passed by the Royal College of Organists in 1881, which are as follows:—

"*That the compass of the pedals to be from* CCC *to F, i. e.,* 30 *notes.—That the pedals be parallel.—That the pedals be concave, with radial top facings; and the arc of concavity be the arc of a circle, having a radius of eight feet six inches.*"

In our own organ, constructed between the years 1865 and 1872, we applied a Willis pedalier; and it was while practising on it that we discovered its inconvenience, chiefly in the direction of its radiation. We then studied the problem of formation from a personal anatomical point of view. The clavier had to be adapted, to as great an extent as practicable, to the natural and unstrained motions of the legs at the hip and knee joints, and, to some extent, at the ankle also; the performer being seated in a central position, and having to move his body as little as possible. Without laying a claim to having devised a perfect pedalier, we submit for serious consideration, by the organ-playing world, the form which we have ventured to call, for the sake of distinction, the Audsley-Willis Pedal Clavier; the form and details of which are accurately shown, to scale, in the accompanying Plate I. We shall fully describe this pedalier under different heads.

Radiation.—First in importance, in connection with the desirable form of the pedal clavier, is the element of radiation; but that which, like all other matters connected with the pedalier, has been seriously neglected, or altogether ignored, by the writers of works on the organ published in Germany, France, Spain, and England.[4] That key radiation is essential to the proper and easy action of the legs and feet in pedaling must be obvious to all who have paid any thoughtful attention to the anatomy of the human body. It is necessary that the performer, steadily seated directly in a central position with respect to the clavier, shall be able to reach and easily depress the extreme keys—CCC and G—without having to change his position on the seat, or turn his body in any unseemly fashion while playing. Though radiation is not the only means to this desirable end it is an important factor, and, accordingly, calls for serious consideration.

[3] Full particulars and correct drawings of the pedalier are given in "The Organ of the Twentieth Century," Chap. VII.

[4] That this statement is not without good foundation is amply proved by the following facts regarding works in which the pedalier is mentioned. In "L'Art du Facteur d'Orgues," sixty-eight lines only are devoted to the pedalier. In "Die Theorie und Praxis des Orgelbaues," only about one page is given to the description of a very crude pedal clavier. In "The Organ," by Hopkins, the subject of the pedal clavier is dismissed, so far as its construction is concerned, in forty-nine lines. In "Organologia," by Merklin (Madrid 1924), the pedalier is touched upon in twenty-two lines. In "Organs and Organ-Building," by C. A. Edwards, thirty-two lines are given to the pedal clavier. In "A Practical Treatise on Organ-Building," by F. E. Robertson (London 1897), a somewhat better state of affairs obtains, fifty-nine lines being devoted to this very important clavier. In "Organs and Tuning," by Thomas Elliston, the pedal clavier is dismissed in fourteen lines. In "Organ Construction," by J. W. Hinton, M.A., Mus. Doc., neither a word of description nor a complete illustration of a pedal clavier is given; truly a remarkable fact in connection with a work bearing so comprehensive a title. In a recently published work entitled "Modern Organ-Building," by Walter & Thomas Lewis, Organ-builders—a quarto of 164 pages—the pedal clavier is dismissed in forty-seven words. One cannot help wondering, while scanning all these works, what views their authors held regarding this all-important clavier. It is certain our views are widely different, for, in "The Art of Organ-Building," twenty-eight quarto pages, fully illustrated, are devoted to the pedal clavier. In "The Organ of the Twentieth Century," eighteen pages are similarly devoted.

Carefully considering the Willis clavier in its more important practical features, we were quickly led to the inevitable conclusion that, at 8 feet 6 inches, the point of radiation from the front of the sharp keys was much too short, chiefly because it brought the keys at the heel-board of the clavier much too close together; and, what was more undesirable, it varied the distance between the natural keys too much at the different playing points in their length. To remove these undesirable conditions, it was evident a much longer radius was necessary. After considerable study and the drawing of full-sized diagrams of radiating claviers, we reached the conclusion that a radius of 13 feet was to be recommended for general adoption. That radius is correctly carried out in the Plan given in Plate I. The radius deciding the noses of the sharp keys is 7 feet, bringing them within easy reach of the performer's feet. The spaces between the natural keys, or the distances between their centers throughout their playing surfaces are so slight as to be hardly perceptible in pedaling—a matter of importance in a clavier in which the keys assume forms differing from those of all other pedaliers.

Concavity.—Of no less importance than Radiation is the matter of Concavity; indeed, the proper treatment of concavity may justly be considered of greater importance than that of radiation, insomuch that it more directly affects the performer in a facile command of the entire clavier. In determining the arc of concavity, the action of the legs, as they swing laterally from the knees, has to be considered; with avoidance, as much as possible, of extreme movements of the thighs, which are not only undesirable in themselves, but have the almost unavoidable effect of disturbing the steady posture of the body so desirable while playing.

While studying the subject of concavity, arcs of different forms presented themselves for consideration. The following extract from "The Art of Organ Building," touches this matter: "It is a question worthy of consideration whether an arc of a circle is the most suitable form for the concavity of the pedal clavier; and whether a curve derived from an ellipse would not be more convenient and comfortable. If the latter were adopted, the central portion of the clavier would be nearly flat, while its ends would rise somewhat higher than in the case of a circular disposition. We are of opinion that the elliptical curve would render the keys throughout the clavier much more easily commanded by the natural movements of the legs and feet." Practical matters had to be considered concerning the difficulties of proper construction, and the almost hopeless task of inducing organ-builders to face these difficulties; so after serious thought we decided to adopt the simpler and safer arc of a circle.

In the Willis pedalier of thirty notes—the original form—the long radius of concavity may be found convenient by a performer with long legs; but for those of the average length of legs, and especially for female organists, the radius of eight feet six inches is much too long. In claviers of thirty-two notes, the inconvenience of the Willis radius is increased; and the desirability of bringing the extreme notes of the pedalier—CCC and G— within easier reach of the performer, while centrally seated, becomes too obvious to be questioned.

Our studies from an anatomical standpoint, combined with careful practical tests, have led us to the conclusion that, in the full compass pedalier, the longest radius of the arc of concavity should be seven feet. This is the arc of the Section shown in the Plate. We feel quite sure that for general adoption the seven feet radius will be found perfectly satisfactory.

Construction.—If there is one thing more than another that strikes us when we examine the pedaliers turned out from the busy, trade-ridden, organ factories to-day, it is the slovenly manner in which they are made and finished. We can see the pitying smile that will illuminate the face of the average organ-builder when he reads this assertion—unhesitatingly made—that the pedal clavier should be as carefully formed, and constructed of as good materials, as a manual clavier. Organists, as a rule, do not realize this, or they would not accept such pedaliers as are commonly thought good enough for their feet: nor would they venture to play them, at any serious performance, wearing their ordinary, sandy, street shoes or boots. The Great Best, the consummate artist on the pedalier of his time, and, so far as our experience and observation extend, without an equal to-day, either in executive skill, or in dignified deportment while playing, never gave a recital on the Organ in St. George's Hall, Liverpool, without having put on a pair of shoes of thin leather, the soles of which were of so soft and pliant a nature as to enable his feet to feel the pedal keys with almost as sensitive a touch as his fingers felt the manual keys. We have examined the shoes he wore, and have watched his pedaling hundreds of times. These facts regarding the shoes should be well considered by the young and ambitious organist.

The keys of the properly formed pedalier should have a finished thickness of one inch at the toe-board; and, as they properly follow the radiation, their thickness will be full three-quarters of an inch at the heel-board, under which they are hinged. In the Willis clavier, the keys were commonly made less than an inch in thickness, and rounded along their playing surfaces. This practice was condemned by Mr. Best, who insisted on the desirability of having the keys one inch in thickness, and their playing surfaces flat, their sharp angles only being removed to prevent chipping. No one knew better than he did what was conducive to clean and effective pedaling. This treatment in the Audsley-Willis pedalier, is clearly shown in the Section at the Toe-board in the Plate. Special attention should be paid to the form of the natural keys, as shown in the lower Section, in which the EE key is given. In connection with this peculiar treatment of the upper surface of the keys, our remarks in "The Organ of the Twentieth Century" may be quoted: "The late George Cooper (1820–1876)—one of the distinguished English organists of his day—in an Article in the *Musical World* for April 14th, 1855, suggested that the natural keys of the pedal clavier should be formed with an ***upward slope*** on their playing surface, so that at the heel-board they should be an inch higher than at the line of the sharp keys. Notwithstanding this valuable suggestion by a man who knew what he was talking about, and who distinctly stated the treatment he advocated, 'to wonderfully facilitate the performance of pedal passages requiring an extensive use of the heel,' no notice seems to have been taken of it by organ-builders; and none is known to have been taken at the remarkable Conference of the Royal College of Organists." No allusion to this key treatment has appeared in any works on the organ save our own: and so obvious was it, that we unhesitatingly incorporated it in the Audsley-Willis pedalier in the manner shown.

The sharp keys in the claviers commonly made by inartistic and careless organ-builders are radically wrong and insufficient in form and size; being practically no better than the toe-pedals of the French organs of the early years of the eighteenth century. Such bull-nosed, stunted, apologies for keys should be condemned by every organist who aspires to become a perfect pedalist. No sharp key should be less than 5¾ inches in length; and in the clavier shown in Plate I that minimum length falls on the DD♯ key. As the toe-board is, in this setting out, straight, all the other sharps, which have their fronts set to the arc of a circle, are elongated; the extreme keys CCC♯ and F♯ being about 8 inches in length. In properly appointed electro-pneumatic organs, toe-pistons or touches are commonly located in the toe-board, and this practice calls for the adoption of a segmental toe-board, following the arc of the sharp keys; and, accordingly, having the radius of seven feet six inches. The shape of the sharp keys and the position of their playing surface to that of the natural keys call for careful consideration, and the conclusions we have arrived at may be stated.

The front of each sharp key should rise above the level of the immediately adjoining natural keys 1½ inches, and its angle should be only slightly rounded: from this, its playing surface should have a decided slope—at the angle of eight degrees from the horizontal—so that the foot may fall upon it as upon a natural key, and without requiring any undesirable motion at the ankle joint. This form is distinctly shown in the DD♯ key in the lower Section in the Plate. It is quite evident that, in the formation of the ordinary organ-builder's style of pedal clavier, matters connected with leg and feet anatomy are ignored. At the front line of the sharp keys, the playing depth or touch in all keys will be three-quarters of an inch, so that when a sharp is depressed its front will be three-quarters of an inch above the natural key level. This will be found perfectly convenient in artistic pedaling.

No wood for universal adoption has been selected by organ-builders for the natural keys: and, accordingly, as little interest has been taken by organists and the purchasers of organs in this direction, it is not to be wondered that unsuitable and objectionable woods have been used, in conjunction with slovenly workmanship, in the construction of the tradesman organ-builder's ideal pedalier.

For the natural keys, a straight- and close-grained light colored wood is desirable, such as beech, maple, lancewood (*Duguetia quitarensis*), sycamore, and boxwood (*Cornus florida*); preference being given to one of light weight, so as to enable an easy and elastic touch to be secured without resort to an undesirably strong recovering-spring. Although we are inclined to favor the wire spring, shown at S in the Plate, some makers prefer the steel heel-spring, which is readily adjusted to any desired strength by a screw.[5] There is no necessity, from a mere practical point of view, that the sharp keys should be made of a wood different from that approved of for the natural keys: but an artistic sense, and a desire to carry out an appearance of sympathy between the manual and pedal claviers, has properly dictated the construction of the playing portion of the sharp keys of a hard and dark-colored wood, such as ebony or rosewood: the wear-resisting properties of these woods strongly recommending their adoption. The remainder of the sharp key, being in no manner touched by the foot, may be formed of some light and tough wood, or the same as that used for the natural keys. Certain organ-builders, to save labor and money, have resorted to sham, by simply staining black the sharp keys. This stain soon wears off on the playing surface, disclosing the fraud. The pedal clavier should, from every point of view, be a work of art.

THE MANUAL CLAVIERS—The successive stages of development through which the Manual Claviers of the organ have passed, from their inception, in the Hydraulic Organ of the ancients, to their standard form of the present day, make a very interesting chapter in the History of the Monarch of all Instruments. The earliest illustrations of organ claviers to be found in a work on organ matters are given by Praetorius in his "Theatrum Instrumentorum seu Sciagraphia"; in which he gives full-size drawings of the remarkable keys of the "Gross Magdeburgisch Clavier," supposed to belong to the eleventh century, and also those of the Halberstadt Organ, built by Nicholas Faber in 1361. The keys of both were of enormous size, and were manipulated in some forcible manner. In the year 1456, an organ was installed in the Church of St. Egidius, at Brunswick, having manual claviers which, clumsy though they were, marked a decided step toward the modern treatment. Praetorius gives a full-size representation of portions of two manual claviers belonging to this instrument, showing keys of different dimensions. The keys, although similar in disposition to those of the modern clavier, were large and clumsy, so much so that an ordinary hand could not comfortably stretch beyond a major sixth.[6] From this time the manual keys were gradually reduced in size, as the compass of the clavier was increased, and the mechanism of the organ was improved and lightened, until we find that in the organ built by Cranz, in the year 1499, for the Church of St. Blaise, at Brunswick, the keys were sufficiently reduced in width to admit of the octave being easily spanned by the hand. The sixteenth century saw the correct or approved scale of the manual keys established, practically in the form now adopted.

As the compass of the manual claviers of the organ has been fixed, and is now adopted for all instruments of any importance, it is only necessary to state that it comprises sixty-one notes, from CC to c^4.

[5] This method is illustrated in Fig. CXII., page 148, Vol. II., of "The Art of Organ-Building."

[6] The Claviers alluded to and illustrated in the "Theatrum Instrumentorum seu Sciagraphia" are reproduced in "The Art of Organ-Building," Vol. II., pp. 60–63.

As the relative disposition of the claviers, directly commanding the tonal resources of the several Divisions of the organ, is of considerable interest to the organist, and of importance in the principal subject of the present dissertation, we cannot do better than give it place here: and, in doing so, we may substantially repeat what has been said on the subject in "The Art of Organ-Building." In the following remarks it will be understood that the claviers are numbered from the lowest one upward; the lowest one being the First Clavier. Each clavier commands a special tonal Division, or special Divisions, of the instrument; and to which a distinctive name is given, more or less expressive of its general character or its office in the tonal economy of the organ.

In the arrangement of two claviers, no diversity of practice obtains; the First Clavier invariably commanding what is called the Great Organ, and the Second Clavier commanding what is usually a subordinate Division, called either the Swell Organ or the Choir Organ; the latter term being used when the Division is of a softer tonality than the Great Organ, and not necessarily expressive, according to common opinion.

In the groups of three claviers, three dispositions are met with. First:—the First Clavier commanding the Great Organ; the Second Clavier, the Choir Organ; and the Third Clavier, the Swell Organ: many examples of this disposition are to be found in consoles at home and abroad. Second disposition:—the First Clavier commanding the Great; the Second Clavier, the Swell; and the Third Clavier, the Choir Organ. This disposition is uncommon and not to be recommended. In the interesting organ erected by Schulze in the Petrikirche, at Soest, in Westphalia, one finds a powerful Great Organ commanded by the First Clavier, and an extremely delicate Choir Organ, voiced on very light wind, commanded by the Third Clavier. The Second Clavier commands a Division of the instrument which in general intensity of tone is intermediate with respect to the tones of the other Divisions. This Second Division should have been rendered expressive: but according to the ideas which obtained in Germany at the time this organ was constructed, both its tonal appointment and clavier disposition left, in the mind of its designer, nothing to be desired. Third disposition:—The First Clavier commanding the Choir Organ; the Second Clavier the Great Organ; and the Third Clavier the Swell Organ. Although this disposition frequently appears in groups of four claviers, it is not to be recommended for triple clavier arrangements. We do not believe that this disposition was ever adopted for the convenience of the performer; but that it necessarily attended the old position of the Choir Division, behind the performer's seat, and the necessity of obtaining a simple tracker action between it and its clavier. Certain distinguished organists, including the late W. T. Best, have advocated the abandonment of this old disposition in favor of the first one, given above, in which the clavier commanding the Choir Organ is placed between those of the Great and Swell Organs. This arrangement has been pronounced convenient because it places the most useful accompanimental clavier immediately under the clavier commanding the Division most suitable for expressive effects, both accompanimental and solo. The old disposition, of

Choir, Great, and Swell, has found many advocates among modern organists; but upon what grounds save that of long usage and familiarity, we have failed to discover.

In the groups of four claviers, five different dispositions may be mentioned as obtaining in certain representative organs. First:—the most desirable disposition, in which the First Clavier commands the Great Division; the Second Clavier the Choir Division; the Third Clavier the Swell Division; and the Fourth Clavier the Solo Division. This disposition obtains in Cavaillé-Coll's Organ in the Albert Hall, at Sheffield, in which the Positif, Récit, and Solo are all expressive, and are commanded respectively by the Second, Third, and Fourth Claviers. The Grand-Orgue is commanded by the First Clavier. Second disposition:—that exemplified by the Willis Organ in St. George's Hall, Liverpool. In this instrument the First Clavier commands the Choir Organ; the Second Clavier the Great; the Third Clavier the Swell; and the Fourth Clavier the Solo. This disposition was adopted by Roosevelt for his important instrument in the Auditorium, at Chicago. This disposition has been adopted by other distinguished organ-builders at home and abroad. Third disposition:—that exemplified by the Organ in the Town Hall of Bolton, Lancashire. In this instrument, which was constructed from the specification of W. T. Best, we find the First Clavier commands the Choir Organ; the Second the Great, the Third the Solo, and the Fourth the Swell. This disposition, so far as the Third and Fourth Claviers are concerned, is, so far as our knowledge extends, unique. The location of the Solo clavier was doubtless suggested by Best's special taste and style in the rendition of orchestral scores on the organ, which so frequently called for the operation of the fingers of one hand on two adjacent claviers at the same time. In the disposition of the claviers of Concert-room Organs, on which complex orchestral compositions are certain to be rendered, such a matter as the above should receive careful consideration, in combination with the tonal appointment of the Divisions affected. It must be mentioned that the Solo Division of the Bolton Organ is rendered expressive by being inclosed in a special swell-box. Fourth disposition:—exemplified by the notable Cavaillé-Coll Organ in the Church of Saint-Ouen, at Rouen. In it the First Clavier commands the Grand-Orgue; the Second Clavier the Bombarde; the Third Clavier the Positif; and the Fourth Clavier the Récit expressif. For organs of four manual claviers, appointed according to the usual modern French method, this disposition has several advantages. In the Organ in Saint-Ouen the Récit expressif is a combination of a Swell and a Solo Organ, while the Positif is well adapted for accompaniment; accordingly, these Divisions are frequently used together. The stop-apportionments of the Grand-Orgue and the Bombarde, make the latter practically a part of the former; accordingly, their claviers are conveniently placed adjacent to each other. As a general rule, Divisions that are closely related in their offices in a tonal scheme, and are more or less dependent on each other, should have their claviers adjoining. This matter should be carefully considered in the disposition of the claviers of a Concert-room Organ.

Fifth disposition:—instituted in the Organ in the Town Hall of Leeds, Yorkshire. In this instrument the First Clavier commands the Choir Organ; the Second Clavier the Swell Organ; the Third Clavier the divided Great; and the Fourth Clavier the Solo Organ. There is also an Echo Organ commanded by the First and Fourth Claviers. The position of the Great Organ clavier is unique; and it is difficult to account for so radical a departure from the commonly approved and certainly more convenient positions. Certain other dispositions may be found in German Organs, but of these it is unnecessary to speak.

In groups of five claviers, three dispositions may be given as presented by notable organs. First disposition:—represented by the Concert-room Organ in the Centennial Hall, at Sydney, N. S. W., in which the First Clavier commands the Choir Organ; the Second Clavier the Great; the Third Clavier the Swell; the Fourth Clavier the Solo; and the Fifth Clavier the Echo Organ. This is the second disposition given in the groups of four claviers, with the addition of the Fifth or Echo Clavier. Second disposition:—that introduced by Cavaillé-Coll in the Organs in Notre-Dame and the Church of Saint-Sulpice, Paris. In these the First Clavier commands the Grand-Chœur; the Second Clavier the Grand-Orgue; the Third Clavier the Bombarde; the Fourth Clavier the Positif; and the Fifth Clavier the Récit expressif. In considering this disposition, it is desirable to bear in mind that the Grand-Chœur is practically a dependent Division, containing the stops, designated by the French builders *jeux de combinaison*, which complete the tonal appointment of the Grand-Orgue. The Grand-Chœur must not be confounded with the Choir Organ, commanded by the First Clavier in many American and English instruments. As will be seen, the Divisions called the Grand-Orgue and the Grand-Chœur may properly be commanded by one clavier, showing their close connection in the tonal scheme. Taking the stop-apportionments of the remaining Divisions of these organs into consideration, and bearing in view the fact that each instrument has only a single expressive Division, it seems questionable if the Récit expressif is commanded by the most convenient clavier. In our opinion no Division of an organ is of more importance than its expressive one; and, accordingly, it should be commanded by a clavier within easy reach of the organist's hands. The highest and farthest away of five claviers cannot be considered a very convenient one for a lengthened use by both hands; while it is adapted for occasional passages, more or less of a solo character by a single hand. Important, according to French ideas, as the Bombarde may be in the production of full effects, it is of secondary importance to the Récit expressif in both the organs under consideration; and might have been given to the Fifth Clavier, allowing the more important Récit to be commanded by the more accessible Third Clavier. Third disposition:—set forth in Cavaillé-Coll's great project for the Organ for St. Peter's, at Rome: in which the First Clavier commands both the Grand-Orgue and the Grand-Chœur;[7] the Second Clavier

[7] Cavaillé-Coll remarks: "Cette 2e partie du premier clavier *Grand-Chœur* serait disposée pour être jouée séparément avec le *Grand-Orgue* sur premier clavier."

PLATE II.

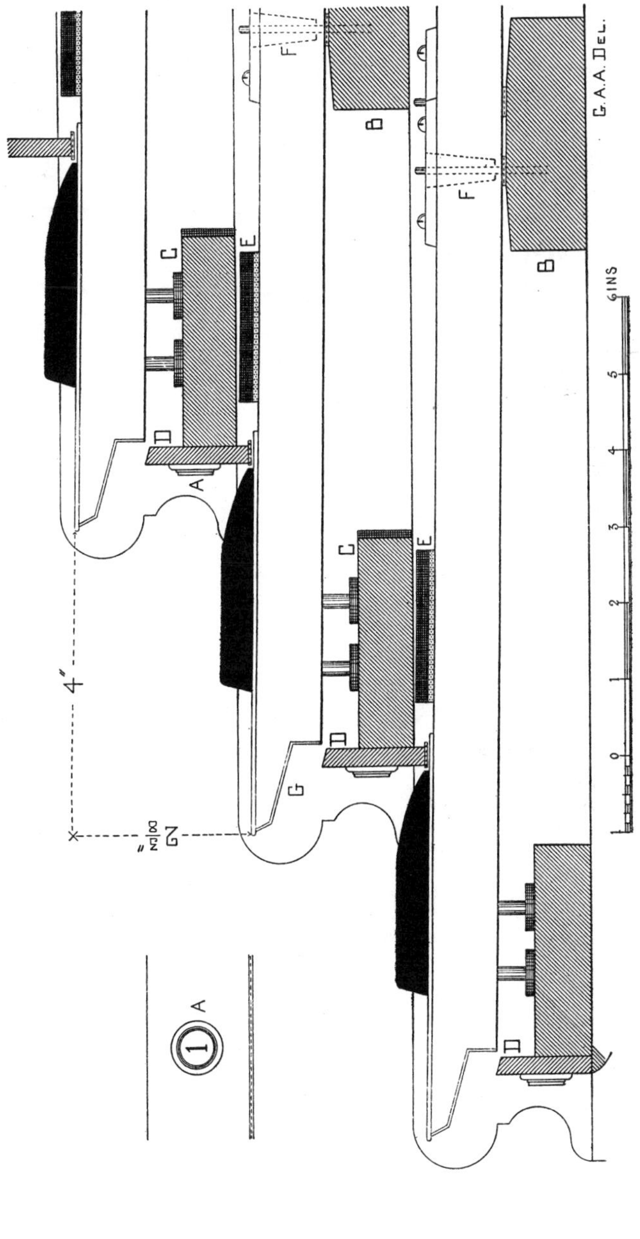

G.A.A. DEL.

commands the Bombarde; the Third Clavier the Positif; the Fourth Clavier the Récit expressif. The relationship between the Grand-Chœur and the Grand-Orgue, already alluded to, is in this tonal scheme clearly shown by placing them under the command of a single clavier. Although the general disposition seemed proper to Cavaillé-Coll, we are of opinion the positions of the Bombarde and Récit should have been reversed.

The preceding notes are sufficient to show the arrangements of the manual claviers and their usual names in organs of importance schemed on old-fashioned tonal systems—systems which are still followed by builders and designers of organs, who, apparently, find it difficult or undesirable, for personal reasons, to strike into new paths of progress which would necessarily lead to more artistic and wider fields for their labors. It is only necessary to read organ specifications, or to glance at the stop-jambs of the consoles of Concert-room, Church, Theater, or Chamber Organs, as still commonly constructed and tonally appointed, to find the same old, time-worn, and largely inappropriate and meaningless divisional nomenclature—nomenclature which will have to be altered, entirely or in part, under advanced systems of tonal structure and divisional stop-apportionment. New names must be introduced as new tonal Divisions are formed and added to the organ; and these names must clearly indicate the tonal character, or special office of the Divisions in the tonal economy of the instrument.

The next matters to be considered are the measurements of the Manual Claviers and their positions, vertically and horizontally, with relation to each other. These details are of the greatest importance to the organist, for they directly concern his ease and comfortable control of the tonal forces of the organ. Fortunately, all matters connected with these claviers have received careful consideration by both organ-builders and players. What seems to be a satisfactory standard for two or more associated claviers has been arrived at through the operations of the Committee on Standardization, composed of members of the American Guild of Organists and the National Association of Organists. Of this committee, the writer had the honor of being a member. The Resolution arrived at in the matters under consideration is as follows:—

"*Resolved—That the distance from the surface of one manual clavier to another, immediately above it, shall be two and three-eighths inches; and that the distance from the front edge of each clavier to that of the clavier immediately above it shall be four inches.*"

The disposition of the claviers, according to the Resolution, is accurately set forth in the accompanying Plate II. The total height between the horizontal playing surfaces of the extreme keys in the group of five claviers will be 9½ inches; and the distance between vertical lines drawn from the front edges of the First and Fifth Claviers will be 16 inches. With the moderate key-overhang of the seven-eighths of an inch, as shown, the distance between the claviers is sufficient to give easy access to the combination thumb-pistons in the key-slips, as indicated at A. The sloping of the sharp keys toward the key-slips.

now wisely done in well formed claviers, also favors an easy approach to the pistons.

Regarding the desirable depth of touch of the manual keys, the following decisions were reached by the Committee on Standardization, after careful consideration and testing: tubular-pneumatic and electro-pneumatic actions only being contemplated:—

"*Resolved—That the fall of the manual keys at their front ends shall be three-eighths of an inch; and that the pressure required to depress them, under the touch of the fingers, shall be equal to the weight of four ounces laid upon the playing portions of the keys.*"

Although no exception can well be taken to these Resolutions, the question regarding weight of touch cannot well be definitely fixed. To some performers it may be too light; to others too heavy: accordingly, it would be desirable, in a perfect console, for means to be provided to change the weight necessary, to suit the touch of the organist. In this important matter too much must not be left to the console maker. The organist, allowing he is a talented and experienced artist, is the best one to judge what is necessary to give him absolute and easy command and control of the tonal forces and effects of his complicated instrument; and his directions on all matters belonging thereto should receive the fullest recognition and practical attention.

Construction.—Although not absolutely necessary in relation to the dominating subject of this Work, a brief description of the general formation of the Manual Clavier may prove interesting to some readers. A single clavier consists of two principal divisions; namely, the key-frame which carries the keys, and which is stationary and rigid; and the keys, which are movable.

The *key-frame* is formed of the following parts:—The *cheeks*, which are the two thick rails, set on edge, which form its sides, and to which the cross rails are securely attached. The cheeks, being always visible in certain portions, are properly made of oak, mahogany, or some other rich wood, carefully finished on all exposed surfaces. The cheeks are commonly of moderate thickness, and finished in front in some ornamental manner, as indicated in Plate II. In large and complicated organ consoles, they may assume a square form of considerable thickness, for the reception of tablets or pistons, controlling certain movements of the instrument: in which case the cheeks are built up hollow in part.

The *mid-rail* is the part of the key-frame which extends across from cheek to cheek, at their lower edges, and, usually, about the center of their length. This rail—also termed the *balance-rail*—serves as the support or fulcrum on which the keys rock. It is properly made of straight-grained oak or other hard, close-grained wood not liable to warp. The mid-rail holds the *mid-pins*, which pass through the centers of the key bodies and on which they rock. The mid-rail is shown, in cross-section, at B in the Plate. In old organs, having tracker actions, the key bodies were commonly pivoted at their rear ends, as shown in the claviers illustrated by Dom Bédos. In this treatment the key-frame has a *back-rail* for the reception of the key-pins.

The *bed-rail* is the portion of the key-frame which extends from cheek to cheek, at or near their front ends, and at their lower edges. This rail holds the *bed-pins*, which retain the keys in position; and it also serves to arrest the descent of the keys. The bed-rail, also termed the *front-rail*, is commonly made of oak or some other very stiff hard wood, strengthened along its back edge by a steel plate, as indicated at C in the Plate.

The *key-slip* or *front-bead* is a thin slip of some choice wood, which extends from cheek to cheek, and is screwed to the front edge of the bed-rail, as shown at D. This slip is chiefly for the purpose of carrying the thumb-pistons, while it is ornamental, and covers the unseemly space between the bed-rail and the under side of the keys.

The *thumper*, though held in position by the cheeks, cannot be considered an integral part of the key-frame. It is either a flat, heavily weighted bar of hardwood, or of steel, covered on its lower surface with soft thick cloth or felt, which is laid upon the key-bodies, a short distance behind the black keys, as shown in section at E in the Plate. Its office is to retain all the keys at the proper level; and to silently arrest the upward motion of the keys when they are released by the fingers of the performer. The thumper is so fitted to the cheeks as to have an up and down motion only.

The *keys* are formed of long quadrangular rods, commonly of the finest straight-grained and thoroughly seasoned white pine. Straight-grained light mahogany, lime, and some other suitable woods have been used; but, except under some special conditions, white pine, open-air seasoned, is commonly preferred; it has no tendency to warp or twist. These rods are termed the *key-bodies* or *key-stocks*. They are pivoted at the mid-rail, as indicated at F; finished in front with *combs*, *platings*, and *nosings;* and attached at their rear ends to the key action of the organ. The combs, or sharp keys, are made of the finest black ebony, prepared by being thoroughly dried in a hot-air chamber, as is the practice in the Steinway Piano Works. They are securely glued to the key-bodies and carefully finished to the desired form and polished. The length of the finished combs varies from 3 inches to 3½ inches, according to requirements. When more than three claviers are associated, the three-inch combs should be adopted. The natural keys are plated with the finest white ivory, which should have a finished thickness of not less than one-twelfth of an inch. In slop-work, celluloid has been used; but this should never be accepted from any organ-builder. The front ends of the keys, or *nosings*, have thin plates of ivory, celluloid, ebony, or some other suitable material attached to them, as indicated by the double lines at G in the Plate. In cheap claviers, the nosings are merely painted and varnished.[8]

THE DRAW-STOP SYSTEM—Although the form and arrangement of the agents or appliances by means of which the performer commands the speech of the numerous stops of the organ, while he is properly and comfortably

[8] The full description of the processes of clavier making, from first to last, is given in "The Art of Organ-Building," Volume II, pp. 71–95.

seated at the console, are of paramount importance, nothing has been achieved toward a general practice or standardization; yet something in that desirable direction is devoutly to be wished by organ players. Everything in this direction seems, at the present time, to be governed by the convenience or caprice of the organ-builder or the person by whom the console is designed.

One form of stop control can surely be dismissed from serious consideration at this late date in organ appointment: we allude to the old-fashioned and time-honored, but very clumsy and inconvenient, draw-stop knobs, commonly closely arranged in rows and tiers on sloping jambs, crowded together in perfect regularity, painful to look at. Perhaps the most awful example of this absurd treatment is to be found in the largest Church Organ in England, recently installed in the Liverpool Cathedral. The arrangement in this instrument is as follows:—On the right sloping jamb, adjoining the five manual claviers, are arranged one hundred and twelve knobs, disposed in eight vertical rows, the outer one of which has eighteen knobs. The bottom knob is placed some inches below the level of the board on which the claviers rest; while the top knob reaches, above the level of the fifth clavier, to a height exceeding that of the five claviers combined. A similar arrangement of one hundred and ten knobs adorns the left jamb. Nothing so terrible as this has been perpetrated in connection with any organ constructed in the United States; although the inconvenient old-fashioned knob treatment is still favored by certain conservative builders. Further comment on this antiquated treatment is unnecessary.

Leaving out of consideration a patented form of draw-stop appliance, not at all likely to come into general or even extensive use, there remain only two forms of stop control immediately commanded by the performer at the console; namely, rocking-tablets and pendant stop-tongues or touches. The adoption of either of these will be largely a matter of personal preference on the part of the builder or organ architect; for there is but little difference on the score of convenience, provided they are conveniently disposed within easy command of the performer's hands. We prefer, on several grounds, the rocking-tablet; chiefly because it can be made more seemly in form and disposition than the pendant tongue, and only requires a simple pushing touch both in bringing on and shutting off a stop. The stop-tongue calls for an awkward flipping-up action of the finger in silencing a stop; and has, however disposed, a somewhat loose appearance. Whichever form is adopted, it is essential that it shall be disposed in a manner perfectly convenient in every way to the performer; avoidance being made of that crowded and extremely ugly semicircular disposition, huddled immediately over the claviers, and seeming to crush them, which has been adopted by certain console designers for instruments of the objectionable "Unit" type. The rocking-tablets can easily be disposed so as to be perfectly accessible to the performer's hands, either on inclined or vertical curved jambs; but no curve should obtain in the length of, or directly over the upper clavier. This straight stretch being devoted to the coupler tablets and other controlling devices.

Color can be applied to the draw-stop tablets or tongues in two ways and for different purposes. First—it may be employed to distinguish the several tonal Divisions or Sub-divisions of the organ commanded by the pedal and manual claviers. This may be termed the *general method;* and is found in full development in the console of the Organ in the Wanamaker Store in Philadelphia, Pa. Secondly—colors may be employed in the tablets or tongues to indicate the different tonalities of the stops contained in the Divisions or Subdivisions of the instrument. This may be termed the *particular method;* and is fully exemplified in the console of the Organ in the Cadet Chapel at West Point, N. Y. In the former method, the colors indicating the different Divisions can properly be applied to the tablets or tongues of the couplers, indicating the Divisions coupled: but in the latter and better method, colors cannot be properly applied to the couplers.

THE COMBINATION PISTONS.—These, for the most part, are located conveniently under the manual claviers, the stops of which they command through the adjustable combination action of the organ. They are commonly known as *thumb-pistons,* being chiefly operated by the performer's thumbs. Two systems of draw-stop action are operated by these pistons, commonly known as the "absolute system" and the "dual system." The former, which dominates the draw-stop action, is so obviously undesirable that it calls for no consideration here. On the other hand, the dual system, being that which should be carried out in all organs, may be fully described, and, in doing so, we cannot do better than quote what we have said on the subject in "The Organ of the Twentieth Century."[9]

The dual system, as the name implies, comprises two practically independent combination actions—that commanded by the draw-stop knobs, rocking-tablets, or other devices, and that commanded by the pistons located under or adjoining the claviers. These combination actions can be used separately or conjointly, as the performer may desire; a convenient means being provided to combine or separate them—preferably by double-acting pistons or touches set in the cheeks of the claviers. Under such conditions, the operation of the pistons in no case moves the draw-stop knobs or devices; nor does it affect in any way the tonal combination prepared on the knobs or draw-stop devices. These are important advantages belonging to a properly constituted dual combination system.

It will be understood that unless the piston release belonging to a clavier has been operated, the combination pistons of that clavier are active; and that their respective tonal combinations will remain available at the command of the performer, regardless of whatever stop or combination of stops belonging to the clavier may be drawn by means of the knobs or draw-stop devices. This is an important condition.

Now, if the two combination actions belonging to a clavier are separated, by means of the double-acting pistons alluded to above, the draw-stop combi-

[9] In this Work, which is now out of print and will not be reprinted, both the systems alluded to are described.

nation will be cut off from the clavier, and all the piston combinations will be available without any tonal alteration. Then, should the performer reverse the double-acting pistons, so as to unite the two combination actions, the tonal combination prepared on the draw-stop knobs or devices will immediately speak on the clavier, along with the tonal combination on any piston of the clavier that the performer may operate. While this connection obtains, any addition to or substraction from the draw-stop combination can be made, by the manipulation of the knobs or devices, at the will of the performer. The value of these methods of producing varied combinational effects with ease and certainty cannot well be overrated, be the organ small or large. They render possible the instantaneous changes of tonality, producing powerful or other pronounced effects, or imparting a special tonal coloring, by the addition of one or more voices, to all the piston combinations that may be brought on the clavier. Now, if the piston release is operated, the draw-stop combination, whatever it may be, will alone remain active on the clavier.

FLEXIBILITY AND EXPRESSION

Flexibility of tone and expressive powers in the organ can only be secured by mechanical appliances and means, under the control of the performer seated at the console, and while playing. Up to the present time, although certain essays have been made to furnish the performer with some easier and more effective means of obtaining desirable results, both in flexibility and expression of tone, all have failed in favor of the Swell-box and its shutter-operating lever, the latter commonly, though not properly, designated the "swell-pedal." Such being the case; what is required, now that the great importance of expression and tonal flexibility and control is becoming fully realized in artistic organ playing, is perfection in Swell-box design and construction, and an absolute control of the mechanism operating the swell shutters. Much has yet to be done in both these directions. Improvements in the construction of the Swell-box are not difficult, if properly understood and undertaken: but considerable difficulty seems to obtain in providing a thoroughly satisfactory control over the opening and closing of the swell shutters, or shades, in large organs. That the only perfect control of the shutters is by means of a direct mechanical connection between them and the expression lever operated by the foot of the performer at the console, must be freely admitted: but such a chain of mechanism is practically impossible in a large organ, containing several Swell-boxes, and having its console located at a considerable distance; or, as in the case of an electro-pneumatic instrument, movable and connected only by a cable.

In the issue of "*The American Organist*" for March, 1894, there appeared an Article, from our pen, entitled, "The Rational Treatment of the Swell-Box." As this contains matter desirable to be mentioned here, we shall repeat our words. We shall start with the emphatic proposition:—

That every Swell-box should be designed and constructed with special regard to the tonal character and power of the pipe-work it is to inclose, and to which it is to impart artistic and effective powers of expression and tonal flexibility.

Nothing in this direction has apparently been dreamt of by any other writer on the organ; certainly not one of them seems to have considered the construction of the Swell-box worthy of serious thought; accordingly, careless organ-builders have crammed beautiful pipe-work into all manner of sound-killing caves of reinforced concrete or brick-work, or into crudely constructed boxes of wood and sawdust; utterly regardless of the destructive effects they may have, and, indeed, are certain to have, on the tones of the inclosed stops.

The logical and common-sense proposition set forth above, would necessarily call for special acoustical conditions to be provided for in the formation of each and every Swell-box in an organ; providing that the proper, and artistically classified stop-apportionment is made in each Division or Sub-division of the organ, in accordance with our system of tonal appointment. This branch of our general subject may be properly closed by the General Principles of Swell-box Construction, given for the first item in organ literature in the pages of the journal named above.

I. That the Swell-box shall be made of sufficient internal width, depth, and height to afford ample space for the accommodation of the inclosed pipe-work in all directions; to give every pipe sufficient room to speak properly; and to provide convenient means of easy access to every pipe, small and large, and labial and lingual, for tuning and regulating.

II. That the Swell-box shall be so constructed of suitable material and thickness, and having shutters of the necessary thickness and form, that when the box is closed a correct *pianissimo* will be obtained without in any degree producing annihilation of tone or destruction of the characteristic quality of any of the stops speaking within the box.

III. That the interior surfaces of the Swell-box shall be such and so finished, as to be of a uniform, hard, and sound-reflecting character: so that all tendency to absorption of sound or the deadening of brilliancy of tone may be avoided. With this aim the surfaces must be left free and unencumbered; and no large wooden pipes are to be planted directly against or very close to them.

IV. That the Swell-boxes of all the tonal Divisions and Sub-divisions of the organ shall be constructed in such a manner and of such materials as to be consistent with the requirements and conditions imposed by the tonal character and penetrating quality of the voices of the pipe-work they inclose. This Principle dictates that every Swell-box, in a properly appointed organ, must be specially devised for the work it has to do in the acoustical development of the instrument.

V. That the Swell-box applied to the Great Organ, or any part thereof, shall, preferably, be shuttered on the front and also on one or both sides. In the case of this Foundation Division, as large a portion of the box should be shuttered as practicable; it is desirable on occasions to have as little obstruction to the free egress of sound as possible. This treatment is not desirable, under ordinary favorable conditions of space and position, in the Swell-boxes of the other Divisions or Sub-divisions of the organ.

VI. That the shutters of the Swell-box shall be of sufficient thickness to secure the desirable *pianissimo* effect when closed; and of sufficient width to produce a gradual *crescendo* in opening, and the minimum of obstruction to the free egress of sound when fully open. They must be built up, so as to retain their true form; and are to be properly carried on steel pivots in bronze plates, and balanced as may be necessary to secure correct and silent action. Under favorable conditions, no shutters should be less than 8 inches in width; and shutters of 15 inches are desirable in large boxes.

Little need be added to what is set forth in the First Principle; for it must be evident to every one acquainted with the conditions attending the proper production of sound by organ-pipes, and its free transmission, that a spacious and properly proportioned Swell-box is essential.

The Second Principle treats of matters of the greatest importance, and should receive the studious attention of the organ architect, and by no means be left to the decision of the ordinary organ-builder. Too much care cannot be taken in the selection of materials for, and their proper use in, the construction of the Swell-boxes suitable for the stop-apportionments of the several Divisions of the organ, as specially set forth in Principle IV. The woods most suitable for the construction of the Swell-box are yellow and white pine: the former for large boxes which are to hold stops, chiefly lingual, which have powerful and penetrating voices, speaking on winds of high pressures; and the latter and finer wood for boxes in which stops of refined and soft intonation, chiefly labial, are to be inclosed. In all Swell-boxes the shutters must be of the lightest and finest white pine, built up of several pieces so as to prevent warping in any manner.

According to the Third Principle, it is necessary for the interior surfaces of the Swell-box to be so treated as to be hard and of a sound-reflecting character. This very important condition requires the entire interior surfaces to be free from irregularities of any sound deflective tendency; and that they shall be perfectly smooth. This desirable condition can be secured by different treatments of the interior of the box; but that which will be found satisfactory can be secured by well gluing stout cotton sheeting, or the finest wall burlap, all over the walls and ceiling; and then painting it with three coats of hard-drying white lead and linseed oil paint, and finishing the same with a full coat of the finest glossy enamel paint. The inside surface of the shutters should be painted, directly on the wood, in the same manner. The exterior of the box should be well painted or varnished.[10]

[10] For a full treatment of matters connected with the Swell in the Organ, the reader is referred to "The Organ of the Twentieth Century," in which Chapter VIII, of twenty-two pages, is devoted to the subject.

We strongly advocate, as a necessary condition of our System, that every tonal Division and Sub-division—main or ancillary— of a perfect organ should, in whole or part, be made flexible and expressive by inclosure in a Swell-box. This advocacy has led us to add the following proposition to the literature of the organ:—

There is no more reason in making any Division of the Organ unexpressive and invariably uniform in strength of its tones, than there would be in destining any division of the Grand Orchestra to deliver its sounds at one unvarying strength and without any expression whatever.

The proposition is perfectly logical; and surely every thoughtful and unprejudiced musician must recognize it the instant its full bearing enters his mind. It is very doubtful, however, if it will appeal to the old-fashioned and naturally prejudiced organist: new ideas and methods are not usually acceptable to him. But things in this direction have made a considerable advance since we practically demonstrated, half a century ago, the importance, from every artistic point of view, of having two independent expressive Divisions commanded by one clavier; introducing for the first time in the history of organ-building compound tonal flexibility and expression. How far further advance can be made is pointed out in the following Parts of this Disquisition.

Having briefly treated of the Swell-box, it is now in order that consideration be given to the appliance by means of which the performer, at the console, opens and closes the shutters of the Swell-box. This appliance we have termed the Expression Lever, preferring it to the old and less appropriate term, "Swell-pedal." In the System of compound expression and flexibility of tone which we advocate, the office of the Expression Lever is twofold. First, it is the means whereby the performer imparts expressive powers or effects to the voices of the inclosed stops, by artistically opening and closing the shutters of the Swell-box in which they are placed. Secondly, it is the means of imparting powers of flexibility of tone to the voices of the inclosed stops, by so adjusting the position of the shutters as to secure any desired strength or softness of speech in the stops, and for any desired length of time. In a properly constructed Swell-box at least ten clearly marked intensities or values of tone can thus be secured to the ear, in the voice of every pipe planted in the box. We maintain that in a properly and artistically designed and stop-apportioned organ, powers of tonal flexibility are as important as those of expression. This contention is fully supported by what is set forth in following pages.

The form of the Expression Lever is a matter of considerable importance, especially so in organs designed on the System set forth in these pages. In instruments having only one Swell Division, the form of the Lever is not of great moment, provided it is convenient for the foot. But in groups of from three to seven, the form, proportions, and relative positions of Levers, call for careful consideration. There is one form which must be condemned; namely, that which imitates the sole of a shoe, with a depression for the heel. Strange to relate, this objectionable form has been adopted for the seven Levers in the great console of the Organ in the Wanamaker Store, in Philadelphia. But it is right to remark that the Divisions of the instrument are carried out according to the old method; and the Levers are used in the old-fashioned single manner. Such being the case, the form of the Levers is not of great importance.

The Committee on Standardization, already alluded to in connection with the manual claviers, gave somewhat scant attention to matters affecting the Expression Lever, only passing the following Resolutions:—

"*Resolved—That the Swell Organ Expression Pedal shall be placed opposite the gap between the DD♯ and FF♯ keys of the Pedal Organ clavier; and that the Choir Organ Pedal shall be placed to the left and the Solo Organ Pedal to the right of it.*

"*That the Crescendo Pedal shall be placed to the right of the Expression Pedals, and separated by being raised slightly above their line.*

"*That the width of each Expression Pedal shall be four inches; and the distance between the Pedals shall be half-an-inch.*

"*That a curved toe-stop shall be placed at the top of each of the Expression Pedals, forming a guide in which the toe can rest.*"

When only three Expression Levers are required, as in the generality of organs of four manual Divisions made to-day on old-fashioned methods of tonal appointment, the positions of the Levers, as decided by the Committee, may be accepted as satisfactory. But for instruments in which there may be from four to ten expressive Divisions, to be commanded by the performer at the console, a provision and an arrangement have to be made, undreamt of by the organists on the Committee. This important matter will be treated fully in the schemes for organs of different tonal appointments and dimensions, given in the following Parts.

Before deciding the most convenient form and dimensions for the Expression Levers, and their position with respect to each other, it is desirable that the conditions which have to be recognized in their formation and operations shall be understood. These are as follows: First—That the playing surface of the Lever shall be of sufficient width and length to accommodate a man's shoe of normal size, and such as should be worn by an organist while playing. Secondly—That the Lever shall have a plain and level surface, so as to offer no obstruction to the movement of foot upon it. Thirdly—That the Levers shall be placed at such a distance apart as to reasonably prevent an accidental moving of a Lever adjoining that being properly operated. Fourthly—That the Levers shall be so disposed that the foot can easily glide from one to another alongside, or to rest on the contiguous portions of two Levers, so as to operate both simultaneously and in similar direction. Fifthly—That the action of the Levers shall be uniform throughout a series; and shall move without a jerk or irregularity of any description; but with just sufficient resistance to be comfortable to the foot and safely responsive to its every pressure. A curvature in length of the Lever, and a toe-stop at its rear end, have been recommended; but as these somewhat interfere with the free and necessary gliding of the foot from one Lever to another, we are decidedly in favor of a plain, flat, playing surface. In our System, the Expression Levers have a very important role; widely different from that necessary in organs as commonly appointed on old lines.

The dimensions which seem desirable, from all points of view, for the standard Expression Lever are four inches in width and ten inches in length: and the distance between their adjacent edges should never exceed three-quarters of an inch. In groups of four or more Levers, the distance should be half-an-inch.

PART SECOND

THE CONCERT-ROOM ORGAN

HAT the Concert-room Organ of the Future will be a widely different instrument in its tonal appointment and means of tonal control, replete with powers of flexibility and expression—simple and compound—to what it is to-day, even at its best, cannot reasonably be questioned. Signs of progress are slowly showing themselves in directions we have pointed out and strongly advocated, and to some extent practically demonstrated the advantage of, during the past half century. When the true Concert-room Organ appears in all its inexhaustible tonal resources and grandeur, then, and then only, will the Organ justly claim to be The Temple of Tone—The Monarch of all Instruments—unsurpassed and unsurpassable.

The first attempt to produce a Concert-room Organ was made in England; and, important though it was, it failed to truly differentiate the instrument—in its tonal appointment—from a large Church Organ. The names of its Divisions failed to indicate a difference of aim and treatment; for they were, as of old, Pedal Organ, Choir Organ, Great Organ, Swell Organ, and Solo Organ. And, what is still more significant, in the stop-apportionments of the Divisions no radical difference obtained between them and those in the large Church Organs that had been constructed previously in England and on the Continent. From the installment of the Organ in St. George's Hall, Liverpool, in the year 1855, commenced what may be considered the era of Concert-room Organ construction in England; and several important instruments were produced, including the Organs for Leeds Town Hall, Albert Hall, London, and Centennial Hall, Sydney, N.S.W.; but in not one of which appeared any indication of advance toward the institution of a new and special tonal treatment imperatively called for in the Concert-room Organ. Even the great Willis failed to see the necessity for a radical departure from Church Organ methods. What can be said, in this direction, of the organ-builders in this country to-day?

Notwithstanding what has been attempted in England in recent years which seems to show an awakening to the advisability of giving up old-world ideas, in favor of more artistic modes of tonal appointment and control, in the construction of the Concert-room Organ; we are convinced that The Temple of Tone, in its grandeur and architecture of sound, will first be built in this country: and that so soon as the younger schools of organ-builders and organists realize what has to be done, and learn how to put it into consistent form. Then, on its frieze can justly be inscribed THE MONARCH OF ALL INSTRUMENTS.

In the present Part we give the results of an earnest study of all matters connected with the general tonal structure and divisional stop-apportionment and control of the true Concert-room Organ—a study which has extended over half a century, and which commenced with a practical demonstration of the two leading principles on which the development of the organ must be founded; namely, divisional and subdivisional contrast of tone, and compound tonal flexibility and expression. These must never be ignored if progress is to be made along artistic lines. We only profess to point a way toward the solution of the problem which besets the proper building of the Temple of Tone; hoping that others, better qualified for the task, will follow us, correcting our mistakes, and carrying the development of the instrument to the highest state of excellence, scientifically and artistically. That we shall not be spared to witness the final achievement is certain; but that conviction does not dishearten us in attempting to contribute toward its fruition.

It is evident from what has already been done in the designing and construction of Concert-room Organs, that a full realization of all their requirements has never been reached by those interested in their production. It is certain that not a single instrument of the class, which has appeared in this country or abroad, can be pronounced as sufficient and satisfactory in all required directions. As we have said on other pages, it must be admitted by all thoughtful musicians that no other class of organ is required to meet so many and varied demands on its tonal resources and powers as that properly designed for the concert-room. The instrument has a threefold office to fulfil, and that to the fullest extent that can be rendered possible in an organ, responding to every thought and mood of an inspired performer. It must be properly equipped tonally for taking part, in conjunction with an orchestra, in the accompaniment of Oratorios and other important choral works. It should be equally suitable for the accompaniment of such works, furnishing a sufficient substitute for the grand orchestra. It must furnish the most exacting musician with the necessary tone-colors, scientifically and artistically grouped, and placed under his certain and easy control, for the adequate and expressive rendition of transcriptions of orchestral scores; and for the artistic performance of all classes of organ music. In short, the true Concert-room Organ must be a two-fold instrument—a perfect organ and a representative orchestra combined. In the latter capacity, in certain tonal developments, surpassing in dignity and impressiveness the grand orchestra.

To what has been said may be added the following quotation from Berlioz's Treatise on Orchestration:—"The organ seems able—like the pianoforte, and even better—to present itself in the instrumental hierarchy under two aspects:—as an instrument belonging to the orchestra, or as being in itself a complete and independent orchestra. It is doubtless possible to blend the organ with the divers constituent elements of the orchestra, and this has been many times done: but it is strangely derogatory to the majestic instrument to reduce it to a secondary place. Moreover, it should be felt that the smooth, equal, and uniform sonorousness of the organ, never entirely melts into the variously characterized sounds of the orchestra, and that there seems to exist between these two musical powers a secret antipathy. The Organ and the Orchestra are both Kings; or rather, one is Emperor, the other Pope; their mission is not the same; their interests are too vast, and too diverse, to be confounded together. Therefore, on almost all occasions when this singular connection is attempted, either the organ much predominates over the orchestra, or the orchestra, having been raised to an immoderate degree of influence almost eclipses its adversary." When Berlioz wrote these words he knew only the severe unexpressive organs of his country and day. He never dreamt of the possibilities another century was to develop.

We think that if the organ designer will endeavor to associate, in his mind, the different great families of musical tones with different colors, he will find considerable assistance given him in the formation of tonal schemes suitable for the appointments of the Divisions and Subdivisions of the Concert-room Organ. Should he happen to have some experience in the production of refined and beautiful colors by the mixing of various pigments, he will find that experience to be helpful in his studies of compound tone-production. We speak from experience in this matter. The following are the colors we have mentally associated with the families of tones produced by labial and lingual organ-pipes:

Organ-tones . .	White
Flute-tones . .	Blue
String-tones . .	Violet
Reed-tones . .	Yellow
Brass-tones . .	Red

As the subject just touched upon must be considered essentially esthetical, and one not likely to be acknowledged by the organ designers of to-day, it is unnecessary to enlarge upon it. To those to whom it may appeal, no enlargement is necessary. But it is desirable, before we enter on the main subject of the present Part, that a few particulars be given regarding the families of tones alluded to above.

ORGAN-TONE

This is the tone peculiar to the organ in so much that it cannot be produced, in its purity, by any other known musical instrument. It, accordingly, stands alone, in its grandeur and beauty, the acknowledged foundation of the Temple of Tone. As it varies in quality under certain pipe treatments it is properly divided into two classes of tone, as follows:—

Pure Organ-tone.—This is produced by the true and properly voiced Diapason, and its direct harmonic series of derivatives, commencing with the

Octave, and carried as far as is practicable in the formation of small pipes possessing the same quality of voice; producing, in combination, what is designated the *Diapason chorus*— the chief glory of the organ. Pure Organ-tone strictly belongs to the foundation Divisions; namely, the Pedal and Grand Organs. Its introduction in other tonal Divisions is not imperative; though it may in some cases be desirable for artistic coloration or support. The second class of Organ-tone is properly designated—

Free Organ-tone.—This embraces a valuable and effective series of voices, which show in combination with Pure Organ-tone certain ameliorating colorations; and also different strengths of intonation. Stops producing Free Organ-tone are commonly and desirably of metal, and vary in scale and shape, assuming cylindrical and direct and inverted conical forms of different proportions. All the stops yielding Free Organ-tone are extremely valuable; their refined and sympathetic voices peculiarly adapting them for accompanimental music; and, in their compound tonality, they are invaluable in enriching and delicately tinting the voices of other differently toned stops. The principal difference obtaining between Free Organ-tone and Pure Organ-tone is created by the presence in the former of certain harmonic upper partial tones. This is especially the case in the voices of the valuable Gemshorn, regarding which Professor Helmholtz says, they have the property of rendering some higher partial tones comparatively stronger than the lower; hence their peculiar importance in artistic registration and coloration, in which clearness and brightness is required, without a cutting quality which tends to destroy repose and refinement of tone.

FLUTE-TONE

The stops yielding Flute-tone are the most numerous in the tonal appointment of the Concert-room Organ, and are of great importance and value. They are primarily divided into two classes—those yielding unimitative Flute Organ-tone, and those yielding imitative Orchestral Flute-tone. The latter class can here be dismissed in a few words, for their voices imitate and represent in the stop-apportionment of the organ those of the Flutes and Piccolo of the orchestra only. The Orchestral Flutes, of eight and four feet pitch, in the organ are formed of open pipes, preferably of wood, and for the larger part harmonic. In the finer examples the imitation of the orchestral Flutes is remarkably true. These valuable stops find their proper places in the Wood-Wind and Solo Divisions of the Concert-room Organ.

The stops yielding unimitative Flute-tone are many and varied in their formations. They, however, group themselves in three families, which produce tones having in their characteristic timbres harmonic upper partial tones differing in nature and number.

The First Family comprises stops formed of open pipes of standard speaking lengths; in the voices of which the first upper partial tone is the octave of the prime tone; tending to the production of clear and penetrating intonations of various strengths, and of great value in the institution of contrasts and in coloration. We have designated this quality as *Open Flute-tone*. The unimitative HARMONIC FLUTES are included in this family; the harmonic pipes of which are approximately double the standard speaking length.

The Second Family, which is of almost equal importance to the first, comprises stops formed of pipes, chiefly of wood, and entirely covered or stopped; in the voices of which the second upper partial tone is commonly more or less evident in combination with the prime tone. The first upper partial cannot be produced by this family; and, accordingly, all its covered pipes yield tones markedly dissimilar to those produced by the open pipes of the first family; these are designated, for the sake of distinction, *Covered Flute-tones*. The value of the several covered stops, in all their many pitches, cannot be overrated: their voices, in which the quint is more or less prominent in combination with the prime tone, as in the QUINTATEN, are of great importance in registration and tonal coloration. While the Open Flute-tone may be symbolized by light pure blue; Covered Flute-tone may be symbolized by slightly impure deep blue. Practically, all the Flute-toned stops of 32 feet and 16 feet pitch belong to this family.

The Third Family embraces a few stops formed of metal and wood, producing what is termed *Half-covered Flute-tone*, from the fact that their covers or tompions are fitted with open tubes or are perforated; thus partially opening the upper end of their interior air-columns to the external air. The tones produced by such pipes are brighter and lighter than those yielded by wholly covered pipes; and, accordingly, hold a position, tonally, between them and the tones of open pipes. The most important stops of this intermediate family is the German ROHRFLÖTE and the French FLÛTE À CHEMINÉE; but the most beautiful is the FLAUTO D'AMORE. The ROHRFLÖTE has been made of several pitches, all of which are valuable in the softer Divisions of the Concert-room Organ.

VIOL ORGAN-TONE

These stops yielding what we have designated, for the sake of distinction, Viol Organ-tone, are, while furnishing string tones in various degrees of assertiveness in combination with other qualities of voice, strictly unimitative; and on this account hold extremely prominent positions in the tonal appointment of the organ.

On the border-line between Pure Organ-tone and Viol Organ-tone is the refined and sympathetic voice of the true SALICIONAL: while the most effective and characteristic stops of this dual tonality are the QUINTATENS, the GRAND VIOL, and the VIOLIN DIAPASON or GEIGENPRINCIPAL. When in registration and coloration a delicate string stain, so to speak, is desired, the artist organist will resort to some one of the stops now under consideration: and provided the organ has been correctly appointed and stop-appointed in its several Divisions and Subdivisions by a master designer, he will doubtless find the suitable stop or stops at his command. But it must be admitted that String-toned stops of all classes have been lamentably neglected by modern organ designers; and they were almost unknown by the old builders.

ORCHESTRAL STRING-TONE

The stops whose voices closely imitate those of the string instruments of the Orchestra may justly be placed in a very prominent position in the tonal structure of the true Concert-room Organ. And we are proud to be able to say that we were the first in the organ-designing world to realize and directly lead to the practical demonstration of this important fact in the constitution of the Concert Organ. The first properly stop-apportioned and independent expressive String Organ was schemed by us, and was carried into effect in the Organ installed in the Festival Hall of the Louisiana Purchase Exposition, at St. Louis, in 1904.[11] Although the absolute necessity of such a complete and independent Division, representing as fully as practicable the fundamental division of the Grand Orchestra, must be evident to every one interested in the tonal development of the Concert Organ, and gifted with a keen musical sense and the perception of tonal values; strange to say, no other attempt has been made to supply an adequate and properly appointed String Organ in any of the Concert-room instruments constructed during the past twenty years, and up to the time of writing (1924). What would seem to be the reason for the short-comings in this direction we must leave to the imagination of the organ lover who reads these words; our views on the subject might be considered somewhat severe.

No organ can be pronounced a true and efficient Concert-room instrument, however large it may be, if it is without a complete and proportionate String Division, commanded by any and every clavier. Our matured ideas regarding its stop-apportionment and control will be seen in the Specifications given in the present Part.

A few words conveying the views evidently held by the designers of the early Concert-room Organs in the matter of String-toned stops will be instructive to those interested in the subject of organ tonal development. In the year 1855, what must be recognized as the first concrete attempt toward the creation of a Concert-room Organ was installed in St. George's Hall, Liverpool. This instrument, of one hundred complete stops, distributed over a pedal and four manual Divisions, was constructed by Henry Willis, who was not only a great organ-builder, but also an accomplished organist. Strange to say, in the tonal appointment of this instrument, the importance of String-toned stops was practically ignored; for not one of a fully imitative character was introduced. As originally appointed, the few unimitative ones were so dispersed that massing of String-tone was all but impossible. The following are how matters stood in this direction: In the Pedal Organ there was a

[11] See "The Organ of the Twentieth Century," Page 505.

VIOLON, 16 FT.; in the Great Organ a VIOLONCELLO, 8 FT. and a VIOLA, 4 FT.; and in the Choir Organ a VIOLA DA GAMBA, 8 FT. and a VIOLA, 4 FT. In neither the Swell nor Solo Organ was there a single String-toned stop of any class.

The next Concert-room Organ, in point of time, is the instrument installed in the Town Hall of Leeds (1859). It was designed by the late Dr. W. Spark and Henry Smart, and constructed by Gray & Davison. It comprises one hundred and one independent speaking stops, and of these only four are String-toned, and distributed in its six Divisions thus: in the Pedal Organ a VIOLON, 16 FT. and a VIOLONCELLO, 8 FT.; in the Great Organ a VIOLA, 8 FT.; and in the Choir Organ a VIOLA DA GAMBA, 8 FT. No stop of approaching a String-tone appears in the Swell, the Orchestral Solo, or Echo Organ.

We may pass over the other organs, including that, of one hundred and eleven speaking stops, built by Henry Willis, and installed in the Royal Albert Hall, London, which show no advance in general tonal appointment, constructed prior to the year 1890, in which the Concert-room Organ, of one hundred and thirty complete stops, was constructed by William Hill & Son, and installed in the Centennial Hall, Sydney, N. S. W. We pass on to this important instrument; because, being built thirty-five years after the construction of the St. George's Hall Organ, it might reasonably be expected to display a decided advance in the all-important matter of the String-toned stops and their necessary grouping, to somewhat represent the massed String forces of the Orchestra. But, alas!—its builders utterly failed to realize the absolute necessity of providing a proper proportion and disposition of String-toned stops, and especially those of an imitative orchestral tonality. The few stops introduced and disposed in the Organ, when it was performed on by Best, at its Inauguration in 1890, were as follows: In the Pedal Organ a VIOLONE, 16 FT. and GAMBA, 16 FT.; in the Great Organ a VIOLA, 8 FT. and GAMBA, 8 FT.; in the Swell Organ a VIOLA DA GAMBA, 8 FT.; in the Solo Organ a VIOLA, 8 FT.; and in the Echo Organ a VIOLE D'AMOUR, 8 FT. and VIOLE D'AMOUR, 4 FT. Nothing obtained in this instrument—the largest Concert-room Organ existing at the time—in the nature of strictly imitative String-tone; and the only possibility of massing such tone as was provided, was by considerable coupling, and the corresponding crippling of the different Divisions in other directions.

Such were the conditions in all the existing Concert-room Organs, when, in 1901, we were called upon to design the largest instrument of the class that had been contemplated up to that time. The opportunity was given us to carry into effect our ideas regarding the appointment of a complete and practically independent String Organ. We, accordingly, schemed an independent Division of eighteen ranks of pipes, which embraced imitative representatives of all the bowed string instruments of the Orchestra, and a Viol harmonic structure. Fortunately all the stops were voiced by one of the most artistic English voicers of String-toned stops. This String Organ was inclosed in a special Swell-box, and formed the Second Subdivision of the Organ commanded by the Third Clavier. In this direction we made a grave mistake: the String Organ should have been an Ancillary, available alike on any one or more of the claviers, alone, or in association with the stop-apportionment of the Divisions specially commanded by the claviers. But as our String Organ was a new thing, perhaps the mistake was pardonable.

A very timid attempt was made, in a similar direction, in the Concert Organ, designed by Dr. Alfred Hollins, and constructed by Norman & Beard, which was installed in the Town Hall of Johannesburg, South Africa, in 1916. In the Orchestral Organ of this instrument, and forming a portion of its appointment of nineteen stops, are the following: CONTRA-VIOLA, 16 FT., VIOLE, 8 FT., VIOLE CÈLESTE (II. Ranks from FF), VIOLE OCTAVIANTE, 4 FT., and VIOLE CORNETTE (III. Ranks). Considering that the instrument has ninety stops, including the few derived stops in the Pedal Organ, it must be admitted that the provision of imitative Orchestral String-tone is lamentably deficient. We wonder at this weakness in this all-important orchestral element, knowing, as we do, the wonderful artistry in interpretation, and refined feeling in tonal coloration, possessed by Dr. Hollins. The Orchestral Organ is playable on any or all of the manual claviers—a step in the right direction. Nothing calling for special comment in the present matter appears in the Concert-room Organs constructed during recent years in this country.

In the String-toned Division of the true Concert-room Organ, all the bowed string instruments of the Orchestra must be represented as fully as possible; and, in addition, a VIOL harmonic structure should be added; for it is impossible to obtain the necessary richness of compound String-tone from the mere multiplication of unison voices—that tone which is, at once, the foundation and the glory of the Grand Orchestra.

ORCHESTRAL REED-TONE

It is essential, in the tonal appointment of the true Concert-room Organ, that the reed instruments of the Orchestra be fully represented by stops of strictly imitative voices. These instruments are the Contrafagotto, Fagotto, Basson-quinte, Oboe, Clarinetto, Corno di Bassetto, Cor Anglais, and Saxophones. Modern skill has developed lingual stops to such a point of excellence that the characteristic tones of these instruments have been imitated with remarkable fidelity. Had this progress not been made a truly satisfactory Concert Organ would have been an impossibility. Now it remains, in scheming the tonal structure of the organ, to dispose them in the most consistent and artistic manner with regard to the other stops of contrasting and analogous tonalities.

The different timbers of the lingual Reed-toned stops render them of great value: those of unison pitch being most effective as solo voices; namely, the OBOE, 8 FT.; CLARINETTO, 8 FT.; FAGOTTO, 8 FT.; CORNO DI BASSETTO, 8 FT.; COR ANGLAIS, 8 FT. and SAXOPHONE, 8 FT. The double and mutation stops are of great importance, being very effective in combination and in darkening coloration. These stops are the CONTRAFAGOTTO, 16 FT.; CONTRA-OBOE, 16 FT.; CONTRA-CLARINETTO, 16 FT.; CONTRA-BASSETT-HORN, 16 FT.; CONTRA-SAXOPHONE, 16 FT.; BASSON-QUINTE, 5⅓ FT. and CLARINETTO QUINTA, 5⅓ FT.

The most satisfactory Reed-toned stop, from an imitative point of view, is the CLARINETTO: and it is eminently so when associated with a soft-toned DOPPELFLÖTE or a LIEBLICHGEDECKT, 8 FT., the harmonic upper partials of which enrich those of the lingual stop. When the CLARINETTO is inserted, as a Solo stop, in the Concert Organ, it should always assume this dual form. The CONTRA-CLARINETTO and CLARINETTO QUINTA are purely organ stops, and of very great value, forming along with the unison CLARINETTO a singularly beautiful Reed-tone family.

The OBOE, 8 FT. is introduced in the Concert-room Organ under two treatments, named respectively OBOE and ORCHESTRAL OBOE. The former, as usually formed and voiced, cannot be considered imitative of the tone of the orchestral instrument, in its somewhat full voice: and the latter is only satisfactory when made of the most approved form, and voiced by a master-hand. It has been found extremely difficult to imitate the "small acid-sweet voice—having a pastoral character, full of tenderness," as Hector Berlioz has accurately described the tones of the orchestral instrument.

The COR ANGLAIS, 8 FT., properly represents in tone the orchestral instrument of the same name, which is really an Alto Oboe; regarding which Berlioz remarks: "its quality of tone, less piercing, more veiled, and deeper than that of the Oboe, does not so well as the latter lend itself to the gaiety of rustic strains. . . It is a melancholy, dreamy, and rather noble voice." The organ stop, if carefully voiced, yields a voice of medium power, extremely valuable in compound tone-production and coloration.

The CORNO DI BASSETTO, 8 FT., represents in tone the Tenor Clarinet of the orchestra. It is, accordingly, when properly scaled and voiced, richer and fuller in tone than the CLARINETTO, 8 FT., and is, on this account, more effective in combination and coloration. The organ stop, the CONTRA-BASSETT-HORN, 16 FT., although it has no counterpart in the orchestra, should find a place in every important Concert-room Organ. As, like the CLARINETTO, its resonators are short it is easily inserted in a Swell-box.

Although the FAGOTTO, 8 FT., and CONTRAFAGOTTO, 16 FT., may be accepted as representing the Fagotto and Contrafagotto of the orchestra, the latter going down to BBBB♭, it must be admitted that the organ stops, so far made, cannot be pronounced strictly imitative in their voices. Notwithstanding this shortcoming, the value of both the stops cannot be overrated, and their insertion in every Concert-room Organ is imperative. The CONTRAFAGOTTO, so scaled and voiced as to yield different intensities and colorations of tone, can with advantage be inserted in more than one manual Division of the Organ, and it is also a valuable Pedal Organ stop.

The SAXOPHONE, 8 FT. and CONTRA-SAXOPHONE, 16 FT. are comparatively late additions to the Reed-toned forces of the organ. The orchestral Saxophones belong to the Clarinet family. Their voices are thus described by Berlioz as possessing: "Most rare and precious qualities. Soft and penetrating in the higher part, full and rich in the lower part, their medium has something profoundly expressive. It is, in short, a quality *sui generis*, presenting vague analogies with the sounds of the Violoncello, of the Clarinet, and Corno Inglese, and invested with a brazen tinge which imparts a quite peculiar accent." Dr. W. H. Stone, commenting on the peculiar Violoncello like intonation, remarks: "It reproduces on a magnified scale something of the Violoncello quality, and gives great sustaining power to the full chorus of brass instruments, by introducing a mass of harmonic overtones." The opinions expressed by these recognized authorities clearly point to what pipe designers and voicers have to accomplish in the production of satisfactory lingual SAXOPHONES. On the other hand, accepting the best stops that have already been produced, the most artistic course to adopt would seem to be to associate with them soft-voiced String-toned stops, rich in "harmonic overtones." This, however, need only be done with the unison SAXOPHONE likely to be made as a solo stop. Such refinement as this is only likely to be resorted to by the artist designer of true Concert-room Organs. The SAXOPHONE has been made with free-reeds, as in the case of the beautiful stop presented to us by the late Hilborne L. Roosevelt, and inserted in the Pedal of our Chamber Organ. A labial wood stop, imitating the voice of the orchestral instrument with remarkable fidelity, has been made.[12]

ORCHESTRAL BRASS-TONE

The lingual stops of the Organ, which yield tones more or less closely imitative of those of the brass wind-instruments of the orchestra and band, are the TROMBONES, HORN, TRUMPET, CORNET, TUBA, OPHICLEIDE, and EUPHONIUM. Although these stops are few in number, they are of immense importance in the tonal structure of the Concert-room Organ: and much depends on the qualities of their voices. Advances have been made by expert voicers in the development of orchestral tones in certain of the stops named, yet much remains to be done. Numerous voicers seem to have come to the conclusion that the production of loud and blatant tones—the product of high-pressure wind and screaming harmonics—is the cure for all ills: losing sight of what the orchestra teaches, and of the all-important elements of refinement and beauty.

In the case of the HORN, 8 FT., pipe-makers and voicers have made noteworthy progress toward the imitation of the characteristic voice of the orchestral instrument; but entire success has not yet crowned their labors. This, however, is not difficult to understand. Berlioz calls the orchestral Horn a "noble and melancholy instrument"; and this seems expressive, for in its finest tones there are no tendencies to bassiness and clang. Indeed, the chief difficulty experienced by the voicer of the lingual stop is getting rid of such

[12] For full particulars of this stop, see "The Art of Organ Building," Vol. II., pp. 484-6.

assertiveness. The closest imitation of the unforced tones of the Horn, produced by a master player, we have ever heard were yielded by the tenor register of a labial stop of the KERAULOPHONE class, of full scale, and voiced on wind of low pressure. The orchestral Horn has two series of sounds, designated the *open* and *closed;* and it is hopeless to expect that both these characteristic tones will ever be imitated in a single stop. Choice of the open tones should, accordingly, be made by the voicer.

The brass wind-instrument of the orchestra which, as a rule, has been most successfully imitated in the lingual stops of the organ is the Trumpet. Two varieties of the stop obtain, which may be designated simply TRUMPET, 8 FT., producing a normal brassy tone of a full and good mixing quality, suitable for insertion in the foundation Division of the organ; and the ORCHESTRAL TRUMPET, 8 FT., yielding the brilliant silvery tones of the orchestral instrument when played by an artist. As the TRUMPET is one of the few stops that can properly be introduced in the tonal appointments of different Divisions of the organ, it is desirable that it should be voiced to yield different intensities and colorings, both on the score of contrast and analogy. Accordingly, it is desirable to add prefixes to the general name, indicating any special or distinguishing tonal qualities or powers the stops may possess. As we have said elsewhere, the TRUMPET must be placed under perfect control. A TRUMPET should never be placed *en chamade*, as in the Organ in the Church of Saint-Ouen, Rouen, and in several of the large Spanish organs. To imagine any orchestral instrument, or its organ representative, played without expression, could only be possible in the brain of a musical ignoramus. The organ DOUBLE TRUMPET, 16 FT., has no counterpart in the orchestra. It is a product of the possibilities afforded by the organ for the creation of new and noble voices; which go far to build up in grandeur, and beyond the possibility of imitation, The Temple of Tone.

The Trombones of the grand orchestra belong to the Trumpet family, furnishing, properly considered, the bass to the true orchestral Slide Trumpet. Their tones carry down, with singular grandeur, the brilliant brazen clang and accurate intonation of the Trumpet. The Alto, Tenor, and Bass Trombones, along with the Trumpet, form the complete enharmonic wind quartet of the orchestra; and thus clearly point the way to the necessary massing of TROMBONES of different pitches in the Concert-room Organ. The stops of this important family are the pedal CONTRA-TROMBONE, 32 FT.; and the manual CONTRA-TROMBONE, 16 FT.; TROMBONE, 8 FT.; TROMBONE QUINT, 5⅓ FT.; and TROMBONE OCTAVE, 4 FT. A TROMBONE TIERCE, 6⅖ FT. can be added if considered desirable; but its value is questionable. As the TROMBONES are of great value in the artistic rendition of orchestral scores, much care must be taken in their scaling, voicing, and regulating.

The Ophicleides of the old orchestras were three in number—the Alto, Bass, and Double-Bass. They are keyed-instruments belonging to the Keyed-Bugle family; and although they are no longer used in the grand orchestra, they were resorted to by certain composers for the production of special tonal effects. For instance, Mendelssohn introduced the Ophicleide in some of his scores; notably in those of "Elijah" and "Midsummer Night's Dream" music. The tones of the Ophicleides are broad and impressive; so much so that, in seeking to reproduce them, Wagner employed in his orchestra both the Bass and Contra-Bass Tubas. As the Ophicleide is no longer used in the orchestra, lingual-pipe voicers of to-day have no opportunity of studying its characteristic tones. That its voice when played by a master was full and impressive is clearly indicated by the instruments Wagner considered necessary to imitate it.

So far as our knowledge extends, the first series of OPHICLEIDES, of double and unison pitch, introduced in the Concert-room Organ, is that distributed in the Pedal, Great, Swell, and Solo Divisions of the Organ in St. George's Hall, Liverpool; and, strange to say, only one of the stops is rendered expressive. That in the Solo, voiced on wind of twenty-two inches, yells with uncontrollable voice. It is strange how this love for this fixed blatant noise is beloved of organ-builders and organists, who are, naturally, supposed to have musical sense and taste. Do they ever give a thought as to how the Ophicleide was played under the baton of an experienced Conductor? The question holds good with reference to any powerfully voiced lingual stop in the organ.

Although the orchestra possesses the Bass-Tuba, which Berlioz designates the "Double-Bass of harmony," and describes it as a species of Bombardon, possessing an immense advantage over all other low wind instruments; it must be recognized that the TUBAS of the organ, while partaking of the tonality of the orchestral instrument, are stops producing tones of a gravity and volume of unsurpassable dignity and power. Such being the case the unison stop has commonly been designated TUBA MIRABILIS. The TUBAS belong, in their grandeur, to The Temple of Tone; in the structure of which they hold all-important places. In the true Concert-room Organ the TUBAS must always be inclosed and rendered flexible and expressive. Similar remarks obtain regarding the TROMBAS, the voices of which occupy a position, in strength of tone, between those of the TRUMPETS and TUBAS; but with a coloring different from both. Accordingly, the TROMBAS afford a wide field for the exercise of musical sense, taste, and skill on the part of the voicer.

The BOMBARDE, beloved of French organ-builders, is a large-scaled stop of 16 feet pitch, and powerful intonation. So much so, that the presence of one is considered sufficient to give the name "Clavier des Bombardes" to the Division in which it is placed. The names CONTRE-BOMBARDE, 32 FT. and QUINTE BOMBARDE, 10⅔ FT. have been given to Pedal Organ stops of these grave pitches. The exact character of the tone of the BOMBARDE has not been determined; but it seems desirable that it should stand midway between the tones of the TUBA and the CONTRAFAGOTTO, and partaking of both. Here is another opportunity for the clever voicer to show his knowledge, taste, and skill. The voicing of the French BOMBARDES leaves something to be desired.

We believe that it is a wise plan for the designer or organ architect, before proceeding to decide the most artistic and effective stop-apportionments of the several distinct tonal Divisions of the organ, and especially of the Concert-room Organ, to prepare a complete tonal scheme, in the form of a list of the necessary or available stops, classified under the different qualities or families of tone—unimitative and imitative—capable of being effectively produced by the labial and lingual pipes at present constructed. No valuable quality of tone must be overlooked; special care being taken to provide an ample force of foundation Pure Organ-tone and a practically complete harmonic structure, of the same tonality, based thereon. Without this foundation, the Temple of Tone cannot be reared. It may be found desirable, or, indeed, necessary, to develop certain other tones, of an unimitative or imitative character, both in lower and higher pitches, as will be shown, than are at present in use (1924). Fortunately no great difficulty presents itself in this direction. Great care must be taken in the production of the tones imitating those of orchestral instruments; for much of the musical value and beauty of the Concert-room Organ will depend on this care.

It is undesirable that any two stops in the organ shall have exactly similar voices. Indeed, it may be accepted as a postulate, in Concert Organ tonal appointment, that there shall be no duplication of stops of similar tonality or strength of voice. Variety of tone is a standard law in artistic organ appointment.

The following is a classified List of Stops, from which selections may be made for the stop-apportionments of the Divisions of Concert Organs of all sizes:

LIST OF STOPS SUITABLE FOR THE TONAL APPOINTMENT OF CONCERT-ROOM ORGANS

MANUAL ORGANS

PURE ORGAN-TONE

Stop		Pitch
Double Diapason, major	M.	16 Feet
Double Diapason, minor	M.	16 "
Grand Quint	M.	$10\frac{2}{3}$ "
Major Diapason	M.	8 "
Diapason (Schulze)	M.	8 "
Minor Diapason	M.	8 "
Diapason (English)	M.	8 "
Echo Diapason	M.	8 "
Diapason	W.	8 "
Quint	M.	$5\frac{1}{3}$ "
Octave, major	M.	4 "
Octave, minor	M.	4 "
Tierce	M.	$3\frac{1}{5}$ "
Twelfth	M.	$2\frac{2}{3}$ Ft.
Septième	M.	$2\frac{2}{7}$ "
Super-octave	M.	2 "
Seventeenth	M.	$1\frac{3}{5}$ "
Nineteenth	M.	$1\frac{1}{3}$ "
Grand Cornet	M.	VII. Ranks

$8'—5\frac{1}{3}'—4'—3\frac{1}{5}'—2\frac{2}{3}'—2\frac{2}{7}'—2'$.

Stop		Pitch
Full Mixture	M.	V. Ranks

FREE ORGAN-TONE

Stop		Pitch
Grossgemshorn	M.	16 Feet
Double Dulciana	M.	16 "
Horn Diapason	M.	8 "
Dulciana	M.	8 "
Dolcan	M.	8 "
Gemshorn	M.	8 "
Dolce	M.	8 "
Keraulophone	M.	8 "

FREE ORGAN-TONE—Continued

Voix Angélique	M.	8 Feet
Voix Éolienne	M.	8 "
Gemshornquinte	M.	$5\frac{1}{3}$ "
Gemshornoctav	M.	4 "
Cœlestina	M.	4 "
Dulcet	M.	4 "
Dulciana Tierce	M.	$3\frac{1}{5}$ "
Gemshorn Twelfth	M.	$2\frac{2}{3}$ "
Echo Quint	M.	$2\frac{2}{3}$ "
Dulciana Fifteenth	M.	2 "
Gemshorn Super-octave	M.	2 "
Grand Dolce Cornet	M.	VII. Ranks
Dulciana Cornet	M.	V. Ranks
Harmonia Ætheria	T.	VI. Ranks

$4'$—$3\frac{1}{5}'$—$2\frac{2}{3}'$—$2'$—$1\frac{3}{5}'$—$1\frac{1}{3}'$—$1'$.

FLUTE ORGAN-TONE

(Open Flute-Tone)

Flûte à Pavillon	M.	8 Feet
Stenterphone	M	8 "
Tibia Plena	W.	8 "
Flauto Maggiore	W.	8 "
Nachthorn	W.	8 "
Flachflöte	W.	8 "
Hohlflöte	W.	8 "
Clarabella	W.	8 "
Waldflöte	W.	8 "
Melodia	W.	8 "
Philomela	W.	8 "
Harmonic Flute	M.	8 "
Spitzflöte	M.	8 "
Flauto Amabile	W.	8 "
Flauto Dolce	W.	8 "
Dolcissimo	W.	8 "
Zartflöte	W.	8 "
Flautone	M.	8 "
Flauto Amoroso	M.	4 "
Spitzflöte	M.	4 "
Claribel Flute	W.	4 "
Waldflöte	W.	4 "
Clear Flute	W.	4 "
Harmonic Flute	M.	4 "

(Open Flute-Tone)—Continued

Flageolet	M.	2 Feet
Spitzflöte Cornet	M.	V. Ranks

(Half Covered Flute-Tone)

Doppelrohrgedeckt	W.	8 Feet
Doppelrohrflöte	W.	8 "
Rohrflöte	W.	8 "
Flûte à Cheminée	M.	8 "
Rohrflötenquinte	M.	$5\frac{1}{3}$ "
Flauto d'Amore	W.	4 "
Rohrnasat	M.	$2\frac{2}{3}$ "

(Covered Flute-Tone)

Manualuntersatz	W.	32 Feet
Grossdoppelgedeckt	W.	16 "
Grossgedeckt	W.	16 "
Bourdon	W.	16 "
Starkgedeckt	W.	16 "
Quintaten	W.	16 "
Bourdon Doux	W.	16 "
Bourdonecho	W.	16 "
Lieblichgedeckt	W.	16 "
Doppelflöte	W.	8 "
Quintaten	W.	8 "
Zartgedeckt	W.	8 "
Doppelgedeckt	W.	8 "
Tibia Clausa	W.	8 "
Lieblichgedeckt	W.	8 "
Gedeckt	W.	8 "
Gedecktquinte	M.	$5\frac{1}{3}$ "
Lieblichflöte	M.	4 "
Divinare	W.	4 "
Zauberflöte	M.	4 "
Gedeckt-Terz	M.	$3\frac{1}{5}$ "

VIOL ORGAN-TONE

Contra-Violone	M.	16 Feet
Contra-Gamba	M.	16 "
Cone Gamba	M.	16 "
Violin Diapason	M.	8 "
Grand Viol	M.	8 "
Viole à Pavillon	M.	8 "
Salicional	M.	8 "
Bass Viol	M.	8 "
Cone Gamba	M.	8 "
Echo Gamba	M.	8 "

VIOL ORGAN-TONE—Continued

Æoline	M.	8 Feet
Viol Quint	M.	5 1/3 "
Gambette	M.	4 "
Salicet	M.	4 "
Geigenoctav	M.	4 "
Cone Gamba	M.	4 "
Viol Octave	M.	4 "
Viol Tierce	M.	3 1/5 "
Viol Twelfth	M.	2 2/3 "
Viole Septième	M.	2 2/7 "
Viol Fifteenth	M.	2 "
Viol Cornet (Sordino) 4′—3 1/5′—2 2/3′—2 2/7′—2′.	M.	V. Ranks
Viol Sesquialtera 2 2/3′—1 3/5′.	M.	II. Ranks

ORCHESTRAL FLUTE-TONE

Orchestral Flute	W.	8 Feet
Orchestral Flute	W.	4 "
Recorder	W.	2 2/3 "
Orchestral Piccolo	M.	2 "
Flûte à Bec	M.	2 "

ORCHESTRAL STRING-TONE

Contrabasso	W.	16 Feet
Contrabasso Sordo	M.	16 "
Viola Bastarda	M.	10 1/3 "
Violoncello	M.	8 "
Violoncello Sordo	M.	8 "
Viola	M.	8 "
Viola Sordo	M.	8 "
Viole d'Orchestre	M.	8 "
Violino	M.	8 "
Violino Sordo	M.	8 "
Violino Vibrato	M.	8 "
Viola Pomposa	M.	8 "
Viola da Gamba	M.	8 "
Viola da Gamba (Sharp)	M.	8 "
Viola d'Amore	T.	8 "
Viola d'Amore (Flat)	T.	8 "
Violetta	T.	4 "
Violetta Sordo	T.	4 "

ORCHESTRAL REED-TONE

Contrafagotto	W.	16 Feet
Contra-Oboe	M.	16 "

ORCHESTRAL REED-TONE—Continued

Contra-Clarinetto	M.	16 Feet
Contra-Bassett-Horn	M.	16 "
Contra-Saxophone	M.	16 "
Fagotto	M.	8 "
Clarinetto	M.	8 "
Orchestral Oboe	M.	8 "
Oboe	M.	8 "
Saxophone	M.	8 "
Dulcian	M.	8 "
Corno di Bassetto	M.	8 "
Scialumo	M.	8 "
Cor Anglais	M.	8 "
Oboe d'Amore	M.	8 "
Basson-quinte	M.	5 1/3 "
Clarinetto Quinta	M.	5 1/3 "
Clarinetto Ottava	M.	4 "
Oboe Ottava	M.	4 "
Musette	M.	4 "

ORCHESTRAL BRASS-TONE

Bombardon	M.	16 Feet
Bombarde	M.	16 "
Contra-Trombone	M.	16 "
Double Trumpet	M.	16 "
Contra-Tuba	M.	16 "
Ophicleide	M.	8 "
Tuba Magna	M.	8 "
Tromba Real	M.	8 "
Tromba	M.	8 "
Trumpet Royal	M.	8 "
Trumpet, Harmonic	M.	8 "
Trumpet	M.	8 "
Trombone	M.	8 "
Horn	M.	8 "
Cornet	M.	8 "
Euphonium	M.	8 "
Tuba Quint	M.	5 1/3 "
Trombone Quint	M.	5 1/3 "
Trumpet Quint	M.	5 1/3 "
Trombone Octave	M.	4 "
Tuba Clarion	M.	4 "
Tromba Clarion	M.	4 "
Clarion	M.	4 "

INDETERMINATE-TONE

Vox Humana	M.	8 Feet
Cornet (Timbre-creating)	M.	VI. Ranks

PERCUSSION-TONE

Carillon	(Hemispherical Bells)
Chimes	(Tubular Bells)
Harp	(Wood Bars)
Celesta	(Metal Plates)

PEDAL ORGAN

ORGAN-TONE

Double Principal	W.	32 Feet
Double Principal	M.	32 "
Contra Dulciana	M.	32 "
Grossquintenbass	M.	$21\frac{1}{3}$ "
Major Principal	W.	16 "
Minor Principal	M.	16 "
Diapason Phonon	M.	16 "
Dulciana	M.	16 "
Gemshornbass	M.	16 "
Quintenbass	W.	$10\frac{2}{3}$ "
Gemshornquinte	M.	$10\frac{2}{3}$ "
Grand Octave	M.	8 "
Gemshornoctav	M.	8 "
Grand Tierce	M.	$6\frac{2}{5}$ "
Gemshornterz	M.	$6\frac{2}{5}$ "
Quint	M.	$5\frac{1}{3}$ "
Gemshornquinte	M.	$5\frac{1}{3}$ "
Septième	M.	$4\frac{4}{7}$ "
Super-Octave	M.	4 "
Compensating Mixture	M.	VI. Ranks

FLUTE-TONE

Untersatz	W.	32 Feet
Bourdon	W.	16 "
Tibia Major	W.	16 "

FLUTE-TONE—Continued

Lieblichgedeckt	W.	16 Feet
Double Melodia	W.	16 "
Quintaten	M.	16 "
Gedecktquinte	W.	$10\frac{2}{3}$ "
Doppelspitzflöte	W.	8 "
Grossflöte	W.	8 "
Flötenbass	W.	8 "
Hohlflöte	W.	4 "

STRING-TONE

Contra-Violone	M.	32 Feet
Contrabasso	W.	16 "
Violon-Basse	W.	16 "
Contra-Salicional	M.	16 "
Violoncello	M.	8 "
Grand Viol	M.	8 "

REED-TONE

Fagottone	W.	32 Feet
Contrafagotto	M.	16 "
Contra-Saxophone	M.	16 "
Contra-Oboe	M.	16 "
Contra-Clarinetto	M.	16 "

BRASS-TONE

Contre-Bombarde	M.	32 Feet
Bombardon	M.	32 "
Contra-Trombone	M.	32 "
Ophicleide	M.	16 "
Bombarde	M.	16 "
Trombone	M.	16 "
Euphonium	M.	16 "
Quinte Bombarde	M.	$10\frac{2}{3}$ "
Trombone	M.	8 "
Ophicleide	M.	8 "
Tuba Sonora	M.	8 "
Tromba	M.	8 "
Clarion (Harmonic)	M.	4 "

Before proceeding further, it is desirable that the nomenclature of the several tonal Divisions of the true Concert-room Organ should be considered—a nomenclature consistent with, and expressive of, their tonal appointments and their offices in the general scheme of the instrument. This necessity does not seem to have assumed any importance in the minds of organ-builders and designers up to present time; probably because it has not yet been fully realized that, in the Concert-room Organ, there is any necessity for the adoption of a tonal appointment widely different from that which has so long been considered proper and sufficient for the Church Organ. Such being the case, it can hardly be wondered at that the terms Great, Choir, Swell, Solo, and Echo, have been used in organs for the concert-room, as in the Church Organ. Accordingly, one finds these old terms in all the Concert-room Organs constructed in the last century; and, indeed, with additions, in organs recently constructed; as in the Johannesburg instrument, designed by Dr. Alfred Hollins, in which are added "Orchestral Organ" and "Bombarde Organ," although in the latter there is no BOMBARDE. In the St. Louis Exposition Organ (1904), the old terms were used; although we desired numbers only to be used for the manual Divisions; not seeing then, as we do now, in our more advanced system of stop-apportionment, the necessity of adopting a new and more expressive nomenclature, indicative of the tonal character and office of each of the Divisions named.

The term Pedal Organ must necessarily be retained; and there is no objection to the retention of the old name Great Organ, but for this all-important manual Division of the Concert-room instrument we prefer Grand Organ or Foundation Organ; for it is, when properly appointed, the foundation of The Temple of Tone. In the true Concert-room Organ the old nomenclature—Choir, Swell, and Echo—is practically meaningless. It is ridiculous to apply the term Swell to any Division of an organ in which every Division is inclosed in a Swell-box: but, in the absence of logical thought, old names continue to be used. The terms which seem suitable to distinguish the manual Divisions of a Concert-room Organ, as we consider they should be stop-apportioned, are Grand (or Foundation) Organ; Accompanimental Organ; String Organ; Wood-Wind Organ; Brass-Wind Organ; and Solo Organ. To which are to be added such names as the stop-apportionments of the Ancillary Organs may suggest. These valuable Divisions are treated on at length in due course.

THE GRAND ORGAN

The Organ, properly designated Grand, ranks first in importance in the entire series of manual organs, as called for in the structure of the Concert-room instrument; and the fact that it properly contains no stops of an imitative or orchestral tonality gives it a distinct position. Its dominant stops are all of Pure Organ-tone, such as can be produced only by organ-pipes of the DIAPASON class. The Grand Organ tonal appointment in association with the Pure Organ-toned portion of the Pedal Organ, forming the firm and sufficient foundation for the entire tonal structure of the instrument, and sustaining and building it up in grandeur and beauty. In the stop-apportionment of this Organ the full complement of DIAPASONS of unison pitch, varying slightly in timbre, and effectively in strength of voice, must be provided; and to these must be added one or two DOUBLE DIAPASONS, 16 FT., voiced slightly subordinate to the unison voices, imparting fullness and impressiveness to the unison tones of the DIAPASONS, without injuriously affecting their dominating pitch. To these stops must be added those which, in their voices, corroborate the harmonic upper partial tones of the prime tones. The harmonic series belonging to the unison DIAPASONS must be as complete as practicable, and all the stops composing it must be of the DIAPASON class, yielding Pure Organ-tone, properly and scientifically graduated in strength in accordance with the natural law of compound-tone production. This scientific graduation, which necessarily entails the exercise of acoustical knowledge, skill, and painstaking labor, is rare indeed, if it is ever to be found, in trade-built organs; accordingly, the organ-playing world has had very little opportunity of learning what a perfectly balanced Diapason Chorus is or should be.

As this matter of graduation of tone in harmonic-corroborating stops seems to be very little understood, and still less attended to, in ordinary organ-building; and because it is of prime importance in artistic organ tonal development; and, further, as the opinions of one who is neither a professional organ-builder nor an organist are little likely to be heeded, we here give the remarks on the matter by the greatest authority who has written on the subject of musical tone, the late Professor Hermann Helmholtz, of the University of Berlin:—

"It is well known that the union of several simple tones into one compound tone, which is naturally effected in the tones produced by most musical instruments, is artificially imitated on the Organ by peculiar mechanical contrivances. The tones of organ-pipes are comparatively poor in upper partials. When it is desirable to use a stop of incisive penetrating quality of tone and great power, the wide pipes (*Principal-register* and *Weitgedackt*) are not sufficient; their tone is too soft, too defective in upper partials; and the narrow pipes (*Geigen-register* and *Quintaten*) are also unsuitable, because, although more incisive, their tone is weak. For such occasions, then, as in accompanying congregational singing, recourse is had to the *compound stops*. In these stops every key is connected with a larger or smaller series of pipes, which it opens simultaneously, and which give the prime tone and a certain number of the first upper partials of the compound tone of the note in question. It is very usual to connect the upper Octave with the prime tone, and after that the Twelfth. The more complex compounds (*cornet*) give the first six partial tones, that is, in addition to the two Octaves of the prime tone and its Twelfth, the higher major Third and the Octave of the Twelfth. This is as much of the series of upper partials as belongs to the tones of a major chord. But to prevent these compound stops from being insupportably noisy it is necessary to reinforce the deeper tones of each note by other rows of pipes, for in all natural tones which are suited for musical purposes the higher partials decrease in force as they rise in pitch. This has been regarded in their imitation by compound stops. These compound stops were a monster in the path of the old musical theory, which was acquainted only with the prime tones of compounds; but the practice of organ-builders and organists necessitated their retention, and when they are suitably arranged and properly applied, they form a very effective musical apparatus. The nature of the case at the same time fully justifies their use. The musician is bound to regard the tones of all musical instruments as compounded in the same way as the compound stops of organs."

Recognizing the great importance of the subject, the same authority adds the following remarks:—

"We have thus been led to an appreciation of upper partial tones, which, as it differs considerably from that previously entertained by musicians, and even physicists, must meet with considerable opposition. The upper partial tones were indeed known, but almost only in such compound tones as those of strings, where there was a favorable opportunity for observing them; but they appear in previous physical and musical works as an isolated accidental phenomenon of small intensity, a kind of curiosity, which was certainly occasionally adduced, in order to give some support to the opinion that nature had prefigured the construction of our major chord, but which on the whole remained almost entirely disregarded. In opposition to this we have to assert, and we shall prove the assertion, that upper partial tones are, with few exceptions, a general constituent of all musical tones, and that a certain stock of upper partials is an essential condition for a good musical quality of tone. Finally, these upper partials have been erroneously considered as weak, because they are difficult to observe, while, in point of fact, for some of the best musical qualities of tone, the loudness of the first upper partial is not far inferior to that of the prime tone itself. There is no difficulty in verifying this last fact by experiments on the tones of strings. Strike the string of a piano or monochord, and immediately touch one of its nodes for an instant with the finger; the constituent partial tones having this node will remain with unaltered loudness, and the rest will disappear. We might just as well touch the node at the instant of striking, and thus obtain the corresponding constituent partial tones from the first, in place of the complete compound tone of the note. In both ways we can readily convince ourselves that the first upper partials, as the Octave and Twelfth, are by no means weak and difficult to hear, but have a very appreciable strength."

Beyond the simple statements in the quotations given, and in certain others of less importance on the same subject, Professor Helmholtz did not venture to be more explicit, or to give, as the results of his investigations, any calculations of the tonal values of the several upper partials with regard to the value or strength of the prime tone. This omission is greatly to be regretted; because, supported by his wide reputation as a careful investigator in all matters of tone production, his calculations would certainly have received respectful consideration by organists, and have been, in all probability, put to practical test by German organ-builders, and have led them to modify the voices of all their harmonic-corroborating stops; reducing their respective assertiveness to accord, as closely as possible, with the natural laws of compound-tone production as then defined. Helmholtz, however, evidently did not give the tonal structure or stop appointment of the organ the study it deserved; and, accordingly, no important, if any, changes were made in the then obtaining traditional and unscientific rule-of-thumb methods. The single octave-, fifth-, and third-sounding harmonic-corroborating stops, and the equally important compound harmonic stops, have continued to be made, without any systematic alteration or attempt toward scientific adjustment, just as they obtained prior to his time, and even up to the present day. There have been a few exceptions which have done little more than prove the rule. Beyond such accomplished artists as the late Aristide Cavaillé-Coll, of Paris, Edmund Schulze, of Paulinzelle, and Thomas C. Lewis, of London, organ-builders, as a rule in all countries, seem to have devoted very little, if any, attention to scientific matters connected with their art. Had they given them due consideration, one would have to-day, in all probability, little fault to find with their treatment of the harmonic-corroborating stops, or to regret the almost total neglect of such stops, which has denuded so many modern organs of the potent means of artistic registration, and, accordingly, of the most effective elements of tone-coloration. Organists, as a rule, little know what this loss amounts to.

Although neither having the favorable opportunities nor possessing the complete apparatus for accurate investigation that Helmholtz enjoyed and had at his command, we have endeavored, in time stolen from the study and practice of an exacting art, and with the limited means of investigation and observation at home and abroad, to arrive at conclusions regarding the relative tonal values of the harmonic-corroborating voices; the prime tone or voice being that produced by the foundation DIAPASON, 8 FT., of full scale and Pure Organ-tone. The calculations have been made assuming the value or strength of the prime tone to be represented by 100. These are set forth in the following Table:—

APPROXIMATE RELATIVE STRENGTHS OF TONE OF THE PRINCIPAL HARMONIC-CORROBORATING STOPS; THE PRIME TONE OF THE DIAPASON BEING REPRESENTED BY 100.

STOPS	*PARTIAL-TONES*	*STRENGTH OF TONES*
DIAPASON, 8 FT.	Prime Tone	100 —
OCTAVE, 4 FT.	1st Upper Partial	85 to 90
TWELFTH, 2⅔ FT.	2nd " "	80 " 85
FIFTEENTH, 2 FT.	3rd " "	70 " 75
SEVENTEENTH, 1⅗ FT.	4th " "	65 " 70
NINETEENTH, 1⅓ FT.	5th " "	60 " 65
SEPTIÈME, 1 1/7 FT.	6th " "	40 " 45
TWENTY-SECOND, 1 FT.	7th " "	45 " 50

The desirable strengths of the voices of the several harmonic-corroborating stops with respect to that of the foundation DIAPASON cannot well be definitely fixed as applicable to all organs, because they will necessarily be affected by the positions the stops occupy and whether they are planted on an open chest or inclosed in a Swell-box. The DIAPASON being, in all cases, understood to be uninclosed. Under our system of stop-apportionment the harmonic corroborating stops gain much value in registration and tone-coloration by being inclosed and rendered flexible.

The stops given in the Table comprise all those belonging to the unison, 8 ft., harmonic series which can be carried unbroken throughout the compass of the manual claviers. If the DOUBLE DIAPASON, 16 FT., is added, the unison DIAPASON assumes the position of first upper partial in the 16 ft. harmonic series; the second upper partial may then be added in the form of the QUINT, 5⅓ FT. The full tone of the DIAPASON, 8 FT., must not be interfered with, as it firmly establishes the unison pitch of the Grand Organ; but the MINOR DIAPASON may be substituted if considered desirable; the inclosed harmonic-corroborating stops being softened to accord.

The compound harmonic-corroborating stops, or MIXTURES, which carry the upper partial tones to the highest point possible or desirable in the tonal structure of the organ, properly follow the principle of graduation of strength of tone, similar to that obtaining in the voicing and regulating of the independent and complete stops, as set forth above. Owing, however, to their complex structure, the variety of pitches and arrangements of their ranks, and the numbers of their breaks, rendered necessary by the impossibility of carrying pipes of high pitches unbroken throughout the compass of the organ, the problem of their tonal graduation and regulation becomes extremely complicated; and artistic sense and a keen appreciation of respective tonal values must take the place of purely scientific adjustment. Science points the way, but art must accomplish the work; as experience taught us forcibly more than half a century ago.

As we have said elsewhere, we feel sure that all accomplished organists, who have had experience of the tonal behavior of such MIXTURES as are commonly found in organs built to-day, will agree with us that their voices are much too loud, and generally crude and unmusical. We feel that it is largely due to these imperfections that musician-organists have willingly allowed organ-builders to omit such screaming MIXTURES from even important stop-apportionments. Under such unfavorable conditions, organists have not had proper opportunities of learning the great value of scientifically and artistically constructed and regulated suitable harmonic-corroborating compound stops. Stops that would furnish them with material for the exercise of skill and taste in registration and tone-coloration; and for the creation of rich compound tones impossible of production on the organs now commonly at their command. If the Organ of the Future is to take its true position as The Temple of Tone, it behooves organists and organ-builders to seriously study the natural laws governing the creation of beautiful compound musical sounds; and, in practical work, to strive to furnish the tonal elements that build up such sounds. The task is not a difficult one if properly understood and earnestly undertaken. It is quite evident that in organs constructed at the present time, a most serious deficiency in their tonal appointments obtains in the direction of harmonic-corroborating stops, simple and compound. But it is to be feared that the dislike of organ-builders for stops calling for the exercise of scientific knowledge and unusual skill, and what to them seems profitless labor, will seriously militate against their proper introduction in organs schemed by them, and by organists who are not awake to their great importance. The old builders were so greatly impressed with their powers in tone-building, that they went, in their introduction in organs, far beyond what artistic tonal appointment demanded and science directed. Moderation in this, as in most other matters, is a virtue.

Having touched, so far, on the MAJOR DIAPASON, 8 FT., and its attendant harmonic chorus, a few words may be said on the MINOR DIAPASON and others of unison pitch that may be considered desirable; and with which the same chorus can be associated, provided it is inclosed in a properly constructed Swell-box and so rendered capable of being adjusted in power to suit the tone of the DIAPASON speaking. This is a matter of scientific value and artistic refinement impossible in a completely uninclosed Grand Organ. While the MAJOR DIAPASON must be a stop of large scale and powerful intonation, with a voice full, round, and dominating, the MINOR DIAPASON, of smaller scale, should have a voice of contrasting quality, rich and somewhat penetrating in character, due to the presence of certain harmonics absent in the voice of the larger stop. This contrast of tone, slight though it may seem to the ear, is of great value, apart from its leading to variety, in preventing tonal sympathy and a consequent loss of power and volume in their combined voices. In a Concert-room Organ of the first magnitude, the stop-apportionment of the Grand Organ will call for the introduction of two or three more DIAPASONS of different qualities of voice, one of which should be placed in the inclosed subdivision.

In addition to the volume of Pure Organ-tone furnished by the DIAPASONS and the harmonic-corroborating stops; other stops, producing tones of contrasting and coloring character, must be provided and distributed in the unexpressive and expressive Subdivisions. All stops of a markedly imitative or orchestral tonality must be omitted from the apportionment of the Grand Organ. Free Organ-tone should be effectively represented; unimitative Flute-tone must be furnished by both open and covered stops, in both Subdivisions; Viol Organ-tone by stops of 16 ft. and 8 ft., also in both Subdivisions; and Brass-tone by lingual stops of the normal TRUMPET class, properly confined to the Expressive Subdivision.

We may conclude this section of our subject with a few additional words on the harmonic-corroborating stops, for their purpose and value should be well understood by the organist. They are inclosed in the Swell-box of the Second Subdivision, and so placed under control as to be capable of having any necessary or desirable degree of softness or flexibility of tone given to them. Now comes the obvious question: What should be the full strength of the complete harmonic series when heard with the Swell-box fully opened? This is easily answered. Let the DIAPASONS of unison pitch, which speak on open wind-chests, be drawn, then let all the stops which form the unison harmonic series be so voiced and regulated as to complete the grand volume of compound tone, known as the Diapason Chorus—a volume of Pure Organ-tone practically impossible of production on the impoverished Great Organs of to-day—but let there be no scream or unmusical sound as the fingers press the keys: on the contrary, let the whole complex structure combine in one grand volume of rich and pure sound, of which the satisfied ear seems never to tire. When such a result is reached, the Grand Organ in its foundational form is secured; and the modifying operation of the Swell-box may enter on its mission—to throw upon the several combinations of unison Pure Organ-tone, garments of subtle and fascinating beauty, changing in brilliancy, coloration, and never-ending variety, at the will of the performer.

Reference to the Grand Organ, as set forth in the first Specification which follows these remarks, will enable the organist to form a correct conception of the practically inexhaustible possibilities in varied tone production. Let him try to realize what can be done by the skilful and musicianly handling of the stationary and flexible tones or voices of the Subdivisions, by the occasional resort to the means of expression at his command. On due study he will, in all probability, realize that our Grand Organ, in conjunction with the foundational stops of the Pedal Organ forms a complete instrument, on which the giant fugues of Bach and the compositions of the strict Organ School could be artistically and impressively rendered. Leaving untouched the other Divisions and Subdivisions of the Organ, with their unique resources for the production of musical effects, as endless as they are unknown in organ-playing to-day.

THE ACCOMPANIMENTAL ORGAN

This Division of the Concert-room Organ holds practically the same relative position with respect to the Grand Organ—just treated of—that the Choir Organ does to the Great Organ in the Church instrument. We do not use the time-honored term Choir Organ here, because it has no correct significance in an instrument specially designed for the concert-room.

In scheming the general tonal appointment and the special, contrasting, stop-apportionments of this Accompanimental Organ, in its divided treatment, certain important conditions have to be recognized. First, as to its relation to the tonal appointment of the Grand Organ. Secondly, as to its value and equipment as an independent Division. Thirdly, as to its place and principal office in the complete tonal scheme of the instrument. Fourthly, as to its special relation, as an attendant on the other Divisions which are chiefly orchestral in tonal character.

In the contrasting and expressive Subdivisions of the Accompanimental Organ, stops yielding Free Organ-tone, and others more or less unimitative in their voices, are to be favored. At the same time, stops are to be preferred which admit of a well-marked separation into effective groups, yielding at all times, and under all conditions of registration, contrasting tonalities, which impart force and musical life to compound flexibility and expression in this Organ. At this point, the interested reader would do well to compare the conditions just defined with those which necessarily obtain in the undivided and heterogeneously stop-apportioned Choir Organs, so called, which have hitherto been introduced in Concert-room instruments.

The reader must steadily bear in mind that throughout every branch of our tonal system, the great and revolutionary principles of divisional compound tonal flexibility and expression are strictly observed. As has already been stated elsewhere: we were the first in the art of organ-building to practically introduce these principles, and so demonstrate their value; and the first and only writer on the organ to propound them and advocate their adoption. They are now gradually becoming recognized as deserving serious consideration: but as organ-builders are very reluctant to depart from the time-worn, one-ply, methods followed by their great-grandfathers; and as organists have had little, if any, experience of what our system offers them in artistic interpretation; it can only be hoped that time, with an awakening knowledge and a consequent abatement of prejudice, will bring our system into general appreciation. It is the chief aim of the present treatise to thoroughly elucidate the system, in its different treatments, as applied to organs of all classes and of various dimensions.

At the risk of repeating what we may have said in advocating our system, we desire it to be clearly realized that the principle of primal importance insists, on both logical and practical grounds, that each manual Organ and its Subdivisions shall have special and well defined tonal characteristics, sharply marking its position and office in the general scheme of the Concert-room instrument in particular, and substantially in all other organs. The present prevailing old-world and antiquated method of Divisional stop-apportionments, which favors undesirable and unnecessary repetition of stops, and which practically makes each manual Division (save, perhaps, the Solo, when such a Division is introduced) independent and little better than a tonal replica of the other Divisions, except in the matter of strength of tone, or in being open or inclosed, is obviously undesirable and insufficient; and necessarily results in a great loss of tonal variety and concentration, and, consequently, in a serious sacrifice of utility and beauty, affecting the musical properties of the entire instrument.

The necessity, from an artistic point of view, of the Concert-room Organ having distinctive and contrasting tonal powers and colorings in all its manual Divisions and their Subdivisions; and that they shall, separately, be endowed with controllable powers of flexibility and expression, must be obvious to every organist who can claim to be considered a *musician*. Yet we regret to say, that we know many master performers who seem so supinely satisfied with the prevailing method (we cannot call it system) of divisional tonal appointment (or disappointment) that they cannot stretch their imaginations to anything better, or that would furnish them with the certain and ready means of producing not only the ordinary musical effects with which they have so long been familiar, but with others, far more beautiful, which are unknown to them; and impossible of production on organs of restricted powers with which they now seem satisfied. Uncontrollable musical noise is the generally accepted order of the day in the organ-building and organ-playing worlds of the present time. This is shown by the preference given by even talented organists for the uncontrollable and ear-splitting roar of exposed TUBAS, on thirty- or forty-inch wind. Vulgarity has too often blotted the fair page of Art, and soiled the palette of the tone painter.

As the properly appointed Accompanimental Organ will, taken as a whole, be the softest or least assertive Division directly commanded by a manual clavier, it is necessary that great care be taken, not only in the selection of its stops, but that, on their selection, their strengths of voice shall be so adjusted as to secure an artistic tonal balance. As great a variety of voices as possible must be selected, having sufficient contrast to render an effective arrangement into two distinct groups possible. The chief rule to be observed in the formation of the Subdivisions is that there shall be no stops similar in quality of voice in both, so that a perfect contrast of single or collective voices shall obtain between them; favoring, to the fullest possible extent, the production of the artistic effects of compound tonal flexibility and expression. The complete stop-apportionment of this Organ must be such as to render it tonally distinct and self-contained, while it is, in all respects, suitable for furnishing effective accompaniments, full of light and shade, to solos of all kinds rendered on the other Divisions of the instrument. Reference to the treatment generally, and to the stop-apportionments of the Subdivisions of the Accompanimental Organ, given in the first Specification, will show the manner in which all requirements are provided for. Further remarks follow the Specification.

THE WOOD-WIND ORGAN

With this important and beautiful tonal Division, properly commanded by the Third Manual Clavier, commences the tonal portion which imparts to the true Concert-room Organ its distinguishing character and purpose. In the hands of the modern organ-builders and according to the schemes of ordinary designers, almost all the Concert-room instruments constructed here and abroad have failed to show radical departures, in tonal appointment and arrangement, from the traditional types of important Church Organs. Yet things look somewhat hopeful; for in certain quarters signs obtain that thoughtful minds are at work; and that a study of the multiple powers and musical effects of the grand orchestra is gradually leading to the conception of a Concert-room Organ, worthy of its name and office in the world of music. It is in the hopes of aiding in the consummation of such an achievement that this book has been written. Recent essays indicate that serious consideration is being given to tonal matters, and the movement is evidently toward a further development, which will inevitably result in the production of organs of all classes, which, in both tonal equipment and artistic means of control, will leave little to be desired. It is hoped that this Work, with its many Specifications for organs of all classes, tonally appointed to accord with their special uses, and varying in size from instruments of over two hundred speaking stops to those of under twenty, will help in the right direction and probably prevent many disappointments. It embodies the results of an earnest study, extending over half a century, and embracing the methods of all the great organ-building countries in the world; and, further, the logical consideration of the desirable tonal relation of the organ to the orchestra—the stage now reached in this essay.

In this third and very important Division, which we have named the Wood-Wind Organ, are continued and clearly marked the principles of tonal contrast and compound flexibility and expression, characteristic of our System, and on which is built up the true fabric of The Temple of Tone. The stop-apportionment provides a palette of beautiful colors, from which the brush of the Musician, scientifically and artistically manipulated, can paint tone-pictures, replete with musical chiaro-oscuro, fancy and pathos, simplicity and complexity, repose and force; while the powers of compound flexibility and expression invest his pictures with indescribable charms.

In this Division are gathered the organ-stops representing the Flutes and the reed instruments of the orchestra; associated with choice unimitative stops, yielding tones which lend themselves, consistently, to the improvement and enrichment of the orchestral voices; and which, at the same time, impart a completeness and self-contained value to the entire Division. To institute the desirable powers of compound tonal flexibility and expression to this Wood-Wind Organ it is necessary, as in the Divisions already commented on, to arrange its stop-apportionment into two groups or Subdivisions, having contrasting tonalities. This arrangement is favored by the fact that a decided contrast of tone naturally obtains between the Flutes and the single and double reed instruments of the orchestra. It must be recognized, however, that no strict balance in volume and strength of tone exists, in the orchestra, between the voices of the Flutes, on the one hand, and those of the Oboes, the several Clarinets, the Corno di Bassetto, and the unison and Double-Bassoons—with their different tonalities and powers—on the other hand. Such being the case so far as the orchestra is concerned, it must be realized that to institute a desirable balance of contrasting tonalities in the Subdivisions of the Wood-Wind Organ, a larger number of unimitative voices must be added to the Subdivision containing the ORCHESTRAL FLUTES than will be called for in that in which the reed instruments are represented. There is another matter to be considered; namely, that although it is not necessary to introduce extensions of the ORCHESTRAL FLUTES, as the unimitative Flute-toned stops meet all requirements; it is very important that the imitative Reed-toned lingual stops be extended to develop their voices both below and above the compass and pitch of the orchestral instruments; accordingly, in the organ, there are available the following important stops yielding impressive voices, CONTRA-OBOE, 16 FT., CONTRA-CLARINETTO, 16 FT., CONTRAFAGOTTO, 16 FT., CONTRA-BASSET-HORN, 16 FT., CONTRA-SAXOPHONE, 16 FT., BASSON-QUINTE, 5⅓ FT., CLARINETTO QUINTA, 5⅓ FT. Each Subdivision will, as in the case of the Accompanimental Organ, be inclosed in a separate Swell-box, specially constructed to suit the tonal powers of the stop-apportionment. This is important to secure the maximum effects of compound tonal flexibility and expression. Mere trade rule-of-thumb work will not do in so complicated an instrument as the Concert-room Organ.

Reference to the appointment of the Wood-Wind Organ in the first Specification, will convey to the interested reader the principle on which the subdivisional stop-apportionments are made, to obtain the desirable contrasts of tone and the full value of compound expression and graduation of power.

THE BRASS-WIND ORGAN

This Division of the true Concert-room Organ is devoted, in the most important portion of its stop-apportionment, to the representatives of the brass-wind instruments of the orchestra, and such stops as the genius of the pipe-maker and voicer has devised to extend the compass and accentuate the harmonics of their several voices, after the manner followed in the Reed-toned stops of the Wood-Wind Organ. Thus imparting singular richness and impressiveness to the musical resources of the entire organ, unapproachable by any other musical instrument.

Although the principal stops of this Division—directly controlled by the fourth manual clavier—are those which place at the command of the performer especially the representatives of the brass-wind instruments of the orchestra, it is necessary that suitable labial stops be introduced to provide the performer with the means, through artistic registration, of producing a great variety of both contrasting and analogous tonalities in the Subdivisions. It must be borne in mind that the principles, involved in the divided stop-apportionment of this powerfully voiced organ, are in every way consistent with those governing the stop-apportionments of the second and third organs already described.

In this fourth organ the brass-wind stops are arranged in two groups, contrasting in tonality to as great a degree as possible, and holding dominating positions in the two Subdivisions, which are endowed with powers of flexibility by being enclosed in separate Swell-boxes. Owing to the extremely assertive quality of the brass-wind voices, a control, as complete as art can secure, is absolutely necessary: this every true musician-performer on the organ must admit. Without this control, which embraces powers of expression and gradation of tone, the general utility of such voices would be bereft of nine-tenths of their value. This is proved by the idiotic practice, commonly followed today, of leaving the most powerful lingual stops, such as the high-pressure TUBAS, in an exposed position, to roar at all times with uncontrollable power. Such a practice can only be accounted for by the lack of musicianly culture and refinement of audition, on the part of those who perpetrate such a blunder, or suffer it to be made in the organ of to-day. There may be some excuse, in this matter, for the inexperienced organist who, probably, has been taught on a miserable Music-school Organ, from which he has formed warped conceptions of tonal right and wrong, while he was studying technique. But, in our opinion, there can be no excuse for the accomplished musician organist. Nothing in the nature of this TUBA blunder will be found in the Specifications in this treatise.

On referring to the appointment of this Division in the first Specification, it will be observed that there are introduced two groups of Brass-toned stops, such as has never appeared in any single Division of a Concert-room Organ hitherto constructed. And it would require but a little exercise of the imagination on the part of a musician-organist, to realize the limitless tonal powers and resources of this separate manual Division, in which every stop could be graduated from a *fortissimo* to a *pianissimo*, in stationary tone; and have imparted to it any degree of expression a performer may desire; contrasting the tonalities of the Subdivisions in any conceivable relation the artistic impulse of the musician may suggest. Until these powers are given to this and every complete Division of the Concert-room Organ, that instrument can lay no unquestioned claim to be called The Temple of Tone.

It will be observed in the first Specification, that in addition to the groups of the Orchestral Brass-toned stops and their extensions and derivatives, a complement of labial stops has been given in each Subdivision, suitable for registration with the lingual stops, for the purpose of giving, to a large extent, completeness and independence to the Subdivisions; and at the same time a sympathetic connection with the tonal appointments of all the other Divisions. Here is a wide field for the exercise of the musical sense and not a little scientific knowledge on the part of the organ-designer, who can divest himself of out-of-date old-fashioned traditions; and cast aside stupid trade methods of how-not-to-do-it.

THE SOLO ORGAN

This Division, directly commanded by the fifth manual clavier, is designated the Solo Organ, because, in its stop-apportionment, it, for the most part, comprises stops specially adapted for the production of distinct tonal effects of an orchestral solo character. It is so appointed with the aim of relieving the other and more important manual Organs from having to be inconveniently or suddenly changed in tonality; and also to render the undesirable resort to coupling unnecessary. It is obviously important, in so complex an instrument as the true Concert-room Organ, that every possible arrangement should be made, in the stop-apportionments of the several manual Organs, to prevent the necessity for a frequent change of stops, or resort to coupling, in any direction, for the production of special and frequently recurring tonal effects. In an artistically schemed and appointed instrument, each manual Organ should have a special place and office in the general tonal economy, and be at all times independent and untrammeled in ordinary playing.

As the true office of this fifth Organ is essentially different from the chief offices of the other four manual Divisions, it is unnecessary to divide its stop-apportionment and impart to it compound flexibility and expression. Every stop, however, must be inclosed in the most responsive and perfectly adapted Swell-box that art can devise; care being taken to avoid any approach to annihilation of sound when the box is closed, and to secure a very gradual and even *crescendo* and *diminuendo;* for upon such necessary conditions depend the beauty and sympathetic character of the special effects this Solo Organ places at the command of the accomplished performer.

Seeing that the chief office of this Division is to furnish solo voices and combinations of a special and distinct tonal character, leaving the four other manual Divisions entirely free for their independent and appropriate rôles in the musical composition that may be under rendition, it is, obviously, necessary that there must appear in its appointment duplications of certain stops which are present in the stop-apportionments of both the Wood-Wind and Brass-Wind Organs. But it is essential, to sustain the solo character, that a pronounced imitative quality be given to each of the orchestral voices.

In this Solo Organ high pressures of wind may be more freely employed than elsewhere in the instrument, for the production of commanding voices. It is here that the powerful Tubas may be inserted, under control in the Swell-box of the Division, enabling them to be used in a musicianly and effective manner.

The peculiarities of the more important stops selected for insertion in this Organ may be briefly described, so that their respective tonal values, and their offices in the complete tonal scheme, may be better realized. The stops which are strictly of a solo character are first in order. The tone of the Viole d'Orchestre must be full and rich, and as highly imitative of that of the Violin of the orchestra as art and skill of the pipe-maker and voicer can accomplish: while that of the Violoncello is to be still fuller and richer; imitative of the full-bodied tone of the orchestral instrument. Our long and close acquaintance with the late William Thynne, of London—the most distinguished English voicer of String-toned stops—who invented the Viole d'Orchestre, has made us familiar with perfect imitations of the highly harmonic-charged tones of the orchestral string instruments. The Orchestral Flute and Piccolo must be brilliant and strictly imitative in their tones; in this direction there is no difficulty. The Orchestral Oboe and Clarinetto are the only Reed-toned stops really necessary in this Organ; and they must have a decided imitative character; the Clarinetto being a dual stop, formed by the association with a small-scaled and softly voiced Doppelflöte, 8 ft., which greatly adds to its orchestral tone. Any Tubas inserted will impart an almost overwhelming grandeur to this important Division. Of the impressive labial stops it is unnecessary to speak here.

THE PEDAL ORGAN

It would have been strictly in order had we treated of the Pedal Organ before entering on the subject of the manual Organs; but we considered it desirable for the interested reader to form some idea of our System of tonal appointment and stop-apportionment before being called upon to consider what, in accordance with that system, is the proper tonal appointment of the Division which may justly be acknowledged as the Sub-foundation of The Temple of Tone. Just as the sub-foundation of an architectural temple must be laid in a manner sufficient to properly support the entire superstructure; so should the Pedal Organ hold a similar relation to the entire tonal superstructure it has to support, or to which it has to form a base. This simple fact—in accordance with the teaching of science and art—is systematically ignored by the majority of the organ-builders and designers of to-day, who seem to think, and act upon the thought, that the Pedal Organ is merely an offspring of the manual portion of the instrument—not its fundamental portion—and, accordingly, of comparatively little importance. How differently the old masters and true founders of the art of organ tonal appointment viewed this serious question. Serious it is when it is realized that the present objectionable practice is laying the axe at the root of the true tonal structure of the Monarch of all Instruments.

The fundamental principles which govern the artistic and necessary tonal appointment of the Pedal Organ of the true Concert-room instrument are simple, and such as must be recognized as reasonable and requisite, in a properly constituted organ, by every one gifted with musical sense and who has given any serious thought to the subject: they are four in number. First, that in its stop-apportionment the Pedal Organ shall be complete and entirely independent of the stop-apportionments of the manual Divisions. Secondly, that in its tonal appointment it shall furnish adequate and effective basses—either analogous or contrasting in tonality—for all the principal voices and combinations of voices in the manual Divisions. Thirdly, that it shall comprise stops suitable for solo passages of a prominent character, quite independent of resort to manual stops. Fourthly, that it shall, to as large an extent as desirable and practicable, be endowed with powers of flexibility and expression. Reasonable and essential as are the conditions set forth in the four Principles, and which must be recognized by every musician and accomplished organist as necessary to obtain in every properly appointed instrument, the fact remains that there is not a Concert-room Organ in existence to-day (1924) in which the Pedal Organ has been schemed in accordance with the four Principles given: and these Principles never will be observed so long as the degradation of the Pedal Organ is countenanced by the apparently don't-care organ-playing world. With what profound respect one regards the works of the German masters, with their majestic Pedal Organs, in which there are neither borrowings nor duplications. Then one turns, with feelings of regret and disgust, to the miserable travesties of Pedal Organs, turned out of modern "up-to-date" organ workshops. Art has gone, and dollars win the day, with which there is mixed much ignorance.

In accordance with the Principles given, the stop-apportionment of the Pedal Organ has to be arranged in two groups, contrasting in general tonality; one of which is to be inclosed in a suitable Swell-chamber, so constructed and shuttered as not to destroy the clear sounds of its pipe-work when closed, and to offer the least possible obstruction to the free emission of sound when the shutters are fully opened. In the exposed Subdivision are to be grouped the more important stops which are strictly and chiefly fundamental in their grave voices and which form, in themselves, the true and firm sub-foundation of the tonal structure of the organ. In the inclosed Subdivision are to be grouped the stops forming the harmonic-corroborating series of 32 ft. and 16 ft.; also, such stops as are of a solo character, and the assertive stops of Reed-tone and Brass-tone, to the voices of which effective control and powers of expression and flexibility are essential if an artistic use is to be made of them.

We were the first, and appear to be still the only writer on organ design and tonal appointment, to advocate, and insist, on logical and artistic grounds, that powers of tonal flexibility be imparted to the voices of the Pedal Organ. It is no exaggeration to say that, for truly artistic and legitimate purposes, the inclosure of powerful lingual stops, and especially those of Brass-tone, thereby rendering them flexible in tone, multiplies their musical value tenfold. How very few Pedal Organs have a softly-toned lingual stop in their appointments; yet the value of such a stop has never been questioned; and many a musician-organist has sighed for one, just as he has desired a softly-voiced labial stop, such as a Double Dulciana. Apart from the ready means of adjusting every inclosed stop to exactly the strength of tone required by the combinations drawn in the manual Organs; the powers of expression provided, impart a richness, impressiveness, and artistic force to the pedal parts, absolutely unknown and impossible on the usual entirely exposed Pedal Organs obtaining to-day, in the largest Concert-room instruments.

In the following Specification all details are given regarding the tonal appointment and the necessary control of the properly designed and complete Pedal Organ.

THE ANCILLARY ORGAN

Before proceeding further with our principal subject, it is desirable that the student reader should become conversant with the nature and purpose of the Ancillary Organ; especially so as neither the name nor the introduction and use of it has ever been mentioned in any published works save our own. As we have said elsewhere:[13] Bearing in mind the immense tonal resources of

[13] "The American Organist," March, 1923.

the organ, the practical impossibility of playing more than five manual claviers; and the convenience and desirability of having only four claviers, except in extreme instances, the question of the adequate and artistic stop-apportionments of the manual stationary Divisions becomes a very serious and far-reaching one. Serious, because it is undesirable to attempt to make the stationary Divisions complete and practically independent, by overloading them with systemless stop-apportionments, involving an unnecessary multiplication of similar stops. This inartistic and old-fashioned method of tonal appointment, which obtains in all recently constructed organs here and abroad, is swept away by our classified System, and by the introduction of specially stop-apportioned Ancillary Organs, which impart hitherto undreamt of powers of tone production to every manual Division.

Neither organ-builders nor organ-players have, up to the present time, grasped the true office and the great importance of the Ancillary Organ, in the various forms and treatments it can be designed to assume, in accordance with its purpose and the calls to be made on its tonal resources. But this is hardly to be wondered at when one realizes the apathy which at present obtains in the organ-designing world in all matters appertaining to the scientific and artistic tonal appointment of the organ, and the true Concert-room Organ in particular. If this lamentable feeling of don't-care-ism did not exist, the present degradation of the Pedal Organ would never be tolerated by the musician organists of to-day. When and where will the organ-builder appear, imbued with scientific knowledge and artistic aspirations, to advance the organ to its true position as The Temple of Tone?

It is very important that all matters connected with the general purpose or office, the tonal appointment, the construction, and the system necessary for the perfect control, tonally and mechanically, of the Ancillary Organs, should be thoroughly understood; for they are destined to hold very important positions in the large instruments of the future. This statement is supported by what has recently been done in a somewhat similar direction. We, accordingly, give the Principles, in accordance with our System, on which the Ancillary Organs should be constructed, tonally appointed, and controlled.

PRINCIPLES OF CONSTRUCTION, APPOINTMENT, AND CONTROL OF ANCILLARY ORGANS

I. The Ancillary Organs are, in general, auxiliaries to the stationary manual tonal Divisions of the organ proper. And, accordingly, in only very special cases is an Ancillary stop-appointed so as to be practically complete in itself, as in the unique case of the complete String Organ. The incomplete Ancillaries are so stop-apportioned as to augment or otherwise aid the stationary tonal appointments of the different manual Divisions with which they are temporarily associated. Their chief offices in the tonal economy of the entire organ are, from both scientific and artistic points of view, highly important and far-reaching.

II. In scheming the stop-apportionments of the Ancillary Organs (with the exception of the Ancillary String Organ), special regard must be paid to the stop-apportionments of the Divisions with which they will properly be associated, and have to enter into more or less extensive combination; adding valuable tonal elements, filling up tonal deficiencies, or furnishing the tonal material for the production of new compound musical sounds or extreme effects; otherwise impossible under ordinary methods of tonal appointment and one-ply stop-apportionment.

III. The Ancillary Organs, be they complete and independent in themselves, or designed as adjuncts to the stationary Divisions or Subdivisions directly commanded by the manual claviers, must have their stop-apportionments of a character requiring no duplication of stops—identical in tone—which have been introduced in the stationary Divisions. In accordance with our System, contrast of tone is to be adopted in all possible cases, as in the String Organ.

IV. All the Ancillary Organs must be rendered tonally flexible and expressive by being inclosed in suitably constructed Swell-boxes. As all these Organs will, necessarily, differ widely in their stop-apportionments, and, accordingly, in their qualities and strengths of tone, it is essential, on artistic grounds, that their Swell-boxes be differently treated, so as to properly control and balance their effects; securing in all cases a perfectly clear and audible *pianissimo*. Anything approaching annihilation of sound, even from the softest stops, must be avoided; and, indeed, rendered impossible, by the proper proportioning of the thicknesses of the walls and shutters of their Swell-boxes, which will, necessarily, have to vary considerably.

V. All the Ancillary Organs are to be brought on and thrown off any one or more of the manual claviers, at the will of the performer; and can be either played alone or with the stop appointments directly commanded by the claviers: in some cases imparting double and in others triple powers of tonal flexibility and expression. Simple means of thus connecting and disconnecting the Ancillary Organs must be provided; preferably in the form of Couplers, immediately associated with the Draw-stops commanding the tonal resources of the Ancillaries. As many Couplers will be required for each Ancillary as there are manual claviers. Thumb-pistons may be used instead if preferred, or may be introduced in addition to the Couplers associated with the Draw-stops.

VI. As the shutters of all the Ancillary Organs have to be operated by the Expression Levers belonging to the actions of the Swell-boxes inclosing the stationary stop-appointments of the manual Organs, Couplers—preferably double-acting—have to be provided, by means of which the swell-actions of the different Ancillary Organs can be connected and released, at the will of the performer, to or from any one or more of the Expression Levers belonging to the stationary Divisions. These Couplers may be in the form of Tablets, Thumb-pistons, or Toe-pistons, as may be considered most convenient.

THE ANCILLARY STRING ORGAN

In the properly appointed Concert-room Organ there can be no Division, of an orchestral character, of more importance than that representing the String forces which form the foundation of the grand orchestra. Such being the case, it may, on first thoughts, be wondered at that a special manual Division was not devoted to it. That position was the one which originally occurred to us as the proper one; and, accordingly, when we designed the first String Organ that had ever been conceived, we located it as the second expressive Subdivision of the Third Organ in the Concert instrument installed in the Festival Hall of the Louisiana Purchase Exposition, at St. Louis, in 1904. This Subdivision comprised eleven stops, having eighteen ranks of imitative and harmonic-corroborating String-toned pipes. Although this position was, at the time, considered generally satisfactory, we subsequently came to the conclusion that making it stationary and under the direct command of a single clavier was undesirable, and a serious narrowing of its all-important artistic office. So, after a careful study of the question from all points of view, the conclusion was reached that it was necessary to make the String Organ an Ancillary or Floating Division, playable from any one or more of the claviers, either alone or in combination with the stationary tonal appointments commanded by the claviers. By this arrangement, the String Organ becomes of prime importance in the tonal structure of the true Concert-room instrument; opening up an entirely new realm of musical resources and effects, and, through double and triple powers of expression, *nuances* impossible on any organ of ordinary construction and appointment in existence (1924).

The following remarks, alluding to the Ancillary now under consideration, are from our Article on the Concert-room Organ, in "The American Organist" of February, 1923. There is no Division of the Concert-room Organ which in its stop-apportionment demands more care and skill on the part of the pipemaker and voicer than that now under consideration. It admits of no half-way work: it can only be a pronounced success or a total failure. So far as our experience extends, we regret to say we have not heard a truly satisfactory imitative VIOLINO or VIOLONCELLO in any organ constructed in this country. The resort to the ridiculously small scales, beloved of organ-builders on account of their saving in expensive metal (preferably tin), which is about one-third that which is required for properly scaled imitative String-toned stops, is to be condemned. To obtain the full and richly colored tones demanded in stops closely imitating the voices of the orchestral Violin, Viola, Violoncello, and Double Bass, liberal scales are absolutely necessary; as has been proved by the practice of the late Edmund Schulze, of Paulinzelle, and William Thynne, of London; the latter one of the most, if not the most, artistic of the voicers of String-toned stops of the nineteenth century. He favored a scale for the CC, 8 ft., pipe of his celebrated VIOLE D'ORCHESTRE measuring closely 3.13 inches in diameter, developed on the ratio 1 · 2.519, halving on the nineteenth pipe. He used a slightly larger scale for his beautiful VIOLONCELLO, 8 FT. It is essential that voices of the VIOLINO, VIOLA, and VIOLONCELLO and their variants, shall be as distinctive in tone as are the corresponding orchestral instruments. The wood VIOLA, 8 FT., and VIOLON BASS, 16 FT., of Schulze, and the metal VIOLE D'ORCHESTRE, 8 FT., and VIOLONCELLO, 8 FT., of Thynne are matchless stops. A complete String Organ formed of this class of stops would be a revelation in the organ world.

To these remarks may be added a passage from our Work, "The Organ of the Twentieth Century." Of all the Ancillary Organs likely to be schemed, the String Organ will certainly remain the most important. Indeed, it is quite important enough to have a clavier specially devoted to it; but that would very seriously limit its utility and tonal value. As a Floating Organ, capable of being connected, immediately and at the will of the performer, with any desirable clavier, there to be played alone or in combination with the tonal forces of the Organ commanded by that clavier, its usefulness can hardly be overrated. Musical results could be obtained by such simple means, that could never be arrived at were the String Organ confined to a special clavier, as can be readily understood. Again, the musical value of the String Organ is vastly increased by its being endowed with powers of expression, and by the fact that those powers can be commanded, as may be desired, by any of the Expression Levers—that belonging to the Organ with which the String Organ is coupled, or with any of the other Expression Levers deemed more conducive to the production of the special musical effects desired. The String Organ can be connected, at the same time, with two or more claviers, and, accordingly, with the Organs they command. The countless beautiful combinations of tone rendered possible by such means almost baffle imagination. The importance and musical value of the Floating String Organ, in the artistic rendition of orchestral compositions, cannot be overestimated.

In the following first Specification will be found complete particulars and details of the tonal appointment and control of the Ancillary String Organ, in its full artistic development.

THE ANCILLARY AËRIAL ORGAN

This Ancillary Organ is a manual Division—endowed with tonal flexibility and expression—which, properly stop-apportioned and artistically treated, may be considered complete in itself and practically independent; more so, indeed, than even the String Ancillary. Accordingly, it can be played from any of the claviers with which it is temporarily connected, while the tonal appointment permanently belonging to the clavier is shut off. Under these conditions, the Aërial Organ assumes great importance, adding a complete tonal Division to the Concert-room instrument, without affecting the number of the claviers—four or five as may be adopted—substituting, for the time, the stationary tonal appointment belonging to the clavier. In addition to this arrangement, the Aërial Organ may take the place of either one of the Subdi visions of the clavier, preferably that of the Accompanimental Organ; being used, in compound expression, with the Subdivision retained at the same time on the clavier.

Some apology is, perhaps desirable for our introduction of the term Aërial Organ into the nomenclature of the tonal Divisions of the Concert-room Organ. We experienced a little difficulty in finding an appropriate and expressive name for an entirely new Division of an extremely soft and refined tonality, such as had never been known in the appointment of the Concert-room Organ. The common term Echo Organ was decidedly undesirable; for we had no intention that this entirely new manual Division should in any manner be confused with the old established form of Echo Organ, which depended for its tonal effects, largely on its location at a considerable distance from the main Organ; or under some conditions which would impart to its tones somewhat the effect of the natural echo; a very useless and senseless expedient in the Monarch of all Instruments.

We remarked above, that the Aërial Organ may be preferably associated with the Accompanimental Organ, taking the place of one of its Subdivisions; thus retaining on the second clavier compound flexibility and expression. Such an association would be productive of remarkable musical effects; because the Aërial Organ, in its great variety and refinement of tonality, would prove an extremely beautiful accompanimental Subdivision, either alone or, in compound tones and expression, associated with the Subdivision of the Accompanimental Organ retained on the clavier. If the Aërial Organ is added to the complete Accompanimental Organ, triple powers of flexibility and expression will be instituted; and, accordingly, wonderful accompanimental or other effects will be readily produced by the musician organist; impossible on any organ ever constructed. This will be easily realized on consulting the first Specification.

All the stops of the Aërial Ancillary are to be of the smallest scales suitable for the production of their characteristic voices in their most refined and sympathetic intonations. They are to be voiced on wind of one and a half inches pressure; such as has been used by the great Schulze in the beautiful Echo Division inclosed in the Organ in the Parish Church of Leeds, England. It is probable, however, that the lingual stops, including the VOX HUMANA, may require a slightly higher pressure, say two to two and a half inches. All the five lingual stops in our own Chamber Organ spoke beautifully and promptly on wind of two and three-eighths inches.

It must be understood that the low pressure stated is conditional on the Ancillary being favorably located, close to the stationary Organs; and where no obstruction obtains to the free emission and passage of the sounds from its pipe-work. If, however, there is danger of the tones of so delicate an Organ being seriously interfered with, higher pressures of wind may be found desirable. Care must be taken, in any case, to construct the Swell-box of clear pine, of only sufficient thickness to secure a distinct *piano* effect. Anything approaching the inartistic *annihilating Swell* must here be avoided, as in every other tonal Division.

THE ANCILLARY FANFARE ORGAN

In introducing an entirely new Organ, Ancillary in character, composed of commanding Brass-toned lingual stops, we naturally experienced some difficulty in finding a name that would, as directly as possible, indicate its tonal character, and to some extent its position in the tonal structure of the entire instrument. Our memory flew back to half a century ago, when we listened to the Fanfare of Hunting Horns, in the Summer concerts in the Champs Elysées, Paris. The effects produced by the Horns were extremely impressive; and as we desired to make it possible to produce (under artistic control) equally impressive tonal effects on the Concert-room Organ, we designed the Ancillary and named it Fanfare Organ. It is doubtful if a more expressive name could be given, seeing the name Brass-wind Organ had already been given to the stationary Division commanded by the fourth clavier.

In designing the Fanfare Ancillary, which, apparently, had never before been thought of, our aim was to furnish the complete Concert-room Organ with ready and effective means of producing, under absolute control and powers of tonal flexibility and expression, the most powerful and impressive effects that could possibly be required in the rendition of orchestral scores. Something has been essayed, in a similar direction, in certain large modern organs, but not only in a fast-bound, but in a singularly crude and essentially inartistic manner, altogether unworthy of acceptance by the musician-organist of to-day. How the *virtuosi* now in the organ-playing world suffer such crudities to continue to be foisted upon them, without serious protest, has long been a mystery to us. A Society for the Prevention of Cruelty to Organists ought to be instituted, with a President gifted with sensitive auditory nerves.

The Fanfare Organ, as its name implies, is to comprise, for the most part, a series of lingual stops, of full scales, voiced on winds of high pressures, and yielding exceptionably powerful voices, suitable—being under control and expressive—for solo effects, or for association with the various tonalities of the more powerfully appointed stationary manual Divisions or Subdivisions. This novel Ancillary is practically a floating Brass-wind Organ of a dominating tonality, exceeding in strength of tone the lingual stops of the stationary Brass-wind Organ; so that it would form a valuable addition to that Division. Its presence in the tonal appointment of the instrument, would, happily, render it unnecessary to resort to undesirable high wind-pressures in the stationary Brass-wind Organ; and, accordingly, allow a desirable balance of tone to be established therein, and so increase its value generally in relation to the other Divisions of the instrument. From these points of view, the tonal value of the Ancillary could hardly be overrated. It can, of course, be played, under single expression, alone on any manual clavier.

The Swell-box must be constructed of solid walls, ceiling, and shutters of best straight-grained yellow pine, of sufficient thickness to secure an effective *crescendo* starting from a *piano* tone of perfect clearness and true character. The voices of the inclosed stops are to be subdued, but by no means destroyed on the Swell-box being closed. Power or strength of intonation is an essential element in the Fanfare Organ, and diminution of its audible intensity is to be proportioned properly; otherwise its utility in artistic music will be largely sacrificed. Under such control, the tonal flexibility of this expressive Ancillary will admit of its entering into numberless combinations with the voices of the stationary and the other Ancillary Organs. If the Swell-box of the Fanfare Organ is properly constructed, so as to secure the necessary flexible control, it will be possible, and, perhaps, sometimes desirable, to effectively combine certain of its voices with those of the Accompanimental or Wood-Wind Organs; when it may be necessary or convenient to temporarily connect its Swell-action with that of an Expression Lever directly adjoining and belonging to the manual Organ in use; providing that the Expression Lever is not immediately required for the manual Division to which it strictly belongs. Under a favorable condition, the Ancillary can be used with adjusted stationary tones or in simple or compound expression. These possibilities, with many others open up a very wide and practically unknown field for the exercise of musical knowledge and taste on the part of the organ *virtuoso*.

THE ANCILLARY HARMONIC ORGAN

The name given to this important floating Division of the fully appointed Concert-room Organ clearly indicates its nature and its office in the tonal scheme of the instrument; which is to furnish, in a more or less temporary manner, desirable harmonic-corroborating and enriching combinations of labial stops to the stationary forces of the manual Organs. Thereby rendering it largely unnecessary to insert numerous harmonic-corroborating stops in the stationary Divisions. In addition, as the Ancillary is rendered expressive and flexible in tone by being inclosed in a special Swell-box, its voices can be imparted, in any harmonic tonality and of any desired strength, to accord with any registration drawn in the stationary Division to which they are added.

The organ-builder and organist, on reading these remarks, will, in all probability, question the value of this Ancillary Organ, seeing that the stationary manual Divisions would properly comprise certain harmonic-corroborating stops. Under the present prevailing unsystematic and unscientific methods of stop-apportionment, with its purely modern and ignorant treatment and neglect of the invaluable harmonic-corroborating stops, which, in quarters that ought to know better, is accepted as representing the acme of tonal development, it seems quite reasonable that such a question should arise in the minds of those unfamiliar with the value of harmonic-corroborating stops; and the wonderful facilities for compound tone-production afforded by the Ancillary Organs. The paramount importance of the harmonic-corroborating stops—simple and compound—are generally unrealized, and to the majority of modern organ-builders and organists unknown. An open-minded study of musical acoustics is necessary to the full knowledge and appreciation of the great tonal and tone-creating value and office of such stops.

By means of such an Ancillary Harmonic Organ as here alluded to, and as set forth in the following first Specification, countless tonal effects of a remarkable, beautiful, and almost mysterious character could be produced, in combination with the tonal forces of the different Divisions and Subdivisions commanded by the manual claviers. Imagine the possibility of throwing the combined tones of ten or more ranks of harmonic-corroborating pipes on a single DULCIANA, without affecting its pitch, while investing its voice with a garment of mysterious charm, absolutely impossible of production on any organ hitherto constructed. To give the mere outline of what would be possible in this direction, and under our System, would occupy many pages, and would utterly fail to convey any adequate idea of the tonal effects due to the combinations of the stops of the stationary expressive Organs with series of harmonic stops, loud or soft, in the equally expressive Harmonic Ancillary. They can be better imagined than described.

The musical value of this Ancillary largely depends on the perfection of its stops: their scaling, voicing, and their scientific graduation of tone according to the natural laws of compound musical sounds. It can be made of one complete Division, or of two contrasting tonal Subdivisions, as the general appointment and size of the organ may render desirable. The latter treatment, which is set forth in the First Specification, is formed of two Subdivisions, designated Forte and Piano, providing harmonic series of widely different intensities of tone, produced by ranks of pipes of different forms and scales, voiced on winds of different pressures. The two series, controlled by powers of flexibility and expression, render the Ancillary capable of meeting every demand that could be made upon it in compound-tone production in which harmonic-corroboration is essential and necessarily prominent. To fully realize the value of this Ancillary, it must be borne in mind that it can be coupled with any one or more of the stationary Divisions or Subdivisions of the instrument; and that its swell-action can be coupled with any of the Expression Levers or left uncoupled, with its Swell-box closed, and with any combination of its stops speaking; a condition conducive to the production of many fascinating and almost mysterious musical effects, at present unknown. In this subdued and unexpressive condition, either of the harmonic Subdivisions can be used in combination with any single unison stop in any of the stationary Organs, which may be played as a solo with expression.

Further remarks regarding the stop-apportionments of this Ancillary will follow the full Specification.

THE ANCILLARY PERCUSSION ORGAN

Much as the organ purist may question the propriety of introducing any sounds into the tonal economy of the organ which are foreign to the true nature and constitution of the instrument, it must be admitted that certain sounds produced by *percussion* are now accepted as agreeable, and to a certain extent serviceable in compound-tone production, in combination with the steady tones of labial pipes; and, in special cases, appropriate in solo effects in descriptive music. Of course, percussion stops are admissible in Concert-room, Theater, and Chamber Organs only. There are certain instruments (not stops) which are neither desirable nor possible to be artistically commanded in organ playing; and which, in our opinion, should never be considered constituents of The Temple of Tone. We allude specially to Drums, Cymbals, Triangles, and the like, practically impossible to be artistically commanded by a single performer at the console, while he is fully engaged on the pedal and manual claviers. We were not a little surprised on reading the Specification of the Concert Organ installed in the Town Hall of Johannesburg, and knowing the consummate musicianship of its designer, to find the following:—

> "Bass Drum tap action connected to each of the pedal keys and operated by rocking tablet.
>
> Side Drum tap action connected to each of the pedal keys and operated by rocking tablet.
>
> Bass Drum roll by rocking tablet.
>
> Side Drum roll by rocking tablet.
>
> Triangle connected to each pedal key and operated by rocking tablet."

Unless unmusical noise was aimed at, one is at a loss to understand the introduction of the untunable Drums. It is just possible, however, that the designer of the Organ had some special effects in mind, which he alone could properly produce in some composition of his own. Would that warrant the introduction of such generally useless and necessarily expensive attachments? The only percussion stops in the Organ are a CARILLON of two octaves from G, and GLOCKENSPIEL, from F to c^2.

The introduction of percussion and what may be called mechanical speaking stops is by no means modern, for the old German masters indulged in tonal freaks. In the year 1733, the English organ-builder Thomas Schwarbrook inserted in the organ he installed in the fine Church of St. Michael, at Coventry, three remarkable string stops, designated HARP, LUTE, and DULCIMER, in imitation of the instruments of the same names in use in his time. It is very probable that the HARP and LUTE were sounded, plectrumwise, by a Harpsichord jack-action; while it is certain that the DULCIMER had a percussion or hammer-action. The strings or wires of all the stops were stretched over sound-boards, mounted on resonant boxes, as in the Dulcimer of to-day. Owing to the difficulty of keeping the strings in tune with the organ-pipes, these unique mechanical stops were removed from the organ in 1763, after having been more or less in use for thirty years.

If percussion stops are deemed necessary or desirable in the true Concert-room Organ, by all manner of means let them be of a sympathetic and refined tonal character, favorable to artistic combination with suitable labial voices; or for the production of occasional solo effects in music, more or less, of a descriptive character. If these simple conditions are recognized as reasonable and desirable, very few percussion stops or adjuncts will be found suitable.

CARILLON—The percussion stop most to be wished for in the fully appointed Concert-room Organ, but which, so far as we are aware, has not made its appearance in proper form is a CARILLON formed of true bells, of three or four octaves; on which could be rendered true bell music under control and expression. Such a stop would consist of a series of graduated hemispherical or dish-shaped bells, arranged as closely together as practicable on a central steel rod, supported horizontally, and adjoining which, close to the edges of the bells, is adjusted an electric hammer-action and a damper-movement.

Another form of CARILLON, commonly designated CHIMES, is now frequently introduced in organs of all classes. In its approved form, as made by Mayland or Degan, it is a satisfactory percussion stop, pleasing in tone and effective, under control, in both solo and combinational tonal passages. It is formed of a carefully tuned series of tubular bells, commonly twenty-five or thirty-two in number, freely suspended, and played by an electric hammer-action. Although this stop is usually inclosed in the Swell-box of one of the stationary manual Divisions, and is, accordingly, commanded by one of the claviers; it must be evident that its value would be greatly increased if made an ancillary stop, capable of being connected with any Division or Subdivision of the organ.

HARP—Although not so frequently introduced in the organ as the CHIMES, we consider the percussion stop which closely imitates the tone of the orchestral Harp the most desirable one on the score of refinement and its sympathetic tonality. The HARP stop is formed of a series of bars of sonorous wood, of graduated dimensions, suspended in front of sympathetic and accurately tuned resonators, and sounded by an electric hammer-action. The Degan "Marimba Harp" is a fine example; formed of five octaves of Nagaed wood bars, suspended directly in front of the open ends of scientifically proportioned and correctly tuned brass resonators. The hammers are correspondingly adjusted in size and weight so as to produce the most imitative tones. Like the orchestral Harp, no mechanical dampers are required, for the sounds produced by the bars are necessarily of short duration.

Following, as it were, the lead of Thomas Schwarbrook, who in 1733 introduced in the Organ in the Church of St. Michael, Coventry, a HARP stop, formed of strings, stretched over a sound-board, and plucked by a plectrum-action, a HARP of somewhat similar description has been included in the extension to the Concert Organ we designed, and which was installed in the Festival Hall of the Louisiana Purchase Exposition, now in the Wanamaker Store in Philadelphia, Pa. Whether this stop will be found beset with the imperfection which led to the removal of Schwarbrook's HARP remains to be seen. It must be allowed, however, so far as strict tonal imitation is concerned, to be a step in the right direction; and, accordingly, deserves careful consideration on the part of the organ-builder and organ-designer.

XYLOPHONE—This is another percussion stop of the Degan Harp class, formed of graduated bars of Nagaed wood: made in two treatments, one with and the other without resonators. That which is known as the "Organ Special

Xylophone" is the proper form to be introduced in the organ. It is constructed of forty-nine bars placed over accurately tuned resonators. This stop is not required if the HARP is introduced.

CELESTA—This is a percussion stop of a bright and refined quality of tone, contrasting with that of the more powerful CARILLON or CHIMES. Its best form is the Degan "Harp Celeste." It is formed of sixty-one graduated bars of special alloy steel, suspended in front of accurately tuned sympathetic resonators of brass, and played by a graduated electric hammer-action.

It has been customary heretofore to directly associate such percussion stops, as described above, with the stop-apportionments of the stationary manual Divisions of the organ; but in the properly appointed Concert-room Organ this practice is undesirable for several reasons. Their proper place is, unquestionably, in an expressive Ancillary or Floating Organ; so that they may, according to the requirements of the composition being rendered, be played on any convenient manual clavier, either alone, or in combination with any stop or stops commanded by the clavier. This facility combined with their independent powers of tonal flexibility and expression multiplies their musical value a hundredfold. The Swell-box of the Ancillary Percussion Organ must be made of wood about one and a half inches in thickness, so as to in no manner destroy the percussion tones or effects.

The first Specification, which is for a Concert-room Organ of the first magnitude, now follows in order; and should be carefully studied both in its system of stop-apportionments and its mechanical system of tonal control.

—FIRST SPECIFICATION—

GRAND CONCERT-ROOM ORGAN

AUDSLEY SYSTEM—COMPOUND EXPRESSION
FIVE MANUAL CLAVIERS

—PEDAL ORGAN—

Compass CCC to G—32 Notes

—PEDAL CLAVIER—

UNEXPRESSIVE SUBDIVISION

1. Vox Gravissima (Resultant)		64	Feet
2. Double Principal .	W.	32	"
3. Double Principal .	M.	32	"
4. Contra-Violone (61 pipes) . . .	M.	32	"
5. Contra-Dulciana (61 pipes) . .	M.	32	"
6. Grossquintenbass (44 pipes) . .	W.	$21\frac{1}{3}$	"
7. Major Principal .	W.	16	"
8. Minor Principal .	M.	16	"
9. Gemshornbass . .	M.	16	"
10. Violonbass (From 4)	M.	16	"
11. Dulciana (From 5)	M.	16	Feet
12. Quintenbass (From 6)	W.	$10\frac{2}{3}$	"
13. Grand Octave .	M.	8	"
14. Grossflöte . . .	W.	8	"
15. Super-Octave . .	M.	4	"
16. Compensating Mixture . .	M.	VI.	Ranks
17. Contre-Bombarde	M.	32	Feet
18. Contra-Trombone (61 pipes) . .	M.	32	"
19. Bombarde . . .	M.	16	"
20. Trombone (From 18)	M	16	"
21. Tromba . . .	M.	8	"

EXPRESSIVE SUBDIVISION

Inclosed in Swell-Chamber

22. Untersatz . . .	W.	32	Feet
23. Diapason Phonon .	M.	16	"
24. Contrabasso . .	W.	16	"
25. Gemshornbass . .	M.	16	"
26. Gemshornquint .	M.	$10\frac{2}{3}$	"
27. Doppelspitzflöte .	W.	8	"
28. Violoncello . .	M.	8	"
29. Octave	M.	8	"
30. Gemshornterz . .	M.	$6\frac{2}{5}$	"
31. Gemshornquint .	M.	$5\frac{1}{3}$	"
32. Septième . . .	M.	$4\frac{4}{7}$	Feet
33. Hohlflöte . . .	W.	4	"
34. Grand Cornet	M.	VII.	Ranks
35. Fagottone . . .	M.	32	Feet
36. Contrafagotto .	M.	16	"
37. Contra-Saxophone	M.	16	"
38. Contra-Clarinetto	M.	16	"
39. Tuba Sonora . .	M.	8	"
40. Trombone . . .	M.	8	"
41. Clarion (Harmonic)	M.	4	"

GRAND ORGAN

Compass CC to c⁴—61 Notes

—FIRST CLAVIER—

UNEXPRESSIVE SUBDIVISION

42. Double Diapason Major	M.	16 Feet
43. Contra-Gamba	M.	16 "
44. Double Dulciana	M.	16 "
45. Grand Quint	M.	10⅔ "
46. Major Diapason	M.	8 "
47. Diapason, Schulze	M.	8 "
48. Minor Diapason	M.	8 "
49. Diapason	W.	8 "
50. Flûte à Pavillon	M.	8 Feet
51. Doppelflöte	W.	8 "
52. Quint	M.	5⅓ "
53. Octave Major	M.	4 "
54. Harmonic Flute	M.	4 "
55. Tierce	M.	3⅕ "
56. Twelfth	M.	2⅔ "
57. Super-Octave	M.	2 "

AUXILIARY STOP

58. Dolciano Profundo . . M. 32 Ft. 61 Notes—From Pedal Organ No. 5.

EXPRESSIVE SUBDIVISION

Inclosed in Swell-Box No. 1

59. Starkgedeckt	W.	16 Feet
60. Quintaten	W.	16 "
61. Horn Diapason	M.	8 "
62. Viol Diapason	M.	8 "
63. Clarabella	W.	8 "
64. Grand Viol	M.	8 "
65. Tibia Plena	W.	8 "
66. Flauto Maggiore	W.	8 "
67. Harmonic Flute	M.	8 "
68. Quint	M.	5⅓ "
69. Waldflöte	M.	4 "
70. Octave Minor	M.	4 "
71. Harmonic Flute	M.	4 Feet
72. Gedeckt-Terz	M.	3⅕ "
73. Twelfth	M.	2⅔ "
74. Septième	M.	2²⁄₇ "
75. Super-Octave	M.	2 "
76. Full Mixture	M.	VI. Ranks
77. Grand Cornet	M.	VII. "
78. Double Trumpet	M.	16 Feet
79. Tromba	M.	8 "
80. Trumpet	M.	8 "
81. Tromba Quint	M.	5⅓ "
82. Clarion (Harmonic)	M.	4 "

ACCOMPANIMENTAL ORGAN

Compass CC to c⁴—61 Notes

—SECOND CLAVIER—

FIRST EXPRESSIVE SUBDIVISION

Inclosed in Swell-Box No. 2

83. Bourdon Doux	W.	16 Feet
84. English Diapason	M.	8 "
85. Salicional	M.	8 "
86. Keraulophone	M.	8 "
87. Dolcan	M.	8 "
88. Gemshorn	M.	8 Feet
89. Melodia	W.	8 "
90. Flauto Amabile	W.	8 "
91. Dolce	M.	8 "
92. Flûte à Cheminée	M.	8 "

FIRST EXPRESSIVE SUBDIVISION—Continued

93. Spitzflöte . . .	M.	8	Feet
94. Flautone . . .	M.	8	"
95. Rohrflötenquinte	W.	5⅓	"
96. Gemshornoctav .	M.	4	"
97. Spitzflöte . . .	M.	4	"
98. Salicet . . .	M.	4	Feet
99. Grand Dolce Cornet	M.	VII.	Ranks
100. Horn	M.	8	Feet
101. Cor Anglais . .	M.	8	"

I. Tremolant

SECOND EXPRESSIVE SUBDIVISION

Inclosed in Swell-Box No. 3

102. Lieblichgedeckt .	W.	16	Feet
103. Dulciana . . .	M.	8	"
104. Viole Sourdine .	M.	8	"
105. Lieblichgedeckt .	W.	8	"
106. Viola d'Amore .	M.	8	"
107. Viola d'Amore (Sharp) . . .	M.	8	"
108. Philomela . .	W.	8	"
109. Cone Gamba . .	M.	8	"
110. Dulciana Quint .	M.	5⅓	"
111. Lieblichflöte . .	W.	4	Feet
112. Dulcet . . .	M.	4	"
113. Flauto d'Amore .	W.	4	"
114. Dulciana Twelfth	M.	2⅔	"
115. Dulciana Fifteenth . .	M.	2	"
116. Dulciana Cornet . .	M.	V.	Ranks
117. Euphonium . .	M.	16	Feet
118. Oboe d'Amore .	M.	8	"

II. Tremolant

WOOD-WIND ORGAN

Compass CC to c^4—61 Notes

——THIRD CLAVIER——

FIRST EXPRESSIVE SUBDIVISION

Inclosed in Swell-Box No. 2

119. Bourdon . . .	W.	16	Feet
120. Doppelrohrgedeckt	W.	8	"
121. Flachflöte . .	W.	8	"
122. Hohlflöte . .	W.	8	"
123. Orchestral Flute	W.	8	"
124. Dolce	M.	8	"
125. Gedecktquinte .	M.	5⅓	"
126. Orchestral Flute	W.	4	"
127. Zauberflöte . .	M.	4	Feet
128. Harmonic Flute .	M.	4	"
129. Spitzflöte Cornet	M.	IV.	Ranks
130. Orchestral Piccolo	M.	2	Feet
131. Contra-Bassett-Horn . . .	M.	16	"
132. Saxophone . .	M.	8	"

III. Tremolant

SECOND EXPRESSIVE SUBDIVISION

Inclosed in Swell-Box No. 3

133. Bourdon Doux .	W.	16 Feet	142. Orchestral Oboe	M.	8 Feet
134. Doppelgedeckt .	W.	8 "	143. Orchestral Clarinetto .	M.	8 "
135. Clarabel Flute .	W.	8 "	144. Cor Anglais . .	M.	8 "
136. Melodia . . .	W.	8 "	145. Vox Humana .	M.	8 "
137. Dolce Cornet	M.	IV. Ranks	146. Clarinetto Quinta	M.	5⅓ "
138. Contrafagotto .	M.	16 Feet	147. Clarinetto Ottava	M.	4 "
139. Contra-Clarinetto	M.	16 "	148. Oboe Ottava .	M.	4 "
140. Contra-Oboe .	M.	16 "	149. Musette . . .	M.	4 "
141. Orchestral Fagotto . .	M.	8 "	IV. Tremolant		

BRASS-WIND ORGAN

Compass CC to c⁴—61 Notes

——FOURTH CLAVIER——

FIRST EXPRESSIVE SUBDIVISION

Inclosed in Swell-Box No. 4

150. Grossgedeckt . .	W.	16 Feet	158. Super-Octave .	M.	2 Feet
151. Horn Diapason .	M.	8 "	159. Grand Cornet	M.	V. Ranks
152. Grand Viol . .	M.	8 "	160. Contra-Tromba .	M.	16 Feet
153. Doppelflöte . .	W.	8 "	161. Tromba Real .	M.	8 "
154. Clarabella . .	W.	8 "	162. Ophicleide . .	M.	8 "
155. Gemshorn . . .	M.	8 "	163. Trumpet Royal .	M.	8 "
156. Octave, Major .	M.	4 "	164. Tromba Quint .	M.	5⅓ "
157. Octave Viol . .	M.	4 "	165. Tromba Clarion	M.	4 "

SECOND EXPRESSIVE SUBDIVISION

Inclosed in Swell-Box No. 5

166. Grossdoppelgedeckt	W.	16 Feet	174. Trombone . .	M.	8 Feet
167. Major Diapason .	M.	8 "	175. Trombone Quint	M.	5⅓ "
168. Grossflöte . .	W.	8 "	176. Trombone Octave	M.	4 "
169. Quintaten . .	W.	8 "	177. Orchestral Horn	M.	8 "
170. Gambette . . .	M.	4 "	178. Orchestral Trumpet . .	M.	8 "
171. Bombardon . .	M.	16 "	179. Clarion . . .	M.	4 "
172. Contra-Trombone	M.	16 "			
173. Euphonium . .	M.	8 "			

AUXILIARY STOP

180. Contra-Trombone . M. 32 ft. 61 Notes—From Pedal Organ No. 18.

SOLO ORGAN

Compass CC to c^4—61 Notes

—FIFTH CLAVIER—

EXPRESSIVE

Inclosed in Swell-Box No. 6

181. Quintaten	W.	16 Feet
182. Geigenprincipal	M.	8 "
183. Orchestral Violoncello	Tin	8 "
184. Orchestral Violin	T.	8 "
185. Orchestral Flute	W.	8 "
186. Violetta	T.	4 "
187. Orchestral Flute	W.	4 "
188. Orchestral Piccolo	M.	2 "
189. Dolce Cornet	M.	V. Ranks
190. Orchestral Oboe	M.	8 Feet
191. Orchestral Clarinet	M.	8 "
192. Orchestral Horn	M.	8 "
193. Vox Humana	M.	8 "
194. Orchestral Trumpet	M.	8 "
195. Tuba Magna	M	8 "
196. Tuba Clarion	M.	4 "

V. Tremolant to Labial Stops

ANCILLARY STRING ORGAN

Compass CC to c^4—61 Notes

EXPRESSIVE

Inclosed in Swell-Box No. 7

197. Contrabasso	W.	16 Feet
198. Quintaten	W.	16 "
199. Viola Bastarda	M.	10⅔ "
200. Violin Diapason	M.	8 "
201. Salicional	M.	8 "
202. Melodia	W.	8 "
203. Nachthorn	W.	8 "
204. Violoncello	M.	8 "
205. Violoncello Sordo	M.	8 "
206. Violoncello Vibrato	M.	8 "
207. Viola Pomposa	M.	8 "
208. Viola Sordo	M.	8 "
209. Viola da Gamba	M.	8 "
210. Viola da Gamba (Sharp)	M.	8 "
211. Viola d'Amore	M.	8 "
212. Viola d'Amore (Flat)	M.	8 Feet
213. Viole d'Orchestre	M.	8 "
214. Violino	M.	8 "
215. Violino Sordo	M.	8 "
216. Violino Vibrato	M.	8 "
217. Viol Quint	M.	5⅓ "
218. Violetta	M.	4 "
219. Viol Tierce	M.	3⅕ "
220. Viol Twelfth	M.	2⅔ "
221. Viol Septième	M.	2²⁄₇ "
222. Viol Fifteenth	M.	2 "
223. Viol Cornet Sordo	M.	V. Ranks
224. Viol Sesquialtera	M.	II. "

VI. Tremolant

ANCILLARY AËRIAL ORGAN

Compass CC to c^4—61 Notes

EXPRESSIVE

Inclosed in Swell-Box No. 8

225. Bourdonecho . W. 16 Feet
226. Echo Diapason . M. 8 "
227. Dulciana . . . M. 8 "
228. Gelindgedeckt . W. 8 "
229. Salicional . . T. 8 "
230. Melodia . . . W. 8 "
231. Violino Sordo . T. 8 "
232. Flauto d'Amore . W. 8 "
233. Harmonica . . W. 8 "
234. Æoline . . . M. 8 "
235. Voix Angélique . M. 8 "
236. Voix Céleste (Sharp) M. 8 Feet
237. Cœlestina . . M. 4 "
238. Flauto Amabile . W. 4 "
239. Echo Quint . . M. $2\frac{2}{3}$ "
240. Flautino . . . M. 2 "
241. Harmonia Ætheria T. VI. Ranks
242. Vox Humana . M. 8 Feet
243. Dulcian . . . M. 8 "
244. Scialumo . . . M. 8 "
VII. Tremolant

ANCILLARY HARMONIC ORGAN

Compass CC to c^4—61 Notes

EXPRESSIVE

Inclosed in Swell-Box No. 9

FORTE SUBDIVISION

245. Quintaten . . W. 8 Feet
246. Quint . . . . M. $5\frac{1}{3}$ "
247. Octave . . . . M. 4 "
248. Tierce . . . . M. $3\frac{1}{5}$ "
249. Twelfth . . . M. $2\frac{2}{3}$ "
250. Septième (Soft) . M. $2\frac{2}{7}$ Feet
251. Super-Octave . M. 2 "
252. Twenty-second . M. 1 "
253. Mixture . . M. IV. Ranks

PIANO SUBDIVISION

254. Dolce . . . . M. 8 Feet
255. Dolce Quint . . M. $5\frac{1}{3}$ "
256. Dolce Octave . M. 4 "
257. Dolce Tierce . . M. $3\frac{1}{5}$ "
258. Dolce Twelfth . M. $2\frac{2}{3}$ "
259. Dolce Fifteenth . M. 2 "
260. Dolce Seventeenth M. $1\frac{3}{5}$ Feet
261. Dolce Nineteenth M. $1\frac{1}{3}$ "
262. Dolce Twenty-second . . . M. 1 Foot
263. Dolce Acuta . M. IV. Ranks

ANCILLARY FANFARE ORGAN

Compass CC to c^4—61 Notes

EXPRESSIVE

Inclosed in Swell-Box No. 10

264. Stentorphone . M. 8 Feet
265. Contra-Tuba . M. 16 "
266. Contra-Trumpet (Harmonic) . . 16 "
267. Tuba Magna . M. 8 "
268. Trumpet (Harmonic) M. 8 "
269. Trumpet Quint . M. $5\frac{1}{3}$ Feet
270. Tuba Clarion . M. 4 "
271. Clarion (Harmonic) M. 4 "
272. Trumpet Tierce . M. $3\frac{1}{5}$ "
273. Stentor Cornet M. IV. Ranks

ANCILLARY PERCUSSION ORGAN

EXPRESSIVE

Inclosed in Swell-Box No. 11

274. CARILLON	True Bells 49 Notes	276. CELESTA.	Steel Bars 61 Notes
275. HARP .	Wood Bars 61 "	277. XYLOPHONE	Wood Bars 49 "

CLAVIER COUPLERS

PEDAL ORGAN COUPLERS

First Clavier......to Pedal Clavier, Unison Coupler.
First Clavier......to Pedal Clavier, Octave Coupler.
Second Clavier....to Pedal Clavier, Unison Coupler.
Third Clavier.....to Pedal Clavier, Unison Coupler.
Fourth Clavier....to Pedal Clavier, Unison Coupler.
Fifth Clavier......to Pedal Clavier, Unison Coupler.
Pedal Clavier......on Itself, Octave Coupler.

FIRST CLAVIER COUPLERS

Second Clavier..1st Subdivision..to First Clavier, Unison Coupler.
Second Clavier..1st Subdivision..to First Clavier, Octave Coupler.
Second Clavier..2nd Subdivision..to First Clavier, Unison Coupler.
Second Clavier..2nd Subdivision..to First Clavier, Octave Coupler.
Third Clavier...1st Subdivision..to First Clavier, Unison Coupler.
Third Clavier...1st Subdivision..to First Clavier, Octave Coupler.
Third Clavier...2nd Subdivision..to First Clavier, Unison Coupler.
Third Clavier...2nd Subdivision..to First Clavier, Octave Coupler.
Fourth Clavier..1st Subdivision..to First Clavier, Unison Coupler.
Fourth Clavier..2nd Subdivision..to First Clavier, Unison Coupler.
Fifth Clavier........Undivided...to First Clavier, Unison Coupler
Fifth Clavier........Undivided...to First Clavier, Octave Coupler.

SECOND CLAVIER COUPLERS

Third Clavier...1st Subdivision..to Second Clavier, Unison Coupler.
Third Clavier...1st Subdivision..to Second Clavier, Octave Coupler.
Third Clavier...2nd Subdivision..to Second Clavier, Unison Coupler.
Third Clavier...2nd Subdivision..to Second Clavier, Octave Coupler.
Fourth Clavier..1st Subdivision..to Second Clavier, Unison Coupler.
Fourth Clavier..1st Subdivision..to Second Clavier, Octave Coupler.
Fourth Clavier..2nd Subdivision..to Second Clavier, Unison Coupler.
Fourth Clavier..2nd Subdivision..to Second Clavier, Octave Coupler.
Fifth Clavier......Undivided...to Second Clavier, Unison Coupler.

THIRD CLAVIER COUPLERS

Fourth Clavier . . 1st Subdivision . . to Third Clavier, Unison Coupler.
Fourth Clavier . . 1st Subdivision . . to Third Clavier, Octave Coupler.
Fourth Clavier . . 2nd Subdivision . . to Third Clavier, Unison Coupler.
Fourth Clavier . . 2nd Subdivision . . to Third Clavier, Octave Coupler.
Fifth Clavier . . . . . . Undivided . . . to Third Clavier, Unison Coupler.
Fifth Clavier . . . . . . Undivided . . . to Third Clavier, Octave Coupler.

FOURTH CLAVIER COUPLERS

Fifth Clavier. . . . . . . Undivided. . to Fourth Clavier, Unison Coupler.
Fifth Clavier. . . . . . . Undivided. . to Fourth Clavier, Octave Coupler.

FIFTH CLAVIER COUPLERS

First Clavier . . . . to Fifth Clavier, Unison Coupler.
Third Clavier . . . . . . to Fifth Clavier, Unison Coupler.

ANCILLARY COUPLERS

Five Couplers connecting Ancillary String Organ with First, Second, Third, Fourth, and Fifth Manual Claviers.

Five Couplers connecting Ancillary Aërial Organ with First, Second, Third, Fourth, and Fifth Manual Claviers.

Five Couplers connecting Forte Subdivision of the Ancillary Harmonic Organ with First, Third, Fourth, and Fifth Manual Claviers, and Pedal Clavier.

Four Couplers connecting Piano Subdivision of the Ancillary Harmonic Organ with Second, Third, Fourth, and Fifth Manual Claviers.

Five Couplers connecting Ancillary Fanfare Organ with First, Third, Fourth, and Fifth Manual, and Pedal Clavier.

Four Couplers connecting Ancillary Percussion Organ with Second, Third, Fourth, and Fifth Manual Claviers.

EXPRESSION LEVER COUPLERS

Couplers connecting String Organ Swell-action with Expression Levers II., III., IV., V., VI.

Couplers connecting Aërial Organ Swell-action with Expression Levers II., III., IV., V., VI.

Couplers connecting Harmonic Organ Swell-action with Expression Levers II., III., IV., V., VI.

Couplers connecting Fanfare Organ Swell-action with Expression Levers II., III., IV., V., VI.

Couplers connecting Percussion Organ Swell-action with Expression Levers II., III., IV., V., VI.

Couplers connecting Pedal Organ Swell-action with Expression Levers II., III., IV., V., VI.

EXPRESSION LEVERS

I. Balanced Expression Lever commanding Pedal Organ Swell-action.
II. Balanced Expression Lever commanding action of Swell-Box No. 1.
III. Balanced Expression Lever commanding action of Swell-Box No. 2.
IV. Balanced Expression Lever commanding action of Swell-Box No. 3.
V. Balanced Expression Lever commanding action of Swell-Box No. 4.
VI. Balanced Expression Lever commanding action of Swell-Box No. 5.
VII. Balanced Expression Lever commanding action of Swell-Box No. 6.
A, B, C, D, E, F, G.—Seven double-acting Toe-Pistons, disconnecting and connecting the actions of the Pedal Swell-Chamber and of Swell-Boxes Nos. 1, 2, 3, 4, 5, 6, with the respective Balanced Expression Levers, as tabulated above.

CRESCENDO LEVER

Balanced Crescendo Lever commanding selected groups of Stops in progressive order of tonal power and character. The mechanism of the Lever being so adjusted as to indicate, by well marked changes in resistance to the pressure of the foot, the entry into changes of tonal character and increase of power until the climax is reached. The *decrescendo* follows in the same order downwards. The Lever is placed on the right of the Expression Levers, and at an angle convenient to the foot of the performer.

DIVISIONAL PISTONS

Two Thumb-Pistons—under First Clavier—bringing on and throwing off Expressive Subdivision of Grand Organ.

Two Thumb-Pistons—under Second Clavier—bringing on and throwing off First Expressive Subdivision of Accompanimental Organ.

Two Thumb-Pistons—under Second Clavier—bringing on and throwing off Second Expressive Subdivision of Accompanimental Organ.

Two Thumb-Pistons—under Third Clavier—bringing on and throwing off First Expressive Subdivision of Wood-Wind Organ.

Two Thumb-Pistons—under Third Clavier—bringing on and throwing off Second Expressive Subdivision of Wood-Wind Organ.

Two Thumb-Pistons—under Fourth Clavier—bringing on and throwing off First Expressive Subdivision of Brass-Wind Organ.

Two Thumb-Pistons—under Fourth Clavier—bringing on and throwing off Second Expressive Subdivision of Brass-Wind Organ.

Two Thumb-Pistons—under Fifth Clavier—bringing on and throwing off Solo Organ.

ADJUSTABLE COMBINATION PISTONS

Ten Operating Thumb-Pistons and Release—under First Clavier—commanding Stop-combinations on Grand Organ, Pedal Organ, and Couplers.

Four Double-acting Thumb-Pistons—under First Clavier—bringing on and throwing off Ancillary String, Aërial, Forte Harmonic, and Fanfare Organs.

Ten Operating Thumb-Pistons and Release—under Second Clavier—commanding Stop-combinations on Accompanimental Organ, Pedal Organ, and Couplers.

Four Double-acting Thumb-Pistons—under Second Clavier—bringing on and throwing off Ancillary String, Aërial, Piano Harmonic, and Percussion Organs.

Ten Operating Thumb-Pistons and Release—under Third Clavier—commanding Stop-combinations on Wood-Wind Organ, Pedal Organ, and Couplers.

Five Double-acting Thumb-Pistons—under Third Clavier—bringing on and throwing off Ancillary String, Aërial, Harmonic, Fanfare, and Percussion Organs.

Eight Operating Thumb-Pistons and Release—under Fourth Clavier—commanding Stop-combinations on Brass-Wind Organ, Pedal Organ, and Couplers.

Five Double-acting Thumb-Pistons—under Fourth Clavier—bringing on and throwing off Ancillary String, Aërial, Harmonic, Fanfare, and Percussion Organs.

Six Operating Thumb-Pistons and Release—under Fifth Clavier—commanding Stop-combinations on Solo Organ and Pedal Organ.

Five Double-acting Thumb-Pistons—under Fifth Clavier—bringing on and throwing off Ancillary String, Aërial, Harmonic, Fanfare, and Percussion Organs.

TREMOLANTS

The Seven Tremolants are to be directly commanded by the general Draw-Stop System, by rocking-tablets, pendant touches, or by whatever style of Draw-Stop appliances may be generally adopted for the command of the Stops and Couplers, and are to be immediately associated with them. In addition, the five Tremolants belonging to the Subdivisions of the stationary Organs are to be commanded also by Thumb-Pistons located under the respective Manual Claviers. If preferred, the Pistons can be placed in the fronts of the clavier cheeks.

PEDAL ORGAN TOE-PISTONS

ALL DOUBLE-ACTING

1. Piston coupling First Manual Clavier to Pedal Clavier.
2. Piston coupling First Manual Clavier to Pedal Clavier, in the Octave.
3. Piston coupling Second Manual Clavier to Pedal Clavier.
4. Piston coupling Second Manual Clavier to Pedal Clavier, in the Octave.
5. Piston coupling Third Manual Clavier to Pedal Clavier.
6. Piston coupling Third Manual Clavier to Pedal Clavier, in the Octave.
7. Piston coupling Fourth Manual Clavier to Pedal Clavier.
8. Piston coupling Fourth Manual Clavier to Pedal Clavier, in the Octave.
9. Piston coupling Fifth Manual Clavier to Pedal Clavier.
10. Piston coupling Fifth Manual Clavier to Pedal Clavier, in the Octave.
11. Piston coupling Pedal Organ on itself, in the Octave.
12. Piston coupling String Organ to Pedal Clavier.
13. Piston coupling Harmonic Organ to Pedal Clavier.
14. Piston coupling Fanfare Organ to Pedal Clavier.
15. Piston coupling Percussion Organ to Pedal Clavier.
16. Piston opening and closing all Swell-Boxes.

Other Toe-Pistons may be added for any special purposes deemed desirable by the Organ Architect or Organist in charge.

NOTES ON THE FIRST SPECIFICATION

PEDAL ORGAN—A few remarks are desirable on this all-important Division of the Organ. The absolute necessity, in an artistically appointed instrument, of having, at least, a considerable portion of its Pedal Organ stop-apportionment rendered tonally flexible and expressive, was, as we have already said, first advocated, on logical and artistic grounds, many years ago, by us; and is only now becoming recognized as essential in a properly appointed Concert-room Organ.

It will be observed that out of the forty-one stops, as listed, twenty are rendered flexible and expressive by being inclosed in a Swell-Chamber, and placed under the control of a special Expression Lever. In this Subdivision are located all the higher-pitched single and compound harmonic-corroborating stops, so as to greatly increase their powers in compound-tone production, in combination with the uninclosed stops; as can readily be realized on studying the stop-apportionments of the unexpressive and expressive Subdivisions. The stops which are of a solo character and the contrasting lingual stops are also inclosed, for obvious reasons. The composition of the GRAND CORNET, VII. RANKS, is to be the same as that given in the List, under Pure Organ-Tone; and its pipes are to be of larger scales and of fuller voices than are desirable in the Grand Organ. The compound harmonic-corroborating and tone-clearing stop which we have good reason to include in the stop-apportionment of the unexpressive Subdivision is the almost unknown COMPENSATING MIXTURE,

VI. RANKS.[14] The chief peculiarity of this stop is that all its ranks vary in their compass: all commencing on CCC of the Pedal Organ clavier, but only one extending throughout its compass. Its office is to impart richness, distinctness, and clearness of sound to the necessarily dull and somewhat confused tones of the heavy basses of the grave Pedal stops, without unduly overloading the higher notes of the clavier compass. How this desirable result is secured will be understood from the following:—

PEDAL ORGAN COMPENSATING MIXTURE

CCC to G . . .	SUPER-OCTAVE, 4 FT. . . .	32 Notes.
CCC to D	TIERCE, 3⅕ FT.	27 "
CCC to BB . .	OCTAVE QUINT, 2⅔ FT. . .	24 "
CCC to GG . .	TWENTY-SECOND, 2 FT. . .	20 "
CCC to EE . .	TWENTY-SIXTH, 1⅓ FT. . .	17 "
CCC to CC . .	TWENTY-NINTH, 1 FT. . .	13 "

All the ranks of the stop are formed of pipes of the DIAPASON class; and the scales of the ranks are to be relatively smaller as they rise in pitch; and their scale ratio to be such as to place the half diameter on the thirteenth pipe. In addition to this quick reduction in scale, it is essential to the true tonal office of the stop that the voice of each rank be gradually reduced in strength as it ascends the scale, so as to render the cessation of its voice almost imperceptible to the ear. The effect of a properly regulated stop of this class on a heavy groaning Pedal bass is as remarkable as it is beneficial.

It is hardly possible to give definite instructions regarding the necessary or desirable wind-pressures for the Pedal Organ labial and lingual stops, simply from the fact that the positions they may occupy in a large and necessarily crowded instrument go far to dictate them. It is in all cases very undesirable to resort to inordinate pressures, such as are approved of to-day by the lovers of musical noise. This vitiated taste will largely disappear in the organ-building and playing worlds with the introduction of a more artistic and refined school of organ tonal appointment. The time will come when an organ will not be considered a great work in proportion to "the great noise it can kick up"; and when uncontrollable, roaring TUBAS will no longer be tolerated by educated ears. Under normal conditions, we are of opinion that for the labial stops a pressure of six inches should not be exceeded; and for the exposed lingual stops ten inches, and the inclosed lingual stops fifteen inches should be the limits. All the stops of the Subdivisions are to be of 44 pipes with the exception of the CONTRA-VIOLONE, CONTRA-DULCIANA, and GROSSQUINTENBASS, which are to have 61 pipes.

GRAND ORGAN—This Organ is the only manual Division in which any unexpressive voices obtain. It is subdivided into two contrasting stop-apportionments; one of which is flexible and expressive, for the definite purpose of

[14] For particulars respecting the origin of the stop as developed by us, and introduced in a satisfactory form in two important (and the only two) organs in this country, the reader is referred to "The Organ of the Twentieth Century," pp. 72-74.

multiplying the tonal resources of the Division in a scientific and artistic direction; and so enabling the experienced organist to readily produce combinations of tone of almost inexhaustible variety; utterly impossible on any Great Organ alone, hitherto constructed and arranged on the old-fashioned and inflexible and unexpressive methods of tonal appointment. It only requires the musician organist to consider what it would be possible to do with the Subdivisions, as schemed, to realize what a wide field of new musical effects and *nuances*, invested with expression, this single Grand Organ opens up to him. It was after playing the organ in which our System was first instituted that induced the late Dr. Daniel J. Wood, organist of Exeter Cathedral, to write these words: "*It opened to my imagination quite a vista of new and previously impossible effects in organ playing.*" It is, however, proper to state that the Great Organ, to which he alluded, had three independent Subdivisions—one unexpressive and two expressive inclosed in separate Swell-boxes—multiplying the powers of expressive tonal combination enormously. To obtain such compound and complex tonal effects in the instrument set forth in the Specification, it would only be necessary to couple to the Grand Organ any Division or Subdivision belonging to the other claviers, or any Ancillary Organ: when the organist would have at his command, one all-important unexpressive or stationary series of stops; and, in combination, two or more independent, flexible, and expressive series, of any tonalities he might desire, without having to remove his fingers from the first clavier. Just think of it ye musician organists.

The Grand Organ stands in a similar position to the Pedal Organ in so much that it forms, in association, the foundation of the entire tonal structure of the instrument, as has already been stated. The stops of the First Subdivision, which are foundational in their tones, are advisedly exposed; so that, under no circumstances, can such tones be changed or lose their essential character, whatever the others associated with them may be. In this Subdivision are apportioned the labial stops which yield Pure Organ-tones; such tones as belong exclusively to pipes of the DIAPASON class, and which are impossible of production by any instrument known in the grand orchestra. Added to the stops of Pure Organ-tone are five stops of valuable mixing qualities, calculated to enrich the combinations of the other voices. Lingual stops have been omitted here, in accordance with the principle we advocate; namely, that no lingual stop should be inserted in an unexpressive and inflexible manual Division or Subdivision of an organ. This important principle, which every organist endowed with musical sense and taste must approve, is seriously ignored in organ tonal appointment at the present time. A special feature in this First Subdivision is the introduction of the DOLCIANO PROFUNDO, 32 FT., of full compass, derived from the CONTRA-DULCIANA of the Pedal Organ. It is common, in the present miserable school of organ tonal appointment, to bolster up an insufficient Pedal Organ by a wholesale borrowing from manual stops: but, except in special cases, and when an adequate Pedal has been provided, such borrowing is to be condemned. On the other hand, the addition to a manual

Division of a large Pedal stop, which could not otherwise be conveniently or possibly commanded by a manual clavier, has, as in the present case, a good deal to recommend it both on the score of simplicity of construction and the matter of expense, to say nothing of the great space that would be required for its accommodation. If properly scaled and voiced and copiously supplied with wind no higher pressure than five inches need be used in this Subdivision. The three metal unison DIAPASONS should be voiced on a copious wind not exceeding 3¾ inches.

The stop-apportionment of the Second Subdivision, rendered tonally flexible and expressive by inclosure in Swell-box No. 1, is, in accordance with a basic principle of our System, in strict contrast to that of the First Subdivision. This will be clearly realized on comparing the relative apportionments. Although the Second Subdivision is practically complete in itself, it is a necessary portion of the Grand Organ appointment. Both in its double and unison labial voices, and in its octave and other harmonic-corroborating stops, it forms an essential adjunct to the chief foundation work of the Division; providing invaluable means for artistic and effective registration. In this Subdivision are disposed all the lingual stops of the Grand Organ, in which they are given, through the agency of the Swell-box, the absolutely necessary powers of tonal flexibility and expression; to enable the musician organist to employ their powerful voices in any strength and in any possible manner he may desire. It is needless to say what this power of control means to the artist in the rendition of refined music. The power to adjust or graduate the tones of the harmonic-corroborating stops, and especially of both the GRAND CORNET and FULL MIXTURE, cannot well be overvalued; for it increases their utility in compound tone-production to an almost limitless extent. The GRAND CORNET is to be formed of small scaled DIAPASON pipes, the seven ranks being as given in the List of Stops suitable for the Concert-room Organ. The FULL MIXTURE, VI. RANKS, is to be composed as follows:—

CC to B . .	15 —	19 —	22 —	24 —	26 —	29.
c^1 to b^1. .	8 —	12 —	15 —	17 —	19 —	22.
c^2 to b^2. .	1 —	8 —	12 —	17 —	19 —	22.
c^3 to c^4.	DOUBLE —	1 —	8 —	10 —	12 —	15.

As no octave coupling will be required or desirable in the Grand Organ, all stops in both Subdivisions will extend only to the compass of the clavier—61 notes. Higher wind-pressures will be necessary in this inclosed Subdivision, favoring the production of the characteristic and most desirable qualities of tone in all the stops, both labial and lingual. Accordingly, as repose and refinement are essential in such an organ as here schemed, great care is necessary in adopting only such pressures as are certain to favor artistic voicing, and the avoidance of strained speech, which invariably results in that coarseness which characterizes the general tonality of the large majority of modern organs in which inordinate pressures are resorted to to produce musical noise. In a comprehensive organ, as specified, forced or strained voices are unnecessary and to be avoided.

Volume of tone can be secured by artistic voicing on winds of moderate pressures.[15] For the inclosed labial stops a pressure of 6 inches should not be exceeded, while 10 inches may properly be the limit for the lingual stops.

ACCOMPANIMENTAL ORGAN—The name we have given to this Second Division of the Concert-room Organ clearly denotes its position and chief office in the tonal scheme of the entire instrument: and a glance over its general stop-apportionment will show how carefully it has been devised to meet all legitimate demands that can be made on it in accompanimental music, and, in the production of tonal effects, simple and complex, of a singularly refined character, and of any degree of softness that may be desirable; and this, without the necessity of any resort to methods of tonal annihilation so commonly required in the crudely appointed organs usually constructed to-day.

In strict accordance with our System of compound tonal flexibility and expression, this Organ is formed of two Subdivisions, contrasting in stop-apportionments, and inclosed in separate Swell-boxes—Nos. 2 and 3—in this manner greatly increasing their separate contrasting and combined musical resources. While each Subdivision is practically complete, and can be used separately; in combination they afford the organist entirely new and fascinating means for the production of refined effects and subtle *nuances*, impossible on any manual Division differently constituted. The coupling of the Ancillary Aërial Organ to this Division will greatly increase its tonal resources; placing at the command of the performer three independent and expressive stop-apportionments, on the single Second Clavier. On this subject we have already commented.

It will be observed, on examining the stop-apportionment of the First Subdivision, that the special voices provided are of refined and sympathetic unimitative Flute-tones; which, associated with the other voices of valuable mixing and coloring qualities, impart a distinct individuality and tonal completeness to the Subdivision. These voices contrast effectively with the special voices of the Second Subdivision, which are of delicate String and Free Organ-tones: the latter being furnished by the nine ranks of DULCIANA pipes:—five of which form the beautiful DULCIANA CORNET, thus:—

CC to BB	19 ——	22 ——	24 ——	26 ——	29.
C to B	12 ——	15 ——	17 ——	19 ——	22.
c^1 to b^1	8 ——	12 ——	17 ——	19 ——	22.
c^2 to c^4	1 ——	8 ——	10 ——	12 ——	15.

The composition of the DOLCE CORNET, VII. RANKS, which is inserted in the First Subdivision, is given, under Free Organ-tone, in the List of stops. It should be formed of small-scaled pipes of the inverted conical form, similar to those of the DOLCAN. Its tone should contrast with that of the DULCIANA family. We specially direct attention to the compound harmonic-corroborating

15 The finest stops of the DIAPASON class made during the past seventy years speak on wind of about 3½ inches; and the finest VOX HUMANA we have ever heard was voiced on wind of only 2⅜ inches.

stops for two good reasons. First, because we know from experience how greatly the utility and artistic value and beauty of an organ depend on the proper treatment of such stops: and, secondly, because of their neglect both in number and scientific formation in the hurried trade organ-building at the present time.

Low wind-pressures are desirable for this Accompanimental Organ, for anything in the nature of forced speech should be avoided. For the labial stops winds of from $2\frac{1}{2}$ to $3\frac{1}{4}$ inches should be employed, and for the four refined lingual stops, wind not exceeding five inches should be employed.

WOOD-WIND ORGAN—In this important Division of the true Concert-room Organ the orchestral character and the strictly imitative voices of the instrument commence; still further developing, and demonstrating the importance of, our principles of divisional and subdivisional tonal contrast, flexibility, and compound expression. An examination of the stop-apportionment of this third Organ will show the appropriateness of the name given to it, for in its Subdivisions will be found the organ representatives of the wood Flutes and the single- and double-reed instruments of the grand orchestra, and their organ extensions and derivatives. All of which are of the greatest importance on account of the variety, beauty, and rare coloring qualities of their voices; which gain tenfold by the powers of flexibility and expression given them. Although the Subdivisions differ widely in their respective tonalities, contrasting in a marked degree with each other and all the other Divisions and Subdivisions of the instrument, they are tonally complete and practically independent; and from this fact derive much of their value in the general scheme of the complete organ.

In both Subdivisions care has been taken to provide adequate means for the production of effective compound tones, through artistic registration and the use of single and compound harmonic-corroborating stops. In the First Subdivision, in addition to the quint and octave stops, is a Spitzflöte Cornet, V. ranks; to be formed of small-scaled pipes, of properly graduated tones. As an adequate amount of octave tone is provided by three effective stops, the Cornet may properly be formed of the following ranks:—

Terz $3\frac{1}{5}'$ – Twelfth $2\frac{2}{3}'$ – Fifteenth $2'$ – Nineteenth $1\frac{1}{3}'$ – Twenty-second $1'$.

In the Second Subdivision a compound harmonic-corroborating stop is introduced in the form of a Dolce Cornet, IV. ranks; to be voiced so as to blend perfectly with the voices of all the associated stops. Its coloring powers are of extreme value in a Subdivision which comprises no fewer than twelve lingual stops, representing and extending the voices of the reed instruments of the orchestra. The Cornet to be formed of the following ranks of small-scaled pipes, yielding Free Organ-tone stronger than that of the usual Dulciana:—

Terz $3\frac{1}{5}'$ – Twelfth $2\frac{2}{3}'$ – Septième $2\frac{2}{7}'$ – Fifteenth $2'$.

In this Subdivision, so singularly rich in stops yielding Orchestral Reed-tone, the importance and tonal value of the four stops yielding unimitative Flute Organ-tone must be recognized. They combine, if properly voiced, perfectly with the stops of the Fagotto and Clarinetto families, imparting to their voices fullness and richness, characteristic of the orchestral instruments they represent. The Vox Humana gains much when associated with a softly-toned unison Flute.

Extreme wind-pressures must be avoided in both Subdivisions, for extreme refinement of tone is essential. Unless some very peculiar conditions obtain, no higher pressure for the labial work of the First Subdivision need be used than 3½ inches. For the Saxophones, 6 inches will be ample, especially if they are free-reed stops. For the five labial stops of the Second Subdivision the pressure of 3½ inches will be suitable if they are properly voiced; for anything approaching a coarse and unduly assertive tone would greatly limit their value in combination. For the lingual stops, pressures, wisely selected for their desirable voices, should not exceed 8 inches. The positions the Swell-boxes of the Wood-Wind Organ may occupy, and the character of their construction, must be reckoned as factors in the determination of wind-pressures.

BRASS-WIND ORGAN—Widely different, in its tonal appointment and stop-apportionments, from the preceding, is the Brass-Wind Organ: the name of which clearly indicates its position and office in the scheme of the true Concert-room Organ. Fortunately the great wealth of lingual stops yielding tones more or less closely imitating those of the brass-wind instruments of the orchestra and band, enable the organ designer to form such a specially appointed Division as that now under consideration; giving it an importance and position only secondary to that of the fundamental Grand Organ, while it exceeds it in volume and power of tone.

Like the other manual Organs already commented on, it is appointed in strict accordance with our principles of divisional and subdivisional tonal contrast, and given powers of compound flexibility and expression, increasing the effective tonal value of every stop tenfold; and establishing consistency throughout the scheme of the instrument. This control of the voices of such commanding stops as the Trombas, Trombones, and Trumpets, is essential if artistic music is to be played on the instrument. It may, however, not commend itself to the large majority of organists who seem to think that the production of noise is the path to fame.

The purpose of the labial and lingual stop-apportionments of the two Subdivisions, inclosed in separate Swell-boxes, must be so evident to every one at all conversant with tonal matters and their artistic treatment, that special comment is here unnecessary. But allusion may properly be made to the auxiliary Contra-Trombone, 32 ft., from the Pedal Organ—an addition never before suggested by any organ designer to be commanded by a manual clavier: but which would impart a wonderful dignity and impressiveness to this Brass-

Wind Organ. A further and very important addition is provided, which will be commented on later.

The wind-pressures required for the production of the desirable voices of the labial and lingual stops will, necessarily, vary greatly. For the former no pressure exceeding 5 inches should be employed; while for the lingual stops of double and unison pitch 15 inches may be used; and for the octave and mutation stops pressures of from 7 to 10 inches will be sufficient. The GRAND CORNET, V. RANKS, is to be formed of small-scaled DIAPASON pipes of the following pitches:—

SEPTIÈME $4\frac{4}{7}'$ – OCTAVE 4′ – TERZ $3\frac{1}{5}'$ – TWELFTH $2\frac{1}{3}'$ – FIFTEENTH 2′.

Each rank, as it rises in pitch, to be voiced slightly softer in tone; and each rank is to be regulated softer as it ascends the scale. This general regulation is in accordance with the natural laws of compound musical sounds, and should be observed in the tonal regulation of every compound harmonic-corroborating stop.

SOLO ORGAN—This is the only manual stationary Division that does not call for subdivision; although, on the other hand, it demands the most effective powers of expression that can be imparted to it. A solo without expression is a musical anomaly; and, accordingly, a solo stop in an organ, devoid of expressive powers, is in the same category. Yet how often in modern organ-designing is this obvious fact ignored. The teachings of the human voice in song, and of the orchestra under the baton of a master, seem to be forgotten, if they were ever learnt.

A glance at the Specification of this important Organ will show the aim and scope of its stop-apportionment. Of its sixteen stops, nine are designated Orchestral, clearly indicating that they are intended for solo passages and special effects, not readily produced on the stop-apportionments of the other four manual Organs: and also that it is intended that they shall be, as closely as possible, tonal imitations of the orchestral instruments they represent. It is in this Division that the artist pipe-maker and voicer can show their knowledge and skill.

Although it is generally acknowledged that a fifth clavier is undesirable, owing to its unavoidable distance from the performer, it must be admitted that it is necessary in a fully appointed Concert-room Organ; not only as commanding, as in the present scheme, a special and very valuable Solo stop-apportionment, but, what is of equal importance, as providing the means for the convenient command of any Ancillary Organ temporarily coupled to it; leaving the other four claviers undisturbed.

For further particulars regarding this Organ, the reader is referred to what is said on the subject in the general remarks preceding the Specification.

ANCILLARY ORGANS—As the subject of these Organs has been treated at some length in the general remarks immediately preceding the Specification now under consideration; it is only necessary to allude here to the stop-apportionments of the Ancillaries as set forth in the Specification. The formation and introduction of Ancillary Organs have been urged by us on both artistic and practical grounds; but up to the present time they have received scant attention from organ-builders and organists. Their inclusion, to some extent, is imperative in every properly appointed Concert-room Organ. They have not hitherto formally appeared in the quasi-church, bastard instruments designed for the concert-room; but certain apologies have made their appearance in organs of recent construction, which seem to indicate an awakening to the importance and practical value of true Ancillary Organs. The necessary limitation of the number of claviers renders their introduction in the Concert-room Organ of the future imperative. The Principles of construction, appointment, and control of Ancillary Organs, have been given, at length, in our general remarks.

STRING ORGAN—In the general remarks preceding the Specification are treated with sufficient fullness all matters regarding the position of the Ancillary String Organ in the tonal structure of the Concert-room instrument, its value as a distinct tonal Division, and its relation to the stationary Organs directly commanded by the several claviers; accordingly, it is only necessary here to comment on the stop-apportionment of the Ancillary as set forth in the Specification.

Probably the first thing that will strike the critical reader, conversant with ordinary organ designing and haphazard methods of stop-apportionment, is the comprehensiveness of the String-toned forces in this Ancillary. It will be observed that of the twenty-eight stops only three are not of String-tone, and that these belong to the Flute-tone family. These are introduced for the purpose of imparting fullness and roundness to such combination String-tones as may benefit by their addition. To the two String-toned stops of 16 and 10⅔ feet are added fifteen of 8 feet and also eight harmonic-corroborating stops comprising thirteen ranks of pipes. This complete appointment would furnish a satisfactory representative of the string forces of the orchestra; and also, in varied combinations, all desirable effects commonly produced by the string instruments played by the bow. Much of the true value of this remarkable Ancillary would, naturally, depend on the skilful voicing, on suitable wind-pressures, of all the imitative stops, and also on the refinement and scientific regulation of all the harmonic-corroborating voices. Everything approaching a screaming intonation must be eliminated; and the full and impressive tones, which have characterized the imitative String-toned stops of the best English voicers, must be followed: The soft-toned VIOL CORNET, V. RANKS, and VIOL SESQUIALTERA, II. RANKS, are to be formed of through ranks, of the pitches given in the List of Stops. It is imperative that scientific graduation of tone be observed in the regulation of these delicate stops. Different pressures of wind will be required, but that of 4½ inches must not be exceeded. Very special attention must be given to the formation of the Swell-box of this Ancillary.

AËRIAL ORGAN—While considering the tonal appointment of this refined Ancillary, the interested reader should refer to what is said regarding it in the general remarks preceding the Specification. It is sufficient to say here that a tonal Division of the character here set forth has never appeared, or been even approached, in the scheme of any Concert-room Organ hitherto constructed. We have, in our general remarks, alluded to the term Aërial Organ; and to the fact that the Division is not to be confounded with what has hitherto been called the Echo Organ. The only tonal Division, which in any way approaches this in character, is that of nine stops, voiced on wind of 1½ inches, constructed by Edmund Schulze prior to the year 1889, inserted in the Organ of the Parish Church of Leeds, England.

It will be observed the stop-apportionment makes this Ancillary practically complete and independent; a condition obviously desirable in a Division of so delicate a tonality. But this condition does not limit its usefulness; for it would be a valuable addition to the Accompanimental, Wood-Wind, and Solo Organs. With the String Ancillary, it could be made to produce compound tones never heard on the organ of to-day. The only labial stop which calls for special notice is the HARMONIA ÆTHERIA, VI. RANKS, which should be formed of VOX ANGELICA pipes, in the following composition:—

CC to F♯	.	15 —	17 —	19 —	22 —	26 —	29.
G to f♯	.	12 —	15 —	17 —	19 —	22 —	26.
g^1 to f♯	.	8 —	12 —	15 —	17 —	19 —	22.
g^2 to c^4	.	1 —	8 —	12 —	15 —	17 —	19.

A few words may be said respecting the three lingual stops—VOX HUMANA, DULCIAN, and SCIALUMO—all of which must be of the softest tones producible by reeds voiced on wind of a pressure not exceeding 2½ inches. Refinement and smoothness of voice are essential. Regarding the VOX HUMANA it is only necessary to say that its resonators are to be cylindrical, covered, slotted, and regulated by a slide. The DULCIAN is a stop of small scale, the resonators of which are smaller in scale than those of the FAGOTTO, and shaded; and the SCIALUMO is a very small-scaled stop of the CLARINET family, capped, and slotted, producing an extremely soft and smooth tone, partaking of the chalumeau of the orchestral Clarinet.

HARMONIC ORGAN—The reader who has confined his attention so far to this specification should, before proceeding further, turn to the general remarks of an introductory nature, and carefully read what is there said on the subject of the Ancillary Harmonic Organ; for it is essential to a just conception of its importance that a full knowledge of its nature and office in the tonal economy of the true Concert-room Organ should be thoroughly realized. Unlike the other Ancillaries that are specified, which in their stop-apportionments are practically independent; and, accordingly, can be played alone; this Harmonic Ancillary is essentially an adjunct, not complete in itself, and not to be played alone. Herein, however, lies its great importance and value. As an addition to any other Division or Subdivision of the instrument, it immensely increases its powers in the colorations of compound tones which are dependent on the introduction of varied harmonic over-tones.

To meet all possible requirements in combination with the Divisions or Subdivisions, this Ancillary is formed in two groups of harmonic-corroborating stops of different scales and widely different strengths of voice; distinguished by the terms Forte and Piano. The former is composed of one wood stop of compound voice; six single-rank harmonic-corroborating stops, of medium scales, yielding Pure Organ-tone, voiced on wind of 3¼ inches; and one MIXTURE, IV. RANKS of small-scaled pipes of similar tone, composed as follows:—

CC to B♭	19 —— 22 —— 26 —— 29.
B to f	12 —— 15 —— 19 —— 22.
f♯^{2} to b^2	8 —— 12 —— 15 —— 19.
c^3 to c^4	1 —— 8 —— 12 —— 15.

The Piano Subdivision comprises ten DOLCE stops: one of which is of unison pitch, eight single-rank harmonic-corroborating stops, and one four-rank compound stop, termed ACUTA on account of its high pitch. It is composed thus:—

CC to E	26 —— 29 —— 33 —— 36.
F to e^1	19 —— 22 —— 26 —— 29.
f^1 to e^2	15 —— 19 —— 22 —— 26.
f^2 to b^2	12 —— 15 —— 19 —— 22.
c^3 to c^4	8 —— 12 —— 15 —— 19.

This compound stop must be very carefully voiced and evenly regulated, reducing in strength of tone as it ascends the scale.

FANFARE ORGAN—As all matters relating to the origin and purpose of this powerfully toned Ancillary have been gone into in the general remarks preceding the Specification, it is unnecessary to go over similar ground here. This Organ comprises ten stops, two of which are labial—the STENTORPHONE, 8 FT., formed of pipes of large scale and very thick metal, voiced on wind of 8 inches, yielding the most powerful Flute-tone possible; and the STENTOR CORNET, IV. RANKS, of large scaled pipes, and full intonation. The ranks to be unbroken and of the following pitches:—

OCTAVE, 4′ – TIERCE, 3⅕′ – TWELFTH, 2⅔′ – FIFTEENTH, 2′.

These labial stops would impart great body, firmness, and harmonic richness to the tones of the lingual stops. The HARMONIC TRUMPETS to be voiced on 15 inch, and the TUBAS to be voiced on 20 inch wind. A very powerful tone can safely be given to the latter stops as their voices are under control.

PERCUSSION ORGAN—As a full dissertation on all important matters connected with this Ancillary is given in the general remarks, it is quite unnecessary to say further on the subject here, beyond reminding the reader that it is a purely mechanical tonal adjunct, not strictly belonging to the constitution of the organ proper.

It is unnecessary to make any special remarks on the numerous mechanical appliances provided in the Specification to enable the organist to have complete and easy command of the vast tonal forces of the Organ. All the appliances are clearly detailed and classified according to their nature and office, so as to prevent any confusion in the mind of the reader. We may, accordingly, pass on to the consideration of schemes of lesser size.

The Second Specification is cast in a smaller mold than that just descanted on, but embraces all the principles involved in its tonal structure and special stop-apportionments. While the First Specification sets forth the full development of our System in a Concert-room Organ of the first magnitude, it is obviously too extensive in its general appointment to be adopted, except, perhaps, on some extraordinary occasion. The Second Specification, somewhat more moderate in size, is still for an instrument of noble proportions and of the front rank. It, however, points the way to further reductions, tonal and mechanical.

—SECOND SPECIFICATION—

GRAND CONCERT-ROOM ORGAN

AUDSLEY SYSTEM—COMPOUND EXPRESSION
FIVE MANUAL CLAVIERS

PEDAL ORGAN

Compass CCC to G—32 Notes

—PEDAL CLAVIER—

UNEXPRESSIVE SUBDIVISION

1. Vox Gravissima (Resultant) . . . 64 Feet
2. Double Principal . W. 32 "
3. Contra-Violone (44 pipes) . . M. 32 "
4. Contra-Dulciana (61 pipes) . . M. 32 "
5. Major Principal . W. 16 "
6. Minor Principal . M. 16 "
7. Violonbass (From 3) M. 16 "
8. Dulciana (From 4) M. 16 Feet
9. Bass Flute . . . W. 8 "
10. Octave . . . . M. 8 "
11. Compensating Mixture . M. IV. Ranks
12. Contra-Trombone (44 pipes) . . M. 32 Feet
13. Trombone (From 12) M. 16 "
14. Tromba . . . M. 8 "

EXPRESSIVE SUBDIVISION

Inclosed in Swell-Chamber

15. Untersatz . . . W. 32 Feet
16. Grand Principal . M. 16 "
17. Quintaten . . . W. 16 "
18. Contrabasso . . W. 16 "
19. Lieblichgedeckt . W. 16 "
20. Quintenbass . . W. 10⅔ "
21. Violoncello . . M. 8 "
22. Grand Octave . M. 8 "
23. Grossflöte . . . W. 8 "
24. Grand Cornet M. VII. Ranks
25. Fagottone (44 pipes) M. 32 Feet
26. Contrafagotto (From 25) . . M. 16 "
27. Contra-Clarinetto M. 16 "
28. Bombarde . . . M. 16 "
29. Euphonium . . . M. 16 "
30. Tuba Sonora . . M. 8 "

GRAND ORGAN

Compass CC to c^4—61 Notes

—FIRST CLAVIER—

UNEXPRESSIVE SUBDIVISION

31. Double Diapason Major . . . M. 16 Feet
32. Contra-Gamba . M. 16 "
33. Double Dulciana. M. 16 "
34. Grand Quint . . M. 10⅔ "
35. Major Diapason . M. 8 "
36. Minor Diapason . M. 8 Feet
37. Diapason . . . M. 8 "
38. Doppelflöte . . W. 8 "
39. Octave Major . M. 4 "
40. Cornet . . . M. V. Ranks

AUXILIARY STOP

41. Dolciana Profundo. . M. 32 ft. 61 Notes—From Pedal Organ, No. 4.

EXPRESSIVE SUBDIVISION

Inclosed in Swell-Box No. 1

42. Starkgedeckt . . W. 16 Feet
43. Horn Diapason . M. 8 "
44. Grand Viol . . M. 8 "
45. Diapason . . . W. 8 "
46. Clarabella . . W. 8 "
47. Tibia Plena . . W. 8 "
48. Quint . . . . M. 5⅓ "
49. Octave Minor . M. 4 "
50. Harmonic Flute . M. 4 "
51. Tierce . . . . M. 3⅕ Ft.
52. Twelfth . . . M. 2⅔ "
53. Super-Octave . . M. 2 "
54. Grand Cornet M. VII. Ranks
55. Double Trumpet . M. 16 Feet
56. Trumpet (Harmonic) M. 8 "
57. Tromba . . . M. 8 "
58. Tromba Quint . M. 5⅓ "
59. Clarion (Harmonic) M. 4 "

ACCOMPANIMENTAL ORGAN

Compass CC to c^4—61 Notes

—SECOND CLAVIER—

FIRST EXPRESSIVE SUBDIVISION

Inclosed in Swell-Box No. 2

60. Lieblichgedeckt . W. 16 Feet
61. English Diapason. M. 8 "
62. Gemshorn . . . M. 8 "
63. Salicional . . . M. 8 "
64. Flauto Amabile . W. 8 "
65. Dolce . . . . M. 8 "
66. Voix Angélique . M. 8 "
67. Voix Éolienne (Sharp) . . . M. 8 "
68. Viole Sourdine . M. 8 Feet
69. Dolce Quint . . M. 5⅓ "
70. Salicet . . . . M. 4 "
71. Flauto Amoroso . M. 4 "
72. Dolce Sesquialtera M. V. Ranks
73. Flautino . . . M. 2 Feet
74. Oboe d'Amore. . M. 8 "

I. Tremolant

SECOND EXPRESSIVE SUBDIVISION

Inclosed in Swell-Box No. 3

75. Gelindgedeckt . .	W.	16 Feet
76. Dulciana . . .	M.	8 "
77. Lieblichgedeckt .	W.	8 "
78. Viola d'Amore .	M.	8 "
79. Viola d'Amore (Sharp) . . .	M.	8 "
80. Lieblichflöte . .	M.	4 "
81. Dulciana Octave .	M.	4 "
82. Dulciana Twelfth	M.	$2\frac{2}{3}$ Ft.
83. Dulciana Cornet .	M.	V. Ranks
84. Dulciana Fifteenth	M.	2 Feet
85. Clarinetto . .	M.	8 "
86. Cor Anglais . .	M.	8 "
87. Musette . . .	M.	4 "
II. Tremolant		

WOOD-WIND ORGAN

Compass CC to c^4—61 Notes

—THIRD CLAVIER—

FIRST EXPRESSIVE SUBDIVISION

Inclosed in Swell-Box No. 2

88. Bourdon Echo .	W.	16 Feet
89. Orchestral Flute	W.	8 "
90. Tibia Clausa . .	W.	8 "
91. Quintaten . . .	M.	8 "
92. Melodia . . .	W.	8 "
93. Suave Flute . .	W.	8 "
94. Rohrflöte . . .	M.	8 "
95. Rohrquinte . .	M.	$5\frac{1}{3}$ Ft.
96. Orchestral Flute	W.	4 "
97. Harmonic Flute .	M.	4 "
98. Dolce Tierce . .	M.	$3\frac{1}{5}$ "
99. Spitzflöte Cornet .	M.	V. Ranks
100. Orchestral Piccolo .	M.	2 Feet
III. Tremolant		

SECOND EXPRESSIVE SUBDIVISION

Inclosed in Swell-Box No. 3

101. Echo Diapason .	M.	8 Feet
102. Harmonica . .	W.	8 "
103. Flauto Dolcissimo	W.	8 "
104. Fernflöte . . .	M.	4 "
105. Flageoletta . .	M.	2 "
106. Contrafagotto .	M.	16 "
107. Contra-Clarinetto	M.	16 "
108. Orchestral Clarinetto .	M.	8 "
109. Orchestral Oboe	M.	8 Feet
110. Orchestral Fagotto . .	M.	8 "
111. Vox Humana .	M.	8 "
112. Clarinetto Quinta	M.	$5\frac{1}{3}$ "
113. Oboe Ottava .	M.	4 "
IV. Tremolant		

BRASS-WIND ORGAN

Compass CC to c⁴—61 Notes

—FOURTH CLAVIER—

FIRST EXPRESSIVE SUBDIVISION

Inclosed in Swell-Box No. 4

114. GROSSGEDECKT . . W. 16 Feet
115. HORN DIAPASON . M. 8 "
116. GEIGENPRINCIPAL . M. 8 "
117. DOPPELROHRGEDECKT W. 8 "
118. GEMSHORN . . . M. 8 "
119. OCTAVE MAJOR . M. 4 "
120. GRAND CORNET M. V. Ranks
121. CONTRA-TROMBA . M. 16 Feet
122. TROMBA REAL . M. 8 "
123. TRUMPET, HARMONIC M. 8 "
124. TROMBA QUINT . M. 5⅓ "
125. TROMBA CLARION M. 4 "

SECOND EXPRESSIVE SUBDIVISION

Inclosed in Swell-Box No. 5

126. STENTORPHONE . M. 8 Feet
127. GROSSFLÖTE . . W. 8 "
128. OCTAVE MAJOR . M. 4 "
129. TRIPLETTE M. 3⅕—2⅔—2 "
130. BOMBARDON . . M. 16 "
131. CONTRA-TROMBONE M. 16 "
132. TROMBONE . . M. 8 "
133. TROMBONE QUINT M. 5⅓ Ft.
134. TROMBONE OCTAVE M. 4 "
135. ORCHESTRAL HORN M. 8 "
136. ORCHESTRAL TRUMPET . . M. 8 "
137. CLARION, HARMONIC M. 4 "

SOLO ORGAN

Compass CC to c⁴—61 Notes

—FIFTH CLAVIER—

EXPRESSIVE

Inclosed in Swell-Box No. 6

138. STENTORFLÖTE . . W. 8 Feet
139. DOPPELFLÖTE . . W. 8 "
140. ORCHESTRAL VIOLONCELLO . M. 8 "
141. ORCHESTRAL VIOLIN M. 8 "
142. ORCHESTRAL FLUTE W. 8 "
143. ORCHESTRAL FLUTE W. 4 "
144. ORCHESTRAL PICCOLO M. 2 "
145. ORCHESTRAL OBOE M. 8 "
146. ORCHESTRAL CLARINET . M. 8 "
147. ORCHESTRAL HORN M. 8 Feet
148. ORCHESTRAL TRUMPET . . M. 8 "
149. VOX HUMANA . M. 8 "
150. TRUMPET ROYAL . M. 8 "
151. OPHICLEIDE . . M. 8 "
152. TUBA MAGNA . M. 8 "
153. TUBA CLARION . M. 4 "

V. TREMOLANT to Labial Stops

ANCILLARY STRING ORGAN

Compass CC to c^4—61 Notes

EXPRESSIVE

Inclosed in Swell-Box No. 7

154. CONTRABASSO . .	W.	16 Feet
155. VIOLIN DIAPASON .	M.	8 "
156. GRAND VIOL . .	M.	8 "
157. SALICIONAL . .	M.	8 "
158. VIOLONCELLO (Orchestral) .	M.	8 "
159. VIOLONCELLO (Sordo)	M.	8 "
160. VIOLA (Orchestral)	M.	8 "
161. VIOLA SORDO . .	M.	8 "
162. VIOLINO (Orchestral)	M.	8 "
163. VIOLINO SORDO .	M.	8 "
164. VIOLINO VIBRATO	M.	8 Feet
165. VIOLA DA GAMBA	M.	8 "
166. VIOLA DA GAMBA (Sharp) . . .	M.	8 "
167. VIOL QUINT . .	M.	5⅓ "
168. VIOLETTA . . .	M.	4 "
169. VIOL TIERCE (Sordo)	M.	3⅕ "
170. VIOL TWELFTH .	M.	2⅔ "
171. VIOL FIFTEENTH .	M.	2 "
172. VIOL CORNET	M.	V. Ranks
VI. TREMOLANT		

ANCILLARY PERCUSSION ORGAN

EXPRESSIVE

Inclosed in Swell-Box No. 8

173. CARILLON.	Tubular Bells	37 Notes
174. HARP .	Wood Bars	61 "
175. CELESTA .	Steel Bars	61 Notes
176. XYLOPHONE.	Wood Bars	49 "

CLAVIER COUPLERS

PEDAL ORGAN COUPLERS

First Clavier . .	to Pedal Clavier, Unison Coupler.
First Clavier . .	to Pedal Clavier, Octave Coupler.
Second Clavier .	to Pedal Clavier, Unison Coupler.
Third Clavier . .	to Pedal Clavier, Unison Coupler.
Fourth Clavier .	to Pedal Clavier, Unison Coupler.
Fifth Clavier . .	to Pedal Clavier, Unison Coupler.
Pedal Clavier . .	on Itself, Octave Coupler.

FIRST CLAVIER COUPLERS

Second Clavier .	1st Subdivision.	to First Clavier, Unison Coupler.
Second Clavier .	1st Subdivision.	to First Clavier, Octave Coupler.
Second Clavier .	2nd Subdivision.	to First Clavier, Unison Coupler.
Second Clavier .	2nd Subdivision.	to First Clavier, Octave Coupler.
Third Clavier .	1st Subdivision.	to First Clavier, Unison Coupler.
Third Clavier .	1st Subdivision.	to First Clavier, Octave Coupler.

Third Clavier .	2nd Subdivision.	to First Clavier, Unison Coupler.
Third Clavier .	2nd Subdivision.	to First Clavier, Octave Coupler.
Fourth Clavier .	1st Subdivision.	to First Clavier, Unison Coupler.
Fourth Clavier .	2nd Subdivision.	to First Clavier, Unison Coupler.
Fifth Clavier . .	Undivided.	to First Clavier, Unison Coupler.
Fifth Clavier . .	Undivided.	to First Clavier, Octave Coupler.

SECOND CLAVIER COUPLERS

Third Clavier .	1st Subdivision .	to Second Clavier, Unison Coupler.
Third Clavier .	1st Subdivision .	to Second Clavier, Octave Coupler.
Third Clavier .	2nd Subdivision .	to Second Clavier, Unison Coupler.
Third Clavier .	2nd Subdivision .	to Second Clavier, Octave Coupler.
Fourth Clavier .	1st Subdivision .	to Second Clavier, Unison Coupler.
Fourth Clavier .	1st Subdivision .	to Second Clavier, Octave Coupler.
Fourth Clavier .	2nd Subdivision .	to Second Clavier, Unison Coupler.
Fourth Clavier .	2nd Subdivision .	to Second Clavier, Octave Coupler.
Fifth Clavier . .	Undivided .	to Second Clavier, Unison Coupler.

THIRD CLAVIER COUPLERS

Fourth Clavier .	1st Subdivision .	to Third Clavier, Unison Coupler.
Fourth Clavier .	1st Subdivision .	to Third Clavier, Octave Coupler.
Fourth Clavier .	2nd Subdivision .	to Third Clavier, Unison Coupler.
Fourth Clavier .	2nd Subdivision .	to Third Clavier, Octave Coupler.
Fifth Clavier . .	Undivided .	to Third Clavier, Unison Coupler.
Fifth Clavier . .	Undivided .	to Third Clavier, Octave Coupler.

FOURTH CLAVIER COUPLERS

Fifth Clavier .	Undivided .	to Fourth Clavier, Unison Coupler.
Fifth Clavier .	Undivided .	to Fourth Clavier, Octave Coupler.

ANCILLARY COUPLERS

Five Couplers connecting Ancillary String Organ with First, Second, Third, Fourth, and Fifth Manual Claviers.

Five Couplers connecting Ancillary Percussion Organ with First, Second, Third, Fourth, and Fifth Manual Claviers.

EXPRESSION LEVER COUPLERS

Couplers connecting String Organ Swell-action with Expression Levers II., III., IV., V., VI.

Couplers connecting Percussion Organ Swell-action with Expression Levers II., III., IV., V., VI.

EXPRESSION LEVERS

I. Balanced Expression Lever commanding Pedal Organ Swell-action.
II. Balanced Expression Lever commanding action of Swell-Box No. 1.
III. Balanced Expression Lever commanding action of Swell-Box No. 2.
IV. Balanced Expression Lever commanding action of Swell-Box No. 3.
V. Balanced Expression Lever commanding action of Swell-Box No. 4.
VI. Balanced Expression Lever commanding action of Swell-Box No. 5.
VII. Balanced Expression Lever commanding action of Swell-Box No. 6.
A, B, C, D, E, F, G.—Seven double-acting Toe-Pistons, disconnecting and connecting the actions of the Pedal Swell-Chamber, and of Swell-Boxes Nos. 1, 2, 3, 4, 5, 6, with the respective Balanced Expression Levers as tabulated above.

CRESCENDO LEVER

Balanced Crescendo Lever commanding selected groups of Stops in progressive order of tonal power and character. The mechanism of the Lever being so adjusted as to indicate, by well marked changes in resistance to the pressure of the foot, the entry into changes of tonal character and increase of power until the climax is reached. The *decrescendo* follows in the same manner downwards. The Lever is placed on the right of the Expression Levers, and at an angle convenient to the foot of the performer. Where there are so many Expression Levers it is necessary that the position of the Crescendo Lever shall be carefully adjusted, so as to be easily operated.

DIVISIONAL PISTONS

Two Thumb-Pistons—under First Clavier—bringing on and throwing off Expressive Subdivision of Grand Organ.

Two Thumb-Pistons—under Second Clavier—bringing on and throwing off First Expressive Subdivision of Accompanimental Organ.

Two Thumb-Pistons—under Second Clavier—bringing on and throwing off Second Expressive Subdivision of Accompanimental Organ.

Two Thumb-Pistons—under Third Clavier—bringing on and throwing off First Expressive Subdivision of Wood-Wind Organ.

Two Thumb-Pistons—under Third Clavier—bringing on and throwing off Second Expressive Subdivision of Wood-Wind Organ.

Two Thumb-Pistons—under Fourth Clavier—bringing on and throwing off First Expressive Subdivision of Brass-Wind Organ.

Two Thumb-Pistons—under Fourth Clavier—bringing on and throwing off Second Expressive Subdivision of Brass-Wind Organ.

Two Thumb-Pistons—under Fifth Clavier—bringing on and throwing off Solo Organ.

ADJUSTABLE COMBINATION PISTONS

Eight Operating Thumb-Pistons and Release—under First Clavier—commanding Stop-combinations on Grand Organ, Pedal Organ, and Couplers.

Two Double-acting Thumb-Pistons—under First Clavier—bringing on and throwing off Ancillary String and Percussion Organs.

Eight Operating Thumb-Pistons and Release—under Second Clavier—commanding Stop-combinations on Accompanimental Organ, Pedal Organ, and Couplers.

Two Double-acting Thumb-Pistons—under Second Clavier—bringing on and throwing off Ancillary String and Percussion Organs.

Eight Operating Thumb-Pistons and Release—under Third Clavier—commanding Stop-combinations on Wood-Wind Organ, Pedal Organ, and Couplers.

Two Double-acting Thumb-Pistons—under Third Clavier—bringing on and throwing off Ancillary String and Percussion Organs.

Six Operating Thumb-Pistons and Release—under Fourth Clavier—commanding Stop-combinations on Brass-Wind Organ, Pedal Organ, and Couplers.

Two Double-acting Thumb-Pistons—under Fourth Clavier—bringing on and throwing off Ancillary String and Percussion Organs.

Six Operating Thumb-Pistons and Release—under Fifth Clavier—commanding Stop combinations on Solo Organ and Pedal Organ.

Two Double-acting Thumb-Pistons—under Fifth Clavier—bringing on and throwing off Ancillary String and Percussion Organs.

TREMOLANTS

The Six Tremolants are to be directly commanded by the general Draw-Stop System, by rocking-tablets, pendant touches, or by whatever style of Draw-Stop appliances may be generally adopted for the command of Stops and Couplers, and are to be immediately associated with them. In addition, the Tremolants belonging to the Subdivisions of the stationary Organs are to be commanded also by Thumb-Pistons located under the respective Manual Claviers. If preferred, the pistons can be placed in the clavier cheeks.

PEDAL ORGAN TOE-PISTONS

ALL DOUBLE-ACTING

1. Piston coupling First Manual Clavier to Pedal Clavier.
2. Piston coupling First Manual Clavier to Pedal Clavier, in the Octave.
3. Piston coupling Second Manual Clavier to Pedal Clavier.
4. Piston coupling Third Manual Clavier to Pedal Clavier.
5. Piston coupling Third Manual Clavier to Pedal Clavier, in the Octave.
6. Piston coupling Fourth Manual Clavier to Pedal Clavier.

7. Piston coupling Fourth Manual Clavier to Pedal Clavier, in the Octave.
8. Piston coupling Fifth Manual Clavier to Pedal Clavier.
9. Piston coupling Fifth Manual Clavier to Pedal Clavier, in the Octave.
10. Piston coupling Pedal Organ on itself, in the Octave.
11. Piston coupling String Organ to Pedal Clavier.
12. Piston coupling Percussion Organ to Pedal Clavier.

Other Toe-Pistons may be added for any special purposes deemed desirable by the Organ Architect or Organist in charge. It is undesirable, however, to overcrowd appliances to be operated by the feet.

NOTES ON THE SECOND SPECIFICATION

PEDAL ORGAN—It will be observed that out of the thirty stops, as listed in this Specification, sixteen are rendered flexible in strength of voice and expressive by being inclosed in a Swell-Chamber, and placed under the control of a special Expression Lever. In accordance with the principle of tonal control in our System, in this Subdivision are placed the stops whose voices properly call for powers of expression; and the harmonic-corroborating GRAND CORNET, VII. RANKS, composed as given in the List of Stops under Pure Organ-Tone, which, with different strengths of voice, is invaluable, in compound-tone production in association with the stationary voices of the stops of the Unexpressive Subdivision.

The only stop in the Unexpressive Subdivision, which calls for notice here is the almost unknown but very valuable COMPENSATING MIXTURE. A description of this compound harmonic and clearing stop is given in the Notes on the First Specification, accordingly, it is only necessary to give the composition of the IV. Rank stop here.

PEDAL ORGAN COMPENSATING MIXTURE

CCC to G,	SUPER-OCTAVE, 4 FT.	32 Notes
CCC to C,	TIERCE, 3⅕ FT.	25 "
CCC to GG,	OCTAVE QUINT, 2⅔ FT.	20 "
CCC to DD,	TWENTY-SECOND, 2 FT.	15 "

All the ranks of this stop are formed of pipes of the DIAPASON class; and the scales of the ranks are to be relatively smaller as they rise in pitch; and their scale ratio to be such as to place the half diameter on the thirteenth pipe. It is essential that each rank of this important stop shall markedly decrease in strength of tone as it ascends the scale, as already stated in the Notes on the First Specification. In these Notes will also be found comments on the desirable wind-pressures for the Pedal Organ, which should be referred to. All the stops of the Subdivisions are to be of 44 pipes with the exception of the CONTRA-VIOLONE and CONTRA-DULCIANA, which are to have, respectively, 44 and 61 pipes.

GRAND ORGAN—As in the case of the First Specification, and in accordance with our System, this is the only manual Division in which any inflexible and unexpressive voices obtain. Its subdivision into two tonally contrasting stop-apportionments, one of which is inclosed, and rendered flexible and expressive, for the purpose of multiplying the tonal effects of the entire Division to an almost unlimited extent in a scientific and artistic direction. Further remarks, of interest to the organist, are made in the Notes on the First Specification. These should be referred to and seriously considered by every one interested in the improvement of the organ.

One feature in relation to the tonal resources of the First Subdivision is the addition of the DOLCIANO PROFUNDO, 32 FT., of full compass, derived, complete, from the CONTRA-DULCIANA of the unexpressive Subdivision of the Pedal Organ. This new method of stop derivation effectively solves the problem of adding to a manual Division—preferably the fundamental Grand Organ—an open labial stop of 32 feet. That the increase of dignity and impressiveness thus imparted to the Grand Organ foundation tone is of the greatest value in tone combination no musician will question. Although specially connected with the Unexpressive Subdivision, it can enter into effective combination with the stops of the Expressive Subdivision.

As further remarks on the tonal appointment of the Grand Organ would, necessarily, be duplicating what is said in the Notes appended to the First Specification, the interested reader is referred to them in so far as they apply to this smaller Specification.

ACCOMPANIMENTAL ORGAN—As in the case of the Grand Organ, the Division which, for obvious reasons, we have named Accompanimental Organ is fully commented on in the Notes on the First Specification. Accordingly, it is only necessary here to pass remarks on what is of special interest in this Second Specification. In the general tonal appointment our System is strictly followed; divisional and subdivisional contrast of tone and compound flexibility and expression are provided. The only stop calling for particular description is the compound DOLCE SESQUIALTERA, V. RANKS, formed of DOLCE pipes, slightly larger in scale than that of the standard DULCIANA. The following is its composition; the asterisks showing the sexts in each break:—

CC to F	15 —	19*—	22 —	24*—	26.
F♯ to f¹	12*—	15 —	17*—	22 —	24.
f♯¹ to c³	8 —	12*—	15 —	17*—	22.
c♯³ to c⁴	1 —	5*—	8 —	10*—	12.

The composition of the DULCIANA CORNET, V. RANKS, is given in the Notes on the First Specification, alluding to the Accompanimental Organ. This CORNET, voiced and scientifically regulated according to the method we introduced more than half a century ago, is one of the most valuable and beautiful tone-producing stops in the organ: but is one that will never be favored by the tradesman organ-builder; it demands too much knowledge, skill, and time in its voicing and regulating, to accord with the rapid, anyhow, methods prevalent in many modern schools of organ-building.

The desirable wind-pressure for the Accompanimental Organ is from 2½ to 3¼ inches for the twenty-four labial stops; and for the four refined lingual stops a pressure of 5 inches should not be exceeded.

WOOD-WIND ORGAN—As has been said in the preceding series of Notes, it is in this important Division of the Concert-room Organ that the orchestral character and the strictly imitative voices of the instrument commence, establishing the great importance and artistic value of our System of contrast in stop-apportionment and control.

It will be observed in the Specification under consideration, that the stop-apportionments of the Subdivisions are of such a nature as to render the name given to this orchestral Division of the Organ an expressive and appropriate one. The First Subdivision contains the representatives of the Flutes and the Second Subdivision those of the single and double reed instruments of the orchestra. Notwithstanding the sharp contrast thus instituted, each Subdivision is stop-apportioned to be practically complete and suitable for use independently in different strengths of tone, or, in combination, in either single or compound expression; producing effects of endless variety and beauty. In the First Subdivision are placed all the labial mutation and harmonic-corroborating stops necessary for the entire Division; and can, accordingly, be associated with the stops in the Second Subdivision at the will of the performer. The composition of the SPITZFLÖTE CORNET, V. RANKS, is given in the Notes on the First Specification, and need not be repeated here. For further remarks on the tonal appointment of this important Division of the Concert-room Organ, the interested reader is referred to the comments made on the Wood-Wind Organ in the Notes on the First Specification.

BRASS-WIND ORGAN—The name given to this Division of the true Concert-room Organ is as logical as that given to the immediately preceding Division. It originated from the fact that in it were congregated the representatives of the brass-wind instruments of the orchestra. These are grouped in the Subdivisions to enable the performer to command, at will, their powerful voices, under perfect control and expressively, without the undesirable resort to coupling, and the accompanying interference with the freedom of the other claviers and their special offices in the tonal scheme of the instrument.

In addition to the imitative and other, supporting, lingual stops, a sufficient complement of labial stops is added; suitable for combination with the Brass-toned stops, to the voices of which they impart firmness, increase of richness, and desirable variety. The introduction of the two compound harmonic-corroborating stops will go far in registration to produce tones of complex and beautiful qualities. The composition of the GRAND CORNET, V. RANKS, is given and described in the Note on the Brass-Wind Organ of the First Specification. The desirable wind-pressures for this Organ are also given in the Note.

SOLO ORGAN—To save the interested reader the necessity or trouble of referring directly to what is said respecting this important Division of the Concert-room Organ in the Notes appended to the First Specification, we may here briefly touch on the more important subjects there somewhat fully treated of; but with special reference to the lesser scheme of tonal appointment of the Solo Organ set forth in this Second Specification.

Although this is the only Division directly commanded by a manual clavier that does not call for subdivision, it is the one, above all others, that demands extreme powers of tonal flexibility and expression. As we have said; a solo without expression is a musical anomaly; and stops designed for the production of solo effects and artistic *nuances*, devoid of powers of tonal flexibility and expression, are certainly in the same category. Of the sixteen stops in the Division, nine are strictly imitative in their voices of orchestral instruments essentially of a solo character, although commonly used in combination with other instruments in the orchestra. The convenience and desirability of having these stops available, when required, for solo passages can be readily realized by every organ *virtuoso*. In this Division there is no call for the insertion of combinational or harmonic-corroborating stops: but when any of its stops are desired in combination with those of the other Divisions, resort to the manual Couplers are necessary. The value of this important Organ will depend on the knowledge and skill of the pipe-maker and voicer.

STRING ORGAN—In the general remarks which precede and the Notes which follow the First Specification, everything that is necessary is said regarding this all-important Ancillary Organ, with special allusion to its introduction and office in the tonal structure of the true Concert-room Organ. Accordingly, it is only desirable here to comment on the stop-apportionment of the Ancillary in the Specification now under consideration. It will be seen that it differs in no essentials from the Ancillary String Organ set forth in the First Specification. Indeed, whatever the size of the Concert-room Organ may be, it is imperative that this Division shall be adequately stop-apportioned. Without this provision, in the manner we instituted on its first introduction, an organ designed for the Concert-room will always remain an imperfect and insufficient instrument.

It will be observed that every one of the nineteen stops in this Ancillary is String-toned—either imitative or unimitative—and it is imperative that every one shall be voiced to yield a pure and unstrained tone; absolutely every trace of a screaming intonation must be eliminated. Brilliancy and clearness is secured by the introduction of the three mutation stops and the five-ranked VIOL CORNET. In the formation of the pipes throughout this Ancillary, liberal scales and the ratio 1 : 2.519, halving on the nineteenth pipe, should be used. High class metal must be used for all stops, preferably tin for the orchestral ones. In the voicing, the best English school should be followed.

PERCUSSION ORGAN—As what is said respecting this mechanical Ancillary in the Notes on the First Specification is in every way applicable to the similar Ancillary in the Specification now under consideration, it is unnecessary to repeat the remarks here.

Nor is it necessary to make any comment on the numerous mechanical appliances provided in the Specification to enable the organist to have absolute control and easy command of the tonal forces of the entire instrument: they are all so clearly described and grouped, according to their nature and office, as to prevent any confusion in the mind of the reader.

—THIRD SPECIFICATION—

CONCERT-ROOM ORGAN

AUDSLEY SYSTEM—COMPOUND EXPRESSION
FOUR MANUAL CLAVIERS

PEDAL ORGAN

Compass CCC to G—32 Notes

—PEDAL CLAVIER—

UNEXPRESSIVE SUBDIVISION

1. Double Principal . W. 32 Feet
2. Contra-Dulciana (61 pipes) . . . M. 32 "
3. Major Principal . M. 16 "
4. Dulciana (From 2). M. 16 "
5. Octave . . . . M. 8 Feet
6. Compensating Mixture M. III. Ranks
7. Contra-Trombone. M. 16 Feet
8. Tromba . . . . M. 8 "

EXPRESSIVE SUBDIVISION

Inclosed in Swell-Chamber

9. Grand Principal . M. 16 Feet
10. Bourdon . . . W. 16 "
11. Contrabasso (44 pipes) . . W. 16 "
12. Violoncello (From 11) . . W. 8 "
13. Grossflöte . . . W. 8 "
14. Grand Cornet M. VI. Ranks
15. Bombarde . . . M. 16 Feet
16. Contrafagotto (44 pipes). . . M. 16 "
17. Fagotto (From 16) M. 8 "
18. Tuba Sonora . . M. 8 "

GRAND ORGAN

Compass CC to c^4—61 Notes

——FIRST CLAVIER——

UNEXPRESSIVE SUBDIVISION

19. Double Diapason .	M.	16 Feet
20. Major Diapason .	M.	8 "
21. Minor Diapason .	M.	8 "
22. Grand Viol . .	M.	8 "
23. Doppelrohrgedeckt	W.	8 "
24. Quint	M.	$5\frac{1}{3}$ Feet
25. Octave Major .	M.	4 "
26. Octave Minor .	M.	4 "
27. Diapason Cornet	M.	V. Ranks

AUXILIARY STOP

28. Dolciano Profundo . . M. 32 ft. 61 Notes—From Pedal Organ, No. 2.

EXPRESSIVE SUBDIVISION

Inclosed in Swell-Box No. 1

29. Starkgedeckt . .	W.	16 Feet
30. Horn Diapason .	M.	8 "
31. Geigenprincipal .	M.	8 "
32. Tibia Plena . .	W.	8 "
33. Doppelflöte . .	W.	8 "
34. Harmonic Flute .	M.	4 "
35. Twelfth	M.	$2\frac{2}{3}$ Ft.
36. Super-Octave . .	M.	2 "
37. Full Mixture .	M.	V. Ranks
38. Double Trumpet .	M.	16 Feet
39. Trumpet (Harmonic)	M.	8 "
40. Clarion (Harmonic)	M.	4 "

ACCOMPANIMENTAL ORGAN

Compass CC to c^4—61 Notes

——SECOND CLAVIER——

FIRST EXPRESSIVE SUBDIVISION

Inclosed in Swell-Box No. 2

41. Lieblichgedeckt .	W.	16 Feet
42. English Diapason .	M.	8 "
43. Dulciana . . .	M.	8 "
44. Lieblichgedeckt .	W.	8 "
45. Dolcan	M.	8 "
46. Flauto Amabile .	W.	8 "
47. Gemshorn . . .	M.	4 Feet
48. Flauto Amoroso .	M.	4 "
49. Dolce Mixture	M.	III. Ranks
50. Flautino . . .	M.	2 Feet
51. Oboe d'Amore . .	M.	8 "
I. Tremolant		

SECOND EXPRESSIVE SUBDIVISION

Inclosed in Swell-Box No. 3

52. Gelindgedeckt . .	W.	16 Feet
53. Salicional . . .	M.	8 "
54. Melodia . . .	W.	8 "
55. Viola d'Amore .	M.	8 "
56. Viola d'Amore (Sharp) . . .	M.	8 "
57. Violetta . . .	M.	4 "
58. Flageoletta . .	M.	2 Feet
59. Dulciana Cornet	M.	V. Ranks
60. Dulcian . . .	M.	16 Feet
61. Cor Anglais . .	M.	8 "
62. Musette . . .	M.	4 "
II. Tremolant		

ORCHESTRAL ORGAN

Compass CC to c^4—61 Notes

—THIRD CLAVIER—

FIRST EXPRESSIVE SUBDIVISION

Inclosed in Swell-Box No. 4

63. Bourdonecho . .	W.	16 Feet	72. Harmonia Ætheria	M.	IV. Ranks
64. Quintaton . . .	M.	8 "	73. Contrafagotto .	M.	16 Feet
65. Flûte à Cheminée	M.	8 "	74. Fagotto . . .	M.	8 "
66. Dolce	M.	8 "	75. Orchestral Clarinetto . .	M.	8 "
67. Harmonica . .	W.	8 "	76. Orchestral Oboe .	M.	8 "
68. Orchestral Flute	W.	8 "	77. Clarinetto Quinta	M.	5$\frac{1}{3}$ "
69. Flauto Dolcissimo	W.	8 "	78. Oboe Ottava . .	M.	4 "
70. Orchestral Flute	W.	4 "			
71. Orchestral Piccolo	M.	2 "			

III. Tremolant

SECOND EXPRESSIVE SUBDIVISION

Inclosed in Swell-Box No. 5

79. Grossgedeckt . .	W.	16 Feet	87. Contra-Trombone	M.	16 Feet
80. Stentorphone . .	M.	8 "	88. Trombone . . .	M.	8 "
81. Grossflöte . . .	W.	8 "	89. Ophicleide . . .	M.	8 "
82. Clarabella . .	W.	8 "	90. Orchestral Horn	M.	8 "
83. Octave	M.	4 "	91. Orchestral Trumpet	M.	8 "
84. Claribel Flute .	W.	4 "	92. Tromba Quint .	M.	5$\frac{1}{3}$ "
85. Triplette .	M.	3$\frac{1}{5}$, 2$\frac{2}{3}$, 2 "	93. Tromba Octave .	M.	4 "
86. Grand Cornet	M.	V. Ranks	94. Clarion (Harmonic)	M.	4 "

SOLO ORGAN

Compass CC to c^4—61 Notes

—FOURTH CLAVIER—

EXPRESSIVE

Inclosed in Swell-Box No. 6

95. Tibia Plena . .	W.	8 Feet	101. Solo Horn . .	M.	8 Feet
96. Stentorflöte . .	W.	8 "	102. Trumpet Royal .	M.	8 "
97. Solo Violin . .	T.	8 "	103. Solo Trombone .	M.	8 "
98. Solo Violoncello	T.	8 "	104. Tuba Magna .	M.	8 "
99. Vox Humana .	M.	8 "	105. Tuba Clarion .	M.	4 "
100. Solo Clarinet .	M.	8 "	106. Chimes .	Tubular Bells	8 "

IV. Tremolant

ANCILLARY STRING ORGAN

Compass CC to c⁴—61 Notes

EXPRESSIVE

Inclosed in Swell-Box No. 7

107. CONTRABASSO . .	W.	16 Feet
108. GEIGENPRINCIPAL .	M.	8 "
109. VIOLONCELLO . .	M.	8 "
110. VIOLONCELLO VIBRATO . .	M.	8 "
111. VIOLA	M.	8 "
112. VIOLINO . . .	M.	8 "
113. VIOLINO SORDO .	M.	8 Feet
114. VIOLINO VIBRATO	M.	8 "
115. VIOLETTA . . .	M.	4 "
116. VIOL TWELFTH .	M.	2⅔ "
117. VIOL FIFTEENTH .	M.	2 "
118. VIOL CORNET .	M.	V. Ranks
V. TREMOLANT		

CLAVIER COUPLERS

PEDAL ORGAN COUPLERS

First Clavier	to Pedal Clavier, Unison Coupler.
First Clavier	to Pedal Clavier, Octave Coupler.
Second Clavier . . .	to Pedal Clavier, Unison Coupler.
Third Clavier	to Pedal Clavier, Unison Coupler.
Fourth Clavier . . .	to Pedal Clavier, Unison Coupler.
Pedal Clavier	on Itself, Octave Coupler.

FIRST CLAVIER COUPLERS

Second Clavier .	1st Subdivision .	to First Clavier, Unison Coupler.
Second Clavier .	1st Subdivision .	to First Clavier, Octave Coupler.
Second Clavier .	2nd Subdivision .	to First Clavier, Unison Coupler.
Third Clavier .	1st Subdivision .	to First Clavier, Unison Coupler.
Third Clavier .	2nd Subdivision .	to First Clavier, Unison Coupler.
Fourth Clavier .	Undivided .	to First Clavier, Unison Coupler.

SECOND CLAVIER COUPLERS

Third Clavier .	1st Subdivision .	to Second Clavier, Unison Coupler.
Third Clavier .	2nd Subdivision .	to Second Clavier, Unison Coupler.
Fourth Clavier .	Undivided .	to Second Clavier, Unison Coupler.

THIRD CLAVIER COUPLERS

Fourth Clavier .	Undivided .	to Third Clavier, Unison Coupler.
Fourth Clavier .	Undivided .	to Third Clavier, Octave Coupler.

ANCILLARY COUPLERS

Four Couplers connecting Ancillary String Organ with First, Second, Third, and Fourth Manual Claviers.

EXPRESSION LEVER COUPLERS

Couplers connecting Ancillary String Organ Swell-action with Expression Levers II., III., IV., V., VI.

EXPRESSION LEVERS

I. Balanced Expression Lever commanding Pedal Organ Swell-action.
II. Balanced Expression Lever commanding action of Swell-Box No. 1.
III. Balanced Expression Lever commanding action of Swell-Box No. 2.
IV. Balanced Expression Lever commanding action of Swell-Box No. 3.
V. Balanced Expression Lever commanding action of Swell-Box No. 4.
VI. Balanced Expression Lever commanding action of Swell-Box No. 5.
VII. Balanced Expression Lever commanding action of Swell-Box No. 6.

A, B, C, D, E, F, G.—Seven double-acting Toe-Pistons connecting and disconnecting the actions of the Pedal Swell-Chamber, and of Swell-Boxes Nos. 1, 2, 3, 4, 5, 6 with the respective Balanced Expression Levers as tabulated above.

CRESCENDO LEVER

Balanced Crescendo Lever commanding selected groups of Stops in progressive order of tonal power and character. The mechanism of the Lever being so adjusted as to indicate, by well marked changes in resistance to the pressure of the foot, the entry into changes of tonal character and power until the climax is reached. The *decrescendo* follows in the same manner downwards. The Lever is placed on the right of the Expression Levers, and at an angle convenient to the foot of the performer.

DIVISIONAL PISTONS

Two Thumb Pistons—under First Clavier—bringing on and throwing off Expressive Subdivision of Grand Organ.

Two Thumb-Pistons—under Second Clavier—bringing on and throwing off First Expressive Subdivision of Accompanimental Organ.

Two Thumb-Pistons—under Second Clavier—bringing on and throwing off Second Expressive Subdivision of Accompanimental Organ.

Two Thumb-Pistons—under Third Clavier—bringing on and throwing off First Expressive Subdivision of Orchestral Organ.

Two Thumb-Pistons—under Third Clavier—bringing on and throwing off Second Expressive Subdivision of Orchestral Organ.

Two Thumb-Pistons—under Fourth Clavier—bringing on and throwing off Solo Organ.

ADJUSTABLE COMBINATION PISTONS

Seven Operating Thumb-Pistons and Release—under First Clavier—commanding Stop-combinations on Grand Organ, Pedal Organ, and Couplers.

One Double-acting Thumb-Piston—under First Clavier—bringing on and throwing off the Ancillary String Organ.

Eight Operating Thumb-Pistons and Release—under Second Clavier—commanding Stop-combinations on Accompanimental Organ, Pedal Organ, and Couplers.

One Double-acting Thumb-Piston—under Second Clavier—bringing on and throwing off the Ancillary String Organ.

Ten Operating Thumb-Pistons and Release—under Third Clavier—commanding Stop-combinations on Orchestral Organ, Pedal Organ, and Couplers.

One Double-acting Thumb-Piston—under Third Clavier—bringing on and throwing off the Ancillary String Organ.

Five Operating Thumb-Pistons and Release—under Fourth Clavier—commanding Stop-combinations on Solo Organ and Pedal Organ.

One Double-acting Thumb-Piston—under Fourth Clavier—bringing on and throwing off the Ancillary String Organ.

PEDAL ORGAN TOE-PISTONS

ALL DOUBLE-ACTING

1. Piston coupling First Manual Clavier to Pedal Clavier.
2. Piston coupling First Manual Clavier to Pedal Clavier, in the Octave.
3. Piston coupling Second Manual Clavier to Pedal Clavier.
4. Piston coupling Third Manual Clavier to Pedal Clavier.
5. Piston coupling Fourth Manual Clavier to Pedal Clavier.
6. Piston coupling Fourth Manual Clavier to Pedal Clavier, in the Octave.

Other Toe-Pistons may be added for any special purposes deemed desirable by the Organ Architect or Organist in charge. It is undesirable, however, to overcrowd appliances to be operated by the feet.

TREMOLANTS

The Five Tremolants are to be commanded by the general Draw-Stop System, by rocking-tablets, pendant touches, or by whatever style of Draw-Stop appliances may be generally adopted for the command of the Stops and Couplers, and are to be immediately associated with them. In addition, the Tremolants belonging to the Subdivisions of the stationary Organs are to be commanded also by Thumb-Pistons located under the respective Manual Claviers. If preferred the Pistons can be placed in the clavier cheeks.

NOTES ON THE THIRD SPECIFICATION

Although the true Concert-room Organ schemed in this Specification has less than one-half the stop appointment of that set forth in the First Specification, and has only about two-thirds the stop appointment of the organ set forth in the Second Specification, it is still an instrument of the first rank. Its tonal appointment is larger, by eighteen stops, than that of the Organ installed in St. George's Hall, Liverpool, and, by seven stops, than the Organ installed in the Royal Albert Hall, London, as constructed by Henry Willis. Its tonal appointment is less, only by twenty-two stops, than that of the Sydney Town Hall Organ, as built by Hill; and by forty-four stops than that of the St. Louis Exposition Organ, as designed by us, in 1902.

The system followed in the process of reduction in size can readily be realized by comparing the stop-apportionments of the Pedal and Manual Organs, as set forth in the three Specifications. These will guide the organ designer in effectively scheming lesser instruments, while retaining the true concert-room character and orchestral properties. Care must be taken, however, to avoid serious injury to the dominant principle of Divisional and Subdivisional tonal contrast, and the necessary powers of tonal flexibility and expression. It is as essential, as it is desirable, that the Ancillary String Organ shall not be seriously denuded. It is very questionable if, under any conditions, it should have a stop-apportionment less effective than that given in this Third Specification. It is greatly to be regretted that the organ-pipe makers and voicers of this country have paid so little study and care to the production of truly artistic and highly imitative String-toned stops; for, assuredly, these have, up to the present time (1924), been successfully fabricated in England only, by such artists as Thynne, Whitely, and Pendlebury; and by Edmund Schulze, who placed his masterpieces in English organs. While on this subject, we must again impress on the organ designer the absolute necessity of providing the String Organ with a properly constructed Swell-Box, which will sufficiently subdue, without annihilating, the tones of the inclosed stops, when entirely closed. The artless methods followed by modern organ-builders in Swell-Box construction are little short of brutal.

It is very doubtful if it is desirable to appoint a true Concert-room Organ with less than four Manual Claviers; for the convenience they provide, in facilitating the rapid changes in tonality and in the production of necessary orchestral effects and *nuances*, is unquestionable. In the event of the space, provided by the Architect of the concert-room, being insufficient for the accommodation of an instrument having the number of manual Divisions our System calls for, the Solo Organ, reduced to the minimum stop-apportionment, may be added to the appointment of what we have designated the Orchestral Organ, commanded by the Third Clavier, as set forth in the Specification now under consideration. Under such an arrangement, it may be found necessary to somewhat reduce the stop-apportionments of the Subdivisions of the Orchestral Organ as set forth in the Third Specification. The altered instrument will, under the conditions, require only five Swell-boxes, including that of the Ancillary String Organ. Providing the height of the organ-chamber is sufficient, as it must be to accommodate stops of 32 feet, the Swell-boxes may be placed on two levels, as has been done in the Cavaillé-Coll Organ in the Albert Hall, Sheffield.[16]

The Notes on the several Divisions of the Concert-room Organ which are appended to the First and Second Specifications being sufficiently full and ex-

[16] The Plan showing this disposition, is given in "The Art of Organ-Building," Vol. I., p. 344; and in "The Organ of the Twentieth Century," p. 276.

plicit, it is quite unnecessary to go over similar ground in relation to the reduced tonal appointment set forth in this Third Specification, beyond a few general remarks on the reduction of the stop-apportionments. It will be observed, on comparing the tonal appointments of the Divisions and Subdivisions in all the three Specifications, that the fundamental principles embraced in our System are fully adhered to. Indeed, the strict observance of these principles, as already descanted on, is imperative, if the Concert-room is to be worthy of the high appellation—The Temple of Tone. Unless tonal flexibility and adequate powers of expression are carried throughout every Division of the instrument, the result will be a failure so far as the true Concert-room type of Organ is concerned. In these important directions, reference to, and observance of, the teachings of the grand orchestra must be strictly observed.

It will be realized, on careful comparison of the corresponding Divisions and Subdivisions of the Second and Third Specifications, that the stops omitted in the latter have not seriously denuded the lesser instrument of the tonal and controlling elements which constitute the true Concert-room Organ. In its appointment are provided tonal resources that no organist, or a thousand organists, could exhaust in a lifetime, even should they confine themselves to the resources of a single Division of the instrument.[17]

The mechanical accessories and appliances for the complete control of the instrument set forth in this Third Specification are precisely similar to those detailed in the preceding Specifications, though, necessarily, slightly less in number. The wind-pressures given in the preceding Notes, are equally suitable for the stops given in this Third Specification.

17 Alluding to the stop-apportionments of the Subdivisions of the Third Organ of the instrument installed in the Festival Hall of the Louisiana Purchase Exposition (1904), we remark, in a description of the Organ: A book could be written on the tonal effects possible on this compound, expressive Division alone. It may be interesting to learn that with the thirty-four speaking stops contained in this compound Division, no fewer than seventeen billion, one hundred and seventy-nine million, eight hundred and sixty-nine thousand, one hundred and eighty-three (17,179,869,183) distinct tonal and expressive combinations or effects are possible, without resort to octave or sub-octave coupling, or any multiplying device whatever. Some idea can be formed of the number of tonal effects given above, when it is calculated, if a different combination was drawn every minute, day and night, it would require above thirty-two thousand, six hundred years to complete the performance.

PART THIRD

THE CHURCH ORGAN

HE appointment of the true and sufficient Church Organ is to-day a question demanding serious consideration on the part of those who have the welfare of the instrument at heart; for the clouds of conservatism, old-fashioned ideas, and trade interests hang over it, obscuring the illuminating rays of science and art which should now be heralding the dawn of a brighter day in the organ-building world. In almost all quarters things are going on in the age-crusted style of our great grandfathers; just as if everything, beyond some mechanical matters, had reached a full development, and the organ had become a perfect instrument. Trade interests, on the one hand, and apathy on the part of organists who have not taken the pains to study the construction and tonal structure of the organ, on the other, have effectively blocked the way of progress and development in important tonal directions, and, likely, will continue to do so for some time to come.

We have done our best during more than half a century of devoted study and labor to point the way to better things, and have written so fully regarding the appointment of the Church Organ, that in this final essay on the subject we shall find it very difficult to avoid repeating much that we have necessarily said in preceding works. This, however, will not be undesirable, for this treatise will fall into the hands of many organists and organ-lovers, perhaps, who have never seen, or paid any attention to, what our larger works contain. Therefore, we shall not hesitate to reiterate here what we have said elsewhere on the subject now under consideration.

In the general design and especially in the tonal scheme of the true Church Organ a problem has to be solved, widely different from that presented by the appointment of the true Concert-room Organ, as set forth in the preceding Part. It is a remarkable fact that in the entire range of the literature of the organ—French, German, and English—prior to our taking up our pen on the subject, no serious essays were made, if any, to render the Church Organ a truly flexible and expressive instrument. Not a single writer on the subject, so far as we have been able to discover, had previously contemplated or advised the introduction of more than a single Swell-box, so as to secure more general flexibility of tone and extended powers of expression. Even to-day, Church Organs, almost without number, are being constructed, at home and abroad, with only one insufficient expressive and flexible Division; and these are accepted by church organ committees and indifferent organists as suitable and sufficient instruments. The term Swell Organ being retained, indicating that there is only one expressive Division.

An important question may properly be asked before practical matters are fully entered upon, it is this: What is a true Church Organ? Great as its importance is, this question has appeared to trouble the minds of organ-designers and organ-builders very little, if at all. To the tradesman organ-builder, a Church Organ is simply the largest instrument, constructed tonally on time-honored old-world lines, that money is forthcoming to pay for, and which can be fabricated on a purely commercial basis; and which, by the exercise of ingenuity, can be crammed into the place in the church the architect has thought proper to provide for it. Other matters, such as refinement of tone in all the stops, and the provision of adequate means for the production of tonal flexibility and musical expression, are, comparatively, of little importance. To the organist, if he has any control over the design of the instrument, the desirable Organ is that which most fully embodies his personal ideas of tonal appointment and control, and upon which he can most effectively display his special skill in execution and in the production of musical *tours de force*. To him the essential requirement is that the Organ be fully appointed for recital work. There can be no possible objection to such an instrument in its proper place: but is its proper place in a church? Has nothing of the true and essential qualities and requirements of the proper Church Organ been sacrificed so that such a tonal appointment might be secured? We know full well that, in the large majority of Church Organs, such requirements have been sacrificed for what was neither necessary nor desirable in a perfect Church Organ. When a large instrument is desired, beyond normal requirements, and the church is spacious, it may be deemed expedient to give it a dual office; namely, that of a Church Organ, on the one hand, and a Concert Organ, on the other; care being taken to have every requirement of the Church Organ fully and properly met. But when it is of a moderate and sufficient size only, the instrument should, in every way, be a true Church Organ, perfectly appointed for the place it occupies and the office it has to fulfil. We venture to think that this latter statement is incontrovertible.

The important question—What is a true Church Organ?—has now to be answered; so that the designer and the purchaser of such an instrument may be guided aright, to the saving of money and the prevention of disappointment.

The true Church Organ is primarily and essentially an accompanimental instrument. Its characteristics are grandeur, impressiveness, and repose, secured by the greatest possible richness and refinement of tone, endowed with full powers of flexibility and expression; so that it may adequately meet all demands in the artistic accompaniment of choral and congregational singing, and in the rendition of voluntaries and other incidental music of an ecclesiastical and dignified character. Beyond this it is not necessary to provide. Provision for the execution of florid music and the display of executive skill on the part of the organist being of no importance. Organists will not agree with us in this dictum; but, as they disagree with us in so many other equally important questions, it is of little moment, as time will show.

When one recognizes the religious ethos which should pervade all the musical services of a church, it becomes quite obvious that noisiness and every element of coarseness should be eliminated from the instrument employed in such services. The Organ must, accordingly, comprise in its tonal structure, stops having rich, pure, and sympathetic intonations; such as are characteristic of the Pure Organ-toned foundation stops—the DIAPASONS and their derivatives and harmonic attendants—and those refined labial and lingual stops which most effectively and artistically accompany and support the voice in its full range of expression.

How seldom one finds, on testing the stop-apportionments of modern Church Organs, that the conditions just alluded to have been realized and properly fulfilled; and how often one finds that the true Church Organ has been largely sacrificed for the introduction of certain stops that are practically valueless and out of place in such an instrument. All matters connected with the tonal appointment of the Organ call for serious consideration on the part of those concerned in its production. Utility and Beauty are the standards which must never be abrogated. As a corollary to what has just been said, we may here give the remarks on the subject from the pen of an English writer of experience and good judgment—commending them to the attention of organists and all interested in the production of true and sufficient Church Organs.

"In the first place, the Organ should be of a size and power proportionate to the building and the congregation it will contain. We see in some churches Organs erected out of all proportion to the requirements of the service; as an instance, let that of St. Mary at Hill, London, be adduced—a very fine instrument is to be found there; but it is far too large and noisy for the comparatively small church. This instrument, although possessing great merit, is not a Church Organ in its true sense. The same fault applies to the recently-erected Organ at St. Andrew's, Well-street, London; the instrument is far too large and noisy for the size of the church, placed, as it is, near the congregation. One more example, by way of contrast: take St. Alphage, London Wall: here is a small church, and an Organ designed for the church—a Church Organ *par excellence.* It is unnecessary to go farther into detail upon this point: a Church Organ is an Organ designed to accompany the voices, and to be at the same time capable of rendering with effect the voluntaries before and after service. When the musical demands of an ordinary Sunday service are considered, and the large proportion of accompaniment to voice-singing in which it consists, it is certain that noise is not the attribute best suited to the Church Organ, but rather the more mellow tones of the foundation-stops—the DIAPASONS, and those registers which best accompany the voice. Now, the stops of this class are much more costly than the chorus and mutation stops, and a properly-constructed Organ of this type, with, say, twenty musical and well-balanced registers, would cost as much as an Organ of forty stops upon the quantity principle of endless small pipes. This may be explained more clearly by stating that the last twelve notes of the 8 ft. register on the keyboard cost about as much as the remaining forty-nine pipes, and hence, in the cumbrous 'church-warden's Organ', it will be noticed how often the foundation-stops are cut off at tenor C, 4 ft., and grooved into a common bass, or left altogether incomplete, without any bass at all; while a number of ranks of small pipes are introduced without any proper counterbalance of the foundation-tone either upon the Pedal Organ or keyboards. We now see why one specification of an Organ costing the same money may apparently represent a much more extensive instrument. Again, a Church Organ requires that in its design the tone of the Pedal Organ should be commensurate with the rest of the Organ; the Pedal Organ ought to carry down the last octave of the keyboard an octave lower without any very apparent break in the tone. Comparatively few of our present church instruments have any Pedal Organ at all. A single 16 ft. open wooden stop of a deep booming sound has to do duty alike for the full Chorus Organ and the soft Choir Organ vocal accompaniment. It is very rare to find a properly balanced Pedal Organ, even upon the most recently constructed Church Organs. The fact is, the cost of a proper Pedal Organ nearly equals that of the Organ it has to balance on the keyboard. Our present Church Organs are, as a rule, ill-constructed instruments; and, more or less, are erected in a commercial spirit, and form a transaction like the placing of bricks, stones, and mortar of the building. No one takes special interest, partly from a want of the necessary knowledge, and partly because 'it is no one's business.' What is wanted is a portion of that pure artistic spirit which animated the 'Father Schmidts' and other builders and organists of former days: men whose aim was too high for mere money-getting, and who gloried in the progress of the sublimest of all the constructive arts."—*Musical Standard*, June 23, 1877.

The strictures of this writer, well versed in organ matters, were well deserved at the time they were written—forty-eight years ago—and one regrets to have to say that they are, if anything, better deserved to-day. With his remarks anent the general neglect and poverty of the Pedal Organs we fully agree. But what would he have said had he been acquainted with our organ-builders' latest trade methods of constructing Pedal Organs *on paper*, without resorting to the time-honored and truthful practice of providing actual pedal pipes? Organs had not quite reached that stage of tonal degradation when he wrote; and organ-builders had not lost all sense of artistry and musical sense.

We cannot do better, at this stage of our subject, than practically repeat what we have said elsewhere. A Church Organ should be schemed throughout on sound scientific and artistic principles: there should be no ambition on the part of its designer to make an aimless display in the form of a great number of speaking stops; but, on the contrary, a determination to produce, in every possible way, a work of art—developed on the most serviceable lines, and true and perfect in all materials and workmanship. The tonal structure of the instrument, be it small or large, should be characterized by gravity, dignity, and refinement:—gravity, secured by an adequate, and properly balanced Pedal Organ; dignity, by volume of double and unison foundation Pure Organ-tone in the basic Divisions of the instrument; and refinement, by perfect intonation, secured by skilful voicing, on copious, low-pressure wind. Dignity combined with refinement cannot be secured by insufficient and small-scaled foundation unisons in both the Pedal Organ and manual Divisions, numerous ear-tickling and unnecessary stops, many ranks of high-pitched pipes, and blatant reeds, blown by high-pressure wind until they scream a coarse apology for their shortcomings. Gravity combined with refinement cannot be secured by a borrowed Pedal Organ, or by a single master-of-all-work pedal stop—a "booming" DIAPASON, 16 FT., or a large-scaled tubby-toned BOURDON, without control as regards strength of voice and expression.

In the tonal appointment or structure of the true and sufficient Church Organ suitable representatives of the different families of tones produced by organ-pipes—labial and lingual—will, necessarily, be present; but only of such a character in timbre and strength of voice, and to such an extent, as may be necessary for the office and scope of the instrument. These different families of tones are described in the introductory portion of the preceding Part Second, and may properly be referred to at this point, if any question arises in the mind of the reader.

In the institution of an entirely new system of stop-apportionment—divisional and subdivisional—and of tonal control imparting powers of flexibility and expression throughout the organ, it becomes obvious that the old terminology of the portions of the instrument commanded by the several manual claviers must be somewhat changed. Instead of the old terms Great, Choir, and Swell, for three claviers, we adopt the terms Grand, Accompanimental, and Solo, the term Swell Organ being valueless in an instrument in which all the manual Divisions are entirely or partially inclosed in Swell-boxes. In an instrument of four manual Divisions, commanded by four claviers, we use the terms Grand, Accompanimental, Choir, and Solo. The reasons for the adoption of these terms will be made clear as we proceed.

Before proceeding to consider the Stops which are essential and desirable for the tonal structure of the true and efficient Church Organ, and for apportionment in its several Divisions, we may properly give, as concisely as possible, the General Principles on which such an instrument can be schemed in accordance with the advanced System here set forth. They are as follows:—

GENERAL PRINCIPLES OF THE TONAL APPOINTMENT OF THE CHURCH ORGAN

I. That the Grand Organ, commanded by the First Clavier, shall be constituted the Fundamental Division of the Organ, by being built on Pure Organ-tone furnished by the DIAPASONS of 16 ft. and 8 ft., attended by as full a series of Organ-toned single and compound chorus and harmonic-corroborating stops as the proportions of Organ will admit of.

II. That to this essential Foundation-work shall be added sympathetic and contrasting stops, the voices of which shall further support, and add elements of variety and richness to, the pure foundation-tone. No stops of an orchestral or strictly imitative tonality shall be introduced to mar the grandeur, purity, and repose of this all-important Division of the instrument.

III. That to the harmonic-corroborating stops, with, perhaps, the exception of the MAJOR OCTAVE, 4 FT., corroborating the first upper partial tone of the unison or 8 ft. harmonic series, and the third upper partial of the double or 16 ft. series, and all the chorus, compound, and subsidiary stops shall be inclosed in a special Swell-box; thus rendering their voices flexible and expressive, and, accordingly, multiplied many times in tonal and combinational value, beyond what they could possibly possess under the crude, exposed, and inflexible treatment hitherto commonly followed. The Swell-box of the Grand Organ to be distinguished as Number 1, operated by Expression Lever No. 2.

IV. That the Accompanimental Organ, commanded by the Second Clavier, shall in its general tonal character present a decided contrast to that of the Grand Organ. In its appointment, Pure Organ-tone must be markedly less in quantity and assertiveness than that characteristic of the Grand Organ, although here it must assume a certain foundational position. The general tonal character of this all-important Division must be that most suitable for the accompaniment and support of the voice in sacred song; and this implies extreme purity and refinement.

V. That due care shall be taken, in the selection of the stops for this Division, to provide as full a harmonic-corroborating series as is practicable in the size of the Organ. This tonal element is of extreme value, providing it is scientifically proportioned and characterized by a proper quality and by artistic regulation and graduation of strength of voice.

VI. That the Accompanimental Organ shall be completely endowed with powers of compound tonal flexibility and expression, according to our System. The stops properly selected shall be arranged in two groups—preferably equal in size—contrasting in their general tonalities to the greatest degree possible. These Subdivisions shall be inclosed in separate Swell-boxes, designated Swell-box No. 2, and Swell-box No. 3. These shall have their shades operated by balanced Expression Levers, Nos. 3 and 4, located close together and immediately to the right of Expression Lever No. 2.

VII. That the Solo Organ, commanded by the Third Clavier, shall in its tonal appointment present a decided contrast in quality and strength to the tonalities of the Grand and Accompanimental Organs. In this Division much more freedom may be exercised in the selection of the stops; which, however, must be suitable for the music of church services. Selection can be made from the more refined stops yielding Free Organ-tone, Flute-tone, Viol-tone, Reed-tone, and, but very sparingly, Brass-tone.

VIII. That to secure the maximum powers of tonal flexibility and expression, the stops of this Third Division shall be arranged in two groups—preferably of equal size—having a decided contrast of tonality; and to secure the great advantage of compound flexibility and expression, the contrasting groups shall be inclosed in separate Swell-boxes, designated Swell-box No. 4 and Swell-box No. 5. But we have found it sufficient, in the case of a Church Organ of moderate size, to inclose the groups in Swell-boxes, Nos. 2 and 3, which contain the contrasting groups of the Accompanimental Organ. This latter arrangement places two contrasting groups in each Swell-box; and establishes a compound contrast of great tonal value, absolutely unknown in the one-ply school of organ-building commonly followed to-day.

IX. That in the instrument having four manual claviers, there shall be the Division designated the Choir Organ, which shall be commanded by the Third Clavier—the Solo Organ being commanded by the Fourth Clavier. The Choir Organ shall be tonally the softest and most refined Division of the Church Organ, amplifying its accompanimental resources to an immense extent; being endowed with compound flexibility and expression. Its stop-apportionment shall differ in every respect from those of the other Divisions. Only stops of the most refined and sympathetic tonality, speaking on wind of low pressure, shall be introduced in this Division. They shall, according to the System, be arranged in two contrasting groups, which shall be inclosed in Swell-boxes Nos. 2 and 3, along with the Subdivisions of the Accompanimental Organ. The Solo Organ occupying Swell-box No. 4.

X. That the Pedal Organ, commanded by the Pedal Clavier, shall be treated as the Sub-Foundation of the tonal structure of the entire Organ. It shall be practically complete in itself, not necessarily deriving any aid from the stop-apportionments of the manual Divisions. The importance of an entirely independent Pedal Organ cannot be overrated.

XI. That in its stop-apportionment the Pedal Organ shall provide proper and adequate basses for the principal stops in the manual Divisions, and, accordingly, for their important combinations.

XII. That the Pedal Organ shall, in addition to its unison equipment, in all possible cases comprise a complete stop of 32 ft. pitch, desirably of open wood, yielding Pure Organ-tone. That it shall be adequately furnished with open and covered labial stops of unison or 16 ft. pitch, yielding Pure Organ-tone, Flute-tone, and Viol-tone: Brass-tone and Reed-tone may properly be represented by lingual stops of 16 ft. and 8 ft., of a rich and refined intonation.

XIII. That the Pedal Organ shall, in addition to the foundation stops, be provided with sufficient harmonic-corroborating ranks of pipes, of Pure Organ-tone, to effectively enrich and impart clearness of intonation to the grave and somewhat indeterminate voices of the 32 ft. and 16 ft. stops. This is a matter of importance, for it is generally admitted that below EE, of the Contrabasso of the orchestra, the ear refuses to recognize sounds as musical. Accordingly, there are sixteen notes below this pitch in a stop of 32 ft. Matters of this scientific import are being ignored in the slip-shod methods followed to-day in this country, in which the all-important Pedal Organ is undergoing a process of degradation—a branch of the cancer that, under crude trade methods, is eating away the true science and art of organ-building.

XIV. That the Pedal Organ shall, in all cases where it is possible, be endowed with powers of tonal flexibility and expression, after the simple method directed for the Grand Organ. There is no possible reason why such desirable powers should be denied the Pedal Organ. They may, however, in even the largest instruments, be confined to the harmonic-corroborating, solo, and lingual stops.

As the different families, in which the tones produced by labial and lingual organ-pipes are properly grouped, are treated on with sufficient fullness in the preceding Part Second; and as such Notes as may be necessary or desirable on the several Divisions and Subdivisions of the Church Organ will appropriately follow the Specifications; we may at this point, adopting the method introduced with respect to the Concert-room Organ, give a List of the Stops most suitable for the tonal structure of the Church Organ—according to our System, and the limitations we consider proper to be observed.

In the List will necessarily be omitted many stops that belong peculiarly to the tonal appointment of the true Concert-room instrument. This omission is obviously desirable for several reasons, and especially so at this time, when the craze for musical noise and uncontrollable blatant voices is widely spread among organists; and the equally uncontrollable scream, produced from lingual pipes, inartistically voiced on inordinate wind-pressures, seems to be considered by organ-builders the *ne plus ultra* of artistic tone production; while, in truth, it is an evidence of a vitiated musical sense and lack of refinement in the ear.

LIST OF STOPS SUITABLE FOR THE TONAL APPOINTMENT OF CHURCH ORGANS

MANUAL ORGANS

PURE ORGAN-TONE

Double Diapason	M.	16 Feet
Diapason (Schulze)	M.	8 "
Diapason (English)	M.	8 "
Diapason (Wood)	W.	8 Feet
Echo Diapason	M.	8 "
Quint	M.	$5\frac{1}{3}$ "
Octave, Major	M.	4 "
Octave, Minor	M.	4 "

PURE ORGAN-TONE—Continued

Tierce	M.	3⅕ Ft.
Twelfth	M.	2⅔ "
Super-Octave	M.	2 "
Seventeenth	M.	1⅗ "
Cornet	M.	V. Ranks
4′—3⅕′—2⅔′—2²⁄₇′—2′.		
Full Mixture	M.	V. Ranks

FREE ORGAN-TONE

Double Dulciana	M.	16 Feet
Horn Diapason	M.	8 "
Dolce	M.	8 "
Dolcan	M.	8 "
Dulciana	M.	8 "
Gemshorn	M.	8 "
Voix Angélique	M.	8 "
Voix Éolienne	M.	8 "
Gemshornquinte	M.	5⅓ "
Gemshornoctav	M.	4 "
Dulciana Octave	M.	4 "
Cœlestina	M.	4 "
Dulcet	M.	4 "
Dulciana Tierce	M.	3⅕ "
Gemshorn Twelfth	M.	2⅔ "
Echo Quint	M.	2⅔ "
Dulciana Fifteenth	M.	2 "
Gemshorn Fifteenth	M.	2 "
Dolce Cornet	M.	VI. Ranks
4′—3⅕′—2⅔′—2′—1⅗′—1′.		
Dulciana Cornet	M.	V. Ranks
Harmonia Ætheria	T.	VI. Ranks

FLUTE ORGAN-TONE

(Open Flute-Tone)

Flautone	W.	8 Feet
Flauto Tedesco	W.	8 "
Nachthorn	M.	8 "
Harmonic Flute	M.	8 "
Hohlflöte	W.	8 "
Tibia Plena	W.	8 "
Portunalflöte	W.	8 "
Harmonieflöte	W.	8 "
Flauto Traverso	W.	8 "
Clarabella	W.	8 "

OPEN FLUTE-TONE—Continued

Melodia	W.	8 Feet
Harmonica	W.	8 "
Spitzflöte	M.	8 "
Flauto Amabile	W.	8 "
Flauto Dolce	W.	8 "
Dolcissimo	W.	8 "
Flauto Amoroso	M.	4 "
Spitzflöte	M.	4 "
Waldflöte	W.	4 "
Clarabel Flute	W.	4 "
Flageolet	M.	2 "

(Half Covered Flute-Tone)

Doppelrohrflöte	W.	8 Feet
Rohrflöte	W.	8 "
Flûte à Cheminée	M.	8 "
Flauto d'Amore	W.	4 "

(Covered Flute-Tone)

Bourdon	W.	16 Feet
Bourdon Doux	W.	16 "
Doppelgedeckt	W.	16 "
Lieblichgedeckt	W.	16 "
Doppelflöte	W.	8 "
Zartgedeckt	W.	8 "
Zartflöte (Whitely)	M.	8 "
Lieblichgedeckt	W.	8 "
Tibia Clausa	W.	8 "
Quintaten	M.	8 "
Gedecktquinte	M.	5⅓ "
Lieblichflöte	M.	4 "
Divinare	W.	4 "
Zauberflöte	M.	4 "

VIOL-TONE

Contra-Gamba	M.	16 Feet
Cone Gamba	M.	16 "
Geigenprincipal	M.	8 "
Grand Viol	M.	8 "
Salicional	M.	8 "
Violoncello	M.	8 "
Violino	M.	8 "
Viola d'Amore	M.	8 "
Viola d'Amore (Sharp)	M.	8 "
Æoline	M.	8 "

VIOL-TONE—Continued

Viol Quint	M.	5⅓ Ft.
Gambette	M.	4 "
Salicet	M.	4 "
Geigenoctav	M.	4 "
Viol Twelfth	M.	2⅔ "
Viol Fifteenth	M.	2 "
Viol Cornet (Sordino)	M.	V. Ranks

REED-TONE

Contrafagotto	W.	16 Feet
Contra-Oboe	M.	16 "
Fagotto	M.	8 "
Oboe	M.	8 "
Clarinetto	M.	8 "
Corno di Bassetto	M.	8 "
Cor Anglais	M.	8 "
Oboe d'Amore	M.	8 "
Oboe Ottava	M.	4 "
Musette	M.	4 "

BRASS-TONE

Contra-Trombone	M.	16 Feet
Double Trumpet	M.	16 "
Tromba Real	M.	8 "
Trumpet	M.	8 "
Trombone	M.	8 "
Horn	M.	8 "
Tromba Clarion	M.	4 "
Clarion	M.	4 "

INDETERMINATE-TONE

Vox Humana	M.	8 Feet

PERCUSSION-TONE

Chimes	(Tubular Bells)
Harp	(Wood Bars)

PEDAL ORGAN

ORGAN-TONE

Double Principal	W.	32 Feet
Major Principal	W.	16 "

ORGAN-TONE—Continued

Minor Principal	M.	16 Feet
Dulciana	M.	16 "
Gemshornbass	M.	16 "
Quintenbass	W.	16 "
Grand Octave	M.	8 "
Dulciana Octave	M.	8 "
Quint	M.	5⅓ "
Super-Octave	M.	4 "
Grand Cornet	M.	V. Ranks
Compensating Mixture	M.	VI. Ranks

FLUTE-TONE

Untersatz	W.	32 Feet
Bourdon	W.	16 "
Lieblichgedeckt	W.	16 "
Quintaten	M.	16 "
Grossflöte	W.	8 "
Flötenbass	W.	8 "
Hohlflöte	W.	4 "

VIOL-TONE

Violon-Basse	W.	16 Feet
Contra-Salicional	M.	16 "
Violoncello	M.	8 "
Grand Viol	M.	8 "

REED-TONE

Contrafagotto	W.	16 Feet
Contra-Clarinetto	M.	16 "
Contra-Oboe	M.	16 "
Fagotto	M.	8 "

BRASS-TONE

Trombone	M.	16 Feet
Bombarde	M.	16 "
Euphonium	M.	16 "
Trombone	M.	8 "
Dulcian	M.	8 "
Clarion	M.	4 "

The following Specifications given in this Part furnish tonal and controlling appointments for true Church Organs; all direct indications of a dual treatment, in which an approach to the Concert-room type of instrument is essayed, being studiously avoided. This is desirable, for the important instruments, designed to accord with the ideas and wishes of organists who desire them to be suitable for recital purposes, are supposed by many persons to be ideal Church Organs. This desire has led to the construction of instruments in which the prime purpose and essential tonal treatment of the true accompanimental Church Organ have been largely sacrificed if not entirely ignored. Such instruments are, accordingly, neither sufficient Concert-room Organs nor satisfactory Church Organs.

——FOURTH SPECIFICATION——

CHURCH ORGAN

AUDSLEY SYSTEM—COMPOUND EXPRESSION
FOUR MANUAL CLAVIERS

PEDAL ORGAN

Compass CCC to G—32 Notes

——PEDAL CLAVIER——

UNEXPRESSIVE SUBDIVISION

1. Double Principal (44 pipes) . . .	W. 32 Feet	4. Minor Principal .	M. 16 Feet
2. Double Dulciana (61 pipes) . . .	M. 32 "	5. Dulciana (From 2).	M. 16 "
3. Major Principal (From 1) . . .	W. 16 "	6. Violon-Basse . .	M. 8 "
		7. Grand Octave . .	W. 8 "
		8. Compensating Mixture . .	M. IV. Ranks

EXPRESSIVE SUBDIVISION

Inclosed in Swell-Chamber

9. Bourdon	W. 16 Feet	18. Hohlflöte . . .	W. 4 Feet
10. Lieblichgedeckt .	W. 16 "	19. Grand Cornet	M. V. Ranks
11. Quintaten . . .	M. 16 "	20. Bombarde . . .	M. 16 Feet
12. Grand Viol . .	M. 8 "	21. Euphonium . . .	M. 16 "
13. Doppelflöte . .	W. 8 "	22 Contrafagotto .	W. 16 "
14. Violoncello . .	M. 8 "	23. Contra-Oboe . .	M. 16 "
15. Flötenbass . . .	W. 8 "	24. Fagotto	M. 8 "
16. Quint	M. 5⅓ "	25. Tromba	M. 8 "
17. Super-Octave . .	M. 4 "	26. Clarion	M. 4 "

GRAND ORGAN

Compass CC to c^4—61 Notes

—FIRST CLAVIER—

UNEXPRESSIVE SUBDIVISION

Stop			Stop		
27. Double Diapason .	M.	16 Feet	33. Doppelflöte . .	W.	8 Feet
28. Diapason (Schulze)	M.	8 "	34. Quint	M.	$5\frac{1}{3}$ "
29. Diapason (English)	M.	8 "	35. Octave, Major .	M.	4 "
30. Diapason (Wood) .	W.	8 "	36. Tierce	M.	$3\frac{1}{5}$ "
31. Grand Viol . .	M.	8 "	37. Twelfth . . .	M.	$2\frac{2}{3}$ "
32. Quintaten . . .	M.	8 "	38. Super-Octave . .	M.	2 "

AUXILIARY STOP

39. Dolciana Profundo. M. 32 ft. 61 Notes—From Pedal Organ No. 2.

EXPRESSIVE SUBDIVISION

Inclosed in Swell-Box No. 1

Stop			Stop		
40. Bourdon . . .	W.	16 Feet	48. Gemshorn Twelfth	M.	$2\frac{2}{3}$ Ft.
41. Gemshorn . . .	M.	8 "	49. Gemshorn Fifteenth	M.	2 "
42. Harmonic Flute .	M.	8 "	50. Cornet . . .	M.	V. Ranks
43. Hohlflöte . . .	W.	8 "	$4'$—$3\frac{1}{5}'$—$2\frac{2}{3}'$—$2\frac{2}{7}'$—$2'$.		
44. Clarabella . .	W.	8 "	51. Full Mixture .	M.	V. "
45. Gemshornquinte .	M.	$5\frac{1}{3}$ "	52. Double Trumpet .	M.	16 Feet
46. Gemshorn Octave	M.	4 "	53. Trumpet . . .	M.	8 "
47. Spitzflöte . . .	M.	4 "	54. Clarion . . .	M.	4 "

ACCOMPANIMENTAL ORGAN

Compass CC to c^4—61 Notes

—SECOND CLAVIER—

FIRST EXPRESSIVE SUBDIVISION

Inclosed in Swell-Box No. 2

Stop			Stop		
55. Lieblichgedeckt .	W.	16 Feet	61. Flauto d'Amore .	W.	4 Feet
56. Echo Diapason .	M.	8 "	62. Dulcet	M.	4 "
57. Geigenprincipal .	M.	8 "	63. Dulciana Fifteenth	M.	2 "
58. Dulciana . . .	M.	8 "	64. Dolce Cornet .	M.	VI. Ranks
59. Clarabella . .	W.	8 "	65. Clarinetto (Soft) .	M.	8 Feet
60. Harmonieflöte .	W.	8 "	66. Musette . . .	M.	4 "

I. Tremolant

SECOND EXPRESSIVE SUBDIVISION

Inclosed in Swell-Box No. 3

67. Salicional . . .	M.	8 Feet
68. Dolcan	M.	8 "
69. Violoncello (Sordo)	M.	8 "
70. Flauto Amabile .	W.	8 "
71. Zartflöte (Whitely)	M.	8 "
72. Salicet	M.	4 "
73. Dolcette . . .	M.	4 Feet
74. Dulciana Cornet	M.	V. Ranks
75. Contrafagotto .	M.	16 Feet
76. Horn (Soft) . .	M.	8 "
77. Corno di Bassetto	M.	8 "
78. Oboe	M.	8 "

II. Tremolant

CHOIR ORGAN

Compass CC to c^4—61 Notes

—THIRD CLAVIER—

FIRST EXPRESSIVE SUBDIVISION

Inclosed in Swell-Box No. 2

79. Dolce	M.	8 Feet
80. Melodia . . .	W.	8 "
81. Viola d'Amore .	M.	8 "
82. Viola d'Amore (Sharp) . . .	M.	8 "
83. Dolcissimo . . .	W.	8 Feet
84. Voix Éolienne . .	M.	8 "
85. Divinare . . .	W.	4 "
86. Contra Clarinetto	M.	16 "
87. Oboe d'Amore . .	M.	8 "

III. Tremolant

SECOND EXPRESSIVE SUBDIVISION

Inclosed in Swell-Box No. 3

88. Bourdon Doux .	W.	16 Feet
89. Flauto Dolce . .	W.	8 "
90. Zartgedeckt . .	M.	8 "
91. Harmonica . .	W.	8 "
92. Voix Angélique .	M.	8 "
93. Æoline	M.	8 Feet
94. Cœlestina . . .	M.	4 "
95. Harmonia Ætheria .	T.	V. Ranks
96. Vox Humana . .	M.	8 Feet

IV. Tremolant

SOLO ORGAN

Compass CC to c^4—61 Notes

——FOURTH CLAVIER——

EXPRESSIVE

Inclosed in Swell-Box No. 4

97. CONTRABASSO . .	W.	16 Feet
98. VIOLONCELLO . .	M.	8 "
99. VIOLINO . . .	M.	8 "
100. FLAUTO TRAVERSO	W.	8 "
101. ZAUBERFLÖTE . .	M.	4 "
102. FLAUTO TRAVERSO	W.	4 "
103. PICCOLO . . .	M.	2 "
104. VIOL CORNET .	M.	V. Ranks
105. CONTRA TROMBONE	M.	16 Feet
106. TROMBONE . .	M.	8 Feet
107. TROMBA REAL .	M.	8 "
108. FAGOTTO . . .	M.	8 "
109. OBOE (Orchestral)	M.	8 "
110. CLARINETTO . .	M.	8 "
111. COR ANGLAIS . .	M.	8 "
112. TROMBA CLARION	M.	4 "
113. CHIMES . Tubular Bells		49 Notes
114. HARP . Wood Bars		61 "

CLAVIER COUPLERS

PEDAL ORGAN COUPLERS

First Clavier. to Pedal Clavier, Unison Coupler.
First Clavier. to Pedal Clavier, Octave Coupler.
Second Clavier. . . . . to Pedal Clavier, Unison Coupler.
Third Clavier. . . . . to Pedal Clavier, Unison Coupler.
Fourth Clavier. . . . . to Pedal Clavier, Unison Coupler.

FIRST CLAVIER COUPLERS

Second Clavier. . 1st Subdivision. . . to First Clavier, Unison Coupler.
Second Clavier. . 1st Subdivision. . . to First Clavier, Octave Coupler.
Second Clavier. . 2nd Subdivision. . . to First Clavier, Unison Coupler.
Second Clavier. . 2nd Subdivision. . . to First Clavier, Octave Coupler.
Third Clavier. . . 1st Subdivision. . . to First Clavier, Unison Coupler.
Third Clavier. . . 2nd Subdivision. . . to First Clavier, Unison Coupler.
Fourth Clavier. . Undivided. . . . . to First Clavier, Unison Coupler.

SECOND CLAVIER COUPLERS

Third Clavier. . 1st Subdivision. . to Second Clavier, Unison Coupler.
Third Clavier. . 1st Subdivision. . to Second Clavier, Octave Coupler.
Third Clavier. . 1st Subdivision. . to Second Clavier, Sub-oct. Coupler.
Third Clavier. . 2nd Subdivision. . to Second Clavier, Unison Coupler.
Third Clavier. . 2nd Subdivision. . to Second Clavier, Octave Coupler.
Third Clavier. . 2nd Subdivision. . to Second Clavier, Sub-oct. Coupler.
Fourth Clavier. Undivided. . . . . . . to Second Clavier, Unison Coupler.

FOURTH CLAVIER COUPLERS

First Clavier. . 1st Subdivision. . to Fourth Clavier, Unison Coupler.
First Clavier. . 2nd Subdivision. . to Fourth Clavier, Unison Coupler.

EXPRESSION LEVER COUPLERS

Couplers connecting Pedal Organ Swell-action with Levers II., III., IV.

EXPRESSION LEVERS

I. Balanced Expression Lever commanding Swell-action of Pedal Organ.
II. Balanced Expression Lever commanding action of Swell-Box No. 1.
III. Balanced Expression Lever commanding action of Swell-Box No. 2.
IV. Balanced Expression Lever commanding action of Swell-Box No. 3.
V. Balanced Expression Lever commanding action of Swell-Box No. 4.
A, B, C, D, E.—Five double-acting Toe-Pistons, disconnecting and connecting the actions of the Pedal Swell-Chamber and of the Swell-Boxes Nos. 1, 2, 3, 4 with the respective Balanced Expression Levers as tabulated.

CRESCENDO LEVER

Balanced Crescendo Lever, situated on the right of the five Expression Levers. commanding a selected series of Stops in progressive order of tonal power and character; operated from the First Clavier.

DIVISIONAL PISTONS

Two Thumb-Pistons—under First Clavier—bringing on and throwing off Expressive Subdivision of Grand Organ.

Two Thumb-Pistons—under Second Clavier—bringing on and throwing off First Subdivision of Accompanimental Organ.

Two Thumb-Pistons—under Second Clavier—bringing on and throwing off Second Subdivision of Accompanimental Organ.

Two Thumb-Pistons—under Third Clavier—bringing on and throwing off First Subdivision of Choir Organ.

Two Thumb-Pistons—under Third Clavier—bringing on and throwing off Second Subdivision of Choir Organ.

ADJUSTABLE COMBINATION PISTONS

Five Operating Thumb-Pistons and Release—under First Clavier—commanding Stop-combinations on Grand Organ, Pedal Organ, and Couplers.

Eight Operating Thumb-Pistons and Release—under Second Clavier—commanding Stop-combinations on Accompanimental Organ, Pedal Organ, and Couplers.

Six Operating Thumb-Pistons and Release—under Third Clavier—commanding Stop-combinations on Choir Organ, Pedal Organ, and Couplers.

Six Operating Thumb-Pistons and Release—under Fourth Clavier—commanding Stop-combinations on Solo Organ, Pedal Organ, and Couplers.

TREMOLANTS

The Four Tremolants are to be commanded directly by the general Draw-Stop-System, by rocking-tablets, pendant touches, or by whatever style of Draw-Stop appliances may be generally adopted for the command of the Stops and Couplers, and are to be immediately associated with them. They are also to be commanded by Thumb-Pistons located under the respective Claviers.

PEDAL ORGAN TOE-PISTONS

ALL DOUBLE-ACTING

1. Piston coupling First Clavier to Pedal Clavier.
2. Piston coupling Second Clavier to Pedal Clavier.
3. Piston coupling Third Clavier to Pedal Clavier.
4. Piston coupling Fourth Clavier to Pedal Clavier.

Other Toe-Pistons may be added for any special purposes deemed desirable by the Organ Architect or Organist in charge.

NOTES ON THE FOURTH SPECIFICATION

The stop appointment set forth in this Specification clearly indicates the tonal differentiation which constitutes the true Church Organ in its peculiar and proper office as an accompanimental instrument in the musical services of a church. Such being the case, it may be desirable for the Organ Architect and interested Organist to compare the stop-apportionments of its several Divisions with those given in the foregoing Specifications for Concert-room Organs. This Specification is for an instrument of the first magnitude; greatly in excess of the tonal appointments of the largest Church Organs commonly constructed. It is given with the view of furnishing a complete exponent of our System of tonal appointment and control, invested with extreme powers of compound tonal flexibility and expression, so far as are necessary in the Church Organ.

It is very seldom that, for one reason or another, architects provide sufficient accommodation for the proper reception of organs in the churches they design; and their very general ignorance regarding the nature and requirements of the instrument has led to the installation of organs of very undesirable character. Organ-builders, anxious for business, cannot do the impossible, although, in their enthusiasm, they frequently essay the task—and fail. Something has to give way, and of necessity science and art has to be sacrificed, to the production of what is commonly musical noise. It is unnecessary to say that an organ designed according to our System demands ample and special accommodation, considerably in excess of that required for the reception of the one-ply, old-fashioned type of instrument, of the same number of stops, in which one expressive Division is considered sufficient; and in which compound tonal flexibility and expression are impossible.

PEDAL ORGAN—It will be observed that out of the twenty-six stops of this Division eighteen are rendered flexible and expressive by being inclosed in a Swell-chamber, the action of which is commanded by a special Expression Lever. In this Expressive Subdivision are the stops whose voices call for powers of flexibility and expression and the GRAND CORNET, V. RANKS—$5\frac{1}{3}'$—$4'$—$3\frac{1}{5}'$—$2\frac{2}{3}'$—$2'$. All the lingual stops are properly inclosed, placing them under control and imparting powers of expression to their commanding voices.

The only labial stops calling for special notice are the DOUBLE DULCIANA, 32 FT., and the COMPENSATING MIXTURE, IV. RANKS. The former is extended to 61 Notes for two purposes. First, that the unison DULCIANA may be derived from it. Secondly, so that it may furnish a valuable and suitable Auxiliary stop to the Grand Organ, imparting to it great impressiveness and grandeur. The COMPENSATING MIXTURE is composed as follows:—

PEDAL ORGAN COMPENSATING MIXTURE—IV. RANKS

CCC to G, SUPER-OCTAVE, 4 FT.	32 Notes
CCC to D, TIERCE, $3\frac{1}{5}$ FT.	27 Notes
CCC to GG, OCTAVE QUINT, $2\frac{2}{3}$ FT.	20 Notes
CCC to EE, TWENTY-SECOND, 2 FT.	17 Notes

All the ranks are to be formed of medium-scaled pipes yielding Pure Organ-tone; and the scales of the ranks are to be relatively smaller as they rise in pitch; and their scale ratio to be such as to place the half diameter on the thirteenth pipe. It is essential that to fulfil its office each rank shall decrease in strength of voice as it ascends the scale. The aim of the stop is that it shall chiefly enrich and impart clearness to the graver tones of the larger stops, and then seem to almost die away as it approaches the higher notes of the Pedal Organ compass. The result is highly satisfactory. The wind-pressures for the labial stops should not exceed 6 inches, and for the inclosed lingual stops they may properly range from 7 to 10 inches. Higher pressures are undesirable in the Church Organ.

GRAND ORGAN—There is no essential difference in the tonal constitution and position of the Grand Division of the Church Organ from that of the true Concert-room instrument, save, in all likelihood, that of size and gravity of tone. In both instruments, when properly stop-apportioned, the Grand Organ is the foundation of the entire superposed tonal structure. This fact has been fully insisted on in the preceding pages and need not be enlarged upon here: but it is desirable to impress upon the Organ Architect and interested Organist the absolute necessity of recognizing the position of the Grand Organ and of providing in it a fundamental stop-apportionment. Without that no organ can be recognized as worthy of consideration. In all cases, the proper proportion of fundamental Pure Organ-tone, common to both the Pedal and Grand Organs, will be commensurate with the size or scope of the entire tonal scheme of the instrument. True proportion of parts in the tonal structure of an organ is as essential as it is in every other perfect work of science and art: in so much as this principle of proportion is departed from will the imperfection of the organ be evident.

The only feature in relation to the tonal resources of the Unexpressive Subdivision is the addition of the Auxiliary DOLCIANO PROFUNDO, 32 FT., of full compass, derived complete from the Pedal Organ. The addition of so grave and refined a voice imparts a singular dignity and grandeur to the foundation tone of this all-important Subdivision. As before alluded to, the idea of deriving an important element in the constitution of the tonal appointment of a manual Division directly from a Pedal Organ stop—properly extended—is a new one; but is deserving of the serious consideration of all concerned in the tonal development of the organ.

It will be observed, in the stop-apportionment of the Expressive Subdivision, that we have adopted a method which is very uncommon; namely, that of introducing a practically complete tonal family. In this instance formed by the GEMSHORN stops of 8, 5⅓, 4, 2⅔, and 2 feet. Thus furnishing a series possessing tones of great brilliancy and beauty; the harmonic value of which will be secured by the proper graduation in the scales and voices of the stops as they rise in pitch. It is very seldom that the GEMSHORN made to-day receives the careful manipulation it calls for at the hands of the pipe-maker and voicer; yet few stops better repay the exercise of skill and care. The CORNET, V. RANKS, is to be composed of small-scaled DIAPASON pipes, carefully graduated in strength of tone in accordance with the law of harmonic over-tones. The FULL MIXTURE, V. RANKS, is to be composed of DOLCE pipes of full scale, and as follows:—

FULL MIXTURE—V. RANKS

CC to BB	15	19	22	26	29.
C to B	12	15	19	22	26.
c^1 to b^1	8	12	15	19	22.
c^2 to b^2	1	8	12	15	19.
c^3 to c^4	1	5	8	12	15.

The desirable wind-pressure for all the labial stops is 3¾ inches and for the three lingual stops 7 inches. An ample wind supply is essential for all the stops.

ACCOMPANIMENTAL ORGAN—In this Division the principal and all-important office of the true Church Organ is properly provided for, in accordance with our System, by an appointment peculiarly adapted, both in stop-apportionment and in full powers of tonal flexibility and compound expression, for the artistic accompaniment of all classes of choral music, from that of a solo voice to that of a full church choir. Although in these directions it is sufficient within its tonal limits, it is so appointed as to be effectively aided in both soft and loud accompaniments by association with the tonal resources of the Choir

Organ in the one direction and the Grand Organ in the other. In correct and artistic organ tonal appointment, although each Division must be complete in itself, for the special offices it has to fulfil in the economy of the instrument, it is equally necessary that a close tonal relationship shall obtain between it and the other Divisions. Independence is necessary to a large degree for utility and variety; union for strength and grandeur. In the present case, the association of the Choir Organ with the Division now under review, would add inexhaustible resources for the effective accompaniment of a choir of the highest class and of any dimension: while, in association with the Grand Organ, it would furnish perfect and inspiring accompaniments to the combined singing of the choir and congregation. These are conditions requiring serious consideration on the part of the Church Organ designer.

The stop-apportionment of this Accompanimental Organ is arranged, in our usual manner, in two equal Subdivisions of contrasting tonalities, inclosed in separate Swell-boxes, Nos. 2 and 3, providing the essential conditions of compound flexibility of tone and expression. In the First Subdivision are arranged labial stops of 16 ft., 8 ft., 4 ft., and 2 ft., yielding Pure and Free Organ-tone and refined Flute-tone: the former by the ECHO DIAPASON, DULCIANA, and the DOLCE CORNET of six through ranks, and the latter by the open and covered FLUTES of 16 ft., 8 ft., and 4 ft. pitch. The only lingual stops being the CLARINETTO and the MUSETTE, both of which are sympathetic in voice with the tones of the labial stops. In the Second Subdivision are similarly arranged stops of Viol-tone, supported by stops of Free Organ-tone including the beautiful DULCIANA CORNET, and four lingual stops of soft and refined Reed- and Brass-tone. The complete appointment of the Accompanimental Organ covering a wide range of musical sound suitable in every way for the effective accompaniment of vocal music.

The wind-pressure for the labial stops of this Organ should not exceed 3 inches, and that for the lingual stops should be 5 inches.

CHOIR ORGAN—This Division is designed to form, with additional powers of tonal flexibility and compound expression, an important extension of the principal office of the true Church Organ—the accompaniment of the choral services of the church; and in this instance the special accompaniment of the music of the highly trained choir. For this purpose the stop-apportionment is of a peculiarly soft and sympathetic tonality.

The eighteen stops comprised in this Organ are arranged in two Subdivisions of equal dimensions, contrasting in their respective voices, and inclosed in the two Swell-boxes which contain the Subdivisions of the Accompanimental Organ. In this direction uniting in their offices the two kindred Organs, and thus facilitating the production of practically inexhaustible effects in accompanimental music of the most subtle and expressive character.

In the apportionment of the First Subdivision there are four metal labial stops of 8 ft., the most assertive of which is the DOLCE, properly voiced to yield a tone slightly fuller than that of the normal DULCIANA, and of a leaning toward a Horn timbre. The first VIOLA D'AMORE to be tuned true, and the second to be tuned a few beats sharp, producing together a beautiful Viole Céleste effect. The VOIX ÉOLIENNE is to be of tin, of a smaller scale than that of the DOLCE, and voiced to yield a Pure Organ-tone of a singing character. Of the three wood stops, the MELODIA will have the most prominent voice, about equal to that of the DOLCE. The DOLCISSIMO is the softest Flute-toned stop made, and is extremely valuable in combination with the softer voiced lingual stops suitable for accompanimental music. The uncommon DIVINARE may be considered the Octave of the DOLCISSIMO. All the labial stops of this Subdivision are to be voiced on wind of 2½ inches, and the two lingual stops on wind of 4 inches. The latter, if artistically and softly voiced, will introduce valuable contrasting tones in this Organ.

The Second Expressive Subdivision—partaking of the same purpose as the First—is stop-apportioned to contrast as markedly as practicable with it, considering the general soft intonation of the Division, which prevents any vivid or powerful contrasts of tone. In this Subdivision the stops are labial, with the exception of the VOX HUMANA, and are of exceptionally refined voices of Free Organ- and unimitative Flute-tone. All these stops, and including the lingual VOX HUMANA, demand the greatest skill of the pipe-maker and voicer; but, in their beautiful voices, richly repay the care and artistry expended on their formation. The only stop calling for description here is the almost unknown, but beautiful, compound harmonic-corroborating HARMONIA ÆTHERIA, which is properly composed of ÆOLINE pipes, of tin, as follows:—

HARMONIA ÆTHERIA—V. RANKS

CC to F♯	15	19	22	26	29.
G to f♯	12	15	19	22	26.
g^1 to f♯	8	12	15	19	22.
g^2 to c^4	1	8	12	15	19.

Although, as in all other harmonic-corroborating stops, the HARMONIA ÆTHERIA is amenable to the natural law in compound-tone production, which requires it to decrease in strength of voice as it rises in pitch, its very soft intonation hardly admits of any sensible diminution, and, accordingly, in this direction, it must be very carefully treated. All the labial stops of this Subdivision are to be voiced on wind of 2 inches, and the VOX HUMANA on wind of 4 inches.

SOLO ORGAN—Although the name given to this Division certainly defines one of its offices in the tonal economy of the complete instrument, it does not convey a sufficient idea of what must be considered its principal office. In the Concert-room instrument the Solo Organ is a tonal Division of great importance for solo passages and effects which are very frequently necessary in music of an orchestral and concert-room class; but such solo effects are, comparatively, of little value in legitimate church organ music; and, accordingly, this Fourth Division is designed primarily with the view of furnishing the other tonal Divisions with adequate means for the effective rendition of voluntaries and incidental music of an ecclesiastical character. Associated with the Grand Division, it will furnish a most efficient Organ for the production of dignified, refined, and expressive music. Coupled to the Grand Organ, the organist will have on the First Clavier one unexpressive Subdivision of thirteen stops, including the most important in the instrument, and two expressive independent groups numbering, together, thirty-one stops; establishing in this instrument, and on its First Clavier, the system we invented and practically introduced in organ-designing in 1870. A system previously unknown.

In the stop-apportionment of this Solo Organ the principle of tonal variety is carefully observed. In it are provided three imitative String-toned stops and one harmonic-corroborating Viol Cornet, of five complete ranks; three stops of Flute-tone; five stops of Reed-tone; and four stops of Brass-tone. None of which are tonally duplicated in the other Organs. With the forty-three effective and distinctly voiced stops, arranged in three tonally contrasting groups, two of which are separately endowed with powers of flexibility and expression, and all playable on the Grand Organ clavier, the musician organist, on careful consideration, cannot fail to realize the possibilities of musical effects of a remarkable and subtle character, which he had never heard, and which were impossible on any Church Organ, known to him, constructed on the time-honored methods of our great-grandfathers. There is no question anent this: we have heard these effects (on a small scale) on the first Organ ever constructed on which they were possible. Only moderate wind pressures are desirable in this Solo Organ if its general utility is to be established, in the manner just alluded to. For all the labial stops a wind of 3¾ inches should not be exceeded. For the lingual stops of Reed-tone, a wind of 6 to 7 inches will be sufficient; while for those of Brass-tone pressures of from 9 to 12 inches can be used, depending largely on the position occupied by the Division in the general lay-out of the Organ.

——*FIFTH SPECIFICATION*——

CHURCH ORGAN

AUDSLEY SYSTEM—COMPOUND EXPRESSION
THREE MANUAL CLAVIERS

PEDAL ORGAN

Compass CCC to G — 32 Notes

PEDAL CLAVIER

UNEXPRESSIVE SUBDIVISION

1. Double Principal (44 pipes)	W. 32 Feet	5. Minor Principal (From 1)	W. 16 Feet
2. Major Principal	M. 16 "	6. Major Octave	M. 8 "
3. Violon-Basse	W. 16 "	7. Compensating Mixture	M. IV. Ranks
4. Dulciana	M. 16 "		

EXPRESSIVE SUBDIVISION

Inclosed in Swell-Chamber

8. Bourdon	W. 16 Feet	13. Super-Octave	M. 4 Feet
9. Lieblichgedeckt	W. 16 "	14. Grand Cornet	M. V. Ranks
10. Grand Viol	M. 8 "	15. Bombarde	M. 16 Feet
11. Grossflöte	W. 8 "	16. Trombone	M. 8 "
12. Gemshorn	M. 8 "	17. Clarion	M. 4 "

GRAND ORGAN

Compass CC to c^4 — 61 Notes

——FIRST CLAVIER——

UNEXPRESSIVE SUBDIVISION

18. Double Diapason	M. 16 Feet	22. Grand Viol	M. 8 Feet
19. Diapason (Schulze)	M. 8 "	23. Tibia Plena	W. 8 "
20. Diapason (English)	M. 8 "	24. Octave Major	M. 4 "
21. Diapason (Wood)	W. 8 "	25. Hohlflöte	W. 4 "

EXPRESSIVE SUBDIVISION

Inclosed in Swell-Box No. 1

26. Bourdon	W. 16 Feet	32. Harmonic Flute	M. 4 Feet
27. Geigenprincipal	M. 8 "	33. Super-Octave	M. 2 "
28. Gemshorn	M. 8 "	34. Cornet	M. V. Ranks
29. Harmonic Flute	M. 8 "	35. Double Trumpet	M. 16 Feet
30. Quint	M. 5⅓ "	36. Trumpet	M. 8 "
31. Octave Minor	M. 4 "	37. Clarion	M. 4 "

ACCOMPANIMENTAL ORGAN

Compass CC to c^4— 61 Notes

——SECOND CLAVIER——

FIRST EXPRESSIVE SUBDIVISION

Inclosed in Swell-Box No. 2

38. Lieblichgedeckt . W. 16 Feet
39. Echo Diapason . M. 8 “
40. Salicional . . . M. 8 “
41. Clarabella . . W. 8 “
42. Dolcan . . . M. 8 “
43. Spitzflöte . . . M. 8 “
44. Lieblichflöte . . M. 4 “
45. Rohrflöte . . . . W. 4 Feet
46. Salicet . . . . . M. 4 “
47. Flageolet . . . M. 2 “
48. Dolce Cornet . M. V. Ranks
49. Clarinetto . . M. 8 Feet
50. Musette . . . M. 4 “

I. Tremolant

SECOND EXPRESSIVE SUBDIVISION

Inclosed in Swell-Box No. 3

51. Cone Gamba . . M. 8 Feet
52. Melodia . . . W. 8 “
53. Dulciana . . . M. 8 “
54. Harmonieflöte . W. 8 “
55. Viola d'Amore . M. 8 “
56. Viola d'Amore (Sharp) . . . M. 8 “
57. Dulcet . . . . M. 4 “
58. Flauto d'Amore . W. 4 Feet
59. Dulciana Fifteenth M. 2 “
60. Dulciana Cornet M. V. Ranks
61. Contrafagotto . M. 16 Feet
62. Oboe . . . . M. 8 “
63. Oboe Ottava . . M. 4 “

II. Tremolant

SOLO ORGAN

Compass CC to c^4— 61 Notes

——THIRD CLAVIER——

FIRST EXPRESSIVE SUBDIVISION

Inclosed in Swell-Box No. 4

64. Contrabasso . . W. 16 Feet
65. Violoncello . . M. 8 “
66. Violino. . . . M. 8 “
67. Harmonica . . W. 8 “
68. Clarabel Flute . W. 4 “
69. Clarinetto . . M. 8 “
70. Cor Anglais . . M. 8 Feet
71. Fagotto . . . M. 8 “
72. Oboe (Orchestral) . M. 8 “
73. Corno di Bassetto M. 8 “
74. Vox Humana . . M. 8 “

III. Tremolant

SECOND EXPRESSIVE SUBDIVISION

Inclosed in Swell-Box No. 5

75. Doppelgedeckt. . W. 16 Feet
76. Tibia Clausa . . W. 8 “
77. Doppelrohrflöte . W. 8 “
78. Flauto Traverso. W. 4 “
79. Piccolo . . . . M. 2 “
80. Trombone . . . M. 8 Feet
81. Horn . . . . M. 8 “
82. Tromba Real . . M. 8 “
83. Tromba Clarion . M. 4 “
84. Chimes . . . (Tubular Bells)

CLAVIER COUPLERS

PEDAL ORGAN COUPLERS

First Clavier . . . . to Pedal Clavier, Unison Coupler.
First Clavier . . . . to Pedal Clavier, Octave Coupler.
Second Clavier. . . . to Pedal Clavier, Unison Coupler.
Third Clavier . . . . to Pedal Clavier, Unison Coupler.

FIRST CLAVIER COUPLERS

Second Clavier . 1st Subdivision . to First Clavier, Unison Coupler.
Second Clavier . 2nd Subdivision . to First Clavier, Unison Coupler.
Third Clavier . 1st Subdivision . to First Clavier, Unison Coupler.
Third Clavier . 2nd Subdivision . to First Clavier, Unison Coupler.
Third Clavier . 2nd Subdivision . to First Clavier, Octave Coupler.

SECOND CLAVIER COUPLERS

Third Clavier . 1st Subdivision . to Second Clavier, Unison Coupler.
Third Clavier . 1st Subdivision . to Second Clavier, Octave Coupler.

THIRD CLAVIER COUPLERS

First Clavier . 2nd Subdivision . to Third Clavier, Unison Coupler.

EXPRESSION LEVER COUPLERS

Couplers connecting Pedal Organ Swell-action with Expression Levers II., III., IV., V., VI.

EXPRESSION LEVERS

I. Balanced Expression Lever commanding Swell-action of Pedal Organ.
II. Balanced Expression Lever commanding action of Swell-Box No. 1.
III. Balanced Expression Lever commanding action of Swell-Box No. 2.
IV. Balanced Expression Lever commanding action of Swell-Box No. 3.
V. Balanced Expression Lever commanding action of Swell-Box No. 4.
VI. Balanced Expression Lever commanding action of Swell-Box No. 5.

CRESCENDO LEVER

Balanced Crescendo Lever, situated to the right of the six Expression Levers, commanding a selected series of Stops in progressive order of tonal power and character; operated from the First Clavier.

DIVISIONAL PISTONS

Two Thumb-Pistons—under First Clavier—bringing on and throwing off Expressive Subdivision of Grand Organ.

Two Thumb-Pistons—under Second Clavier—bringing on and throwing off First Subdivision of Accompanimental Organ.

Two Thumb-Pistons—under Second Clavier—bringing on and throwing off Second Subdivision of Accompanimental Organ.

Two Thumb-Pistons—under Third Clavier—bringing on and throwing off First Subdivision of Solo Organ.

Two Thumb-Pistons—under Third Clavier—bringing on and throwing off Second Subdivision of Solo Organ.

ADJUSTABLE COMBINATION PISTONS

Five Operating Thumb-Pistons and Release—under First Clavier—commanding Stop-combinations on Grand Organ, Pedal Organ, and Couplers.

Six Operating Thumb-Pistons and Release—under Second Clavier—commanding Stop-combinations on Accompanimental Organ, Pedal Organ, and Couplers.

Six Operating Thumb-Pistons and Release—under Third Clavier—commanding Stop-combinations on Solo Organ, Pedal Organ, and Couplers.

TREMOLANTS

The Three Tremolants are to be commanded in the manner described in the preceding Fourth Specification. Or in any manner the designer of the Console may consider most convenient to the performer.

PEDAL ORGAN TOE-PISTONS

ALL DOUBLE-ACTING

1. Piston coupling First Clavier to Pedal Clavier—Unison.
2. Piston coupling First Clavier to Pedal Clavier—Octave.
3. Piston coupling Second Clavier to Pedal Clavier—Unison.
4. Piston coupling Third Clavier to Pedal Clavier—Unison.

Other Toe-Pistons may be added for any special purposes considered necessary or desirable by the Organ Architect or the designer of the instrument.

NOTES ON THE FIFTH SPECIFICATION

Although this Specification is for an Organ considerably less in size than that set forth in the preceding Fourth Specification, it is still for a true Church instrument of the first magnitude, not only in the number and character of its stops; but, what is of equal importance, in the practically unlimited resources it furnishes the musician organist for the artistic and beautiful accompanimental music—at once the great office and the glory of the true Church Organ—under our System of compound tonal flexibility and expression, combined with the great convenience and advantage of being perfectly commanded and controlled by only three manual claviers. Every feature of the tonal scheme has been dictated with the primal aim and purpose of producing a perfect Church Organ, capable of meeting every possible call that could be made upon its tonal resources in the rendition of the highest class of ecclesiastical music, accompanimental and incidental.

In our System of Differentiation, we desire no confusion to obtain between the Concert-room, or what may be considered the Recital instrument, and the Church or Accompanimental Organ. They are properly distinct in their tonal appointments, just as they certainly are in their purposes and requirements. Quasi Recital and deficient Accompanimental instruments have been placed in many churches, under the advocacy of interested organ-builders and ambitious organists: but as efficient instruments they are more or less artistic failures, for much had to be sacrificed in both directions tonally.

In the present Specification the less number of speaking stops than are provided in the preceding Specification, may be considered as compensated by the additional resources provided for tonal flexibility and expression. In the Fourth Specification four Swell-boxes are given to the manual Organs on the four claviers, while in the present scheme five Swell-boxes are given to the Organs commanded by the three claviers. Let an accomplished musician organist play, in imagination (as we have studiously done in preparing the schemes), the respective Organs as specified, and judge of their relative musical values; bearing in mind that they represent true Church Organs of which no counterparts exist at the present time (1925).

Should it be found necessary or deemed desirable, owing to want of sufficient accommodation or any other reason, to reduce the number of the Swell-boxes, and yet find it possible to admit of the necessary increase in the depth of the boxes Nos. 2 and 3, then the Subdivisions of the Solo Organ can be placed in addition to the Subdivisions of the Accompanimental Organ in the Swell-boxes Nos. 2 and 3; in the manner adopted in the following Sixth Specification.

PEDAL ORGAN—In accordance with our complete System, which requires that powers of tonal flexibility and expression shall be given to every Division of the Organ, ten of the seventeen stops which are apportioned to this Pedal Division are inclosed in a Swell-chamber, the action of which is commanded by a special, balanced, Expression Lever. This will be used chiefly to graduate the tones of the inclosed stops; and, so as to be as distinct as possible from the Expression Levers of the manual Divisions, it is located on the extreme left of the series. This position will also be most convenient when the Subdivision is being used expressively; for the larger and higher portion of the Pedal Organ will be most used and most conveniently played by the right foot of the performer.

In this Expressive Subdivision are the unison, octave, and harmonic-corroborating labial stops required for combination, in different strengths of tone, with the exposed foundation stops; and also the three powerful lingual stops which demand powers of expression to make them valuable and available at all times. The only stops requiring special description here is the GRAND CORNET, V. RANKS, which may appropriately be made of small-scaled DIAPASON pipes of the following pitches, in complete ranks—5⅓′—4′—3⅕′—2⅔′—2′.

In the Unexpressive Subdivision a firm foundation of Pure Organ-tone—double, unison, and octave—is furnished, enriched by the harmonic-charged voice of the VIOLON-BASSE, and the COMPENSATING MIXTURE, IV. RANKS, composed as described in the Notes on the preceding Specification, in which its tonal functions are clearly explained. The wind-pressures for the labial stops should not exceed 5 inches, and for the three inclosed lingual stops they may properly range from 8 to 10 inches, according to the favorable or unfavorable situation of the Swell-chamber. If the situation is necessarily bad a higher pressure may be found desirable.

GRAND ORGAN—The position and office of the Grand Organ are similar in all respects in the general scheme of every properly appointed instrument. It is, as has been fully explained in the preceding pages, in association with the Pedal Division, the foundation of the tonal structure of the entire Organ. This position is fully established in the stop-apportionments of the Unexpressive and Expressive Subdivisions of the Grand Organ now under consideration.

In the Unexpressive Subdivision, Pure Organ-tone is fully provided by the DOUBLE DIAPASON, 16 FT. and the three unison DIAPASONS of different tonal values, the chief of which is that on the Schulze model, voiced on a copious supply of wind, and yielding a voice of extreme grandeur and beauty. That on the English model yielding a less powerful tone, but one of a singing and refined accompanimental character. The DIAPASON of wood, also on the Schulze model, is, if properly made, a valuable tone-builder, devoid of any tendency toward loss of effect through sympathy. It should be carried up in wood for at least three and a half octaves, thence completed in carefully matched metal pipes. Full particulars and an illustration of this stop are given in "Organ-Stops and Their Artistic Registration," pp. 93-4. The desirable harmonics, in relation to the foundation Pure Organ-tone, are furnished by the GRAND VIOL, on the one hand, and by the TIBIA PLENA, on the other; the important first harmonic of the unison tone being corroborated by the OCTAVE MAJOR and the HOHLFLÖTE.

In the stop-apportionment of the Expressive Subdivision the accompanimental office of the true Church Organ has been recognized so far as is necessary in this fundamental Division. At the same time it properly completes the tonal structure of the entire Division. The CORNET is to be formed in the manner described for the corresponding stop in the preceding Specification.

The desirable wind-pressure for all the labial stops, exposed and inclosed, is 3¾ inches, and for the lingual stops, if properly voiced, a wind-pressure of 7 inches will, generally, be found sufficient. Ample shutter space must be provided in the Swell-box of this Organ, the action of which will be controlled by Expression Lever No. 2.

ACCOMPANIMENTAL ORGAN—Recognizing the office of this Division in the true Church Organ, it may justly be considered the most important one in the tonal economy of the entire instrument; calling, in its constitution, for a full and specially varied and refined stop-apportionment, calculated to meet every legitimate call that can be made upon it in the artistic and sympathetic accompaniment of vocal song as it obtains in public worship. Every possible refinement of tone and the fullest command of expression should always be aimed at by the Organ Architect in the design of this chief accompanimental Division in the Church Organ. Although such should be the case in a properly appointed instrument, it must not be considered that this Division is an independent one: on the contrary, it is an integral part of a full and properly appointed tonal scheme, in which, while apparently independent, all the Divisions and Subdivisions are consistent and component parts; building up a Temple of Tone, just as all the many component structural and ornamental parts, in marble, metal, and wood, go to the building of an Architectural Temple.

The stop-apportionment of this Accompanimental Organ is, in accordance with our System, arranged in two equal Subdivisions of contrasting tonalities, thus securing the maximum value of flexibility of tone in both directions, and establishing the principle of compound expression invaluable in this Division. In the First Expressive Subdivision, inclosed in Swell-box No. 2, are arranged stops of medium strength of voice, yielding Pure and Free Organ-tone; open, half-covered, and covered Flute-tone; and refined Reed-tone; which, if artistically voiced and regulated, will furnish tonal colors suitable for combinations of great value in accompanimental music. Harmonic-corroboration is taken care of in the five-rank Dolce Cornet. In the Second Expressive Subdivision, inclosed in Swell-box No. 3, a similar disposition obtains; the stops here yielding soft Free Organ-tone; Viol-tone of a direct and Céleste character; refined open and half-covered Flute-tone; and double, unison, and octave Reed-tone. All of which will combine in compound flexibility and expression with the stops of the First Subdivision, producing tonal combinations of great beauty and variety, and all suitable for accompaniment.

The wind-pressure for all the labial stops in both the Subdivisions should not exceed 3 inches; and that for the five Reed-toned lingual stops should be 6 inches. The Swell-boxes must be carefully adapted to the soft intonation of the Subdivisions.

SOLO ORGAN—As in the case of the preceding Specification, the name given to this third Division defines what in the present tonal scheme may be considered its principal office; namely, that of providing effective solo voices, or those required for tonal combinations of a more or less assertive or commanding character. But it must not be considered that its office is thus limited. On the contrary; it has been schemed as an important adjunct to the Accompanimental Organ; introducing elements calculated to greatly increase the resources of tonal coloration and powers of flexibility of tone and compound expression. For example: couple either of the Subdivisions of the Solo to the clavier of the Accompanimental Organ, and immediately the performer will find at his command, on that single clavier, three independent contrasting and expressive tonal groups, under easy control by contiguous Expression Levers, which can be operated singly or in adjoining couples by a single foot. Under this arrangement, the performer will have for registration thirty-six suitable and differently voiced stops, under triple expression. If the complete Solo is similarly coupled, the performer will have at his command, on the Second Clavier, forty-five stops of different tones, under quadruple expression. At this point, let the experienced organist pause, and try to realize what he could do on this single clavier, under the conditions set forth, in accompanimental and incidental music. We venture to think he will soon find himself lost in a maze of imagination, entirely new in his experience.

If the Solo is coupled to the Grand Organ, the performer will have, on the First Clavier, one unexpressive Subdivision of eight stops, including the four principal manual foundation stops in the instrument; and three independent expressive Subdivisions, contributing, together, thirty-three stops of different tonalities, specially rich in Reed-tone and Brass-tone, fully balanced by the volume of Pure Organ-tone furnished by the Diapasons and the rich body of Flute-tone in the three expressive Subdivisions. Under this arrangement, the Accompanimental Organ is left perfectly free to perform its special office.

In the First Expressive Subdivision, inclosed in Swell-box No. 4, Viol-tone of double and unison pitch, is prominently represented by three stops, which may properly be imitative in tone of the orchestral instruments whose names they bear. Apart from their direct value as solo stops, they will be valuable in combination, largely on account of the high harmonic over-tones their voices contribute. But the most important and highly-colored compound tones are furnished by the fine series of lingual stops of imitative Reed-tone, attended by the two stops of soft Flute-tone, which impart singular beauty and fullness to their voices. The remaining stop—the Vox Humana, 8 ft.—of Indeterminate-tone, has essentially a solo voice, to which the Harmonica, 8 ft. will add the vocal quality invariably deficient in the lingual stop as usually made and voiced. This stop requires the Tremolant. When made with long, covered, and slotted resonators, and used without the Tremolant, it is a beautiful and valuable stop in combination with labial stops of all tonalities, as we have practically demonstrated. Two wind-pressures are necessary in this Subdivision: that for the five labial stops to be 3½ inches, and for the lingual stops 6 inches; providing this Subdivision occupies a favorable position in the general lay-out of the instrument.

The Second Subdivision, inclosed in Swell-box No. 5, has two groups of stops of sharply contrasting tonalities; purposely associated on account of their combinational value in the production of rich and beautiful compound tones.

One group of five stops, is entirely of Flute-tone in four different pitches. The other group is formed of lingual stops exclusively of Brass-tone. This Subdivision is, accordingly, the most assertive in the tonal scheme of the instrument: and although on this account it will be comparatively seldom used in the accompaniment of a choir, it will be of great value in that of congregational singing; and especially in the artistic rendition of incidental music. Two wind-pressures are required in this Subdivision: that for the five labial stops to be 5 inches, and for the four lingual stops 10 inches. On the ample provision made to give the performer complete control of the tonal resources of the entire instrument, it is unnecessary to comment, for all the appliances and accessories are carefully tabulated and classified. It will be observed that Octave Couplers operating on the same clavier have been omitted as undesirable and unnecessary. This common coupler—beloved of many organists—is essentially a noise-maker; condemned by the acoustical laws which govern the creation of properly balanced compound musical sounds.

—SIXTH SPECIFICATION—

CHURCH ORGAN

AUDSLEY SYSTEM—COMPOUND EXPRESSION
THREE MANUAL CLAVIERS

PEDAL ORGAN

Compass CCC to G—32 Notes

—PEDAL CLAVIER—

1. Double Principal (44 pipes) . . .	W. 32 Feet	6. Dulciana . . .	M. 16 Feet
2. Major Principal .	M. 16 "	7. Major Octave .	M. 8 "
3. Minor Principal . (From 1) . . .	W. 16 "	8. Grossflöte . . .	W. 8 "
4. Violon Basse . .	M. 16 "	9. Compensating Mixture. . .	III. Ranks
5. Bourdon . . .	W. 16 "	10. Bombarde . . .	M. 16 Feet
		11. Trombone . . .	M. 8 "

AUXILIARY PEDAL ORGAN

EXPRESSIVE

12. Double Trumpet (Derived from No. 28) . . . 16 Feet
13. Lieblichgedeckt (Derived from No. 31) . . . . 16 "
14. Contrafagotto (Derived from No. 47) . . . . 16 "

GRAND ORGAN

Compass CC to c^4— 61 Notes

——FIRST CLAVIER——

UNEXPRESSIVE SUBDIVISION

15. Double Diapason .	M.	16 Feet	18. Grand Viol . .	M.	8 Feet
16. Diapason (Schulze)	M.	8 "	19. Tibia Plena . .	W.	8 "
17. Diapason (English)	M.	8 "	20. Octave Major .	M.	4 "

EXPRESSIVE SUBDIVISION

Inclosed in Swell-Box No. 1

21. Bourdon . . .	W.	16 Feet	26. Octave Minor .	M.	4 Feet
22. Geigenprincipal .	M.	8 "	27. Cornet . . .	M.	V. Ranks
23. Doppelflöte . .	W.	8 "	28. Double Trumpet .	M.	16 Feet
24. Gemshorn . . .	M.	8 "	29. Trumpet . . .	M.	8 "
25. Quint	M.	$5\frac{1}{3}$ "	30. Clarion . . .	M.	4 "

ACCOMPANIMENTAL ORGAN

Compass CC to c^4— 61 Notes

——SECOND CLAVIER——

FIRST EXPRESSIVE SUBDIVISION

Inclosed in Swell-Box No. 2

31. Lieblichgedeckt .	W.	16 Feet	36. Flageolet . . .	M.	2 Feet
32. Dulciana . . .	M.	8 "	37. Dulciana Cornet	M.	V. Ranks
33. Spitzflöte . . .	M.	8 "	38. Clarinetto . .	M.	8 Feet
34. Lieblichgedeckt .	W.	8 "	39. Oboe	M.	8 "
35. Lieblichflöte . .	M.	4 "	I. Tremolant		

SECOND EXPRESSIVE SUBDIVISION

Inclosed in Swell-Box No. 3

40. Echo Diapason .	M.	8 Feet	45. Salicet	M.	4 Feet
41. Salicional . . .	M.	8 "	46. Dolce Cornet .	M.	V. Ranks
42. Viola da Gamba .	M.	8 "	47. Contrafagotto .	M.	16 Feet
43. Harmonica . .	W.	8 "	48. Cor Anglais . .	M.	8 "
44. Viola d'Amore .	M.	8 "	II. Tremolant		

SOLO ORGAN

Compass CC to c⁴— 61 Notes

—THIRD CLAVIER—

FIRST EXPRESSIVE SUBDIVISION

Inclosed in Swell-Box No. 2

49. CONTRABASSO . .	W. 16 Feet	52. CLARABELLA . .	W. 8 Feet
50. VIOLONCELLO . .	M. 8 "	53. SPITZFLÖTE . . .	M. 4 "
51. VIOLINO. . . .	M. 8 "	54. VIOLETTA . . .	M. 4 "

SECOND EXPRESSIVE SUBDIVISION

Inclosed in Swell-Box No. 3

55. DOPPELGEDECKT. .	W. 16 Feet	58. TROMBA REAL . .	M. 8 Feet
56. HARMONIC FLUTE .	M. 8 "	59. HORN	M. 8 "
57. DOLCE	M. 8 "	60. VOX HUMANA . .	M. 8 "

III. TREMOLANT

CLAVIER COUPLERS

PEDAL ORGAN COUPLERS

First Clavier . . . . to Pedal Clavier, Unison Coupler.
First Clavier . . . . to Pedal Clavier, Octave Coupler.
Second Clavier. . . . to Pedal Clavier, Unison Coupler.
Third Clavier . . . . to Pedal Clavier, Unison Coupler.

FIRST CLAVIER COUPLERS

Second Clavier . 1st Subdivision . to First Clavier, Unison Coupler.
Second Clavier . 2nd Subdivision . to First Clavier, Unison Coupler.
Third Clavier . 1st Subdivision . to First Clavier, Unison Coupler.
Third Clavier . 2nd Subdivision . to First Clavier, Unison Coupler.
Third Clavier . 2nd Subdivision . to First Clavier, Octave Coupler.

SECOND CLAVIER COUPLERS

Third Clavier . 1st Subdivision . to Second Clavier, Unison Coupler.
Third Clavier . 1st Subdivision . to Second Clavier, Octave Coupler.

EXPRESSION LEVERS

I. Balanced Expression Lever commanding action of Swell-Box No. 1.
II. Balanced Expression Lever commanding action of Swell-Box No. 2.
III. Balanced Expression Lever commanding action of Swell-Box No. 3.

CRESCENDO LEVER

Balanced Crescendo Lever, situated to the right of the three Expression Levers, commanding a selected series of Stops in progressive order of tonal power and character, effective on the First Clavier.

DIVISIONAL PISTONS

Two Thumb Pistons—under First Clavier—bringing on and throwing off Expressive Subdivision of Grand Organ.

Two Thumb-Pistons—under Second Clavier—bringing on and throwing off First Subdivision of Accompanimental Organ.

Two Thumb-Pistons—under Second Clavier—bringing on and throwing off Second Subdivision of Accompanimental Organ.

Two Thumb-Pistons—under Third Clavier—bringing on and throwing off First Subdivision of Solo Organ.

Two Thumb-Pistons—under Third Clavier—bringing on and throwing off Second Subdivision of Solo Organ.

ADJUSTABLE COMBINATION ACTION

Five Operating Thumb-Pistons and Release—under First Clavier—commanding Stop-combinations on Grand Organ, Pedal Organ, and Couplers.

Five Operating Thumb-Pistons and Release—under Second Clavier—commanding Stop-combinations on Accompanimental Organ, Pedal Organ, and Couplers.

Five Operating Thumb-Pistons and Release—under Third Clavier—commanding Stop-combinations on Solo Organ, Pedal Organ, and Couplers.

TREMOLANTS

The Three Tremolants are to be commanded in the manner described in the Fourth Specification. Or in any manner the designer of the Console may consider most convenient to the performer.

PEDAL ORGAN TOE-PISTONS

ALL DOUBLE-ACTING

1. Piston coupling First Clavier to Pedal Clavier—Unison.
2. Piston coupling First Clavier to Pedal Clavier—Octave.
3. Piston coupling Second Clavier to Pedal Clavier—Unison.
4. Piston coupling Third Clavier to Pedal Clavier—Unison.
5. Piston bringing Double Trumpet, 16 ft. (No. 28) on Pedal Clavier.
6. Piston bringing Lieblichgedeckt, 16 ft. (No. 31) on Pedal Clavier.
7. Piston bringing Contrafagotto, 16 ft. (No. 47) on Pedal Clavier.

Other Toe-Pistons may be added for any special purposes considered necessary or desirable by the Organ Architect or the designer of the instrument.

NOTES ON THE SIXTH SPECIFICATION

This Specification is for an instrument of fifty-six complete speaking stops and four derived stops; which latter are properly confined to the Pedal Organ appointment. Of these three are derived from separate manual Divisions, and constitute a Pedal Organ Expressive Auxiliary, which to no appreciable extent interferes with the tonal independence of the manual appointments. This Expressive Auxiliary has been introduced for the purpose of enriching a necessarily small Pedal Organ in which there is no Expressive Subdivision.

It is very seldom that adequate provision has been made in the planning of churches for the installation of sufficient and properly appointed Organs; and, accordingly, in almost every instance, the Pedal Division, owing to the large size of its pipe-work, is necessarily the one to suffer serious curtailment—too often under the wrong idea that it is, comparatively, of little importance. A widely different opinion was held by the good old German masters, who did not consider one-third or one-fourth of the entire stop appointment of an Organ too much for its Pedal Division. The "Degradation of the Pedal Organ" was not known in their day.

In the present Specification only three independent Swell-boxes are provided, which is the smallest number allowed in our System for an instrument having three manual claviers. This appointment requires that a tonal Subdivision from both the Accompanimental and Solo Organs shall occupy each of two Swell-boxes, as set forth in the Specification, and numbered 2 and 3. The remaining box containing the Subdivision of the Grand Organ, requiring flexibility of tone and expression. Just a passing word on the Swell. It is remarkable that, after centuries of development in almost all directions, the short-sighted belief that a single Swell-box was sufficient for any organ, however large, remained so long in the organ-building world. The fact remains established that it was not until after the year 1855 that any essay was made to introduce more than one Swell-box in an organ and so increase its powers of expression. The first essay was a very timid one, so far as we have been able to ascertain. In the Organ installed in the concert-room of the Town Hall of Leeds, Yorkshire, in the year 1858. In this important instrument a small Solo Organ of nine stops, inclosed in a special Swell-box, was added to the Swell Organ proper. Nothing further was done until we took the matter up, and, in 1872, very practically demonstrated to a don't-care organ-building world the advantage and the necessity, on artistic grounds, of almost all the tonal forces of an organ being rendered flexible, in strength of intonation, and expressive. All the Specifications in this Treatise show to what extent our early contention has led us in organ-designing.

As a corollary to what has just been stated, a few remarks regarding our System of contrasting subdivision of the several Organs commanded by the pedal and manual claviers, may not be uninteresting to the organist who has not fully considered the subject. On first thoughts, it may seem of little importance, and likely to lead to confusion. Nothing, however, is further from established fact. The importance is very great and far-reaching; and absolute simplicity pervades the entire System of contrasting tonal flexibility and expression, simple and compound. The System opens up a new world of possible tonal effects and musical artistry, impossible of production on any organ hitherto constructed and appointed on old lines. Just a few facts may be stated here.

In the Specification of the comparatively small Organ now under consideration there are five distinct and contrasting tonal Subdivisions; each of which, under the control of an Expression Lever, can be made to yield at least ten distinctly marked different and stationary strengths of tone to any of the voices speaking. This simple fact multiplies, for artistic purposes, the tonal resources of each Subdivision tenfold, without trenching upon the equally valuable and additional powers of tonal expression. Without considering the operations of the Subdivisions on each uncoupled clavier, let one try to realize what the performer has at his command on the First Clavier with the other two coupled to it, say in the unison only. He has directly under his command and tonal control by means of three easily operated Expression Levers, six distinct Subdivisions of contrasting tonalities. What can the performer do with these? By means of the Thumb-Pistons operating on the Subdivisions only, he can bring under his hands, confined to the First Clavier, no fewer than six single and separate Subdivisions and fifty-seven different groups of Subdivisions, producing sixty-three distinct tonal combinations without changing the stops originally drawn. Further, he can use all these combinations in stationary tones of different strengths; partly stationary in tone and partly expressive; or entirely expressive, excepting the unexpressive Subdivision of the Grand Organ. On what organ constructed on the old-fashioned and still popular one-ply style of tonal appointment, could resources such as have just been outlined be placed at the command of the musician organist and organ *virtuoso?* Yet they are tonal resources in one direction only, and which by no means exhaust those provided in our fully developed System; which, collectively, revolutionize the tonal structure of the organ and its special means for artistic control, which are so radical and constructive as to suggest the formation of a new and advanced school of composition of music for The Temple of Tone. This is no exaggeration, as time will show.

PEDAL ORGAN—In this Specification a stop-apportionment is provided that does not imperatively call for subdivision; but to which, as already commented on, an Auxiliary of three expressive stops is added, imparting valuable and rich tonal coloring to the foundation bass voices. Organ-tone, Flute-tone, Viol-tone, Reed-tone, and Brass-tone are represented in the general appointment. The only stop requiring description is the harmonic-corroborating and brightening compound COMPENSATING MIXTURE, composed of small-scaled DIAPASON pipes, as follows:—

PEDAL ORGAN COMPENSATING MIXTURE—III. RANKS

CCC to G, SUPER-OCTAVE, 4 FT.	. . . . . .	32 Notes.
CCC to D, NINETEENTH, 2⅔ FT.	. . . . . .	27 "
CCC to G, TWENTY-SECOND, 2 FT.	. . . . . .	20 "

The great acoustical properties and value of this compound stop has, notwithstanding our long advocacy and practical demonstration of its great tonal importance, not received the attention it deserves. Perhaps this is not to be wondered at when one observes the very general apathy in organ-building quarters regarding scientific compound-tone production. The stop was first introduced, as might be expected, in Germany; but in a primitive and insufficient form. Our studies in Acoustics led us to understand its tonal importance and the necessity of its being fully developed. It was introduced for the first time, outside Germany, in the Organ we designed, and which was installed in the Festival Hall of the Louisiana Purchase Exposition in 1904. It was in its full development of six graduated ranks of pipes. It was introduced, for the second time, but of three ranks, in the Organ we designed for the Church of Our Lady of Grace, Hoboken, New Jersey.[18]

The wind-pressures for the labial stops should not exceed 6 inches, and for the BOMBARDE and TROMBONE 8 inches will be sufficient to secure rich and refined tones, if medium scales are used and their voicing is artistically executed. It is to be regretted that much too high pressures are in general favor in voicing rooms to-day; due to the impression that loudness and assertiveness are more to be desired than refinement and repose in the organ-tones. This impression evidently obtains in the more vulgar schools of organ-building.

GRAND ORGAN—It is unnecessary to comment, at any length, on the general tonal appointment or stop-apportionment of this Organ, for it differs in no essential from the Grand Organ, except in dimensions, as set forth in the preceding Specification. Fundamental Pure Organ-tone is provided in the Unexpressive Subdivision; and in the Expressive Subdivision sufficient harmonic-corroborating voices are provided by the QUINT, OCTAVE, and CORNET, comprising seven complete ranks of pipes. The other labial stops, in both Subdivisions, are selected, of different pronounced tonalities, to effectively color the normal Pure Organ-tone of the foundation stops. The three lingual stops of different pitches, yield tones of a brilliant unimitative character, perfectly suitable to enrich without impairing the importance and value of the foundation tone. The desirable wind-pressure for all the labial stops, exposed and inclosed, is 3¾ inches; and for the lingual stops, if properly voiced, a wind-pressure of 7 inches will, generally, be found suitable.

ACCOMPANIMENTAL ORGAN—For a brief dissertation on the constitution and office of this Division of the true Church Organ we may refer the interested reader to the Notes on the preceding Fifth Specification; in

[18] Full particulars regarding the COMPENSATING MIXTURE are given in "The Organ of the Twentieth Century, pp. 72-4.

which we say all that is necessary to show its all-important position in the tonal structure of the complete instrument. Accordingly, it is only necessary to make a few remarks here regarding the stop-apportionment of the smaller Division set forth in this Specification. A glance at the entire stop-apportionment will show the musician that it is sufficient, sympathetic, and refined in its several tonalities; and in every way suitable for the artistic accompaniment of a highly-trained choir; eminently so, on account of its complete powers of compound tonal flexibility and expression, which no organ of ordinary construction possesses. This Division is commanded by the Second Clavier, which is the most convenient one for it in all properly appointed Church Organs.

That refined Flute-tones, and especially those produced by stops of the LIEBLICHGEDECKT family, are highly suitable for the accompaniment of choral music is readily acknowledged; and next to these are the tones of softly-voiced DIAPASONS and the stops yielding Free Organ-tones. To prevent monotony and to impart firmness and harmonic richness, the contrasting voices of the more refined VIOL stops are required for combination; and to these must be added the more refined and sympathetic compound harmonic-corroborating stops. All these desirable stops are present in the appointment of this Division, and to them are added four stops of Reed-tone of medium power. In accordance with our System, the stop-apportionment is disposed in two groups, contrasting in general tonality to as marked an extent as possible without destroying the desirable balance; and are inclosed in separate Swell-boxes—Nos. 2 and 3—thereby establishing compound flexibility of tone and expression.

The wind-pressure for all the labial stops in both the Subdivisions should not exceed 3 inches; and that for the four lingual, Reed-toned stops should not exceed 5 inches.

SOLO ORGAN—The opening remarks regarding the Solo Organ made in the Notes appended to the preceding Fifth Specification are applicable, in every sense, to the Division now under consideration; so repetition of what is there stated is unnecessary, as the reader, interested in the subject, has only to turn back a few pages and consult what we state in the Note on the Solo Organ. It is desirable, however, to point out that there is a considerable difference in the size of the stop-apportionments of the two Solo Organs; that in the Fifth Specification having twenty-one, while that in this Sixth Specification has only twelve stops. There is another difference that may be alluded to; namely, that the Subdivisions of the Solo Organ in the former Specification are inclosed in special Swell-boxes, Nos. 4 and 5; while the Subdivisions in the Organ now under consideration are inclosed in the Swell-boxes Nos. 2 and 3, which also contain the Subdivisions of the Accompanimental Organ. Of necessity these different dispositions affect to some extent the powers of compound flexibility and expression in the different Organs; but the disposition adopted in the present lesser instrument affords ample powers in both directions. The twelve stops of the present Solo Organ are divided into equal groups of pronounced contrasting tonalities; and are inclosed in Swell-boxes Nos. 2 and 3, in which they associate with the Subdivisions of the Accompanimental Organ, and with which they contrast in tone, as required by our System. This simpler arrangement, which dispenses with two Swell-boxes, is to be recommended for Church Organs of moderate size, and which will, in all probability, have to be adopted in a large majority of cases, on account of the insufficient accommodation provided by Architects in churches designed without a sufficient knowledge of the nature and requirements of the organ.

It may be pointed out that the inclosure of the Subdivisions of the Solo Organ in the Swell-boxes which contain the Subdivisions of the Accompanimental Organ does not in any direct way interfere with the independence of the four tonal groups which the boxes contain. When the two Organs are uncoupled and played on their special claviers, their Subdivisions are tonally commanded, separately, and in a perfectly distinct manner, by the two Expression Levers connected with the actions of the Swell-boxes. This important fact has been proved by actual demonstration.

Two wind-pressures are necessary in this Solo Organ. For the six labial stops in the First Subdivision, and the three in the Second Subdivision, a pressure of 3½ inches will be sufficient if the stops are artistically voiced: and for the three lingual stops in the Second Subdivision a pressure of 6 inches will be sufficient. In the case of the Vox Humana a lower pressure may be found desirable. If the stop is of proper formation and artistically voiced a pressure of 3½ inches will be desirable. The most beautiful Vox Humana we have ever heard sang on wind of only 2⅜ inches. A full equipment of all the appliances and accessories necessary to give the performer perfect control of the entire instrument is given and classified so as to prevent misunderstanding and confusion.

—SEVENTH SPECIFICATION—

CHURCH ORGAN

AUDSLEY SYSTEM—COMPOUND EXPRESSION
THREE MANUAL CLAVIERS

PEDAL ORGAN

Compass CCC to G—32 Notes

PEDAL CLAVIER

1. Principal (44 pipes)	W. 16 Feet	5. Violoncello (From 2)	W. 8 Feet
2. Contrabasso (44 pipes) . . .	W. 16 "	6. Dolce (From 3) . .	M. 8 "
3. Dulciana (44 pipes)	M. 16 "	7. Trombone (44 pipes)	M. 16 "
4. Octave (From 1) .	W. 8 "	8. Trombone (From 7)	M. 8 "

AUXILIARY PEDAL ORGAN

EXPRESSIVE

9. Double Diapason, 16 ft. (Derived from No. 12).
10. Lieblichgedeckt, 16 ft. (Derived from No. 22).
11. Contrafagotto, 16 ft. (Derived from No. 42).

GRAND ORGAN

Compass CC to c^4— 61 Notes

—FIRST CLAVIER—

UNEXPRESSIVE SUBDIVISION

12. Double Diapason .	M. 16 Feet	14. Diapason (English)	M. 8 Feet
13. Diapason (Shulze) .	M. 8 "	15. Octave	M. 4 "

EXPRESSIVE SUBDIVISION

Inclosed in Swell-Box No. 1

16. Tibia Plena . .	W. 8 Feet	19. Cornet . . .	M. V. Ranks
17. Geigenprincipal .	M. 8 "	20. Double Trumpet .	M. 16 Feet
18. Clarabella . .	W. 8 "	21. Tromba Real . .	M. 8 "

ACCOMPANIMENTAL ORGAN

Compass CC to c^4— 61 Notes

——SECOND CLAVIER——

FIRST EXPRESSIVE SUBDIVISION

Inclosed in Swell-Box No. 2

22. Lieblichgedeckt .	W. 16 Feet	25. Quintaten . . .	M. 8 Feet
23. Salicional . . .	M. 8 "	26. Lieblichflöte . .	M. 4 "
24. Melodia . . .	W. 8 "	27. Dolce Cornet .	M. V. Ranks

SECOND EXPRESSIVE SUBDIVISION

Inclosed in Swell-Box No. 3

28. Echo Diapason .	M. 8 Feet	31. Triplette . .	M. III. Ranks
29. Flauto Amabile .	W. 8 "	32. Clarinetto . .	M. 8 Feet
30. Viola d'Amore .	M. 8 "	33. Oboe	M. 8 "

I. Tremolant

SOLO ORGAN

Compass CC to c^4— 61 Notes

——THIRD CLAVIER——

FIRST EXPRESSIVE SUBDIVISION

Inclosed in Swell-Box No. 2

34. Contrabasso . .	W. 16 Feet	37. Gemshorn . . .	M. 8 Feet
35. Grand Viol . .	M. 8 "	38. Flauto Traverso .	W. 8 "
36. Violino	M. 8 "	39. Violetta . . .	M. 4 "

II. Tremolant

SECOND EXPRESSIVE SUBDIVISION

Inclosed in Swell-Box No. 3

40. Horn Diapason .	M. 8 Feet	43. Trombone . . .	M. 8 Feet
41. Doppelflöte . .	W. 8 "	44. Horn	M. 8 "
42. Contrafagotto .	M. 16 "	45. Tromba Clarion .	M. 4 "

As all the accessories and mechanical appliances requisite for the complete control of the tonal resources of the Organ as schemed in this Seventh Specification are similar in all respects to those set forth in the preceding Sixth Specification, it is quite unnecessary to repeat them here. The interested reader has, accordingly, only to refer to them to grasp all matters necessary for the complete understanding of this seventh scheme.

NOTES ON THE SEVENTH SPECIFICATION

An attempt is made in this Specification to furnish a scheme for a Church Organ of moderate dimensions, in which all the leading principles and demands of our advanced System are observed to as full an extent as practicable under the conditions of size. Of necessity, some desirable features present in the preceding larger schemes have had to be modified or omitted; but without seriously crippling the tonal resources or the important methods of control which characterize our complete System of compound tonal flexibility and expression; and which distinguish it from all the one-ply old methods of organ-building and appointment followed abroad, and generally and blindly adopted in this country. It may be remarked, however, that owing to the recent adoption—timidly and half-heartedly—of certain of the expedients, either practically introduced or formulated by us and recorded in our writings, improvements have appeared in some instruments constructed here; affording a hopeful sign of better things to come, when the artistic constitution and resourceful tonal appointment of the organ are thoroughly understood by organists and the purchasers of organs.

PEDAL ORGAN—In very many cases the accommodation, provided by the church architect for the reception of an organ, is found insufficient to permit of the installation of an instrument of the necessary or desirable dimensions; accordingly, some portions of the organ have to suffer, in some fashion, to meet existing conditions. As might be expected, the Pedal Organ, is, on account of the large size of its pipe-work, the first to suffer diminution in every possible direction. Under such conditions, it is obvious that not only will its stop-apportionment be necessarily small, but that the impossibility of constructing a Swell-chamber must be recognized. Such, then, are the conditions which have dictated the special tonal appointment of the Pedal Organ set forth in the Specification now under consideration.

We are averse, on true acoustical principles, to the deriving of octaves from unison stops; and consider it only admissible in the case of large and grave stops in the Pedal Organ, in which the gravity and somewhat indeterminate quality of tone covers the acoustical insufficiency. In the manual Organs such a practice of octave deriving is to be seriously condemned in all labial stops; and in only exceptional cases is the practice of such deriving to be tolerated in lingual stops. To find the practice of wholesale deriving carried to its limit, one must go to that unscientific and inartistic abomination, known as the "Unit Organ"—the blot on the time-honored organ-builder's art to-day.

In the Pedal Organ now under consideration, there are four important extended stops, of 16 ft., representing Pure Organ-tone, Free Organ-tone, String-tone, and Brass-tone; from which effective Octaves are derived, valuable as solo voices as well as in combination. To the true Pedal Organ is added the expressive Auxiliary of three derived stops, furnishing Pure Organ-tone, Flute-tone, and Reed-tone; all of 16 ft. pitch. The appointment may be accepted as forming an efficient and effective Pedal Organ, requiring only a moderate space for its accommodation. The wind-pressures for the PRINCIPAL DULCIANA, and CONTRABASSO to be 5 inches, and for the TROMBONE 8 inches will be sufficient.

GRAND ORGAN—This foundation Division has, in accordance with the principles of our System, its stop-apportionment arranged in two groups of contrasting tonalities. The First Subdivision is unexpressive, and is formed of foundation Diapason-work, sufficient to support the tonal structure of the manual organs. The Expressive Subdivision has two stops of Flute-tone, one of Viol-tone, and two of Brass-tone, and a valuable harmonic-corroborating CORNET, composed of five complete ranks of small-scaled DIAPASON pipes; completing, in combination with the labial stops of the First Subdivision, the Diapason Chorus. The CORNET is composed as follows:—

I. OCTAVE	. . . .	M. 4 FEET.
II. TIERCE	. . . .	M. 3⅕ "
III. OCTAVE QUINT	. . . . .	M. 2⅔ "
IV. SEPTIÈME	. . . .	M. 2²⁄₇ "
V. SUPER-OCTAVE	. . . . .	M. 2 "

For this compound stop to be of full value in the composition of the true Diapason Chorus, it has to be carefully regulated in the following manner: In the first place, the first rank must yield a tone only slightly less powerful than that of the OCTAVE in the Unexpressive Subdivision; then the other ranks are to be graduated softer in their numerical order. Finally, each rank must be regulated so as to become gradually and slightly softer in tone as it ascends the scale. If this method of regulation is properly carried out, the tonal result of the combination of the CORNET and the three DIAPASONS will be brilliant and impressive. Under the control of the Swell the CORNET can be used with any one of the DIAPASONS. The proper wind-pressure for all the labial stops, exposed and inclosed, is 3¾ inches; and for the two lingual stops a pressure of 7 inches will generally be found sufficient.

ACCOMPANIMENTAL ORGAN—If considered as complete in itself, it is probable that the exacting organist will deem this important Division, of only twelve stops, insufficient to meet all the calls of accompanimental music. It is probable, because in the one-ply and unexpressive tonally inflexible old-style of Choir Organ, with which he has long been familiar, such a limited stop-apportionment might justly be considered insufficient. But, in the first place, it must be borne in mind that, under our System, all the voices of this Division can be employed in at least ten different and effective degrees of strength: and, secondly, it must be recognized that, in the general scheme of the instrument, the Solo Organ, commanded by the Third Clavier, serves, at the will of the performer, and by simple unison coupling, as a potent Auxiliary Accompanimental Organ; also flexible in tone and expressive, and furnishing tonal elements more than sufficient, in combination with those of the Accompanimental Organ, to meet every demand that could properly be made in the rendition of artistic accompanimental music.

It must not be overlooked that when the Solo Organ is coupled to the Accompanimental, the performer has at his command and under easy control, while playing on the Second Clavier only, four practically independent and tonally contrasting Subdivisions of six stops each—an Accompanimental Organ of twenty-four stops, representing all the varieties of tonality belonging to the modern organ.

It is unnecessary to enlarge on the tonal qualities of the stops comprised in this Accompanimental Division; their names are sufficient to show that they have been selected with proper regard to the office they have to fulfil in the tonal economy of the instrument. All their voices are amongst the most refined and beautiful produced by organ-pipes, and are peculiarly adapted to association with the human voice in song. One stop, however, may be described; namely, the TRIPLETTE, a harmonic-corroborating stop of three ranks, introduced in the Second Expressive Subdivision for special combination with the Pure Organ-tone ECHO DIAPASON; to the voice of which it will impart richness and brilliancy. The TRIPLETTE has commonly been made of ranks of high pitched pipes; but in the present scheme such a treatment would be undesirable. The stop required is formed of small-scaled DIAPASON pipes, carefully voiced to yield the soft, singing tones of the old English DIAPASON, and of the following complete ranks:—

I.	OCTAVE	M. 4 FEET.
II.	OCTAVE QUINT	M. 2⅔ "
III.	SUPER-OCTAVE	M. 2 "

The introduction of the VOX HUMANA in the same Subdivision may seem somewhat strange. Not so, however; for if the stop is of its proper form and tonality,[19] and is used without the TREMOLANT, its voice is one of the most valuable in accompanimental music, as we have proved beyond question. Of course, we are not alluding to the miserable things that go by the name, commonly introduced in organs built in this country to-day.

The wind-pressures for all the labial stops in both the Subdivisions should be 2¾ inches; and for the two lingual stops 3½ inches.

SOLO ORGAN—Although this Division is stop-appointed so as to furnish all solo effects that would be necessary or desirable in the artistic rendition of any voluntary or incidental music of an ecclesiastical character; and, in this office, is sufficient in a Church Organ of the size specified; it has another office of more importance, as has already been commented on; namely, to serve as an Auxiliary to the Accompanimental Organ; adding to it valuable tonal colorings, imparting to it character and force, and firmly establishing the primal

[19] This form of VOX HUMANA is described and illustrated in pages 474-5 of "The Organ of the Twentieth Century."

office of the true Church Organ. Its stop-apportionment, which comprises eight important labial stops, of Free Organ-tone, Flute-tone, and String-tone, and four lingual stops of Reed-tone and Brass-tone, is arranged in two groups of markedly contrasting qualities of voice; each group or Subdivision being, separately, flexible and expressive. No harmonic-corroborating voices are required in this Solo Organ, sufficient being provided by the OCTAVE, DOLCE CORNET, and TRIPLETTE in the Accompanimental Organ.

The desirable wind-pressures for all the labial stops are 3½ inches, and for the lingual stops 6 inches.

THE GREGORIAN ORGAN

Twenty years ago there appeared in the pages of a New York Musical Journal an Article from our pen (dated November 26, 1905), captioned, "The Organ as required for the Music of the Roman Catholic Church." This was the first time that such an important subject had been approached in the literature of the Organ in the English language: and, so far as we are aware, no special dissertation on the construction and tonal appointment of the Organ designed exclusively for the accompaniment of Gregorian Chant has appeared in any foreign language; but our knowledge in this direction is necessarily very limited.

It must be obvious to every musician fully conversant with all the schools of ecclesiastical music, that there is a pressing call, under the present prevailing and commonplace practice of organ designing and construction, for an instrument adapted in every essential for the proper accompaniment of Gregorian Chant, rendered as that solemn and impressive Song should be rendered in the services of the Roman Catholic Church, and as the Church has always intended that it should be. Although not a musician, we certainly held that view when we wrote the following words twenty years ago:—

Whatever the opinions of organists and organ-builders may be with reference to the tonal appointment of organs for Protestant Church services, there can, one ventures to think, be only one consistent opinion respecting the tonal appointment of the organ suitable for the accompaniment of the dignified music now ordered to be used by the Roman Catholic Church. From certain passages in the "*Motu proprio*," or "Instruction on Sacred Music," issued from the Apostolic Palace, at the Vatican, on the Feast of Saint Cecilia, November 22, 1903, one may form a tolerably clear conception of what the new type of Church Organ should be. In this "Instruction," sacred music is properly defined as a complementary part of the solemn liturgy of the Church, contributing to the edification of the faithful, and to the splendor and decorum of the ecclesiastical ceremonies, clothing with suitable melody and adding greater efficacy to the liturgical text, that through it the faithful may be moved to deeper devotion. It must be "holy" and "true art," to the exclusion of any element of "profanity," both in itself and in the manner in which it is executed; otherwise it will be impossible for it to exercise on the minds of the worshippers who listen to it that efficacy which the Church aims at in associating with her liturgy the art of music. The "Instruction" clearly orders the adoption of Gregorian music in preference to every other form, the Gregorian Chant being proper to the Roman Church, and that which has always been regarded as the supreme model for sacred music.

It must be obvious from what has been set forth above that for the proper accompaniment of such music an organ differing in several respects from the ordinary modern church instrument, and even from the advanced form we advocate, is to be desired. In the "Instruction" the organ is clearly defined as purely an accompanimental instrument, whose voice should sustain and never oppress the vocal chant; while its tone must participate in all the qualities proper and belonging to the sacred music of the Church. These remarks point to organs possessing extreme dignity and refinement of tone, combined with full powers of flexibility and expression, and not necessarily of large size, rather than to immense instruments, built on the present prevailing trade lines, crammed with unnecessary and fancy stops, and deficient in those expressive powers which impart to an instrumental accompaniment one of its chief elements of perfection and beauty.

Although in the "*Motu proprio*" no directions are given respecting the form and tonal character of the organ most suitable for use in the accompaniment of the Gregorian Chant, it cannot be difficult for one versed in organ matters to read between the lines and arrive at a tolerably clear conception of what the tonal character and appointment of the true Accompanimental Gregorian Organ should and must be to be in perfect accord with the full meaning of the words and signification of the "Instruction." As we have already said, such an Organ must possess extreme dignity and refinement of tone, combined with full powers of tonal flexibility and expression, such as our System of compound control alone places at the command of the accompanist.

Subsequent to the appearance of our Article on the subject in 1905, a very commendable essay was made by a distinguished Organ-building Firm to devise and introduce, on a commercial basis, "Gregorian Organs" of various dimensions; which were intended to meet all the demands considered necessary for the appropriate accompaniment of ecclesiastical Plain Song; and which went far, although not far enough, to solve the problem of the necessary tonal and mechanical appointment of the true and sufficient Gregorian Organ. It was a valuable proof, however, in so far that it recognized the fact that a special instrument was necessary for the proper accompaniment of Gregorian Chant;[20] just as was contended in the first essay published on the subject in the English language.

The Gregorian Organ is not merely a subject for discussion, which, from difference of opinion and lack of general interest, would fall short of desirable results in any practical directions. On the contrary, at this time, when the noble Art of Organ-building is suffering a serious decadence under the hands of too many inartistic, know-little, and don't-care tradesmen, it calls for the careful consideration and serious study by all who respect true ecclesiastical music, hallowed by the use of thirteen centuries, and desire to see the instruments, which accompany it, in every way worthy of the high office they have to fulfil.

Of those known to us who take a learned and whole-hearted interest in Gregorian Music, and necessarily in the proper construction and tonal appointment of the Organ suitable for the artistic, expressive, and refined accompaniment of the same, the most able and distinguished is the Reverend Gregory

[20] Formulated and established for universal use in the Church by Pope Gregory, the Great, 590-604. The Life of whom was written by Denis de Sainte-Marthe, 1697.

Hügle, of the Order of Saint Benedict,[21] Director of Music, of Conception Abbey, Conception, Mo., to whom we owe much in connection with the preparation of this important Section of the present Treatise. Under these favorable conditions, the interested reader may rest assured that what is here furnished is worthy of his acceptance.

Before proceeding to consider the Stops which are essential in certain directions, and desirable in others, to the necessary tonal appointment of the true Gregorian Organ, as designed under the inspiration of the dignified and impressive musical offices and services of the Catholic Church, we may properly give, as concisely as possible, the General Principles on which such a Church Organ should be schemed, consistent with our System of tonal appointment and control. They may be summarized as follows:—

GENERAL PRINCIPLES OF THE TONAL APPOINTMENT AND CONTROL OF THE GREGORIAN ORGAN

I. That the Organ shall be designed and tonally appointed with the primary intent that it shall, under able hands, be sufficient in every way to fulfil its essential office in the accompaniment of the Gregorian Chant; and that in a manner replete with religious ethos—full of repose, grandeur, refinement, and expression.

II. That the Organ shall, in its secondary, but still very important office, afford sufficient tonal resources, of a dignified and effective character, for the rendition, in a manner consistent with the sacred offices and ceremonies of the Church, of such special music as may be called for in the Pontifical Escort on great Feasts, which demands rich and solemn strains; and in incidental music during the Consecration at High Mass, and during Benediction after Vespers. All such music must be of an impressive and elevating character; inducing in the mind religious aspiration.

III. That the voices of all the stops in the Organ shall be characterized by extreme richness, refinement, and individuality of tone; scientifically and artistically balanced to as great an extent as practicable, so as to render it impossible to produce, in combination, undesirable compound tones. To this end, the fullest powers of tonal flexibility must be present in the Organ.

IV. That, to secure the necessary richness, refinement, and individuality of tone in all the stops, properly adjusted scales, copious supplies of winds of low and moderate pressures, high-class artistic voicing, and perfect tonal regulation, are essential; and shall be provided and carried into effect.

V. That the stops selected for the special accompaniment of the Gregorian Chant, and the proper rendition of incidental music, as alluded to in Principles

[21] To this great and industrious Order the organ-building world owes a deep debt; for the greatest practical Work on the Art of Organ-building the world has ever seen was written by "D. François Bédos de Celles, Bénédictin de la Congrégation de Saint-Maur, dans l'Abbaye de Saint-Denys en France."

I. and II., shall necessarily be of different classes of tonality. No undue liberty, however, shall be taken in the selection of the former group of stops; for the proper and sympathetic accompaniment of Plain Song has demands that cannot be ignored by the designer of a true Gregorian Organ. On the other hand, in designing the latter group, no severe restrictions are imposed. An artistic and keen musical sense shall here be the guide in the right direction: but the designer must not overlook the necessity that both groups, combined, must constitute a complete and well-balanced instrument.

VI. That in every Gregorian Organ there shall be a properly formed Pedal Clavier of 32 notes: and in the larger instruments there shall be three, and in the smaller two Manual Claviers of the full compass of 61 notes.

VII. That the Pedal Organ shall comprise a satisfactory stop-apportionment which will furnish appropriate basses to all the important stops and combinations of stops in the Manual Divisions of the instrument.

VIII. That the First Organ, commanded by the First Clavier, shall comprise the foundation stops of Pure Organ-tone, associated with such other stops of kindred and contrasting tonalities as will assist in forming compound tones of great richness and beauty. The number of these subordinate stops, labial and lingual, will, of necessity, be dictated by the general dimensions of the instrument. The stop-apportionment of this First Organ is to be arranged in two groups. The first group to comprise the principal foundation stops, and to be planted on an exposed wind-chest. All the other stops of the Division to be inclosed in a Swell-box, and rendered tonally flexible and expressive. This First Organ, accordingly, forms the foundation of the Accompanimental Gregorian Organ.

IX. That the Second Organ, under general conditions, shall be stop-apportioned so as to fulfil a dual office. In the first place, it shall contribute refined and expressive voices to the accompanimental forces of the Organ: and, in the second place, it shall furnish what is desirable for the rendition of the incidental music required in the services of the Church. The stop-apportionment of this Organ is, in accordance with our System, to be arranged in two tonally contrasting groups, which are to be inclosed in separate Swell-boxes, constituting compound flexibility and expression.

X. That the Third Organ in large instruments, commanded by the Third Clavier, shall be stop-apportioned, in two groups of contrasting tonalities, suitable for the rendition of accompanimental and incidental music of the most impressive character. The groups to be inclosed in the Swell-boxes which contain the Subdivisions of the Second Organ.

XI. That, under the conditions stated above, the stops selected for the Third Organ shall be from those, in the available list, which yield the most expressive and sympathetic voices, and are of sufficient variety to meet all demands that may be made on them in the proper music of the Church. The Subdivisions shall not only contrast in their special tonalities, but also, within desirable bounds, in their relative strengths. Proper wind-pressures and artistic voicing will be very important factors in these matters.

XII. That care shall be taken in the selection of the stops for all the Divisions of the Organ to provide as full a harmonic-corroborating support as practicable in the size of the instrument; for this tonal element is of the utmost importance, providing it is of proper quality and not unduly assertive. A compound harmonic-corroborating stop is very desirable and should be such as to accord with any unison stop or combination of stops in the Division.

XIII. That great care shall be taken to construct the Swell-boxes, so that they shall secure the desirable range of tonal flexibility and expression, without in any way destroying distinctness of tone when closed. That their actions shall be controlled by balanced Expression Levers of approved form, placed three-quarters of an inch apart, and occupying a central position over the Pedal clavier.

XIV. That the Console shall be so constructed and appointed with all the appliances and accessories necessary to give the performer, seated at the claviers, complete and easy command of all the tonal resources of the Organ, and control of its powers of tonal flexibility and expression. The desirable forms which the appliances and accessories shall assume must be left to the judgment of the designer of the Console. The arrangement of the playing portions of the Console is a matter of the utmost importance to the organist.

The following is a classified List of Stops, from which selections may be made for the stop-apportionments of the Divisions of Gregorian Organs of all sizes:

LIST OF STOPS SUITABLE FOR THE TONAL APPOINTMENT OF GREGORIAN ORGANS

MANUAL ORGANS

PURE ORGAN-TONE

Principale Doppio . .	M.	16 Feet
Principale Maggiore .	M.	8 "
Principale	W.	8 "
Principale Minore .	M.	8 "
Principale Dolce . .	M.	8 "
Quinta	M.	5⅓ "
Ottava Maggiore .	M.	4 "
Ottava Minore . .	M.	4 "
Duodecima	M.	2⅔ "
Decima Quinta . .	M.	2 "
Cornetto Dolce .	M.	V. Ranks

4′—3⅕′—2⅔′—$2\frac{2}{7}$′—2′.

FREE ORGAN-TONE

Dolce	M.	8 Feet
Dulciana	M.	8 "
Corno Dolce . . .	M.	8 "
Keraulophone . .	M.	8 "
Voce Angelica . .	M.	8 "
Voce Celeste . . .	M.	8 "
Ottava Dolce . . .	M.	4 "
Duodecimo Dolce . .	M.	2⅔ "
Ottavina Dolce . .	M.	2 "
Cornetto Dolcissimo	M.	IV. Ranks

4′—3⅕′—2⅔′—2′.

Armonia Eterea .	M.	V. Ranks
Ripieno di Cinque .	M.	V. Ranks

FLUTE-TONE

Bordone	W.	16 Feet
Bordone Amabile	W.	16 "
Bordone	W.	8 "
Bordone Dolce	M.	8 "
Flauto Maggiore	W.	8 "
Flauto Doppio	W.	8 "
Flauto Tedesco	W.	8 "
Flauto Traverso	W.	8 "
Flauto Amabile	W.	8 "
Flauto Dolce	M.	8 "
Flauto a Camino	M.	8 "
Flautone	W.	8 "
Unda Maris	W.	8 "
Melodia	W.	8 "
Pastorita	M.	8 "
Philomela	W.	8 "
Flauto Dolcissimo	M.	8 "
Flauto Angelico	M.	8 "
Flauto Quinto	M.	5⅓ "
Flauto Traverso	W.	4 "
Flauto Amoroso	M.	4 "
Flauto d'Amore	W.	4 "
Flauto Piccolo	M.	2 "
Flautino	M.	2 "
Flageoletta	W.	2 "

VIOL-TONE

Contrabasso	W.	16 Feet
Violoncello	M.	8 "
Violino	M.	8 "
Viola da Gamba	M.	8 "
Viola d'Amore	T.	8 "
Salicionale	M.	8 "
Viola Sorda	M.	8 "
Dolce Gamba	M.	8 "
Eolina	T.	8 "
Eolina (Sharp)	T.	8 "
Violetta	T.	4 "
Violetta (Sharp)	T.	4 "

REED-TONE

Contrafagotto	W.	16 Feet
Fagotto	M.	8 "
Corno di Bassetto	M.	8 "

REED-TONE—Continued

Corno Inglese	M.	8 Feet
Clarinetto	M.	8 "
Oboe	M.	8 "
Scialumò	M.	8 "
Oboe d'Amore	M.	8 "
Clarinetto Quinta	M.	5⅓ "
Oboe Ottava	M.	4 "

BRASS-TONE

Tromba Bassa	M.	16 Feet
Tromba	M.	8 "
Corno	M.	8 "
Euphonium	M.	8 "
Trombetta	M.	4 "

PEDAL ORGAN

ORGAN-TONE

Contra-Principale	W.	32 Feet
Principale Grande	W.	16 "
Principale Dolce	M.	16 "
Ottava	W.	8 "
Ottava Dolce	M.	8 "

FLUTE-TONE

Bordone	W.	16 Feet
Flautone	W.	16 "
Flautobasso	W.	8 "

STRING-TONE

Contrabasso	W.	16 Feet
Violone	M.	16 "
Violoncello	M.	8 "

REED-TONE

Contrafagotto	W.	16 Feet
Contra-Clarinetto	M.	16 "
Contra-Oboe	M.	16 "

BRASS-TONE

Contra-Trombone	M.	16 Feet
Contra-Tromba	M.	16 "
Trombone	M.	8 "
Tromba	M.	8 "

It is perhaps desirable at this point to allude to our adoption of a consistent stop nomenclature, in one language, in the List given above; which we consider especially suitable with regard to the stop-appointment of the Gregorian Organ, in which it furnishes a distinctive element of differentiation. We freely admit that it would be undesirable as it would be impracticable, as matters obtain at the present time, to attempt to formulate a consistent stop nomenclature, in any one language, for important Concert-room, Church, and Theater Organs; but the difficulty seems to disappear in the proper stop-appointment of the desirable Gregorian Organ as conceived by us. This, the List of Stops of all tonalities, given above, clearly proves.

The subject is by no means a new one to us; for in the year 1886 we contributed a series of five Articles to "The English Mechanic and World of Science," captioned, "Suggestions for the Introduction of a Systematic Organ-Stop Nomenclature." These were suggested by an interesting Article from the pen of the late Frederick Archer, in "The Keynote," New York, July 26, 1884, in which he says:—

"With respect to the nomenclature of stops much confusion exists, mainly on account of the desire of some builders to differ from their contemporaries in this particular. The system indeed, whereby the English and American builders distinguish the various classes of organ registers is radically wrong in principle, having no logical foundation, and much of the evil referred to may be primarily attributed to this circumstance."

Subsequent to the publication of our Articles, Mr. Archer, in "The Keynote," of June 12, 1886, remarks: "Mr. Audsley is entitled to the thanks of all interested, in the subject of organ-building, for his thoughtful and suggestive Articles, dealing with the present method, in vogue here and in England, of naming the various speaking stops. The importance of a well defined system of universal application is abundantly obvious, but it cannot be denied that there are formidable obstacles in the way of the reformer, many of which Mr. Audsley has overlooked." The correctness of these remarks we freely admit.

It is, however, unnecessary to enlarge on the subject here, in support of the adoption of the systematic stop nomenclature in Italian for the Gregorian Organ. But any reader desiring particulars on the subject may consult Chapter XIV., in Volume I. of "The Art of Organ-Building."

Having decided to adopt, so far as is possible, an Italian stop nomenclature for the Gregorian Organ; the next question, requiring consideration, is what names shall be employed to designate the different tonal Divisions of the instrument? Those we have applied to the Divisions of the usual Church Organ are to a certain extent suitable to those of the instrument now under consideration; but as the Gregorian Organ is primarily and in its chief office an accompanimental instrument, it seems undesirable to apply the name Accompanimental Organ to any one Division. It is intended that, in accordance with our scheme, the tonal appointments of the Divisions commanded by the First and Second Claviers shall constitute the proper accompanimental portion of the instrument, necessarily in conjunction with the Pedal Organ tonal appointment;

assistance on only very special occasions being sought from the tonal forces commanded by the Third Clavier. On the other hand, the Third Division will only necessarily be resorted to, in association with certain portions of stop-apportionments of First and Second Divisions and the Pedal Organ, in the rendition of such incidental music as may be called for in the solemn and impressive services of the Church. Accordingly, the Third Division is stop-apportioned to a large degree in conformity with the apportionments of the other Divisions.

We are strongly disinclined, as the remarks already made indicate, to favor the retention of the old and familiar terms Great Organ, Choir Organ, Swell Organ, and Solo Organ, which are still adhered to, inappropriate as they are in certain respects, by old-fashioned builders and organists. And for the specially appointed instrument now under consideration, we are disposed to abandon the more apposite terms we have used for the manual Divisions of the advanced form of the Church Organ; namely, Grand Organ, Accompanimental Organ, Choir Organ, and Solo Organ. We abandon these, simply because we consider the properly schemed Gregorian Organ, in its united and complete form, to be generally a Grand Organ; connectedly a perfect Accompanimental Organ; and, under similar conditions, an efficient Solo Organ. Thus forming a congruous tonal structure, divided into groups of contrasting tonalities, solely for the purpose of obtaining the maximum of tonal flexibility and compound expression; securing thereby the complete control by means of which the Organ can alone justly claim to be a satisfactory musical instrument for the accompaniment of the human voice in sacred song. In all cases the term Pedal Organ will necessarily be retained.

Under the considerations set forth above, it seems desirable that all special names, which more or less clearly indicate special or distinct uses or offices, shall be omitted in the terminology of the tonal Divisions of the Gregorian Organ. Accordingly, we have adopted the sufficiently distinctive names Pedal Organ, commanded by the Pedalier; First Organ, commanded by the First Clavier; Second Organ, commanded by the Second Clavier; and Third Organ, commanded by the Third Clavier. If Italian is considered desirable; then the names will be Pedale, Organo Primo, Organo Secondo, and Organo Terzo. The tonal appointments of these Divisions may be briefly described, commencing with the First Organ.

FIRST ORGAN — ORGANO PRIMO

The First Organ is first in importance in the tonal scheme of the instrument, in so much that its appointment comprises the most important manual stops; namely, those which form the foundation of the entire tonal structure. These stops yield Pure Organ-tone in sufficient volume (without undue assertiveness) to form a ground-work on which any combinations of compound tone can be built up in grandeur and beauty; and which, in themselves, furnish that full, rich, and refined volume of tone—commonly known as Diapason-tone—which is appropriate for the sympathetic accompaniment and support of the Gregorian Chant and devotional song. These foundation tones, yielded, for the most part, by uninclosed stops, are further enriched and modified by association with the sub-foundational voices of the Pedal Organ stops, and the flexible and expressive voices of the inclosed Subdivision of this First Organ. They are further enriched and modified, when, by the coupling to the First Organ the Subdivisions (in any desirable relation) of the Second and Third Organs, compound tones, practically inexhaustible, are at the command of the organist; suitable in every respect for the accompanimental and incidental music called for in the several services of the Church.

The stops apportioned to this First Organ are arranged in two groups, unequal in size and power, in accordance with our general System; the larger and less assertive in volume of tone being inclosed in a special Swell-box (Number 1), which imparts flexibility of tone and powers of expression, absolutely essential in an instrument fitted for the artistic and sympathetic accompaniment of the human voice. The entire voice of the First Organ must be characterized by gravity, tonal repose, richness of harmonic structure, and refinement.

SECOND ORGAN — ORGANO SECONDO

The tonal appointment of the Second Organ may be accepted as furnishing a softly-toned accompanimental Division, complete in itself; comprising, as it does (when properly stop-apportioned), Subdivisions of contrasting tonalities, endowed, independently, with powers of flexibility and expression, as required by our System. But it must not be viewed from this standpoint only. In fact, it is a subordinate part of the entire accompanimental scheme—connected and complete. It can, and will, be used alone in soft accompanimental passages and incidental music; but its chief value will be evident when, in combination and compound-tone production with the voices of the First and Third Organs—between which it furnishes a bond of sympathy—it fuses together in the musical crucible, as it were, widely different tonalities, producing tonal alloys of great beauty and diversified coloration.

The stop-apportionment of this Second Organ is arranged in two groups having, to as marked a degree as practicable, contrasting tonalities; each of which is inclosed in a separate Swell-box, imparting compound tonal flexibility and expression to the entire Division, as set forth in the following Specifications. The nature and office of this Organ demands that its stops shall be masterpieces of the pipe-maker's and voicer's arts. Its true value and general usefulness depend on the perfection of its voicing and tonal regulation. The last named factor, on account of the time and care necessary in its proper execution, is too often hurried over and neglected by modern organ-builders. Smoothness and perfect accord can never be attained in compound-tone production in an insufficiently regulated instrument. Regulation should be attended to every time an organ is tuned; and the organist should see that it is attended to.

THIRD ORGAN — ORGANO TERZO

In its tonal appointment the Third Organ has a dual office to fulfil in the economy of the properly constituted Gregorian Organ: the chief of which is to provide special resources for the adequate rendition of incidental music suitable for the services of the Church. For this purpose it may be used alone, but preferably in conjunction with the tonal forces of the First Organ, in the rendition of music of a pompous character suitable for certain functions of the Catholic Church: and, in the other direction, in association with the less assertive voices of the Second Organ, in the production of music of a highly refined and appealing character. In a lesser degree, the tonal appointment of the Third Organ furnishes certain means for effectively coloring, enriching, and adding accentuation to the accompanimental music rendered by the other two Manual Organs, separately or in combination.

As in the case of the other Divisions, and in conformity with our basic Principles of tonal appointment, the stops of this Third Organ are arranged in two groups having contrasting tonalities. These are inclosed in the Swell-boxes which contain the Subdivisions of the Second Organ. On first thoughts, this arrangement may seem undesirable to the organist accustomed to the school of one-ply organ appointment in matters of tonal control and expression; but experience has proved its convenience and effectiveness; and in the production of compound tonal flexibility and expression to be satisfactory in every respect.

PEDAL ORGAN — PEDALE

The proper tonal appointment of Pedal Organ of the Gregorian instrument differs in no essential from that of the same important Division of the ordinary Church Organ, unless it is its being desiredly endowed with a greater refinement, combined with a restrained rather than a pronounced assertiveness. Its office is distinctly twofold; namely, it has to furnish the sub-foundational bass in both restrained accompanimental and freer and more varied incidental music. Both these offices could be easily fulfilled were the entire stop-apportionment of the Pedal Organ inclosed in a Swell-chamber; and, accordingly, placed under control and rendered tonally flexible. But the large size of the double and unison labial stops renders such an inclosure almost, if not altogether, impracticable. The smaller stops and the lingual stops which readily admit of mitering to any necessary extent, can and should be inclosed in some effective manner and rendered both tonally flexible and expressive.

EIGHTH SPECIFICATION

GREGORIAN ORGAN

AUDSLEY SYSTEM — COMPOUND EXPRESSION
THREE MANUAL CLAVIERS

PEDALE

Compass CCC to G — 32 Notes

— PEDAL CLAVIER —

UNEXPRESSIVE SUBDIVISION

1. Contra-Principale.	W. 32 Feet	4. Violone	M. 16 Feet
2. Principale Grande (44 pipes) . . .	W. 16 "	5. Bordone	W. 16 "
3. Principale Dolce (44 pipes) . . .	M. 16 "	6. Ottave Maggiore (From 2) . . .	W. 8 "
		7. Ottava (From 3) .	M. 8 "

EXPRESSIVE SUBDIVISION

Inclosed in Swell-Chamber

8. Contrabasso . .	W. 16 Feet	13. Cornetto . .	M. IV. Ranks
9. Flauto Maggiore	W. 8 "	14. Contra-Trombone	M. 16 Feet
10. Violoncello . .	M. 8 "	15. Contra-Oboe . .	M. 16 "
11. Bordone . . .	W. 8 "	16. Contra-Clarinetto	M. 16 "
12. Quinta	M. 5⅓ "	17. Tromba . . .	M. 8 "

ORGANO PRIMO

Compass CC to c⁴ — 61 Notes

— FIRST CLAVIER —

UNEXPRESSIVE SUBDIVISION

18. Principale Doppio.	M. 16 Feet	20. Principale Minore	M. 8 Feet
19. Principale Maggiore . .	M. 8 "	21. Flauto Maggiore	W. 8 "

EXPRESSIVE SUBDIVISION

Inclosed in Swell-Box No. 1

22. Bordone . . .	W. 16 Feet	26. Viola da Gamba .	M. 8 Feet
23. Principale . . .	W. 8 "	27. Flautone . . .	W. 8 "
24. Salicionale . .	M. 8 "	28. Bordone . . .	W. 8 "
25. Keraulophone. .	M. 8 "	29. Flauto Quinto .	M. 5⅓ "

30. Ottava Maggiore	M.	4 Feet	34. Cornetto Dolce	M.	V. Ranks
31. Flauto Amoroso .	M.	4 "	35. Contrafagotto .	W.	16 Feet
32. Duodecimo . . .	M.	2⅔ "	36. Euphonium . . .	M.	8 "
33. Flautino . . .	M.	2 "	37. Oboe Ottava . .	M.	4 "

ORGANO SECONDO

Compass CC to c4— 61 Notes

—— SECOND CLAVIER ——

FIRST EXPRESSIVE SUBDIVISION

Inclosed in Swell-Box No. 2

38. Bordone Amabile.	W.	16 Feet	43. Ottava Dolce. .	M.	4 Feet
39. Principale Dolce .	M.	8 "	44. Duodecimo . . .	M.	2⅔ "
40. Flauto Dolce . .	W.	8 "	45. Ottava Dolce. .	M.	2 "
41. Flauto Tedesco .	W.	8 "	46. Armonia Eterea	M.	V. Ranks
42. Voce Angelica .	M.	8 "	47. Corno	M.	8 Feet

SECOND EXPRESSIVE SUBDIVISION

Inclosed in Swell-Box No. 3

48. Bordone Dolce .	M.	16 Feet	54. Violetta . . .	M.	4 Feet
49. Dulciana . . .	M.	8 "	55. Cornetto Dolcissimo	M.	IV. Ranks
50. Flauto a Camino.	M.	8 "	56. Oboe d'Amore. .	M.	8 Feet
51. Unda Maris . .	W.	8 "	57. Clarinetto Dolce	M.	8 "
52. Viola Sorda . .	M.	8 "			
53. Eolina	M.	8 "			

ORGANO TERZO

Compass CC to c4— 61 Notes

—— THIRD CLAVIER ——

FIRST EXPRESSIVE SUBDIVISIONS

Inclosed in Swell-Box No. 2

58. Principale . . .	M.	8 Feet	62. Flauto Amoroso .	M.	4 Feet
59. Bordone . . .	W.	8 "	63. Flauto Piccolo .	M.	2 "
60. Flauto Traverso.	W.	8 "	64. Corno Inglese. .	M.	8 "
61. Corno Dolce . .	M.	8 "	I. Tremolant		

SECOND EXPRESSIVE SUBDIVISION

Inclosed in Swell-Box No. 3

65. Viola Principale	M. 8 Feet	69. Corno di Bassetto	M. 8 Feet
66. Violoncello	M. 8 "	70. Tromba	M. 8 "
67. Violino	M. 8 "	71. Trombetta	M. 4 "
68. Tromba Bassa	M. 16 "	II. Tremolant	

CLAVIER COUPLERS

PEDAL ORGAN COUPLERS

First Clavier....................to Pedal Clavier, Unison Coupler.
First Clavier....................to Pedal Clavier, Octave Coupler.
Second Clavier..................to Pedal Clavier, Unison Coupler.
Third Clavier...................to Pedal Clavier, Unison Coupler.

FIRST CLAVIER COUPLERS

Second Clavier..1st Subdivision..to First Clavier, Unison Coupler.
Second Clavier..2nd Subdivision..to First Clavier, Unison Coupler.
Third Clavier ..1st Subdivision..to First Clavier, Unison Coupler.
Third Clavier ..2nd Subdivision..to First Clavier, Unison Coupler.

SECOND CLAVIER COUPLERS

First Clavier...1st Subdivision...to Second Clavier, Unison Coupler.
First Clavier...2nd Subdivision...to Second Clavier, Unison Coupler.
Third Clavier..1st Subdivision...to Second Clavier, Unison Coupler.
Third Clavier..2nd Subdivision...to Second Clavier, Unison Coupler.

EXPRESSION LEVERS

I. Balanced Expression Lever commanding action of Pedal Swell-Chamber.
II. Balanced Expression Lever commanding action of Swell-Box No. 1.
III. Balanced Expression Lever commanding action of Swell-Box No. 2.
IV. Balanced Expression Lever commanding action of Swell-Box No. 3.

CRESCENDO LEVER

Balanced Crescendo Lever, situated, conveniently, to the right of the four Expression Levers, commanding an adjustable series of Stops in progressive order of tonal value, such as may be considered desirable in the rendition of the sacred music of the Catholic Church. To be effective on either the First or Third Claviers.

DIVISIONAL PISTONS

Two Thumb-Pistons—under First Clavier—bringing on and throwing off Expressive Subdivision of Organo Primo.

Two Thumb-Pistons—under Second Clavier—bringing on and throwing off First Subdivision of Organo Secondo.

Two Thumb-Pistons—under Second Clavier—bringing on and throwing off Second Subdivision of Organo Secondo.

Two Thumb-Pistons—under Third Clavier—bringing on and throwing off First Subdivision of Organo Terzo.

Two Thumb-Pistons—under Third Clavier—bringing on and throwing off Second Subdivision of Organo Terzo.

ADJUSTABLE COMBINATION ACTION

Five Operating Thumb-Pistons and Release—under First Clavier—commanding Stop-combinations on Organo Primo, Pedale, and Couplers.

Eight Operating Thumb-Pistons and Release—under Second Clavier—commanding Stop-combinations on Organo Secondo, Pedale, and Couplers.

Five Operating Thumb-Pistons and Release—under Third Clavier—commanding Stop-combinations on Organo Terzo, Pedale, and Couplers.

TREMOLANTS

The Two TREMOLANTS are to be commanded by double-acting Thumb-Pistons conveniently located under the Third Clavier; or associated with the Draw-stops of the Organo Terzo.

PEDALE TOE-PISTONS

ALL DOUBLE-ACTING

1. Piston coupling First Clavier to Pedal Clavier—Unison.
2. Piston coupling First Clavier to Pedal Clavier—Octave.
3. Piston coupling Second Clavier to Pedal Clavier—Unison.
4. Piston coupling Third Clavier to Pedal Clavier—Unison.

NOTES ON THE EIGHTH SPECIFICATION

The Organ set forth in this Specification is of dimensions and tonal appointment sufficient to meet the requirements of the musical services, of the most impressive and elaborate character, proper to the Catholic Church. It fulfils its all-important dual offices to the fullest extent required. First, that of an instrument adapted in every way for the expressive and sympathetic accompaniment of the Gregorian Chant in its purest form. And, secondly, that of an organ—with extended powers of tonal flexibility and expression—suitable to the fullest desirable extent for the artistic rendition of the appropriate incidental music required in the impressive services of the Church. Under such exacting calls on its tonal resources, it is obvious that richness, purity, and refinement must characterize the voices of every Division of the instrument. A careful analysis of the general tonal appointment, and the special stop-apportionments of the different Organs and their Subdivisions, as set forth in the Specification, will show the organ expert how all the demands on the tonal resources have been anticipated and provided for. And a further and more searching analysis will show the practically limitless powers of compound tone production and expression our System imparts to every Division of the Organ. No instrument such as is here schemed has ever before been contemplated for a Catholic Church.

It is a composite Gregorian Organ of the first magnitude; designed on the Principles we have established in tonal appointment and control; and is given as a standard and guide to those who may be called upon to design important organs suitable for the Catholic Church. The following remarks on the several Divisions will go far to assist the Organ Architect in matters of detail.

PEDALE—In the proper tonal appointment of the Gregorian Organ—whatever its size may be—the stop-apportionment of the Pedale must be commensurate with that of the other Divisions of the instrument; for on the fullness and firmness of the sub-foundational tones largely depend the dignity and value of the accompanimental office of the organ in Gregorian Chant. In the present Specification a sufficient bass is furnished by one stop of 32 ft. and eight stops of 16 ft. pitch; introducing Pure Organ-tone, Free Organ-tone, Flute-tone, Viol-tone, Reed-tone, and Brass-tone. Harmonic-corroboration being taken care of, in the Expressive Subdivision, by the QUINTA, 5⅓ FT., and the CORNETTO, IV. RANKS —4′— 3⅕′— 2⅔′— 2′.

Softness and extreme refinement of tone is secured, in the Unexpressive Subdivision, by the PRINCIPALE DOLCE, 16 FT.—an open metal stop, equivalent in every respect to the English DOUBLE DULCIANA—and the derived OTTAVA, 8 FT. In the Expressive Subdivison, every desirable gradation of tone, from a whisper to the full volume of compound tone, is rendered possible by the inclosure and complete control of the stops. All these conditions are imperative in a composite Gregorian Organ, such as is set forth in the present scheme. The wind-pressure for the stops of the Unexpressive Subdivision should be 5 inches, and for the labial stops of the Expressive Subdivision 4 inches and the lingual stops 8 inches. If the Subdivisions are unfavorably located, higher pressures may be desirable; but any tendency to coarseness of voice must be avoided.

ORGANO PRIMO—In this all-important Division are—in accordance with our established System of appointment—the stops of Pure Organ-tone which form the foundation of the tonal structure of the entire instrument. These stops are apportioned to the uninclosed Subdivision, and, accordingly, speak at all times with their full richness and sonority. They are of double and unison pitches; and form, as it may be said, the rock of sound on which can be built up any structures of effective, refined, and sympathetic compound tonalities, suitable for the accompanimental music of the dignified Gregorian Chant and free sacred song. The inclosed Subdivision, which furnishes flexibility of tone and powers of expression—absolutely essential to artistic accompanimental music—is formed of stops yielding Pure Organ-tones, Flute-tones, Viol-tones, Reed-tones, and Brass-tone; combined with a sufficient harmonic-corroborating structure of nine complete ranks of pipes: all of which stops—under the control of Swell-box No. 1, are capable of being used in ten well-marked different strengths of voice.

Although the Organo Primo is practically complete in itself, and is productive, under artistic registration, of a large range of effective and beautiful compound and differently colored tones; it is so stop-apportioned as to furnish a groundwork for countless tonal combinations when associated, by means of the several Couplers, with any one or more of the contrasting, flexible, and expressive Subdivisions of the other manual Organs. We have, in the preceding pages, spoken on this matter of Divisional and Subdivisional combination, and it is hardly necessary to enlarge on it here. The experienced organist has only to scan the Specification to realize the practically inexhaustible resources in accompanimental tonalities this Gregorian Organ would place at his command. One interesting fact may here be stated, to save reference to what is said elsewhere; namely, that when the Subdivisions of the Organo Secondo and Organo Terzo are coupled, in the unison, to the Organo Primo, the performer will have under his hands, on the First Clavier, six tonally contrasting Subdivisions, five of which are flexible and expressive, and in these important directions under the control of three Expression Levers. This fact may not, immediately, seem of importance: but it means that the six Subdivisions, played from the First Clavier, only, admit of no fewer than sixty-three separate and different combinations of whatever stops may be drawn in them, and left unchanged. The wind-pressure for the labial stops in both Subdivisions to be 3½ inches, and for the three lingual stops 7 inches.

ORGANO SECONDO—This Organ is so stop-appointed as to form the principal Accompanimental Division of the instrument. It comprises twenty stops, chosen on account of their softly-toned, perfectly mixing, and sympathetic voices; capable of being combined so as to form compound tones of singularly smooth and appealing qualities, in every way suited for the appropriate accompaniment of the impressive and prayerful Gregorian Chant. The stops are arranged in two equal groups, contrasting in tonality to as large a degree as possible, considering the pervading character of the Division, and are inclosed in separate Swell-boxes—Nos. 2 and 3—imparting the necessary flexibility of tone and expression, independently, to each Subdivision, in accordance with our System.

The First Subdivision contains stops yielding Pure Organ-tone of a soft and singing quality, refined Open and Covered Flute-tóne, including the BORDONE AMABILE, 16 FT.; three softly-voiced harmonic-corroborating stops, comprising seven ranks; and one of pure and smooth Brass-tone—the CORNO, 8 FT.—imitating the orchestral Horn played softly.

The Second Subdivision contains stops which contribute tones differing in certain directions from those of the First Subdivision. It furnishes, in the BORDONE DOLCE, 16 FT., a Covered Flute-tone of great value; the deep and impressive character of which is enriched by the addition of the voice of the unison FLAUTO A CAMINO, which is similar to the French FLÛTE À CHEMINÉE, and, occasionally, with that of the UNDA MARIS, which is a softly-voiced open wood Flute-toned stop, tuned a few beats flat, producing, in combination with the FLAUTO A CAMINO, a slow wave-like, intonation, sometimes valuable in accompanimental passages of a pathetic character; but which, like all vibrating sounds in instrumental and vocal music, must be sparingly resorted to. To prevent objectionable effects in this direction, the TREMOLANT has been omitted in the appointments of the Organo Primo as well as in the Division now under consideration. The Subdivision also contains three stops of soft Viol-tone; a harmonic-corroborating compound stop, of four ranks, and of extremely delicate tonality; and the two softest Reed-toned lingual stops introduced in the organ. The importance of this Accompanimental Division in association with the Foundation Division is pointed out in the preceding Notes on the Organo Primo.

It is essential that great care shall be taken in the voicing and regulating of all the stops in this Accompanimental Division; and that low-pressure wind shall be used. That special skill is necessary in voicing stops on low pressures is well known; and, accordingly, they are seldom, if ever, favored in the voicing-rooms of to-day in this country. The reason is easy to understand. Irregularities and other imperfections in the delicate and refined voices of stops voiced on wind of low pressure are much more easily detected, and are much more offensive to the educated ear, than similar imperfections are in the loud and necessarily harsher voices of stops on high-pressure winds. Rapidity of production, not tonal excellence in work produced, is the slogan in the organ workshops of to-day in this country; and also, to a large extent, abroad. But it is here only that organ-building has assumed proportions never before known in the history of the art. Unless under stern expert guidance and the unyielding directions of a fully detailed Specification, it is hopeless to secure true art in the tonal appointment of organs constructed in this time of hurried production and conservative trade methods.

The desirable wind-pressure for all the labial stops in both the Subdivisions of the Organo Secondo is 2½ inches, and for the lingual stops 5 inches.

ORGANO TERZO—On examining the stop-apportionments of the Subdivisions of this Organ, as set forth in the Specification, it will be observed that certain tonal elements are introduced which seem to lead away from the chief accompanimental purpose of the instrument. Such is strictly the case; for this Division is, as it were, an appendix to the main tonal structure, introducing elements of an enriching and orchestral tonality, valuable in the rendition of music of an incidental and solo character. For this purpose, it will be most effective when associated with the tonal resources of the Organo Primo; leaving those of the Organo Secondo free for special and contrasting effects of a refined and, probably, of an accompanimental nature. It can, of course, be associated with the Organo Secondo, forming an efficient instrument for incidental music; leaving the Organo Primo free to assume its foundational office. In both cases it forms a highly flexible and expressive Organ of four contrasting Subdivisions. Couplers being provided to enable these combinations to be made in any desirable manner.

The tonal appointment of the Organo Terzo is characterized by its wealth in assertive String- and Brass-tones of an orchestral tendency; both of which are undesirable in the accompanimental Divisions. The arrangement of the stop-apportionment into two groups of contrasting tonalities, and the inclosure of them in the Swell-boxes—Nos. 2 and 3—multiplies the musical resources and utility of this Organ at least tenfold. The desirable wind-pressure for the labial stops of both Subdivisions is 3¼ inches, and for the lingual stops 7 inches.

——NINTH SPECIFICATION——

GREGORIAN ORGAN

AUDSLEY SYSTEM — COMPOUND EXPRESSION
THREE MANUAL CLAVIERS

PEDALE

Compass CCC to G — 32 Notes

PEDAL CLAVIER

1. Principale Grande (44 pipes) . . . W. 16 Feet
2. Principale Dolce . M. 16 "
3. Bordone . . . . W. 16 "
4. Violone (44 pipes) . M. 16 "
5. Violoncello (From 4) M. 8 Feet
6. Flautobasso . . W. 8 "
7. Ottava (From 1) . W. 8 "
8. Contra-Oboe . . M. 16 "

AUXILIARY PEDALE — EXPRESSIVE

9. Bourdone Dolce, 16 ft., derived from No. 24.
10. Contrafagotto, 16 ft., derived from No. 36.
11. Contrabasso, 16 ft., derived from No. 49.

ORGANO PRIMO

Compass CC to c^4— 61 Notes

—— FIRST CLAVIER ——

12. Principale Doppio	M.	16 Feet
13. Principale Minore	M.	8 "
14. Principale Dolce .	M.	8 "
15. Salicionale . .	M.	8 "
16. Dulciana . . .	M.	8 "
17. Bordone Dolce .	M.	8 "
18. Melodia . . .	W.	8 Feet
19. Flauto a Camino	M.	8 "
20. Viola Sorda . .	M.	8 "
21. Ottava Minore .	M.	4 "
22. Flauto Amoroso .	M.	4 "
23. Cornetto Dolce	M.	V. Ranks

ORGANO SECONDO

Compass CC to c^4— 61 Notes

—— SECOND CLAVIER ——

FIRST EXPRESSIVE SUBDIVISION

Inclosed in Swell-Box No. 1

24. Bordone Dolce .	W.	16 Feet
25. Principale Maggiore . .	M.	8 "
26. Flauto Maggiore	W.	8 "
27. Bordone . . .	W.	8 "
28. Flauto Tedesco .	W.	8 Feet
29. Ottava Maggiore	M.	4 "
30. Duodecima . . .	M.	$2\frac{2}{3}$ "
31. Ripieno di Cinque	M.	V. Ranks

SECOND EXPRESSIVE SUBDIVISION

Inclosed in Swell-Box No. 2

32. Principale . . .	W.	8 Feet
33. Keraulophone . .	M.	8 "
34. Melodia . . .	W.	8 "
35. Viola d'Amore .	M.	8 "
36. Contrafagotto .	W.	16 Feet
37. Corno di Bassetto	M.	8 "
38. Euphonium . . .	M.	8 "
39. Corno	M.	8 "

ORGANO TERZO

Compass CC to c^4— 61 Notes

—— THIRD CLAVIER ——

FIRST EXPRESSIVE SUBDIVISION

Inclosed in Swell-Box No. 1

40. Bordone Amabile .	W.	16 Feet
41. Principale Dolce .	M.	8 "
42. Flauto Amabile .	W.	8 "
43. Flauto a Camino	M.	8 "
44. Flauto Dolcissimo	M.	8 "
45. Ottava Minore .	M.	4 "
46. Cornetto Dolcissimo . .	M.	IV. Ranks
47. Oboe d'Amore . .	M.	8 Feet
48. Oboe Ottava . .	M.	4 "
I. Tremolant		

SECOND EXPRESSIVE SUBDIVISION

Inclosed in Swell-Box No. 2

49. CONTRABASSO . .	W. 16 Feet	54. FLAUTO D'AMORE .	W. 4 Feet
50. BORDONE DOLCE .	M. 8 "	55. ARMONIA ETEREA	M. V. Ranks
51. VIOLONCELLO SORDO	M. 8 "	56. CLARINETTO . .	M. 8 Feet
52. CORNO DOLCE . .	M. 8 "	57. CORNO INGLESE . .	M. 8 "
53. VOCE ANGELICA .	M. 8 "	II. TREMOLANT	

CLAVIER COUPLERS

PEDAL ORGAN COUPLERS

First Clavier....................to Pedal Clavier, Unison Coupler.
First Clavier....................to Pedal Clavier, Octave Coupler.
Second Clavier..................to Pedal Clavier, Unison Coupler.
Third Clavier...................to Pedal Clavier, Unison Coupler.

FIRST CLAVIER COUPLERS

Second Clavier .1st Subdivision..to First Clavier, Unison Coupler.
Second Clavier..2nd Subdivision..to First Clavier, Unison Coupler.
Third Clavier ..1st Subdivision..to First Clavier, Unison Coupler.
Third Clavier ..2nd Subdivision..to First Clavier, Unison Coupler.

SECOND CLAVIER COUPLERS

First Clavier...Undivided......to Second Clavier, Unison Coupler.
Third Clavier..1st Subdivision..to Second Clavier, Unison Coupler.
Third Clavier..2nd Subdivision..to Second Clavier, Unison Coupler.

EXPRESSION LEVERS

I. Balanced Expression Lever commanding action of Swell-Box No. 1.
II. Balanced Expression Lever commanding action of Swell-Box No. 2.

CRESCENDO LEVER

Balanced Crescendo Lever, situated to the right of the two Expression Levers, commanding an adjustable series of Stops in progressive order of tonal value, such as may be considered desirable.

DIVISIONAL PISTONS

Two Thumb-Pistons—under Second Clavier—bringing on and throwing off First Subdivision of Organo Secondo.

Two Thumb-Pistons—under Second Clavier—bringing on and throwing off Second Subdivision of Organo Secondo.

Two Thumb-Pistons—under Third Clavier—bringing on and throwing off First Subdivision of Organo Terzo.

Two Thumb-Pistons—under Third Clavier—bringing on and throwing off Second Subdivision of Organo Terzo.

ADJUSTABLE COMBINATION ACTION

Five Operating Thumb-Pistons and Release—under First Clavier—commanding Stop-combinations on Organo Primo, Pedale, and Couplers.

Eight Operating Thumb-Pistons and Release—under Second Clavier—commanding Stop-combinations on Organo Secondo, Pedale, and Couplers.

Eight Operating Thumb-Pistons and Release—under Third Clavier—commanding Stop-combinations on Organo Terzo, Pedale, and Couplers.

TREMOLANTS

The Two Tremolants are to be commanded by Double-acting Thumb-Pistons conveniently located under the Third Clavier, or associated with the Draw-stops of the Organo Terzo.

PEDAL TOE-PISTONS

ALL DOUBLE-ACTING

1. Piston coupling First Clavier to Pedal Clavier—Unison.
2. Piston coupling First Clavier to Pedal Clavier—Octave.
3. Piston coupling Second Clavier to Pedal Clavier—Unison.
4. Piston coupling Third Clavier to Pedal Clavier—Unison.

NOTES ON THE NINTH SPECIFICATION

The Specification now under consideration is for an Organ of considerable importance, comprising in its four Divisions fifty-three complete stops—simple and compound—exclusive of the five derived stops in favor of the Pedale, and which introduce expressive powers in that Division. The powers of compound tonal flexibility and expression are in this scheme confined to the special Accompanimental Divisions; neither the Pedale nor the Organo Primo having any of their stops inclosed. The purpose of this treatment is to unite as closely as possible, while observing the basic principle of tonal contrast, the tonal appointments of the three manual Organs; so as to form a grand accompanimental instrument, suitable, in every direction, for the sympathetic and impressive accompaniment of the dignified Gregorian Chant in its full and perfect development. It will be observed that, differing from the usual practice, the chief foundational Pure Organ-toned stops are apportioned to the Organo Secondo, where they are under control by inclosure in the Swell-boxes. The advantage of this disposition must be obvious to the experienced accompanist; for it multiplies the tonal value of such assertive and dominating voices to an almost limitless extent. Care has been taken, in the stop-apportionment of the exposed Organo Primo, to include therein Pure Organ-toned stops, of the foundational character, which are of comparatively soft intonation, and do not imperatively call for control.

Indeed, in association with the many flexible and expressive compound tones furnished by the four contrasting Subdivisions of the Organo Secondo and Organo Terzo, the stationary tones of the Organo Primo will be of special value. To the tone colorist the stationary and receptive tone of the Organo Primo will fulfil an office similar to that which the stretched and receptive canvas fulfils to the painter.

We have pointed out, in the foregoing remarks, the prime importance of providing, in the true Gregorian Organ, the fullest possible means for the rendition of accompanimental music called for in all the sacred offices of the Catholic Church. Accordingly, we may, at the risk of somewhat undesirable repetition, allude to the remarkable powers our System provides for the easy production of the simple and compound tonal effects called for in truly impressive and elevating accompanimental music. As already stated, in the present scheme the Organo Primo is undivided and all its voices are stationary and devoid of direct powers of flexibility and expression. Both the Organo Secondo and Organo Terzo have two Subdivisions of different tonalities, flexible and expressive. These four Subdivisions can be coupled to the tonal forces of the Organo Primo. When this is done, the performer has at his command, on the First Clavier, five distinct and contrasting groups of stops, four of which are under control by two contiguous Expression Levers, which can be operated, in any manner, separately or together. These five groups admit of thirty-one changes—five entirely separate and twenty-six in different combinations. This arrangement affords what may be considered inexhaustible accompanimental resources, especially when one realizes the tens of thousands of changes of tonalities the different associations of even a few stops create.

Matters such as those just alluded to go far to show the necessity for careful consideration in the scheming of the tonal forces and their control in so important an instrument as a true and sufficient Gregorian Organ: and which also go far to show the crudity and insufficiency of the countless organs already installed in Catholic churches in this land, instruments carelessly appointed on the inartistic, commercial, and trade-bound methods prevalent to-day.

PEDALE—The tonal appointment of this Sub-foundational Division of the Organ is purposely confined within the smallest limits consistent with reasonable efficiency. Along with the three Auxiliary expressive stops it furnishes voices of all desirable classes: Brass-tone being purposely omitted on account of its undue assertiveness when in an uncontrollable condition. Pure Organ-tone, Covered and Open Flute-tone, Viol-tone, and Reed-tone are furnished in the voices of stops selected on account of their full and refined tonalities. The only stop regarding which any question could be reasonably raised is the CONTRA-OBOE, 16 FT. But if this is of small scale, and voiced to yield a refined and singing quality of tone, it will be found suitable in impressive passages of accompanimental music, and extremely valuable in incidental music.

From these remarks it must not be supposed that we advocate undue softness or lack of foundational character in the voices of the Pedale. As we have said in preceding Remarks; on the firmness and fullness of the sub-foundational tone largely depend the dignity and value of the Pedale in the accompanimental office of the Gregorian Organ.

It would seem, on testing the tonal qualities of the majority of Church Organs, produced under the hurried factory methods and commercial spirit of the present epoch of the art, that organ-builders consider the scaling and voicing of Pedal Organ stops to be, in comparison with those of the manual Divisions, of secondary importance. A greater mistake was never made in organ tonal appointment. What would have happened, from a musical point of view, had the great German masters and others held such an opinion when they constructed their noble and commanding Pedal Organs? The stop-apportionments of which frequently approached, and, indeed, in some cases exceeded, half those of the manual Divisions, as the following list shows:

ORGAN	MANUAL STOPS	PEDAL STOPS
Cathedral Church, Ulm	76	31
SS. Peter and Paul, Goerlitz . . .	36	19
St. Stephen, Vienna	28	13
St. Vincent, Breslau	30	15
Lutheran Church, Vienna	15	8

When we first wrote on this important subject—thirty-eight years ago—we said: The true office of the Pedal Organ is to provide a perfectly suitable bass for all the important stops and combinations of stops of the several manual departments. To fulfil this office in a satisfactory manner, it is necessary that the Pedal Organ should be furnished with well-selected stops, numbering about the fifth part of the entire list of stops contained in the instrument. We have found no cause to change our opinion. The stops of the Pedale of the Gregorian Organ should be scaled in strict accord with the scaling of the chief manual stops to which they furnish suitable basses. For the instrument under consideration the scale of PRINCIPALE GRANDE, 16 FT., should give the interior of the CCC pipe a width of 9 inches and a depth of 10½ inches. The wind-pressure for all the labial stops of the Division proper should be 5 inches, and for the CONTRA-OBOE, 16 FT., 7 inches.

ORGANO PRIMO—As the character and office of this manual Division have been commented on at some length in the preceding Notes, it is only necessary here to allude to the stop-apportionment, so far as it is affected by being entirely exposed and, accordingly under no control as regards its strength of voice. This is a condition which dictates, in this accompanimental instrument, a special style of voicing, free from every trace of coarseness.

The PRINCIPALE DOPPIO, 16 FT., which, under its English name, is a DOUBLE DIAPASON, is an open metal stop of medium scale, voiced to yield a full tone of a soft and supporting character, inferior in power only to that of the PRINCIPALE MINORE, 8 FT., the scale of which should be at the CC pipe 5.80 inches in diameter, developed on the ratio 1 : $\sqrt{8}$; and which should be voiced to yield a Pure Organ-tone of medium strength—resembling that of the true English DIAPASON. The PRINCIPALE DOLCE, 8 FT., is another DIAPASON, voiced to yield a tone midway in strength between those of the PRINCIPALE MINORE and the DULCIANA. The tone should possess the refined singing quality of the DIAPASON as voiced by the old English masters. The BORDONE DOLCE, 8 FT., is a covered Flute-toned stop, resembling the so-called STOPPED DIAPASON of the old English builders. The FLAUTO A CAMINO, 8 FT., is in all essentials similar to the French FLÛTE À CHEMINÉE, softly voiced. The CORNETTO DOLCE is to be formed of through ranks of pipes, slightly larger in scale than that of the standard DULCIANA, yielding Pure Organ-tone distinctly stronger than that of the DULCIANA, 8 FT., in the same Division. The five ranks to be of the pitches given in the attendant List of Stops; thus completing the Pure Organ-tone chorus. On account of the uncontrollable voices of the present Organo Primo no lingual stop is included in its apportionment. The desirable wind-pressure for the entire Division is 3¼ inches, a copious supply of wind being furnished to all the foundational stops.

ORGANO SECONDO—On account of the entirely exposed condition of the Organo Primo, the stop-apportionment of the Organo Secondo in the present scheme differs considerably from that of the Organo Secondo set forth in the Eighth Specification. The inclosure of all the stops in both Subdivisions now under consideration has favored the introduction of the more assertive Pure Organ-toned stops—PRINCIPALE MAGGIORE (metal), 8 FT., PRINCIPALE (wood), 8 FT., OTTAVA MAGGIORE, 4 FT., DUODECIMA, 2⅔ FT., and RIPIENO DI CINQUE; to these may be added the four lingual stops, CONTRAFAGOTTO, 16 FT., and the unison CORNO DI BASSETTO, EUPHONIUM, and CORNO. The most important labial stop is the PRINCIPALE MAGGIORE, the CC pipe of which should have an internal diameter of 6.42 inches, developed on the ratio 1 : 2.66 inches; and voiced on a very copious wind of 3½ inches pressure; developing the full Pure Organ-tones which characterize the noble DIAPASONS produced by Edmund Schulze, and found in perfection in his work in England.

It must be realized that, as has already been pointed out in the preceding Notes, the tonal appointment of the Organo Secondo is only an intimate part of the accompanimental system of the entire instrument; standing, effectively, between the appointments of the Organo Primo and Organo Terzo; and linking them together for the fullest and most expressive rendition of both accompanimental and incidental music. At the same time it must be realized that the four contrasting Subdivisions of the Organo Secondo and Organo Terzo, when combined, would form a most effective and resourceful instrument for the refined and impressive accompaniment of the Gregorian Chant: supported, of course, by the Pedale. The wind-pressure for the labial stops in both Subdivisions is 3½ inches and for the four lingual stops 5 inches.

ORGANO TERZO—This is the largest manual Division of the present scheme: comprising, in its two Subdivisions, eighteen stops of soft intonation; two of which are of 16 ft. pitch, eleven of unison pitch, three of octave pitch, and two compound harmonic-corroborating, formed, respectively, of four and five ranks of small-scaled and very softly-voiced pipes. Forming, collectively, a specially beautiful Accompanimental Division, replete with powers of tonal flexibility and compound expression; and, at the same time, comprising tonal elements suitable for the rendition of refined and appealing incidental music. In this latter direction, the following stops present themselves as valuable both in solo and combinational effects: CONTRABASSO, 16 FT., and VIOLONCELLO SORDO, CLARINETTO, OBOE D'AMORE, CORNO INGLESE, all of unison pitch. Both the compound harmonic-corroborating stops, in their soft voicings, are of the greatest value in registration. The CORNETTO DOLCISSIMO is formed of four through ranks of DULCIANA pipes, of the following pitches: 4′—3⅕′—2⅔′—2′. These ranks must be scientifically graduated in strength of tone as they rise in pitch, and in each rank as it ascends the scale. It is desirable that the third-sounding rank be kept the softest in its voice. The ARMONIA ETEREA is to be formed of five ranks of ÆOLINE pipes, having an extremely delicate Viol-tone. The stop is to be composed as follows:—

ARMONIA ETEREA—V. RANKS

CC to F♯	15	19	22	26	29.
G to f♯^{1}	12	15	19	22	26.
g^1 to f♯^{2}	8	12	15	19	22.
g^2 to c^4	1	8	12	15	19.

The extreme delicacy of the tones of this stop practically renders graduation of tone unnecessary. To attempt it would resemble refining pure gold. Of the Pure Organ-toned PRINCIPALE DOLCE and the open and covered Flute-toned stops it is unnecessary to speak here; their voices have been well described in preceding Notes. The desirable wind-pressure for the labial stops of the First Subdivision is 3 inches, and for the lingual stops 5 inches. For the labial stops of the Second Subdivision the wind-pressure is 2½ inches, and for the lingual stops 3½ inches.

We have now to consider the appointment and control of Gregorian Organs, cast in much smaller molds than those set forth in the preceding two Specifications; but which shall be instruments capable of meeting all the demands that can, reasonably, be made on their tonal resources, including the powers of flexibility and expression, absolutely necessary in the artistic accompaniment of the dignified Gregorian Chant. In these comparatively small Organs a modification of our fully developed System will be in order; and will be found to furnish tonal resources far beyond what is possible in organs appointed on the old-fashioned, one-ply method, favored by the organ-builders of to-day, in small organ construction.

We have before us as we write a pamphlet, entitled "The Gregorian Organ," issued by a distinguished organ-building Firm. This records, for the first time known to us, the introduction of the term Gregorian Organ in the English literature of the organ. An admirable plea for the institution of an instrument peculiarly adapted to the accompaniment of Gregorian Chant is furnished by this pamphlet. It contains this incontrovertible statement, which is a basic principle: "One of the chief characteristics of the Gregorian Organ is the *expressive power* of the stops of both manuals." It is to be regretted that in so important a contribution to organ literature the "*expressive power*," in all the seven "Designs" given, is largely crippled in effective operation by the stops of both the manuals being inclosed, together, in a single Swell-box. The imperative necessity of having independent expressive powers given to each manual Division or Subdivision seems to have been unrealized by the designer of all the examples of tonal appointment given in the pamphlet. This trade production clearly shows how difficult it is for the tradition-bound organ-builder, even when confronted by a new problem, to venture in tonal matters beyond what his great-grandfather did.

—TENTH SPECIFICATION—

GREGORIAN ORGAN

AUDSLEY SYSTEM — COMPOUND EXPRESSION
TWO MANUAL CLAVIERS

PEDALE

Compass CCC to G — 32 Notes

PEDAL CLAVIER

1. Principale Grande	W.	16 Feet	3. Flautobasso (From 2)	W.	8 Feet
2. Flautone (44 pipes)	W.	16 "	4. Ottava Dolce . .	M.	8 "

AUXILIARY PEDALE — EXPRESSIVE

5. Contrabasso, 16 ft., derived from No. 22.
6. Bordone Amabile, 16 ft., derived from No. 10.
7. Contrafagotto, 16 ft., derived from No. 31.

ORGANO MANUALE

Compass CC to c^4— 61 Notes

FIRST SUBDIVISION — UNEXPRESSIVE

8. Principale Doppio .	M.	16 Feet	9. Principale Minore	M.	8 Feet

SECOND SUBDIVISION — EXPRESSIVE

Inclosed in Swell-Box No. 1

10. Bordone Amabile.	W.	16 Feet	17. Ottava Maggiore	M.	4 Feet
11. Principale Maggiore	M.	8 "	18. Duodecima. . .	M.	2⅔ "
12. Flauto Maggiore	W.	8 "	19. Flauto Piccolo .	M.	2 "
13. Dulciana . . .	M.	8 "	20. Cornetto Dolcissimo	M.	IV. Ranks
14. Melodia . . .	W.	8 "	21. Corno di Bassetto	M.	8 Feet
15. Unda Maris . .	W.	8 "			
16. Flauto Tedesco .	W.	8 "			

THIRD SUBDIVISION — EXPRESSIVE

Inclosed in Swell-Box No. 2

22. Contrabasso . .	W.	16 Feet	25. Bordone Dolce .	M.	8 Feet
23. Salicionale . .	M.	8 "	26. Viola da Gamba .	M.	8 "
24. Keraulophone. .	M.	8 "	27. Viola Sorda (Sharp)	M.	8 "

28. Violetta . . .	M. 4 Feet	31. Contrafagotto .	W. 16 Feet
29. Ottava Dolce .	M. 4 "	32. Oboe d'Amore .	M. 8 "
30. Ripieno di Cinque	M. V. Ranks	33. Euphonium . . .	M. 8 "

CLAVIER COUPLERS

PEDAL CLAVIER COUPLERS

First Clavier....................to Pedal Clavier, Unison Coupler.
First Clavier....................to Pedal Clavier, Octave Coupler.
Second Clavier..................to Pedal Clavier, Unison Coupler.

FIRST CLAVIER COUPLERS

Second Clavier................to First Clavier, Unison Coupler.
Second Clavier................to First Clavier, Octave Coupler.
Second Clavier................to First Clavier, Sub-octave Coupler.
First Clavier..................Sub-octave Coupler on itself.

SECOND CLAVIER COUPLERS

First Clavier................to Second Clavier, Sub-octave Coupler.
Second Clavier..............Sub-octave Coupler on itself.

EXPRESSION LEVERS

I. Balanced Expression Lever commanding action of Swell-Box No. 1.
II. Balanced Expression Lever commanding action of Swell-Box No. 2.

ADJUSTABLE COMBINATION ACTION

Six Operating Thumb-Pistons and Release—under First Clavier—commanding combinations on all Stops and Couplers.
Six Operating Thumb-Pistons and Release—under Second Clavier—commanding combinations on all Stops and Couplers.

PEDAL TOE-PISTONS

ALL DOUBLE-ACTING

Piston coupling First Clavier to Pedal Clavier—Unison.
Piston coupling First Clavier to Pedal Clavier—Octave.
Piston coupling Second Clavier to Pedal Clavier—Unison.

NOTES ON THE TENTH SPECIFICATION

The reader, and especially if he is an organist, on examining the Specification now under consideration, will observe a disposition widely at variance with that he has been accustomed to, and which is now commonly followed by organ-builders and designers of instruments of two manual claviers, in which the claviers command *separate* and *fixed* stop-apportionments, one of which is rendered expressive by inclosure in a Swell-box. The Divisions so formed are commonly designated the Great Organ and Swell Organ.

On such an examination, the organist will be at a loss to grasp the peculiar tonal resources and remarkable powers of compound-tone production, flexibility, and expression which the Organ, as specified, would place at his command—powers absolutely impossible on any instrument, of the same stop-appointment, constructed on the usual old-fashioned lines.

To make all matters clear regarding the tonal appointment, powers, and control of this Organ, and with as few words as possible, we shall address the imaginary Organist directly.

In all the organs, of the ordinary construction, you have played, you have found, separate, fixed, stop-apportionments, commanded by the different manual claviers, designated Great, Choir, Swell, etc.; and that the only way of combining the stops belonging to these different tonal Divisions was by coupling their claviers; thereby seriously affecting their always desirable independence. There are other disadvantages.

In the System of tonal appointment set forth in the present Specification, matters are widely different, and independence reigns supreme. Every manual stop is at all times equally free to both claviers, neither of which calls for a name indicating a special tonality. For the sake of distinction, however, they may be called First and Second or Lower and Upper Claviers. This, accordingly, means that you have at your command, for combination or registration, twenty-four stops, equally available on each manual Clavier; the combinations being entirely independent—the Claviers being uncoupled. You can, for instance, have all the twenty-four stops drawn on either of the Claviers; while on the other there can be drawn any stop or combination of stops derived from the twenty-four, and having simple or compound tonal flexibility or expression. Thus, you can have, at will, entirely different tonal groups on the Claviers, or groups having one or more stops in common. In short, you can arrange the twenty-four stops in any manner you consider desirable.

Draw the necessary stops on the Lower Clavier, open one or both the Swell-boxes, and you have an exposed Organo Primo. Draw the desirable stops on the Upper Clavier, use the Expression Levers, and you have a simple or compound expressive Organo Secondo. Again; draw the desirable stops—say, of those inclosed in Swell-box No. 2—on the Upper Clavier; and a suitable combination of the stops in Swell-box No. 1, on the Lower Clavier; and you have expressive and tonally contrasting double Accompanimental Organs, or Solo and Accompanimental Organs, at your command, and which can be instantly changed as musical sense may direct.

But these expedients are far from being all that this Organ places at your service; for neither the special powers of compound flexibility nor expression, possessed by the Organ, have been brought fully into play. Now draw the Full Organ, or any combination of stops from the *three* Subdivisions specified, on, say, the Lower Clavier, and you have thereon *three distinct tonal powers* under your command; one necessarily stationary and unexpressive, but dignified and impressive in character; and two which are alike flexible in tone and adjustable to any desirable strength, but which can become expressive on the touch of your foot on the Expression Levers. These Levers are placed close together, in the usual position, and can be operated separately or together by one foot, so as to produce simple or compound expression. One Lever can be so adjusted as to secure any strength of tone in the stops drawn in the Swell-box it commands; while the other Lever can be operated so as to impart expression to the voices of the stops drawn in the Swell-box it controls. In short, by the alternating and the simultaneous operations of the Levers by a single foot; and, in any contrary manner, at the same time, by both feet; countless impressive and beautiful musical effects can be produced while playing on one uncoupled clavier—effects of great value in the artistic rendition of accompanimental music, which are absolutely impossible on any organ designed on the old-fashioned methods of tonal appointment and control.

To give some idea of the tonal resources of this comparatively small organ, created by the mere combinations of its stops, it may be stated—as a matter of curiosity rather than of practical value or interest—that in the stop-apportionment of the Pedale, including the three Auxiliary stops, one hundred and twenty-seven different tones and combinations are possible; every one of which can be effectively resorted to. In each of the Expressive Subdivisions of the Organo Manuale, comprising twelve stops, no fewer than four thousand and ninety-five different tonal effects can be obtained by the combinations of the stops. When the twenty-four stops of the Subdivisions are combined, the number of possible combinations is positively staggering to the imagination—they amount to sixteen million, seven hundred and seventy-seven thousand, two hundred and twelve.

Clavier Couplers are not of great importance in an organ of this class; but those connecting the Claviers in the Octave and Sub-octave are of value when artistically used. We do not favor resort to such Couplers acting on the same clavier; for although they are great tonal noise producers, beloved by organists, they unavoidably upset correct tonal balance. The reason is obvious.

To properly command the tonal resources of this Organ, a special arrangement of the draw-stop action is imperative. This calls for two complete sets of stop-knobs, rocking-tablets, or pendant touches, disposed in precisely the same order and manner: one set bringing all the twenty-four manual stops on the Lower Clavier; and the other set bringing, in like manner, all the manual stops on the Upper Clavier. These sets, including the draw-stops of the Pedale and Couplers, can be similarly arranged on the jambs of the Console; that on the right of the claviers, belonging to the Lower Clavier, and that on the left, to the Upper Clavier. Or they can be arranged, in a similar order, in two horizontal and parallel rows immediately above the claviers. We are of opinion that the latter arrangement is to be preferred, because the stops drawn on the different claviers are always in the direct view of the performer. Color may be applied to the draw-stops to assist the organist in arranging contrasting tonalities on the different claviers.

PEDALE—In this Gregorian Organ, which is specially of an accompanimental character, an assertive Pedale is to be avoided: on the other hand, a foundational bass of a rich, smooth, and unobtrusive tonality is to be desired; so as to add gravity and fullness to the accompanimental music, without dominating it in any inartistic manner. Accordingly, in the Division proper, which is uninclosed, Pure Organ-tone is furnished by a small-scaled PRINCIPALE GRANDE, 16 FT., of wood, and an OTTAVA DOLCE, 8 FT., of metal. Normal Flute-tone, so desirable in Plain Song accompaniment, is furnished by a FLAUTONE, 16 FT., extended so as to admit of a FLAUTOBASSO, 8 FT., being derived from it. By the addition of the Auxiliary Pedale, three very valuable flexible and expressive stops of unison pitch furnish Viol-tone, Covered Flute-tone, and refined Reed-tone. As already stated, the appointment of this Pedale is capable of yielding one hundred and twenty-seven different tones and combinations. The desirable wind-pressure for the four labial stops of the Pedale proper is 5 inches.

ORGANO MANUALE—The stop-apportionment of this Division is subdivided into three groups of contrasting tonalities, but all the voices of which are highly suitable for refined accompanimental music; and are specially arranged to favor the full development of the tonal system instituted in this Specification; which, as has been already explained, permits any possible combination or registration of all the twenty-six manual stops—under the harmonies of analogy and contrast—on either one or both the claviers: multiplying the accompanimental powers or resources to practically an inexhaustible extent, as calculations, stated in the preceding general Notes, go far to show.

Very little use is made, in this Specification, of fixed or unexpressive voices, for such are foreign to the true spirit and purpose of accompanimental music. Yet they are not without their value in compound-tone production; forming, as it may be considered, a pedestal on which to firmly base beautiful and expressive tonal groups. Under these conditions, only two foundation stops are provided, yielding Pure Organ-tone of double and unison pitches, neither of which is unduly assertive in its tonality. These two stops, accordingly, form the First Subdivision of the Organo Manuale; and are uninclosed. The PRINCIPALE DOPPIO is a DOUBLE DIAPASON of a comparatively small scale, having a voice of slightly less power than that of the PRINCIPALE MINORE, which is a DIAPASON of medium scale, voiced to yield a full tone of a rich singing quality; such as is generally considered to be that of the true and full-toned English DIAPASON, 8 FT., voiced on wind of moderate pressure, not exceeding 3¼ inches. This stop is second only in grandeur and purity of tone to the impressive DIAPASON, commonly known in English organ-building circles as the Schulze model; and which, in the present scheme, is represented by the PRINCIPALE

MAGGIORE, 8 FT., in the apportionment of the Second Subdivision, where its majestic voice is under perfect control, enabling it to be used in expressive accompanimental and incidental music.

Beyond the dominant Pure Organ-tone furnished by the important stop just commented on and its attendant harmonic-corroborating OTTAVA MAGGIORE, 4 FT., and DUODECIMA, 2⅔ FT., the prevailing quality of voice throughout this Second Subdivision is double and unison unimitative Flute-tone. Refined and beautiful Free Organ-tone being contributed by the DULCIANA, 8 FT., and the CORNETTO DOLCISSIMO, of four complete ranks—4′—3⅕′—2⅔′—2′. The UNDA MARIS is a MELODIA, of small scale, tuned flat to the MELODIA proper, with which it is drawn, producing a slow and soft tonal undulation. The CORNO DI BASSETTO is an uncommon lingual stop, of the Clarinet family, which, when properly made, produces a fuller and richer quality of tone than the normal CLARINETTO. As we say elsewhere;[22] voiced by a master-hand and with this aim, the CORNO DI BASSETTO becomes invaluable as a timbre-creator in artistic registration; combining perfectly and producing a series of tones with all classes of labial stops. The desirable wind-pressure for all the stops of this Second Subdivision is 3¼ inches.

In the stop-apportionment of the Third Subdivision a sharp contrast of tone is provided to the tones of both the other Subdivisions. Here is introduced no Pure Organ-tone; its place being taken by refined Viol-tone, produced by the CONTRABASSO, SALICIONALE, VIOLA DA GAMBA, VIOLA SORDA and VIOLETTA. Provided these stops are of proper scales, and voiced to yield full tones of medium strength and devoid of high and cutting harmonics, they will be of the greatest value in the tonal structure of the instrument. It will be observed that care is taken, in the five-rank, RIPIENO DI CINQUE, to furnish harmonic-corroborating tones of high pitch, sufficient for the entire tonal scheme. This compound stop is to be formed of full-scaled DULCIANA pipes, carefully voiced and graduated, and composed as follows:—

RIPIENO DI CINQUE —V. RANKS

CC to G	19	22	24	26	29.
G# to g¹	12	15	17	19	22.
g#¹ to g²	8	12	15	17	19.
g#² to c⁴	1	8	10	12	15.

The two lingual stops, yielding refined Reed-tone of a quality highly suitable, as in the case of the CORNO DI BASSETTO, for the accompaniment of the human voice. Brass-tone, which is more valuable in incidental than accompanimental music, is well furnished by the EUPHONIUM; the voice of which in the present tonal scheme, should stand midway between the characteristic voices of the Horn and Trumpet of the grand orchestra. The wind-pressure for all the stops of this Third Subdivision, inclosed in Swell-box No. 2, is 3 inches, provided it is favorably located in the lay-out of the Organ.

22 "Organ Stops and Their Artistic Registration." Pages 78–80. Where the stop is illustrated and fully described.

—— *ELEVENTH SPECIFICATION* ——

GREGORIAN ORGAN

AUDSLEY SYSTEM — COMPOUND EXPRESSION
TWO MANUAL CLAVIERS

PEDALE

Compass CCC to G — 32 Notes

PEDAL CLAVIER

1. PRINCIPALE GRANDE (44 pipes) . . .	W. 16 Feet	3. OTTAVA GRANDE (From 1) . . .	W. 8 Feet
2. PRINCIPALE DOLCE (44 pipes) . . .	M. 16 "	4. OTTAVA DOLCE (From 2) . . .	M. 8 "

AUXILIARY PEDALE — EXPRESSIVE

5. BORDONE DOLCE, 16 ft., derived from No. 9.
6. CONTRAFAGOTTO, 16 ft., derived from No. 23.

ORGANO MANUALE

Compass CC to c⁴— 61 Notes

FIRST SUBDIVISION—UNEXPRESSIVE

7. PRINCIPALE . . .	M. 8 Feet	8. DULCIANA . . .	M. 8 Feet

SECOND SUBDIVISION—EXPRESSIVE

Inclosed in Swell-Box No. 1

9. BORDONE DOLCE .	M. 16 Feet	14. FLAUTO TRAVERSO .	W. 4 Feet
10. FLAUTO DOPPIO .	W. 8 "	15. CORNETTO DOLCISSIMO	M. IV Ranks
11. DOLCE	M. 8 "	16. CORNO INGLESE . .	M. 8 Feet
12. FLAUTO TEDESCO .	W. 8 "		
13. EOLINA	M. 8 "		

THIRD SUBDIVISION—EXPRESSIVE

Inclosed in Swell-Box No. 2

17. PRINCIPALE DOLCE .	M. 8 Feet	22. VIOLETTA . . .	M. 4 Feet
18. SALICIONALE . .	M. 8 "	23. CONTRAFAGOTTO .	W. 16 "
19. VIOLONCELLO . .	M. 8 "	24. EUPHONIUM . . .	M. 8 "
20. DOLCE GAMBA . .	M. 8 "	25. CLARINETTO . .	M. 8 "
21. MELODIA . . .	W. 8 "	26. OBOE OTTAVA . .	M. 4 "

CLAVIER COUPLERS

PEDAL CLAVIER COUPLERS

First Clavier.................... to Pedal Clavier, Unison Coupler.
First Clavier.................... to Pedal Clavier, Octave Coupler.
Second Clavier.................. to Pedal Clavier, Unison Coupler.

FIRST CLAVIER COUPLERS

Second Clavier............... to First Clavier, Unison Coupler.
Second Clavier............... to First Clavier, Octave Coupler.
Second Clavier............... to First Clavier, Sub-octave Coupler.
First Clavier................. Sub-octave Coupler on itself.

SECOND CLAVIER COUPLERS

First Clavier................ to Second Clavier, Sub-octave Coupler.
Second Clavier............. Sub-octave Coupler on itself.

EXPRESSION LEVERS

I. Balanced Expression Lever commanding action of Swell-Box No. 1.
II. Balanced Expression Lever commanding action of Swell-Box No. 2.

ADJUSTABLE COMBINATION ACTION

Five Operating Thumb-Pistons and Release, under First Clavier—commanding combinations on all Stops and Couplers.
Five Operating Thumb-Pistons and Release, under Second Clavier—commanding combinations on all Stops and Couplers.

PEDAL TOE-PISTONS

ALL DOUBLE-ACTING

Piston coupling First Clavier to Pedal Clavier—Unison.
Piston coupling First Clavier to Pedal Clavier—Octave.
Piston coupling Second Clavier to Pedal Clavier—Unison.

NOTES ON THE ELEVENTH SPECIFICATION

Beyond the element of size, the present Specification differs in no essential, in its tonal structure and system of control, from what is set forth in the Notes, appended to the Tenth Specification. Such being the case, it is unnecessary to repeat what has been stated in the general remarks which form so important a part of the Notes alluded to. But unless the interested reader has already consulted those remarks, he should refer to them at this point; so as to grasp the significance of the present scheme.

There is one fact of great importance to the lover of beautiful sounds, and which the true accompanist cannot fail to realize; namely, that while it will be possible to produce, by the simple means at his command, thousands of tonal combinations on the two claviers, it will be impossible to create undesirable noise. We are well aware that the ordinary organist loves *musical noise* at any price: hence we see the general craze with organ-builders and organists, as we have said elsewhere, for uninclosed TUBAS, Octave-couplers on all claviers creating unbalanced noise, and other means of piling sound on sound, regardless of acoustical laws, or, indeed, common-sense. We unhesitatingly say that the organist, whoever he may be, who loves, or even tolerates, the uncontrollable roar of a TUBA MIRABILIS, on twenty to thirty-inch wind, has no true artistic sense. Care has been taken in all the tonal schemes given in this treatise to prevent, so far as is possible, opportunities for the display of bad taste in tonal effects: and in no instrument is this precaution more necessary than in the true Gregorian Organ while fulfilling its prime office—the accompaniment of the dignified and impressive Plain Song.

PEDALE—This Division is of the same dimensions as that of the Tenth Specification, but is slightly different in its tonality; the PRINCIPALE DOLCE, yielding Pure Organ-tone, taking the place of the FLAUTONE of the preceding scheme, which yields an unimitative Flute-tone of a more assertive character. The same relationship obtaining in the derived Octaves. The Auxiliary Pedale is of only two stops, and, accordingly, less in volume of tone. The desirable wind-pressure for the Pedale proper is 4½ inches to 5 inches according to the position the stops occupy in the lay-out.

ORGANO MANUALE—To avoid undesirable and unnecessary repetition, we here suggest that the interested reader shall, before proceeding further in these Notes, carefully scan what is said, under the sub-heading Organo Manuale, in the Notes appended to the preceding Tenth Specification.

In accordance with our System, and although the stop-apportionment of the Organo Manuale is a complete and connected whole entirely devoid of tonal repetitions, it is arranged in three groups of contrasting tonalities, two of which are rendered flexible and expressive by being inclosed in separate Swell-boxes, which multiply their tonal values and artistic effects tenfold and more; meeting every refinement that could possibly be required in the most exacting accompanimental music.

The First Subdivision is in this Specification, as in the preceding one, formed of two exposed stops only, both of which are of Organ-tone; but here of a less assertive tonality and of unison pitch. These beautifully-voiced stops are the only ones belonging to the Organo Manuale that can be properly assigned to an exposed position under our hard and fast System. Their foundational and stationary voices will be of great value in compound-tone production.

The Second Subdivision, which is inclosed in Swell-box No. 1, comprises in its apportionment eight stops; four of which yield double, unison, and octave Flute-tone. To these are added the two unison labial stops—DOLCE and EOLINA—yielding soft voices of great refinement, aiding effective registration and delicate tonal coloration, extremely valuable in artistic and sympathetic accompaniment to the voice. Such refinement is sought for in vain in the hurriedly built and hastily voiced organs of to-day. The principal unison stop is the FLAUTO DOPPIO, commonly known as the DOPPELFLÖTE, which yields, when properly made and voiced, a full-bodied and richly-colored Flute-tone, possessing a rare mixing property; producing beautiful compound tones in combination with all the metal stops of both the Subdivisions; and especially with the lingual stops, to the voices of which it imparts a desirable fullness and smoothness, without objectionably increasing their power. The desirable wind-pressure for this Second Subdivision is 2¾ inches.

The Third Subdivision, which is inclosed in Swell-Box No. 2, comprises in its apportionment stops which in their tonalities contrast effectively with those of both the First and Second Subdivisions. The characteristic tonality of the Subdivision now under consideration is, in its labial voices, a refined Viol-tone; furnished by the VIOLONCELLO, DOLCE GAMBA, SALICIONALE, and VIOLETTA. These stops in combination form an effective String-toned group which necessarily adds interest and completeness to both the accompanimental and solo powers of the instrument. In the lingual stops, which form a prominent tonal feature in the appointment of this Subdivision, the CONTRAFAGOTTO, CLARINETTO, and OBOE OTTAVA satisfactorily furnish pure Reed-tone: while the accompanying EUPHONIUM yields a soft Brass-tone, clothing, as with a garment of warm and genial sound, the other lingual voices of the Subdivision. The PRINCIPALE DOLCE, yielding Pure Organ-tone, and the MELODIA, yielding a beautiful Flute-tone, bind all the tonal forces of the Subdivision together in a rich compound sound of a distinctive character; completing the entire tonal structure of the instrument in a most effective and resourceful manner.

—*TWELFTH SPECIFICATION*—

GREGORIAN ORGAN

AUDSLEY SYSTEM — COMPOUND EXPRESSION
TWO MANUAL CLAVIERS

PEDALE

Compass CCC to G — 32 Notes

PEDAL CLAVIER

1. Principale (44 pipes)	W. 16 Feet	3. Ottava (From 1) .	W. 8 Feet
2. Principale Dolce (44 pipes) . . .	M. 16 "	4. Ottava Dolce (From 2) .	M. 8 "

AUXILIARY PEDALE — EXPRESSIVE

5. Bordone Dolce, 16 ft., derived from No. 9.
6. Contrafagotto, 16 ft., derived from No. 19.

ORGANO MANUALE

Compass CC to c^4— 61 Notes

FIRST SUBDIVISION—UNEXPRESSIVE

7. Principale . . .	M. 8 Feet	8. Dulciana . . .	M. 8 Feet

SECOND SUBDIVISION — EXPRESSIVE

Inclosed in Swell-Box No. 1

9. Bordone Dolce .	M. 16 Feet	13. Flauto Amoroso .	M. 4 Feet
10. Principale Dolce .	M. 8 "	14. Cornetto Dolcissimo	M. IV. Ranks
11. Flauto Doppio .	W. 8 "		
12. Flauto Dolce . .	M. 8 "		

THIRD SUBDIVISION — EXPRESSIVE

Inclosed in Swell-Box No. 2

15. Salicionale . .	M. 8 Feet	18. Violetta . . .	M. 4 Feet
16. Viola Sorda . .	M. 8 "	19. Contrafagotto .	M. 16 "
17. Eolina	M. 8 "	20. Clarinetto . .	M. 8 "

CLAVIER COUPLERS

PEDAL CLAVIER COUPLERS

First Clavier....................to Pedal Clavier, Unison Coupler.
First Clavier....................to Pedal Clavier, Octave Coupler.
Second Clavier..................to Pedal Clavier, Unison Coupler.

FIRST CLAVIER COUPLERS

Second Clavier...............to First Clavier, Unison Coupler.
Second Clavier...............to First Clavier, Octave Coupler.
Second Clavier...............to First Clavier, Sub-octave Coupler.
First Clavier.................Sub-octave Coupler on itself.

SECOND CLAVIER COUPLERS

First Clavier...............to Second Clavier, Sub-octave Coupler.
Second Clavier.............Sub-octave on itself.

EXPRESSION LEVERS

I. Balanced Expression Lever commanding action of Swell-Box No. 1.
II. Balanced Expression Lever commanding action of Swell-Box No. 2.

ADJUSTABLE COMBINATION ACTION

Three Operating Thumb-Pistons and Release, under First Clavier—commanding combinations on all Stops and Couplers.

Three Operating Thumb-Pistons and Release, under Second Clavier—commanding combinations on all Stops and Couplers.

PEDAL TOE-PISTONS

ALL DOUBLE-ACTING

Piston coupling First Clavier to Pedal Clavier—Unison.
Piston coupling First Clavier to Pedal Clavier—Octave.
Piston coupling Second Clavier to Pedal Clavier—Unison.

NOTES ON THE TWELFTH SPECIFICATION

The Organ set forth in this Specification is cast in the smallest mold we would recommend for a really serviceable Gregorian instrument. It comprises sixteen complete stops, and four derived stops which are properly confined to the Pedale, where they support the two important sub-foundation stops of the instrument, and impart to the bass the invaluable element of expression. It is an essential principle in our System of Tonal Appointment that the Pedal Organ shall have powers of flexibility and expression, just as have the bass instruments of the grand orchestra. This is a logical conclusion no argument,

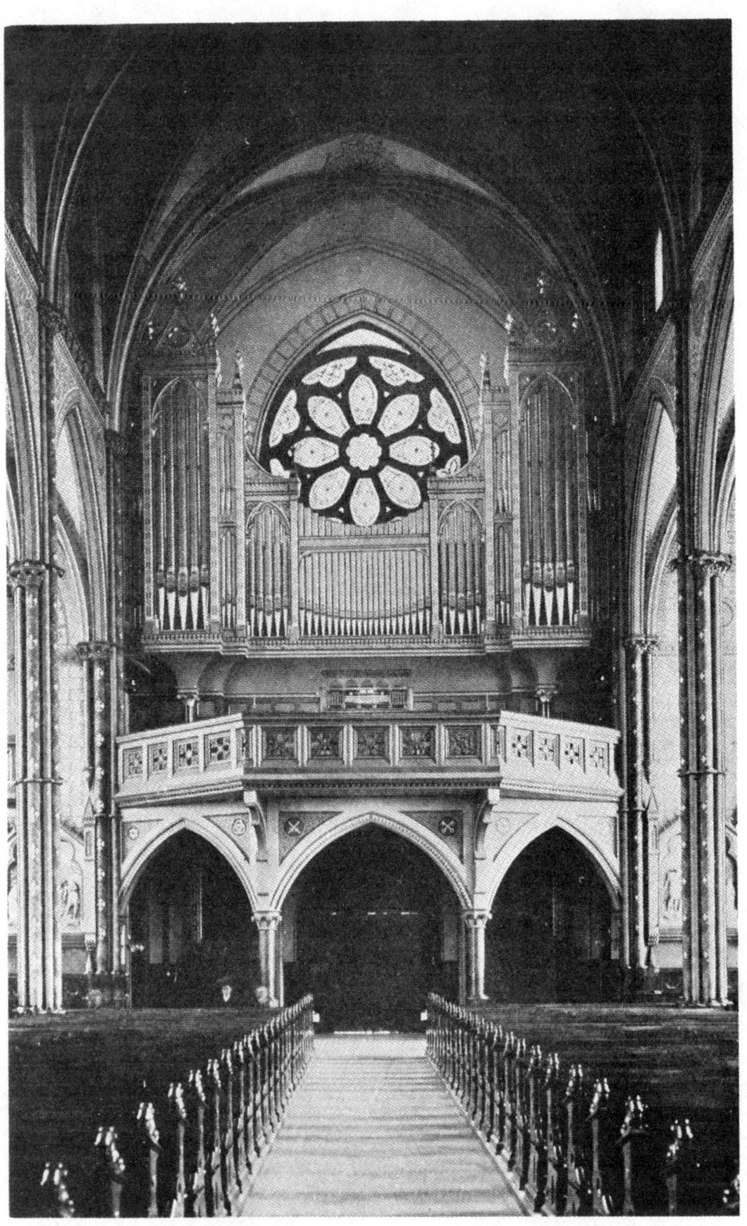

Church of Our Lady of Grace, Hoboken, New Jersey

advanced by the old-fashioned organ-builder, can overthrow. We happen to be the first in the literature of the organ to claim these powers for the Pedal Organ.[23]

The general tonal appointment is strictly refined and sympathetic: and the stop-apportionments in all the Subdivisions are carefully contrasted, both in quality and strength of tone, so as to impart the greatest possible musical resources to the instrument in its all-important office, as an accompanimental organ, suitable in every way for the dignified Gregorian Chant. At the same time, its tonal resources are such, under the means our System furnishes, that they will be found ample for the artistic rendition of any incidental music legitimately called for in the usual services of the Catholic Church. It is but right to remark that all the Organs schemed in this Section of our treatise would require, for the full development of their powers as musical instruments, musician organists, imbued with a rare appreciation of the beautiful in tone and its artistic coloration. Doubtless, with the advent of such organs, the brains to readily grasp their capabilities, and the hands to demonstrate them will be forthcoming.

In the accompanying Plate III. is given a view of the first Church Organ constructed and tonally appointed on our System of Compound Tonal Flexibility and Expression. It was installed in the Church of Our Lady of Grace, Hoboken, New Jersey, about twenty years ago. The following description, which accompanied a view of the instrument, appeared in "Shoppell's Magazine," New York, November, 1908:—

"Notwithstanding the impossibility of obtaining a satisfactory photograph of the organ, against the blaze of light from the rose window behind it, some idea of the architectural design and decorative treatment of the case and displayed pipe-work can be gathered from the accompanying illustration. The case is thirty-four feet in width and thirty-five feet in height, and is so disposed in its several divisions as to interfere as little as possible with the rose window, and that without any sacrifice of architectural effect, and also without having recourse to the intensely ugly and objectionable modern practice of introducing groups of pipes standing without any visible means of support—one of the abominations of every-day, cheap organ-building, and one that was never resorted to by the art-loving old organ-builders. The entire woodwork of the case is harmoniously painted, all architectural features and details being accentuated with contrasting colors and gold. All the displayed pipes, sixty-nine in number, are entirely gilded. Of these, the twenty-one in the central flat are left plain with the exception of their mouths, which are ornamented with patterns in black, and the same treatment obtains in the twenty-four

[23] In the "Cantor Lecture" delivered by the late A. I. Hipkins, F.S.A., before the Society of Arts, London, on Feb. 9, 1891, are these words: "The chief advocate for the extended introduction of the Swell-box in this country is Mr. G. A. Audsley, who has not only urged it on logical grounds in his treatise on 'Concert, Church, and Chamber Organs,' published in the columns of the *English Mechanic* (1886–8), and his recent lectures on 'The Swell in the Organ,' but has practically proved the great advantages to be secured by the multiplication of expressive departments in the organ . . . Mr. Audsley now advocates enclosing a portion of the Pedal Organ to make the bass also expressive."

small pipes which stand, in two tiers, at the sides of the main towers. All the remaining pipes, twenty-four in number, are elaborately ornamented with beautiful Gothic diaper-patterns, executed in black. The contrast presented by this singularly refined pipe decoration associated with the rich polychromatic illumination of the enclosing case-work, is artistically perfect, and is an object lesson that should be studied by all those interested in organ-case designing and pipe decoration. The musical qualities of the instrument are as satisfactory and refined as are the architectural and decorative elements of its case. In certain directions, and notably in its compound powers of expression, this instrument is at present unique. With its forty-five speaking stops and its magnificent thirty-two foot Pedal Organ, it places at the disposal of the accomplished musician and *virtuoso* tonal resources of extreme refinement and endless variety; such, indeed, as are not possible on any other church organ in existence to-day.

"The entire organ was designed and decorated, and its tonal appointment schemed and specified in accordance with his own advanced system of compound expression, by Mr. George Ashdown Audsley, LL.D., Architect, of New York, and author of the standard work, 'The Art of Organ-Building.' The instrument was constructed by The Wirsching Organ Company, of Salem, Ohio, and The Hann-Wangerin-Weickhardt Company, of Milwaukee, Wis., associated. The entire and all-important tonal or sound-producing department being the work of the former firm, on whose tubular-pneumatic system the mechanical portion of the instrument was constructed. The workmanship throughout leaves nothing to be desired."

This instrument was specially designed for a Roman Catholic Church, and is essentially a Gregorian Organ. The Specification is given in "The Organ of the Twentieth Century," pages 482-5.

PART FOURTH

THE THEATER ORGAN

THE Organ suitable in all respects, in its construction and tonal appointment, for the Motion Picture Theater certainly calls for a much more serious consideration than it has yet received by organists and organ-builders. A survey of what has already been done in the installation of Theater Organs, especially in this country, has forcibly led one to the conviction that organ designers have not yet arrived at any definite conclusion regarding the proper and desirable type of instrument, on which can be performed the artistic music required in the sympathetic accompaniment of the moving pictures, for the proper display of which the Theater is erected and appointed.

Indeed, it seems very doubtful if, in the great and hurried demand for organs, the question has received any consideration of a serious nature. Countless evidences of blundering go to prove this idea. Except in some rare instances, the proprietor of a Moving Picture Theater knows little, or nothing, of so complex an instrument as an organ; and is apt to judge its importance by the noise it makes. Accordingly, he is compelled to leave all matters connected with it, save the all-important money ones, to some trusted organist; or is led, more or less blindly, to the ordering point by the persuasive eloquence of some organ-builder or organ-builder's salesman. Doubtless the proprietor has realized the absolute necessity of having an experienced architect to design and superintend the construction of the Theater itself; but has he also realized that, for his own interest and protection, it is quite as important that he should secure the services of a competent organ architect, to design an Organ in every way suitable for his Theater and the office it has to fulfil therein, and to protect his interests in every way? Unless this sensible and businesslike course is followed, the proprietor is at the mercy of the organ-builder, and has to accept what that person chooses to furnish. Had this common-sense and businesslike mode of procedure been generally followed, what a different class of organs would have been installed; and what piles of money would have been spared that have been expended on unnecessarily large, undesirably powerful, and almost invariably coarse and unsuitable instruments, as in the case of all constructed according to the unscientific and inartistic "Unit Organ" manner.

In approaching, with an unbiased mind—if such a mind obtains in organ matters at the present time—one must recognize the necessity of doing so from an entirely new point of view; practically forgetting old-fashioned ideas and prejudices.

As the demands and conditions which necessarily attend the correct and musicianly use of the Theater Organ are essentially different from those which obtain in regard to all other organs, properly differentiated; it surely must be obvious to everyone, gifted with true musical sense, that an instrument of the usual Church Organ type is altogether out of place; and the Concert-room Organ, properly appointed, is to a large extent unnecessary and, for more reasons than one, undesirable in the Theater. It is not to be expected, however, that the advanced organist, who has been accustomed to perform on a large Church or Concert-room Organ, probably more noisy than refined, will agree with the view just expressed: probably he will desire to find in the Theater Organ all the resources for the display of his manual and pedal dexterity; and for the production of the varied and overpowering tonal effects he had so long revelled in; and for which the over-blown and, accordingly, coarsely-voiced organs of to-day furnished ample means.

To the ordinary organist, the problem which besets the music properly called for in the Motion Picture Theater is an altogether novel and perplexing one: and, so far as our experience and observation extend, and notwithstanding the recent efforts that have been made to formulate a school of Theater Organ playing and accompanimental music, no organist has as yet artistically and satisfactorily solved it. Strange to say, the more highly accomplished and dexterous the organist is, the more reluctant he seems to be to attempt the solution. He is too big, and loves grandeur and imposing effects in organ music too dearly, to readily adapt himself to the rendition of the comparatively simple accompanimental music called for by the unique conditions of the moving picture entertainment.

Something must be said regarding many organs—large and costly—that have been installed in important Theaters, so that all the blame may not be laid on the organist if he seems to fail in producing desirable or suitable accompanimental music. We unhesitatingly say that on many of the organs alluded to, an angel from heaven, or Saint Cecilia herself, could not produce refined music.

A survey of even the better class of organs that have been installed in Moving Picture Theaters in this country clearly shows that they have received no serious study from the standpoint of their peculiar purpose and office, which should differentiate them from all other organs.

For the most part, the better class of the Theater Organs which have been constructed here are nothing more than instruments of the old-fashioned Church Organ type, with, in many instances, the addition of some mechanical and more or less vulgar noise-creating accessories. A properly appointed Church Organ has its tonal structure firmly based on Pure Organ-tone, full and dignified, furnished by the DIAPASONS and their important derivatives and attendant harmonic-corroborating families of stops, which form the glory of the instrument. Such a foundation we unhesitatingly say, after years of study of the question, to be unnecessary and largely undesirable in the tonal structure of what may be pronounced the true Theater Organ. In tonal schemes of the larger size, a DIAPASON may be introduced in the stop-apportionments of the Pedal and Grand Organs: but in both cases it is important that it should be different in volume of tone from the foundation Diapason-tone of the Church Organ.

The Theater Organ, when properly considered from all the important points connected with its special position, office, and correct use, which differ from those of all other organs, properly calls for the development of a tonal structure adapted in every way to the artistic office the instrument has to fulfil. The Organ in the Moving Picture Theater is not installed with the view of furnishing, under prevailing conditions, a distinct source of entertainment, or of engendering lines of thought conflicting with those naturally created by the passing scenes presented to the eye. On the contrary, its music should be non-obtrusive, and only such, refined and beautiful, as would aid the impression of realism experienced by the intelligent and absorbed observer of the rapidly passing scenic drama or event. This obvious requirement is, so far as our observation has extended, practically ignored by even the most accomplished theater organists: and, in our opinion, the true artist in theater accompanimental music, and the instrument on which it can be artistically rendered, have yet to appear. Unquestionably the creation and institution of the latter would go far to foster the development of the former. It must be recognized that, among other necessary accomplishments, the organist will have to exercise great self-denial in restraining the display of his powers within the bounds imposed by what the musical accompaniments of the scenes and actions portrayed on the screen call for.

The tonal appointment, stop-apportionments, and control of the Theater Organ present an interesting problem to organ designers; and one which seems, so far, to have been neglected by all the organists and organ-builders of this country. The latter being, naturally, quite content to go on constructing organs on everyday trade methods; or on such as may prove most profitable, and, accordingly, the larger the better. On the other hand, organists seem to have favored the style of organ with which they have, from their pupilage, been familiar, and on which they can best display their technical accomplishments and perform to their own satisfaction. It seems to us that neither of these conditions is likely to foster the production of the true and sufficient Theater Organ.

No one, up to the present time, appears to have fully realized that a decided differentiation is called for in the tonal structure of the Theater Organ, in contrast to the present prevailing method followed in the appointment of the ordinary Church Organ; and that a very special divisional stop-apportionment and expressive control is necessary to adequately meet the unique conditions created by the silent moving pictures on the screen. Powerfully, and in many instances very coarsely, voiced instruments, largely deficient in powers of tonal flexibility and expression, have been unwisely installed in Theaters: and these naturally lend themselves to performances unduly noisy and, for the most part, inartistic and frequently ludicrous and clap-trap. Such musical blundering is entirely out of place in the Theater; distracting and irritating to persons who desire to enjoy, in calmness of mind, the silent drama and thought-creating incidents passing before the eye. The desirable condition of mind, under similar conditions, is clearly expressed by Le Queux in his "Three Knots," in which he says: "There, in the semi-darkness, with soft music playing, and pictures passing ever before her eyes, she found her faculty of mental concentration wonderfully stimulated."

The true Theater Organ is, like the true Church Organ, an accompanimental instrument; but how widely different is the nature of their accompanimental offices. The Church Organ accompanies, in the first place, a highly-trained choir; and, in the second place, a large mass of powerful voices: while the Theater Organ, under entirely different conditions, is used to accompany that which is absolutely silent and provocative of definite and ever-changing trains of thought. Accordingly, the accompanimental music of the latter instrument, under the control of a skilful performer, should always be in full sympathy with the actions or events set forth in the pictures passing on the screen; blending with them, as closely as possible, in tonal harmony and expression; supporting what must be occupying the mind of the intelligent observer, without demanding separate and special attention. To him, the organ music should flow on as an integral part of what is passing before his vision, adding to his mental enjoyment—not breaking in upon its current with unsympathetic and distracting sounds, not always musical, and seldom appropriate.

To neither organ-builders nor organists of to-day will the remarks just made be acceptable. To the former they will seem to destroy—in the event of their being recognized as logical and proper—their hopes of being able to continue the profitable business of furnishing ordinary and more or less nondescript instruments to trusting Theater owners. To the organist, proud of his accomplishments and executive skill, the apparent narrowing of his performances will not be altogether welcome. Is he not there to show off the organ—whatever its class may be—and display his exuberant skill on its attention-compelling keys? Anyway, he almost invariably does so, whatever the cost may be to those present who may desire to enjoy, in thoughtful repose, the silent, pictured drama.

If what has been advanced is proper and desirable, it would seem evident, as already said, that both the true Theater Organ and its master performer have yet to make their appearance. We are strongly of opinion that the creation of the former will go a long way to bring to the front the latter; and lead to the development of an appropriate school of Theater Organ Music. Such a school would imperatively call for the acquisition of considerable skill in improvisation on the part of the theater organist; for, although for certain definite calls of an ordinary class set musical compositions may be found serviceable, it stands to reason that for special and highly expressive accompanimental music, dependence must be laid on voluntary improvisation, under the immediate inspiration of the dramatic events portrayed on the screen. Of course, such improvisation may be the result of a thoughtful study of the drama. Under such conditions, it is obvious that the artist organist requires a highly responsive and expressive instrument, just as the violin and violoncello *virtuosi* require instruments which respond to every touch of the finger and the bow.

The study of the old-fashioned stop-lists of the ordinary Church and Concert-room Organs in existence in this and other countries will go far to confuse and lead the designer of a proper and sufficient Theater Organ astray. In the former he will find much unsuitable tonal material and an undesirable divisional stop-apportionment: and in the latter he will be embarrassed, in all probability, by a superfluity of tonal resources, the large majority of which would not only be unnecessary but positively objectionable in a refined, tonally flexible, and highly expressive instrument, suitable for its true office in the Moving Picture Theater.

Although we would rather pass over, in dignified silence, the distasteful subject of the so-called "Unit Organ"—the name of which condemns it—to do so would be liable to a misconstruction; and it is our desire that the position we take regarding it shall be clearly understood. Unfortunately that monstrosity of the organ-building world, born of ignorance in matters scientific and artistic, and trade interests; in the tonal appointment of which every law of acoustical science and every canon in artistic tone-production are outraged, for the sake of dollars and cents, has been, and is still being installed in important Moving Picture Theaters. It is strongly pressed by cunning salesmen, whose specious representations are accepted as gospel by purchasers, whose ignorance in organ matters is only exceeded by their ready gullibility. The "Unit Organ" is at present a standing disgrace to the time-honored and almost sacred art of organ-building: and, as its construction is perpetrated only in this country, it behooves every American organist, who can claim to be, and desires to be considered a musician, to firmly protest against the production of this miserable and unsuitable instrument; and unless compelled by circumstances he should decline to peril his reputation by publicly performing on one. Why the "Unit Organ" is advocated by purely tradesmen builders is easily understood; and it is hopeless to expect them to cease the construction of such profitable instruments so long as ignorant purchasers can be found. But the time is coming when knowledge and artistic sense in organ matters will demand the consignment of such instruments to the junk heap. Already there is a wave of disfavor passing in certain higher ranks of the organ-playing world in this country: and very fortunately the distinguished organ-builders here will have nothing to do with the "Unit Organ." With these few remarks, no further allusion to this objectionable instrument will be made in these pages.

Before proceeding to consider and tabulate the Stops which are essential and desirable for the tonal structure of what we suggest as the true and sufficient Theater Organ, we may properly give, as concisely as possible, the general conditions and principles on which the instrument should be constructed and appointed. They are as follows:—

GENERAL CONDITIONS AND PRINCIPLES OF THE CONSTRUCTION AND APPOINTMENT OF THE THEATER ORGAN

I. That the Organ shall be designed on the most liberal lines, consistent with its general proportions and the accommodation provided for its reception: which latter should be such as to render objectionable cramping or crowding of any of the sound-producing portions of the instrument altogether unnecessary; providing, at the same time, ample means for the free egress of sound from every portion of the pipe-work. This provision is essential to enable the voicing of all the stops to be unforced on winds of moderate pressures: resulting in refinement and repose of tonality throughout the instrument.

II. That it is desirable in all possible cases for the Organ to occupy a central position with respect to the seated portion of the Theater. If that is not practicable, a single lateral position is to be desired; for a divided organ, located on both sides of the Theater is objectionable. It is distracting to the sensitive ear, and, hence, to the mind, to hear different musical sounds, apparently without any reason or connection, jumping from side to side of the Theater. Concentration of musical sounds is as desirable in the organ as in the orchestra.

III. That the Organ shall have a complete mechanical equipment, comprising all convenient means for the absolute command of all the sound-producing and sound-controlling portions and devices of the instrument. And these means shall be such, in their nature and disposition, as to be devoid of all unnecessary complexity, and the demand for any special and inconvenient physical exertion on the part of the performer seated at the console. This is a matter of great importance in an instrument in which many and rapid changes of tonality and expression have to be rendered certain and easy.

IV. That in the Design of the Console, every appliance and sound-controlling portion and device shall be so placed and arranged, with reference to each other, as to be conveniently reached by the hands and feet of the performer, without compelling him to change his proper central position on the organ-seat, or move his body in any awkward manner while playing. An undignified deportment, much too often indulged in by organists, and in all probability first engendered by the use of badly designed consoles or playing appointments, is to be studiously avoided, for it is most unbecoming. It is necessary to so locate the Console as to give the organist an unobstructed view of the screen on which the pictures are thrown, while he is, as much as possible out of the sight of the persons in the Theater.

V. That in the Appointment of the Console, the old-fashioned and objectionable draw-stop and coupler knobs, arranged in vertical and splayed jambs extending from the clavier cheeks, shall be abandoned, as presenting the maximum of inconvenience, and notwithstanding their still being favored by many organists and some conservative organ-builders. That either centrally-pivoted rocking-tablets, or pendant tablets pivoted at the upper end, shall be adopted, and either disposed on quadrant jambs, or in a semi-elliptical curve, immediately over and embracing the claviers; thus bringing every tablet within immediate reach of the performer. That the several Tonal Divisions and Subdivisions of the instrument shall be indicated by differently tinted tablets. That the Console shall be furnished with a convenient Adjustable Combination Action; and each clavier shall have a sufficient number of Combination Pistons connected therewith. Such other pistons, or finger and toe touches shall be provided as may be required to command the mechanical appliances and accessories the Organ may possess.

VI. That the Manual Claviers shall be of the standard compass of sixty-one notes; and of the approved overhanging pattern, the distance from the surface of one clavier to that of another, immediately above it, to be two and three-eighths inches. The natural keys to be plated with ivory not less than one-twelfth of an inch finished thickness. No imitation ivory to be used in any portions touched by the finger. The sharp keys to be of the best, stove-dried, black ebony. All carefully finished.

VII. That the Pedal Clavier shall be of the radiating and concave pattern known as the "Audsley-Willis Pedal Clavier" (described and illustrated in "The Organ of the Twentieth Century," pages 184–7, Plate XXVI.). This differs widely from the commonplace, more or less inconvenient, and cheaply made claviers, usually furnished by organ-builders, unless otherwise directed.

All the necessary Toe-pistons and Levers for the Pedal Organ Couplers and for the control of the several mechanical accessories of the Organ, are to be provided and located in convenient positions adjoining the clavier, so as to be easily reached by the feet of the performer.

VIII. That the Wind-chests shall be constructed in accordance with the requirements of the most reliable electro-pneumatic action; and shall be of ample dimensions to provide proper speaking-room, and a copious supply of wind, for all the pipe-work planted thereon. With the low and moderate pressures desirable, there must be no shortage or irregularity in the wind supply. To furnish this ample supply, an efficient blowing apparatus and ample reservoirs and wind-trunks shall be provided.

IX. That all the Swell-boxes shall be constructed of suitable materials and in a manner that will secure the production of a proper *crescendo* and *diminuendo*. When closed a perfect *pianissimo* must obtain, without in any way destroying the character or audibility of the sounds of the inclosed pipework.

This is an essential condition, very commonly neglected in this time of inartistic organ-building and tonal appointment.

Proper mechanical means shall be instituted, between the Expression Levers and the shutters of the Swell-boxes, to enable the performer to produce an even and perfectly graduated *crescendo* and *decrescendo*. This condition is imperative.

X. That the entire Tonal Structure of the Organ shall be characterized by a perfect acoustical balance and the greatest refinement possible. All unduly assertive or blatant voices being strictly avoided in favor of those pure voices which combine to produce a sympathetic and resourceful volume of tone throughout the instrument. This quality is essential in the true accompanimental Theater Organ; but that which has evidently been ignored by the builders of the many noisy and undesirable instruments installed in Moving Picture Theaters all over the country.

XI. That the entire Stop Appointment of the true Theater Organ shall afford the largest possible variety of suitable tones, including those of orchestral coloring. Duplication of stops of similar tonality being both unnecessary and undesirable. Stops belonging to the same family, when of different pitches, correctly graduated in strength of voice, and of good mixing qualities, are, however, suitable in instruments of sufficient size to receive them.

XII. That the Divisional and Subdivisional Stop-apportionments, inclosed in the separate Swell-boxes and commanded by different Claviers, shall be so arranged as to furnish distinct groups of leading tonalities as closely as practicable on an orchestral model. These groups will, accordingly, provide the largest possible range of contrasting and analogous voices for the production of effective tonal colorings under artistic registration and compound tonal flexibility.

In Organs of small or moderate size, the Stop-apportionments should be such as to render it almost impossible to form an undesirable tonal combination. Such a scientific and artistic adjustment and fine regulation of tones demand a degree of skill and labor that organ-builders, in these hurried and commercialized times of organ-building, do not dream of exercising. So the ordinary inartistic, rule-of-thumb trade methods go on in the usual unsatisfactory manner; and the organ-playing world in this country to-day seems quite content to accept what trade-bound builders choose to give them.

XIII. That in the Theater Organ, full powers of compound tonal flexibility and expression shall be given to the voices of all the Stops, commanded by the manual Claviers, that can be effectively inclosed: and in every possible case flexibility and expression shall be extended to the voices of the Pedal Organ Stops. Expression is essential in accompanimental music. Flexibility, which means the power of graduating the strength of stationary tones, increases to an almost limitless extent the tonal resources of the Organ; and is especially desirable in instruments of moderate dimensions.

There are other matters than those touched upon in the preceding Principles, which are of some importance in connection with the appointment of the true Theater Organ; but these will present themselves when the Specifications of differently schemed organs are commented on.

The following Specifications for Theater Organs, of different dimensions and tonal resources, will probably assist the organ designer in the production of instruments suitable for Theaters of any dimensions or needs. They set forth what we are convinced are the principles which should govern all such designing.

In the meantime, however, following the method instituted in the preceding Parts, we furnish here a List of Stops of all tonalities, suitable for the tonal appointment of Theater Organs, from which the Organ Architect can select stops desirable for his Specifications for instruments of all sizes.

LIST OF STOPS SUITABLE FOR THE TONAL APPOINTMENT OF THEATER ORGANS

MANUAL ORGANS

PURE ORGAN-TONE

Diapason	M.	8 Feet
Echo Diapason	M.	8 "
Quint	M.	5⅓ "
Octave	M.	4 "
Twelfth	M.	2⅔ "
Super-Octave	M.	2 "
Cornet	M.	IV. Ranks

FREE ORGAN-TONE

Double Dulciana	M.	16 Feet
Dulciana	M.	8 "
Dolcan	M.	8 "
Dolce	M.	8 "
Keraulophone	M.	8 "
Gemshorn	M.	8 "
Echo Dulciana	M.	8 "
Voix Angélique	M.	8 "
Voix Éolienne	M.	8 "
Dolce Quint	M.	5⅓ "
Gemshornoctav	M.	4 "
Dulciana Octave	M.	4 "
Cœlestina	M.	4 "
Dolcette	M.	4 "
Dulciana Tierce	M.	3⅕ "
Gemshorn Twelfth	M.	2⅔ "

FREE ORGAN-TONE—Continued

Dulciana Twelfth	M.	2⅔ Ft.
Dolce Fifteenth	M.	2 "
Gemshorn Fifteenth	M.	2 "
Dulciana Cornet	M.	V. Ranks
Harmonia Ætheria	T.	VI. Ranks

FLUTE ORGAN-TONE

(Open Flute-tone)

Flauto Traverso	W.	8 Feet
Clarabella	W.	8 "
Melodia	W.	8 "
Harmonica	W.	8 "
Fernflöte	M.	8 "
Flauto Amabile	W.	8 "
Spitzflöte	M.	8 "
Harmonic Flute	M.	4 "
Clarabel Flute	W.	4 "
Flauto Amoroso	M.	4 "
Flauto Dolce	M.	4 "
Cœlestina	M.	3⅕ "
Flautino	M.	2⅔ "
Piccolo d'Amore	M.	2 "

(Half Covered Flute-tone)

Doppelrohrflöte	W.	8 Feet
Rohrflöte	W.	8 "
Flûte à Cheminée	M.	8 "
Flauto d'Amore	M.	4 "

FLUTE ORGAN-TONE—Continued

(Covered Flute-tone)

Bourdon Doux	W.	16 Feet
Lieblichgedeckt	W.	16 "
Bourdonecho	W.	16 "
Doppelflöte	W.	8 "
Lieblichgedeckt	W.	8 "
Stillgedeckt	W.	8 "
Zartgedeckt	M.	8 "
Quintaten	M.	8 "
Gelindgedeckt	W. & M.	8 "
Gedecktquinte	M.	$5\frac{1}{3}$ "
Lieblichflöte	M.	4 "
Divinare	W.	4 "

VIOL-TONE

Geigenprincipal	M.	8 Feet
Salicional	M.	8 "
Cone Gamba	M.	8 "
Geigenoctav	M.	4 "
Salicet	M.	4 "
Viol Tierce	M.	$3\frac{1}{5}$ "
Viol Twelfth	M.	$2\frac{2}{3}$ "
Viol Fifteenth	M.	2 "
Viol Cornet (Sordino)	M.	IV. Ranks

ORCHESTRAL STRING-TONE

Contrabasso	W.	16 Feet
Violoncello	M.	8 "
Violino	M.	8 "
Violino Sordo	M.	8 "
Violino Vibrato	M.	8 "
Viola d'Amore	M.	8 "
Viola d'Amore (sharp)	M.	8 "
Violetta	M.	4 "

ORCHESTRAL REED-TONE

Contrafagotto	M.	16 Feet
Contra Clarinetto	M.	16 "
Fagotto	M.	8 "
Clarinetto	M.	8 "
Corno di Bassetto	M.	8 "
Orchestral Oboe	M.	8 "

ORCHESTRAL REED-TONE—Continued

Cor Anglais	M.	8 Feet
Oboe d'Amore	M.	8 "
Clarinetto Quinta	M.	$5\frac{1}{3}$ "
Oboe Decima	M.	$3\frac{1}{5}$ "
Musette	M.	4 "

ORCHESTRAL BRASS-TONE

Double Trumpet	M.	16 Feet
Trumpet	M.	8 "
Orchestral Horn	M.	8 "
Dulcian	M.	8 "
Euphonium	M.	8 "
Tromba Batalha	M.	8 "
Tromba Real	M.	8 "
Clarin Sordino	M.	4 "

INDETERMINATE-TONE

Vox Humana	M.	8 Feet

PERCUSSION-TONE

Carillon	Tubular Bells
Harp	Metal Bars
Celesta	Metal Plates
Xylophone	Wood Bars

PEDAL ORGAN

Major Principal	W.	16 Feet
Minor Principal	M.	16 "
Bourdon	W.	16 "
Violon Basse	M.	16 "
Dulciana	M.	16 "
Grand Quint	W.	$10\frac{2}{3}$ "
Violoncello	M.	8 "
Bass Flute	W.	8 "
Octave	M.	8 "
Grand Cornet	M.	V. Ranks
$5\frac{1}{3}'$—$4'$—$3\frac{1}{5}'$—$2\frac{2}{3}'$—$2'$.		
Contra-Trombone	M.	16 Feet
Contra-Oboe	M.	16 "
Tromba Real	M.	8 "
Trombone	M.	8 "

It has been clearly pointed out in the introductory portion of the present Part of this treatise, that in the general tonal appointment of the Organ suitable for the Moving Picture Theater a special differentiation has to necessarily obtain, to render the production of the sympathetic and appropriate class of accompanimental music, called for by the silent and dramatic doings on the screen, both possible and easy by the able organist and *improvisatore*. This class of organ imperatively calls for all that our System of compound tonal flexibility and expression can accomplish; aided, necessarily, by stop-apportionments in which high-pressure noise is eliminated, and true tones reign supreme.

The List furnishes the names of a carefully considered series of Stops, from which selections may be made for the tonal appointments of organs of all dimensions desirable for the Theaters in which they are to be installed. In the selection of Stops for the separate Divisions of an organ, special consideration should be given to their proper tones, with the view of securing as great a range of contrasting and perfectly mixing voices as possible; thereby securing a satisfactory balance throughout the instrument.

The present trend, and, indeed, the prevailing practice, in Theater Organ construction in this country is diametrically opposite to that advocated in these pages; as is evidenced by the more or less coarse and generally noisy instruments installed in Theaters throughout the land. It is but just to remark, however, that in certain instances no feeble attempts have been made to get away from this prevailing type of instrument, and to produce organs which go far beyond what is legitimately called for in the Theater. Such instruments may be justly considered a cross between a Concert-room Organ and a Church Organ, occupying positions in Theaters of the front rank. Even there, unless used for recital work, their tonal appointments are greatly beyond what are required, or should be resorted to, in their true accompanimental office.

Attention may now be directed to schemes for organs adapted to the requirements of Theaters of different classes and dimensions, carried out in accordance with the Principles enunciated, and stop-apportioned from the List given. It stands to reason that, although very large and expensive instruments are in no cases necessary, organs should in all cases be artistically and, indeed, to as great an extent as possible, scientifically schemed and proportioned with reference to the dimensions and acoustic properties of the Theaters in which they are to be installed. In designing an organ, it should be clearly understood whether it is to be invariably used alone, or at times along with an orchestra. If the latter, greater gravity and richer Pure Organ-tone will be required.

—THIRTEENTH SPECIFICATION—

THEATER ORGAN

AUDSLEY SYSTEM—COMPOUND EXPRESSION

THREE MANUAL CLAVIERS

PEDAL ORGAN

Compass CCC to G — 32 Notes

PEDAL CLAVIER

UNEXPRESSIVE SUBDIVISION

1. MAJOR PRINCIPAL (44 pipes) . . . W. 16 Feet
2. MINOR PRINCIPAL (39 pipes) . . . M. 16 "
3. DULCIANA . . . M. 16 Feet
4. GRAND QUINT (From 2) . . . M. $10\frac{2}{3}$ "
5. OCTAVE (From 1) . W. 8 "

EXPRESSIVE SUBDIVISION

Inclosed in Swell-Chamber

6. BOURDON . . . . W. 16 Feet
7. BASS FLUTE . . . W. 8 "
8. VIOLONCELLO . . M. 8 "
9. GRAND CORNET M. V. Ranks
10. CONTRA-TROMBONE M. 16 Feet
11. TROMBA REAL . . M. 8 "

AUXILIARY PEDAL ORGAN

EXPRESSIVE

12. LIEBLICHGEDECKT, 16 Ft. Derived from No. 30.
13. CONTRABASSO, 16 Ft. Derived from No. 55.
14. CONTRAFAGOTTO, 16 Ft. Derived from No. 75.

FIRST ORGAN

Compass CC to c⁴— 61 Notes

— FIRST CLAVIER —

Inclosed in Swell-Box No. 1

15. DIAPASON . . . M. 8 Feet
16. GEIGENPRINCIPAL . M. 8 "
17. KERAULOPHONE . . M. 8 "
18. CONE GAMBA . . M. 8 "
19. DOPPELFLÖTE . . W. 8 Feet
20. CLARABELLA . . W. 8 "
21. QUINT . . . . M. $5\frac{1}{3}$ "
22. OCTAVE . . . . M. 4 "

23. Harmonic Flute	M.	4 Feet
24. Twelfth	M.	2⅔ "
25. Fifteenth	M.	2 "
26. Cornet	M.	IV. Ranks
27. Double Trumpet	M.	16 Feet
28. Trumpet	M.	8 "
29. Carillon		Tubular Bells

SECOND ORGAN

Compass CC to c^5— 73 Notes

—— SECOND CLAVIER ——

FIRST EXPRESSIVE SUBDIVISION

Inclosed in Swell-Box No. 2

30. Lieblichgedeckt	W.	16 Feet
31. Echo Diapason	M.	8 "
32. Dolcan	M.	8 "
33. Stillgedeckt	W.	8 "
34. Melodia	W.	8 "
35. Flauto Amabile	W.	8 "
36. Spitzflöte	M.	8 Feet
37. Salicional	M.	8 "
38. Flauto Dolce	M.	4 "
39. Salicet	M.	4 "
40. Piccolo d'Amore	M.	2 "
41. Cor Anglais	M.	8 "

I. Tremolant

SECOND EXPRESSIVE SUBDIVISION

Inclosed in Swell-Box No. 3

42. Dulciana	M.	8 Feet
43. Viola da Gamba	M.	8 "
44. Harmonica	W.	8 "
45. Viola d'Amore	M.	8 "
46. Viola d'Amore (sharp)	M.	8 "
47. Dulciana Octave	M.	4 "
48. Dulciana Twelfth	M.	2⅔ Ft.
49. Dulciana Fifteenth	M.	2 "
50. Dulciana Cornet	M.	V. Ranks
51. Oboe d'Amore	M.	8 Feet
52. Dulcian	M.	8 "
53. Corno di Bassetto	M.	8 "
54. Harp		Metal Bars

II. Tremolant

THIRD ORGAN

Compass CC to c^5— 73 Notes

—— THIRD CLAVIER ——

FIRST EXPRESSIVE SUBDIVISION

Inclosed in Swell-Box No. 4

55. Contrabasso	W.	16 Feet
56. Dolce	M.	8 "
57. Violoncello	M.	8 "
58. Violino	M.	8 Feet
59. Gemshorn	M.	8 "
60. Flauto Traverso	W.	8 "

61. Fernflöte . . . M. 8 Feet
62. Voix Angélique . M. 8 "
63. Gemshornoctav . M. 4 "
64. Violetta . . . M. 4 "
65. Harmonia Ætheria T. VI. Ranks
66. Orchestral Horn M. 8 Feet
67. Clarinetto . . M. 8 "
68. Vox Humana . . M. 8 "

III. Tremolant

SECOND EXPRESSIVE SUBDIVISION

Inclosed in Swell-Box No. 5

69. Bourdonecho . . W. 16 Feet
70. Quintaten . . . M. 8 "
71. Doppelrohrflöte . W. 8 "
72. Zartgedeckt . . M. 8 "
73. Dolce Quint . . M. 5⅓ "
74. Cœlestina . . . M. 4 "
75. Contrafagotto . M. 16 "
76. Orchestral Oboe . M. 8 Feet
77. Fagotto . . . M. 8 "
78. Tromba Batalha . M. 8 "
79. Euphonium . . . M. 8 "
80. Musette . . . M. 4 "
81. Clarin Sordino . M. 4 "
82. Celesta . . . . Metal Plates

CLAVIER COUPLERS

PEDAL ORGAN COUPLERS

First Clavier.....................to Pedal Clavier, Unison Coupler.
First Clavier.....................to Pedal Clavier, Octave Coupler.
Second Clavier..................to Pedal Clavier, Unison Coupler.
Third Clavier....................to Pedal Clavier, Unison Coupler.

FIRST CLAVIER COUPLERS

Second Clavier..1st Subdivision..to First Clavier, Unison Coupler.
Second Clavier..1st Subdivision..to First Clavier, Octave Coupler.
Second Clavier..2nd Subdivision..to First Clavier, Unison Coupler.
Third Clavier...1st Subdivision..to First Clavier, Unison Coupler.
Third Clavier...2nd Subdivision..to First Clavier, Unison Coupler.
Third Clavier...2nd Subdivision..to First Clavier, Octave Coupler.

SECOND CLAVIER COUPLERS

Third Clavier..1st Subdivision..to Second Clavier, Unison Coupler.
Third Clavier..1st Subdivision..to Second Clavier, Octave Coupler.
Third Clavier..2nd Subdivision..to Second Clavier, Unison Coupler.

DIVISIONAL PISTONS

Two Thumb-Pistons—under Second Clavier—bringing on and throwing off First Subdivision of Second Organ.

Two Thumb-Pistons—under Second Clavier—bringing on and throwing off Second Subdivision of Second Organ.

Two Thumb-Pistons—under Third Clavier—bringing on and throwing off First Subdivision of Third Organ.

Two Thumb-Pistons—under Third Clavier—bringing on and throwing off Second Subdivision of Third Organ.

ADJUSTABLE COMBINATION ACTION

Six Operating Thumb-Pistons and Release—under First Clavier—commanding Stop-combinations on First Organ, Pedal Organ, and Couplers.

Eight Operating Thumb-Pistons and Release—under Second Clavier—commanding Stop-combinations on Second Organ, Pedal Organ, and Couplers.

Eight Operating Thumb-Pistons and Release—under Third Clavier—commanding Stop-combinations on Third Organ, Pedal Organ, and Couplers.

EXPRESSION LEVERS

I. Balanced Expression Lever commanding action of Swell-Box No. 1.
II. Balanced Expression Lever commanding action of Swell-Box No. 2.
III. Balanced Expression Lever commanding action of Swell-Box No. 3.
IV. Balanced Expression Lever commanding action of Swell-Box No. 4.
V. Balanced Expression Lever commanding action of Swell-Box No. 5.

CRESCENDO LEVER

Balanced Crescendo Lever, situated to the right of the Expression Levers, commanding a selected series of Stops in progressive order of tonal power and character, effective on the First Clavier.

PEDAL ORGAN TOE-PISTONS

ALL DOUBLE-ACTING

1. Piston coupling First Clavier to Pedal Clavier—Unison.
2. Piston coupling First Clavier to Pedal Clavier—Octave.
3. Piston coupling Second Clavier to Pedal Clavier—Unison.
4. Piston coupling Third Clavier to Pedal Clavier—Unison.
5. Piston bringing Lieblichgedeckt, 16 ft. (No. 30) on Pedal Clavier.
6. Piston bringing Contrabasso, 16 ft. (No. 55) on Pedal Clavier.
7. Piston bringing Contrafagotto, 16 ft. (No. 75) on Pedal Clavier.

Other Toe-Pistons may be added for any special purposes considered desirable by the Organ Architect or the designer of the instrument.

NOTES ON THE THIRTEENTH SPECIFICATION

The foregoing Specification is for an instrument suitable for a Moving Picture Theater of the larger class, in which the organ will be used chiefly in its true accompanimental office. At the same time, sufficient tonal resources are provided to render it suitable, in combination with other instruments, to take an effective part in concerted orchestral music. It may, to some extent, take the place of an orchestra in the rendition of any incidental or independent solo music that may be required when any entertainments are provided beyond that furnished by the moving pictures.

The instrument, as specified, comprises seventy-seven complete speaking stops and five derived stops; which latter are properly confined to the appointment of the Pedal Organ. They are derived from different manual Divisions, and constitute a Pedal Organ Expressive Auxiliary, which in no appreciable manner interferes with the tonal independence of the manual appointments. This Auxiliary greatly enriches the Expressive Subdivision of the comparatively small Pedal Organ.

In the scheme under review, there are, in addition to the Pedal Organ Swell-chamber, five Swell-boxes—the maximum number called for, according to our System, in the appointment of a straight three clavier instrument. In the stop-apportionment of the First Organ one Swell-box (No.1) is required, as little would be gained by dividing its fifteen stops. On the other hand, the stop-apportionment of the Second Organ calls for tonally contrasting Subdivisions, and, accordingly, inclosure in separate Swell-boxes (Nos. 2 and 3). The same conditions obtain in the stop-apportionment of the Third Organ, commanded by the Third Clavier. Here our fundamental principle of tonal contrast is still more firmly established, through its twenty-eight stops being effectively grouped and inclosed in separate Swell-boxes (Nos. 4 and 5).

The dispositions of the stops set forth in this Specification, and the ample means for the production of tonal flexibility and compound expression, should be studied by the designer of true Theater Organs.

There are very important facts connected with the tonal resources imparted to organs, designed in accordance with our System of compound flexibility and expression, that must not be overlooked in considering the present Specification. These facts have necessarily been set forth in the preceding pages; but as it is undesirable for the reader, immediately interested, to divert the current of his thoughts, by referring to what has been said elsewhere in relation to organs of a different class to that now under consideration, and which may have no immediate interest to him, we venture at the risk of being accused of undue verbosity, to repeat what has substantially been said on the subject.

According to the present Specification, the Organ, commanded by the three manual claviers, has five tonally contrasting and expressive Subdivisions. The importance of this subdivision may not be immediately realized by an organist not conversant with our principles of tonal appointment: indeed, this subdivision may seem of little importance, and likely to lead to some confusion. Nothing is further from what has been proved to obtain in actual practice. The importance is great and far-reaching; and simplicity pervades the entire System of contrasting tonal flexibility and expression, simple and compound. Our System opens up to the musician organist a new world of refined musical effects and subtle *nuances* of immense value in the accompanimental music of the Moving Picture Theater. Tonal effects and *nuances* absolutely impossible of production on any organ hitherto constructed, or which ever will be constructed, on old-fashioned methods.

Just a few salient facts may be stated here. In the Specification of the Organ now under consideration there are five distinct and contrasting tonal Subdivisions, in which no stop is duplicated; each of which, under the control of a special Expression Lever, can be made to give at least ten distinctly marked different and stationary strengths of tone to any of its voices speaking. This simple fact multiplies, for artistic purposes, the tonal resources of each of the five Subdivisions tenfold; without trenching upon the equally valuable and additional powers of tonal expression possessed by each.

Without considering the operations of the Subdivisions on each uncoupled clavier, let one try to realize what the performer has at his command on the First Clavier with the other two claviers coupled to it, say in the unison only. He has directly under his command and control, tonally, through the agency of easily operated and conveniently arranged Expression Levers, five distinct Subdivisions of different qualities and values of tone. What can the performer do with them? By means of the Thumb-Pistons operating on the Subdivisions alone, he can bring under his fingers—confined to the First Clavier—no fewer than five single and separate Subdivisions and twenty-six different groups of Subdivisions, producing thirty-one distinct tonal combinations without changing the stops originally drawn in the Subdivisions. Further, he can use all these combinations in stationary tones of any desirable and different strengths; partly stationary in tone and partly expressive; or entirely expressive in any desirable groups.

As we have questioned elsewhere: On what organ constructed on the old-fashioned and one-ply style of tonal appointment, still largely popular, could resources such as have just been outlined be placed at the command of the organ *virtuoso?* Yet they are tonal resources in one direction only, and which by no means exhaust those provided in our fully developed Tonal System; which, collectively, revolutionize the tonal structure of the organ and especially the means for its complete and artistic control, which are so radical and constructive as to suggest the possibility of the introduction of a new class of composition of music for the Monarch of all Instruments.

PEDAL ORGAN—In this Specification, which provides a tonal appointment suitable for a true Accompanimental Organ of the class under consideration, neither a large nor noisy Pedal Organ is necessary or desirable. The three complete labial stops of the Unexpressive Subdivision should be of medium scales, voiced to yield three graded strengths of tone; that of the MINOR PRINCIPAL standing midway between the voices of the other two. The GRAND QUINT, derived from the extended MINOR PRINCIPAL, will in combination with the MAJOR PRINCIPAL, generate the Differential Tone of the 32 feet pitch—sometimes, and not inaptly, designated the Acoustic Bass. The OCTAVE, 8 FT., derived from the extended MAJOR PRINCIPAL, completes the only exposed, inflexible, and unexpressive pipe-work in the Organ.

The six effective stops contained in the Expressive Subdivision, furnishing compound Pure Organ-tone, and unison and octave Flute-tones, String-tone, and Brass-tones; and the three stops in the Auxiliary Division, furnishing Flute-tone, String-tone, and Reed-tone; are, in combination with the Organ-toned stops, in the Unexpressive Subdivision, sufficient for all calls that may be made on the Pedal Organ, in supplying analogous or contrasting basses to all classes of manual tonal combinations. Seeing that all the expressive stops are distributed over four different Swells, controlled by four different Expression Levers, it is not difficult to imagine the tonal effects and refinements possible on this Pedal Organ.

The introduction of a CORNET, composed of five full ranks of small-scaled DIAPASON pipes, in a Pedal Organ, is, so far as we know, without precedent in organ-building in this country; and if exposed and, accordingly, not under control, it would be of little use, if not altogether objectionable. If properly scaled and regulated, and rendered tonally flexible and expressive, as here intended, it would be productive of tonal effects of very great value and beauty. For instance, combined with any one or all of the exposed unisons and their derivatives, and artistically adjusted in strength of tone, the CORNET would produce remarkable and beautiful chorus effects, unknown in modern and debilitated Pedal Organs. The composition of the CORNET is given in the List of Stops.

The wind-pressure for all the labial stops should be 5 inches and for the two lingual stops 8 inches. A copious supply must be given to the PRINCIPALS.

FIRST ORGAN—Comprising fourteen complete stops, numbering in all seventeen ranks of pipes, this Organ furnishes a suitable foundation for the entire tonal superstructure of the instrument; which is such as, in our opinion, is best suited to the special requirements of a true Theater Organ. It will be observed that in addition to the six unison labial stops yielding Pure Organ-tone, Free Organ-tone, Open and Covered Flute-tone, and String-tone, there is a singularly rich harmonic structure of eight complete ranks of pipes. Such a full and valuable harmonic furnishing will not be found in any tonal Division in any Theater Organ hitherto constructed. Its importance in scientific and artistic registration cannot well be overrated. The value of the entire Division is immensely increased by its complete inclosure in Swell-box No. 1. The desirable wind-pressure for all the labial stops is 3½ inches, and for the two lingual stops 7 inches.

SECOND ORGAN—Comprising twenty-four complete and independent speaking stops, this Organ furnishes what may justly be considered an adequate Accompanimental Division. It is in general tonality of a refined and sympathetic character; affording a practically inexhaustible variety of effective and beautiful combinations of tone, suitable for the accompaniment of moving pictures of all classes—reposeful or restless, sad or joyful, comic or tragic. In tragic or warlike scenes, however, recourse may be had to certain lingual stops in the Third Organ.

In accordance with our System, the stops of the Second Organ are arranged in two groups of contrasting tonalities, inclosed in separate Swell-boxes, Nos. 2 and 3. The stops in the First Expressive Subdivision furnish Pure Organ-tone, Free Organ-tone, Open and Covered Flute-tone, Viol-tone, and Reed-tone. The stops in the Second Expressive Subdivision furnish Free Organ-tone, String-tone, and Reed-tone. The stop-apportionments in the Subdivisions are such as not to establish a very pronounced tonal contrast between them normally; but such contrast as obtains would be effectively increased through the tonal flexibility imparted by the double Swells, chiefly when in contrary motion. The tonal appointments of both the Subdivisions of this Second Organ are in strict accordance with the Tenth Principle given in the preceding General Conditions and Principles of Construction and Appointment of Theater Organs. Too much care and study cannot be devoted to the problems involved in designing organs, in the tonal structure of which great musical resources are required, and which must be endowed with great refinements of tone, and with extreme powers of flexibility and expression.

The wind-pressure for all the stops of the First Subdivision to be 3 inches, and for all the stops of the Second Subdivision 2¾ inches. These pressures favor liberal wind-supply without endangering purity of tone.

THIRD ORGAN—This Organ is a very important addition to the accompanimental resources of the instrument: furnishing, at the same time, voices of Reed- and Brass-tones of different degrees of assertiveness, suitable for the rendition of highly effective music.

In the First Subdivision, inclosed in Swell-box No. 4, Orchestral String-tones, of double, unison, and octave pitches, are provided, and enriched by the beautiful compound harmonic-corroborating tones of the six-ranked HARMONIA ÆTHERIA. This stop is also of immense value in combination with all the other labial stops in both Subdivisions; and also with the lingual stops, not excluding the VOX HUMANA. Refined Brass- and Reed-tones are sufficiently provided in this Subdivision by the ORCHESTRAL HORN and CLARINETTO. The wind-pressure for the labial stops to be 3 inches, and for the lingual stops 6 inches.

The Second Subdivision, inclosed in Swell-box No. 5, is stop-apportioned in decided contrast to the apportionment of the First Subdivision. It is especially rich in lingual stops, of which there are seven, of double, unison, and octave pitches, yielding full Reed- and Brass-tones of different timbres and strengths of voice, chief of which is the Tromba Batalha or Battle Trumpet. The labial stops have no duplicates in the instrument; and are selected with a special view to combination with the lingual stops, to which they would impart fullness and richness, without impairing their characteristic qualities of tone. The labial stops apportioned to this Subdivision, as, indeed, throughout the entire Organ, clearly indicate the essay made to impart the greatest refinement of tone possible, and that without duplicating a single stop. This is surely a step in the right direction; but a very rare one indeed in modern organ tonal appointment. The wind-pressure for the labial stops to be 3 inches, and for the lingual stops 7 inches.

Before closing the present Notes, it is desirable for a few words to be added regarding the office and operation of the several Swells. These, five in number, are readily controlled by their Expression Levers, which are arranged, from left to right, in numerical order, and having spaces of only half-an-inch between them. By this arrangement, the foot of the performer can operate any adjoining pair, and can move to any one, or from pair to pair, of the series, without any obstruction. The performer can, accordingly, operate any single Lever, either for adjustment of strength of tone or for expression. When used in pairs, he can operate, at the same instant, Swell-boxes Nos. 1 and 2, 2 and 3, 3 and 4, or 4 and 5; and each pair separately for tonal adjustment or alternating expression, or together for either purpose. This system of compound tonal control opens up a new world of musical effects and *nuances* in the organ, absolutely unknown and impossible of production on instruments as at present constructed after the methods of our great-grandfathers.

—*FOURTEENTH SPECIFICATION*—

THEATER ORGAN

AUDSLEY SYSTEM—COMPOUND EXPRESSION

THREE MANUAL CLAVIERS

PEDAL ORGAN

Compass CCC to G — 32 Notes

PEDAL CLAVIER

1. Major Principal (44 pipes) . . . W. 16 Feet
2. Minor Principal (44 pipes) . . . M. 16 "
3. Bourdon . . . . W. 16 "
4. Dulciana . . . M. 16 Feet
5. Violoncello . . M. 8 "
6. Bass Flute (From 1) W. 8 "
7. Octave (From 2) . M. 8 "
8. Contra-Trombone. M. 16 "

AUXILIARY PEDAL ORGAN

EXPRESSIVE

9. Double Trumpet, 16 Ft. Derived from No. 23.
10. Contrabasso, 16 Ft. Derived from No. 43.
11. Contrafagotto, 16 Ft. Derived from No. 59.

FIRST ORGAN

Compass CC to c^4— 61 Notes

— FIRST CLAVIER —

Inclosed in Swell-Box No. 1

12. Diapason . . . M. 8 Feet
13. Geigenprincipal . M. 8 "
14. Keraulophone. . M. 8 "
15. Doppelflöte . . W. 8 "
16. Clarabella . . W. 8 "
17. Spitzflöte . . . M. 8 "
18. Octave . . . . M. 4 "
19. Harmonic Flute . M. 4 Feet
20. Twelfth . . . M. 2⅔ "
21. Fifteenth . . . M. 2 "
22. Cornet . . . M. IV. Ranks
23. Double Trumpet . M. 16 Feet
24. Trumpet . . . M. 8 "
25. Carillon . . . Tubular Bells

SECOND ORGAN

Compass CC to c^5— 73 Notes

—— SECOND CLAVIER ——

FIRST EXPRESSIVE SUBDIVISION

Inclosed in Swell-Box No. 2

26. Lieblichgedeckt .	W.	16 Feet	30. Flauto Dolce . .	M.	4 Feet
27. Echo Diapason .	M.	8 "	31. Piccolo d'Amore .	M.	2 "
28. Melodia . . .	W.	8 "	32. Cor Anglais . .	M.	8 "
29. Flûte à Cheminée	M.	8 "	33. Musette . . .	M.	4 "

I. Tremolant

SECOND EXPRESSIVE SUBDIVISION

Inclosed in Swell-Box No. 3

34. Dulciana . . .	M.	8 Feet	39. Salicet	M.	4 Feet
35. Salicional . . .	M.	8 "	40. Dulciana Cornet	M.	V. Ranks
36. Harmonica . .	W.	8 "	41. Corno di Bassetto	M.	8 Feet
37. Viola d'Amore .	M.	8 "	42. Oboe d'Amore. .	M.	8 "
38. Viola d'Amore (Sharp) . . .	M.	8 "	II. Tremolant		

THIRD ORGAN

Compass CC to c^5— 73 Notes

—— THIRD CLAVIER ——

FIRST EXPRESSIVE SUBDIVISION

Inclosed in Swell-Box No. 2

43. Contrabasso . .	W.	16 Feet	48. Violetta . . .	M.	4 Feet
44. Violoncello . .	M.	8 "	49. Harmonia Ætheria	M.	VI. Ranks
45. Violino. . . .	M.	8 "	50. Orchestral Horn	M.	8 Feet
46. Quintaten . . .	M.	8 "	51. Clarinetto . .	M.	8 "
47. Gemshorn . . .	M.	8 "	52. Vox Humana . .	M.	8 "

III. Tremolant

SECOND EXPRESSIVE SUBDIVISION

Inclosed in Swell-Box No. 3

53. Bourdonecho . .	W. 16 Feet	59. Contrafagotto .	M. 16 Feet
54. Dolcan	M. 8 "	60. Euphonium . . .	M. 8 "
55. Flauto Traverso .	W. 8 "	61. Tromba Batalha .	M. 8 "
56. Zartgedeckt . .	M. 8 "	62. Orchestral Oboe .	M. 8 "
57. Dolce Quint . .	M. 5⅓ "	63. Clarin Sordino .	M. 4 "
58. Dolcette . . .	M. 4 "	64. Harp	Metal Plates

CLAVIER COUPLERS

PEDAL ORGAN COUPLERS

First Clavier....................to Pedal Clavier, Unison Coupler.
First Clavier....................to Pedal Clavier, Octave Coupler.
Second Clavier..................to Pedal Clavier, Unison Coupler.
Third Clavier...................to Pedal Clavier, Unison Coupler.
Third Clavier...................to Pedal Clavier, Octave Coupler.

FIRST CLAVIER COUPLERS

Second Clavier..1st Subdivision..to First Clavier, Unison Coupler.
Second Clavier..2nd Subdivision..to First Clavier, Unison Coupler.
Third Clavier...1st Subdivision..to First Clavier, Unison Coupler.
Third Clavier...2nd Subdivision..to First Clavier, Unison Coupler.
Third Clavier...2nd Subdivision..to First Clavier, Octave Coupler.

SECOND CLAVIER COUPLERS

Third Clavier..1st Subdivision..to Second Clavier, Unison Coupler.
Third Clavier..1st Subdivision..to Second Clavier, Octave Coupler.
Third Clavier..2nd Subdivision..to Second Clavier, Unison Coupler.

DIVISIONAL PISTONS

Two Thumb-Pistons—under First Clavier—bringing on and throwing off First Organ, or any part drawn.

Two Thumb-Pistons—under Second Clavier—bringing on and throwing off First Subdivision of Second Organ.

Two Thumb-Pistons—under Second Clavier—bringing on and throwing off Second Subdivision of Second Organ.

Two Thumb-Pistons—under Third Clavier—bringing on and throwing off First Subdivision of Third Organ.

Two Thumb-Pistons—under Third Clavier—bringing on and throwing off First Subdivision of Third Organ.

ADJUSTABLE COMBINATION ACTION

Six Operating Thumb-Pistons and Release—under First Clavier—commanding Stop-combinations on First Organ, Pedal Organ, and Couplers.

Seven Operating Thumb-Pistons and Release—under Second Clavier—commanding Stop-combinations on Second Organ, Pedal Organ, and Couplers.

Seven Operating Thumb-Pistons and Release—under Third Clavier—commanding Stop-combinations on Third Organ, Pedal Organ, and Couplers.

EXPRESSION LEVERS

I. Balanced Expression Lever commanding action of Swell-Box No. 1.
II. Balanced Expression Lever commanding action of Swell-Box No. 2.
III. Balanced Expression Lever commanding action of Swell-Box No. 3.

CRESCENDO LEVER

Balanced Crescendo Lever, situated to the right of the Expression Levers, commanding a selected series of Stops in progressive order of tonal power and character, effective on the First Clavier.

PEDAL ORGAN TOE-PISTONS

ALL DOUBLE-ACTING

1. Piston coupling First Clavier to Pedal Clavier—Unison.
2. Piston coupling First Clavier to Pedal Clavier—Octave.
3. Piston coupling Second Clavier to Pedal Clavier—Unison.
4. Piston coupling Third Clavier to Pedal Clavier—Unison.
5. Piston bringing Double Trumpet, 16 ft. (No. 23) on Pedal Clavier.
6. Piston bringing Contrabasso, 16 ft. (No. 43) on Pedal Clavier.
7. Piston bringing Contrafagotto, 16 ft., (No. 59) on Pedal Clavier.

Other Toe-Pistons may be added for any special purposes considered desirable by the Organ Architect or the designer of the instrument.

NOTES ON THE FOURTEENTH SPECIFICATION

This Specification is for an instrument in all respects suitable for a Moving Picture Theater of the first class; and is sufficient for the proper rendition of all classes of artistic and legitimate accompanimental music. It comprises fifty-nine complete and independent speaking stops, without a single tonal duplication: this latter is a matter of great importance. In the tonal scheme there are only five derived stops, and these are properly confined to the least sensitive Division of the instrument—the Pedal Organ. It will be observed throughout all the preceding Specifications, that the unscientific, inartistic, and altogether objectionable modern practice of deriving or borrowing stops from one manual appointment to bolster up the deficiencies in others, has been studiously avoided. The practice is diametrically opposed to all the canons of correct organ appointment, and no true artist would adopt it. Of the matter of the Pedal Organ we shall speak in due course.

In addition to the tonal variety, characteristic of the entire stop-apportionments, is the pervading and all important refinement of the whole scheme. This latter was dictated by the chief aim of producing a perfect accompanimental instrument, extremely flexible and expressive. At the same time, however, care was taken to provide sufficient means for the artistic rendition of solo or incidental music of a reposeful and tuneful character.

In this scheme the minimum number of Swell-boxes is introduced that is necessary in an instrument of three manual claviers, appointed in strict accordance with our System. Although this number does not secure the absolute independence of the several contrasting tonal groupings which is obtained by the introduction of the five Swell-boxes, as set forth in the preceding Thirteenth Specification; yet it has been found, in actual practice, to afford ample means for the production of both simple and compound musical effects of a positively inexhaustible number, and sufficiently varied and pronounced to meet all demands of an artistic and refined character in either accompanimental or incidental music.

There is one consideration that tends to favor the employment of the three Swells, and which the ordinary organist is likely to approve of; namely, the necessity of having only three Expression Levers, which are easily operated by the feet in any desirable combination, and in either direct or contrary motion.

In this tonal scheme, as in the preceding larger one, it has been considered desirable to inclose the entire First Organ in Swell-box No. 1. We do not, as a rule, advocate this treatment of the First (or Grand) Organ; but in the case of the true Theater Organ too much tonal control cannot be provided. It is desirable that the Swell-box should not be very obstructive to sound when closed, and should have the largest area of shutter-work possible. As nothing save the pipe-work of the First Organ is inclosed in the Swell-box, and as that is controlled by a special Expression Lever (No. 1), and can be thrown open at any time, the Division can instantly become an exposed Grand Organ; leaving the Second and Third Organs, with their four contrasting Subdivisions to be controlled in any manner by Expression Levers Nos. 2 and 3.

In the notes on the preceding Thirteenth Specification, considerable space is devoted to remarks on the five contrasting expressive tonal Subdivisions, which are there inclosed in five separate Swell-boxes, commanded by five Expression Levers. These remarks should be referred to at this point, for they are largely applicable to the conditions and tonal resources obtaining in the present lesser scheme. In this there are also five contrasting expressive tonal Subdivisions, but which, in strict accord with our System, are inclosed in three

Swell-boxes, commanded by three Expression Levers. Although independence is not so great in this tonal scheme as in that of the Thirteenth Specification, it is ample for all demands likely to be made on it, even by an organ *virtuoso;* and has the advantage of calling into play three Expression Levers only, thereby simplifying the control of the instrument considerably.

PEDAL ORGAN—In the remarks on the Pedal Organ in the preceding Specification, we alluded to the fact that in the true Accompanimental Theater Organ neither a large nor noisy Pedal Organ is necessary or desirable. This is especially the case when the Division is not inclosed and placed under tonal control. In the present Specification, the six carefully selected, complete, and independent stops, supplemented by the two derived octave voices, furnish an adequate Pedal Organ. This is further enriched by the Expressive Auxiliary, comprising three unison stops—String-, Reed-, and Brass-toned—derived from three manual Subdivisions.

The tones produced by the stops in the Pedal Organ proper are Pure Organ-tone, Free Organ-tone, Open and Covered Flute-tone, String-tone, and Brass-tone. These alone, or in combination with those of the Auxiliary, are sufficient for the production of basses suitable for any stops or combinations of stops in the manual Organs.

The wind-pressure for the labial stops should be 5 inches and for the lingual stop 8 inches. A copious supply must be given to the PRINCIPALS.

FIRST ORGAN—This Organ, which may properly be considered the foundation of the tonal structure of the manual Divisions of the instrument, comprises fourteen carefully selected stops, yielding Pure Organ-tone; Open, Covered, and Harmonic Flute-tone; String-tone; and Brass-tone. To which is added Percussion Bell-tone. The foundational Pure Organ-tone is supported and enriched by a harmonic structure comprising seven complete ranks of pipes of the DIAPASON class, properly scaled and scientifically gradated in strength of tone. The CORNET is to be formed of the following four ranks:—

TIERCE	3⅕ Feet
TWELFTH	2⅔ "
SEPTIÈME	2²⁄₇ "
SUPER-OCTAVE	2 "

This Organ is inclosed in Swell-box No. 1, and is controlled by Expression Lever No. 1. The wind-pressure for all the labial stops to be 3½ inches, and for the two lingual stops 7 inches.

SECOND ORGAN—Comprising seventeen complete and independent speaking labial and lingual stops of different analogous and contrasting tonalities, this Second Organ furnishes within its own appointment, what may be considered an Accompanimental Division capable of meeting all demands likely to be made on its tonal resources. These are very greatly increased by the grouping of the stops into two Subdivisions, contrasting in general tonality, and rendered independently flexible and expressive by inclosure in separate Swell-boxes—Nos. 2 and 3. The stops in the First Expressive Subdivision furnish Pure Organ-tone; Open, Covered, and Half-covered Flute-tone, of four pitches; and Reed-tone, of two pitches. The stops in the Second Expressive Subdivision furnish Free Organ-tone, including that of a DULCIANA CORNET, V. RANKS; String-tone, of two pitches; refined Flute-tone; and full Reed-tone. The tonal appointments of both the Subdivisions of this Second Organ are in accordance with the Tenth Principle given in preceding General Conditions and Principles of Construction and Appointment of Theater Organs.

The wind-pressure for all the stops of the First Subdivision to be 3 inches, and for all the stops of the Second Subdivision 2¾ inches. These low pressures favor liberal wind-supply, especially to the lingual stops.

THIRD ORGAN—Comprising twenty-one complete and independent speaking stops—labial and lingual—producing varied and beautiful voices, this Third Organ may, from certain points of view, be considered the most generally useful tonal Division of the instrument. Both its sharply contrasting Subdivisions partake of pronounced orchestral colorings, which are extremely valuable both in combinational and solo effects. Combined with the stops of the First Organ, it produces extremely rich compound tones of great variety, in which orchestral String-, Flute-, Reed-, and Brass-tones enter into artistic combination with Pure and Free Organ-tones, varied building-up Flute-tones, and a rich harmonic structure. Placing at the command of the organ *virtuoso* an almost unlimited range of refined and beautiful tonal colorings, either stationary in any desired degree of intensity; or ever-changing, under the expressive powers of the different Subdivisions engaged.

In combination with the refined stop-apportionments of the Subdivisions of the Second Organ, this Third Organ plays an entirely different rôle. It now becomes an invaluable addition to the accompanimental office of the instrument. In this office the Subdivisions of the Third Organ will rarely be used at their full strength, either in stationary tones or in expression. The Subdivisions are inclosed in the same Swell-boxes as are the Subdivisions of the Second Organ; the principle of contrast being observed in this association of the Subdivisions for the purpose of securing the greatest range possible in tonal colorings and musical effects, with the minimum of trouble in control. The wind-pressure for the labial stops of both Subdivisions to be 3 inches; for the lingual stops of the First Subdivision 5 inches, and of the Second Subdivision 7 inches.

FIFTEENTH SPECIFICATION

THEATER ORGAN

AUDSLEY SYSTEM—COMPOUND EXPRESSION

TWO MANUAL CLAVIERS

PEDAL ORGAN

Compass CCC to G — 32 Notes

PEDAL CLAVIER

1. MAJOR PRINCIPAL .	W. 16 Feet	5. VIOLONCELLO (From 2)	M. 8 Feet
2. VIOLON-BASSE (44 pipes) . . .	M. 16 "	6. BASS FLUTE (From 4)	W. 8 "
3. DULCIANA . . .	M. 16 "	7. CONTRA-TROMBONE (44 pipes) . . .	M. 16 "
4. BOURDON (44 pipes).	W. 16 "	8. TROMBONE (From 7)	M. 8 "

AUXILIARY PEDAL — EXPRESSIVE

9. BOURDON DOUX, 16 ft., derived from No. 18.
10. CONTRABASSO, 16 ft., derived from No. 30.
11. CONTRAFAGOTTO, 16 ft., derived from No. 39.

MANUAL ORGAN

Compass CC to c⁴— 61 Notes

FIRST SUBDIVISION — UNEXPRESSIVE

12. ECHO DIAPASON .	M. 8 Feet	15. CLARABELLA . .	W. 8 Feet
13. GEIGENPRINCIPAL .	M. 8 "	16. QUINTATEN . . .	M. 8 "
14. SPITZFLÖTE . . .	M. 8 "	17. DOLCAN	M. 8 "

SECOND SUBDIVISION—EXPRESSIVE

Inclosed in Swell-Box No. 1

18. BOURDON DOUX .	W. 16 Feet	24. DOUBLE TRUMPET .	M. 16 Feet
19. DIAPASON . . .	M. 8 "	25. TROMBA BATALHA.	M. 8 "
20. KERAULOPHONE. .	M. 8 "	26. CLARINETTO . .	M. 8 "
21. DOPPELFLÖTE . .	W. 8 "	27. OBOE	M. 8 "
22. OCTAVE	M. 4 "	28. CLARIN SORDO . .	M. 4 "
23. CORNET . . .	M. IV. Ranks	29. CARILLON . . .	Tubular Bells

THIRD SUBDIVISION — EXPRESSIVE

Inclosed in Swell-Box No. 2

30. Contrabasso . .	W. 16 Feet	36. Waldflöte. . .	W. 4 Feet
31. Gemshorn . . .	M. 8 "	37. Gemshorn Twelfth	M. 2⅔ "
32. Dulciana . . .	M. 8 "	38. Dulciana Cornet.	M. V. Ranks
33. Flauto Traverso.	W. 8 "	39. Contrafagotto .	M. 16 Feet
34. Violoncello . .	M. 8 "	40. Horn	M. 8 "
35. Violino. . . .	M. 8 "	41. Harp	Metal Bars

I. Tremolant

CLAVIER COUPLERS

PEDAL CLAVIER COUPLERS

First Clavier.............to Pedal Clavier, Unison Coupler.
First Clavier.............to Pedal Clavier, Octave Coupler.
Second Clavier............to Pedal Clavier, Unison Coupler.

FIRST CLAVIER COUPLERS

Second Clavier.........to First Clavier, Unison Coupler.
Second Clavier.........to First Clavier, Octave Coupler.
Second Clavier.........to First Clavier, Sub-octave Coupler.
First Clavier...........Sub-octave Coupler on itself.

SECOND CLAVIER COUPLERS

First Clavier..........to Second Clavier, Octave Coupler.
First Clavier..........to Second Clavier, Sub-octave Coupler.
Second Clavier........Sub-octave Coupler on itself.

ADJUSTABLE COMBINATION ACTION

Six Operating Thumb-Pistons and Release, under First Clavier—commanding combinations on all Stops and Couplers.

Six Operating Thumb-Pistons and Release, under Second Clavier—commanding combinations on all Stops.

EXPRESSION LEVERS

I. Balanced Expression Lever commanding action of Swell-Box No. 1.
II. Balanced Expression Lever commanding action of Swell-Box No. 2.

PEDAL TOE-PISTONS

Piston coupling First Clavier to Pedal Clavier—Unison.
Piston coupling First Clavier to Pedal Clavier—Octave.
Piston coupling Second Clavier to Pedal Clavier—Unison.

Other Toe-Pistons may be added for any special purpose considered desirable by the Organ Architect or the designer of the instrument.

NOTES ON THE FIFTEENTH SPECIFICATION

There is a decided difference, as will be readily realized, in the stop disposition followed in this Specification, from that adopted in the two preceding ones for Theater Organs; and a radical departure also from the dispositions which have been followed in all organs of two manuals hitherto constructed on traditional and antiquated lines. Further, a departure which multiplies to an almost limitless extent, and in an entirely new direction, the possible tonal resources of a two-manual instrument.

The organist or the reader, interested in this matter, will find in the Notes appended to the Tenth Specification, given in the preceding Part Third, a dissertation on this class of organ tonal appointment; fully explaining its peculiarities, its special system of tonal control, and general advantages. If not already read and properly considered, this dissertation should be referred to at this point.

It will be observed on examining the present Specification that although the thirty manual stops are grouped in three Subdivisions—one of which is exposed and the others inclosed in Swell-boxes—not a single stop is specially allotted or confined to either manual clavier: thus establishing the new principle of entire stop independence; which is far-reaching in its capability of producing vast numbers of varied compound tones on either clavier, under the powers of compound flexibility and expression, which specially affect quantity or intensity of tone, stationary or changing. We have just mentioned the possibility of producing vast numbers of varied compound tones on either clavier. Now, as a matter of fact and curiosity, we may add; if all the thirty manual stops are drawn on either clavier, the number of tonal combinations producible thereon, would amount to one billion, seventy-three million, seven hundred and forty-one thousand, six hundred and thirty-one.

Although the reader has been referred to the Notes on the Tenth Specification for an explanatory dissertation on the method of tonal appointment set forth in the Specification now under consideration; we consider it desirable, to secure connected reading and a clear understanding on important matters of tonal control, which do not present themselves for consideration in organs of ordinary construction, to substantially repeat certain remarks that have been made in reference to the disposition set forth in the Tenth Specification.

It will be observed in this Fifteenth Specification that there are only two Divisions named, the Pedal Organ and Manual Organ. The former is not subdivided, the Ancillary Pedal being merely an adjunct forming no part of the Pedal Organ proper. The Manual Organ has three Subdivisions clearly defined. The first Subdivision has its six stops planted on an exposed wind-chest, and is, accordingly, unexpressive. The Second Subdivision, of twelve stops, is inclosed in Swell-box No. 1, and is expressive; and the Third Subdivision, also of twelve stops, is inclosed in Swell-box No. 2, and is expressive. Notwithstanding this systematic subdivision, every manual stop is at all times equally free to both the claviers. In this fact lies the chief characteristic of the treatment adopted. According to this arrangement the claviers call for no special names and are simply designated First and Second Claviers. They may, however, be called Lower and Upper Claviers; or given distinctive names which have no reference to special tonal offices or characteristics; for, if used with the best effect, in these they will be constantly changing.

The arrangement provides means that the performer shall have at his command, for combination or registration, thirty complete and independent stops, of all tonalities and necessary pitches, equally available on each manual Clavier; the combinations being entirely independent—the Claviers being uncoupled. For example, the performer can have all the thirty stops—forming a magnificent Grand Organ—drawn on either of the Claviers; while on the other there can be drawn any stop or combination of stops derived from the complete manual stop-apportionment, which are necessarily also present in the Full Organ commanded, for the time-being, by the First Clavier. Under these conditions, the performer has under his command on the First Clavier *three distinct tonal powers;* one necessarily stationary and unexpressive, but dignified in character; and two which are alike flexible and adjustable to any desirable strength, but which can become expressive on the touch of the foot on the Expression Levers. These Levers are placed close together, in the usual position, and can be operated separately in contrary motion, or together in similar motion, by one foot, so as to produce simple or compound expression. One Lever can be so adjusted as to secure any strength of stationary tone in the stops drawn in the Swell-box it controls; while the other Lever can be operated so as to impart an expressive *crescendo* or *diminuendo* to the voices of the stops drawn in the Swell-box it controls. By the simultaneous and the alternating operations of the Levers by a single foot; and in any contrary manner, at the same time, by both feet, producing, directly, compound expression; countless impressive and beautiful musical effects can be produced while performing on one uncoupled clavier—effects of great value in the artistic rendition of music of an accompanimental or descriptive character, which are absolutely impossible of production on any organ designed on the old-fashioned methods of tonal appointment and control.

To render not only possible, but a very simple matter, the command of the entire tonal resources of the Organ; and to enable the performer to draw all, or any combination he may desire (out of the billion at his command), of the thirty manual stops on either one or both the claviers, it is only necessary to provide two corresponding sets of draw-stops—ordinary knobs, rocking-tablets, or pendant touches—disposed, in a precisely similar manner, on the right and left jambs of the Console, and within easy reach of the performer. The set placed on the right jamb brings all or any of the thirty Manual Organ stops on the First Clavier, and the corresponding set on the left jamb brings, in like manner, the stops on the Second Clavier. In Plate IV. is a Front View of the first Organ, constructed in accordance with our System of tonal appointment, in which the method of stop control that has just been described was introduced. In the open Console the duplication of the draw-stop groups is clearly shown. Although this somewhat old-fashioned jamb arrangement is fairly satisfactory, it is not the only one, nor is it, perhaps, the most convenient. The duplicate sets of draw-stops can be arranged, in similar order, in two horizontal and parallel rows, immediately above the Second Clavier. This arrangement may be preferred, from the fact that it places all the draw-stops in direct view of the performer who can at all times see the relative stop-combinations drawn on the claviers. This is a matter of no small importance, considering that the stop-combinations may be drawn from all the three contrasting Subdivisions of the Manual Organ, and, in all likelihood, differently affected by the operations of the Expression Levers. It is always of importance that the performer's memory shall be taxed as little as possible; and it must be recognized by the console designer that the operations of the eye are of immense value in assisting it. Color is a valuable medium of distinction, and, accordingly, may be properly added to the draw-stops to assist the performer in arranging contrasting tonal groupings on the different claviers.

As couplers are in all cases tone-builders, they should be associated with the draw-stops: but it is safe to say, that in no form of organ are they less necessary than in that just commented on.

PEDAL ORGAN—For a Theater Organ of the moderate size set forth in this Specification, a large or powerful Pedal Organ is unnecessary and, in some directions, undesirable. Refinement of tone is almost as important here as it is in the Manual Organ. On the other hand, it is very desirable that all the families of tone, common to the organ, shall be, to some extent, represented in the Pedal appointment. In the present Pedal Organ proper, Pure Organ-tone, Free Organ-tone, Flute-tone, String-tone, and Brass-tone are provided; while in the Auxiliary Pedal, refined and expressive Covered Flute-tone and Reed-tone are brought into service. The result is a very efficient Pedal Organ.

It is very seldom that in a Theater, room can be found of sufficient dimensions to admit of the formation of a Pedal Organ Swell-chamber; but when that is practicable, it should be attended to. The Pedal Organ proper, as specified, would gain greatly in musical value, if rendered flexible and expressive. The TROMBONES would gain immensely in importance and value.

Music Room in the Residence of the late E. C. Clark, Yonkers, N. Y.

That the scope and tonal importance of this Pedal appointment may be realized, it may be added that, employing the five complete and independent stops only, thirty-one separate tones and combinations of tones are producible, every one of which would be serviceable as a bass. Adding the three derived octave stops, and the number of combinations amounts to two hundred and fifty-five. Then, adding the three auxiliary stops, the number of combinations reaches the total of two thousand and forty-seven; all of which are practicable.

The desirable wind-pressure for the labial stops is 5 inches and for the lingual stop 8 inches.

MANUAL ORGAN—The general stop-apportionment of this grand Division is subdivided into three groups of contrasting tonalities; so arranged that while each group is largely independent in the production of special solo effects and combinations; it shall be equally serviceable, in combination with the tonal resources of the other Subdivisions, in the production of still more effective combinations, under the added powers of compound flexibility and expression provided by our System.

It will be observed that every one of the thirty stops of this Manual Organ is complete and independent; and that there is not a single stop duplication. These are matters of great importance in an organ of moderate dimensions, and, indeed, one may say in an organ of any size. Comparatively little resort is made in this Specification to stationary and unexpressive voices, for such are foreign to the artistic treatment of the accompanimental music desirable in the Moving Picture Theater. As has been said elsewhere; such voices are not without their value in compound-tone production; forming, as it were, a firm pedestal on which to base beautiful and expressive tonal groups. In the present scheme there are six stops apportioned to the First Subdivision, planted on an exposed wind-chest: these yield refined Pure Organ-tone, Free Organ-tone, Viol Organ-tone, and Flute-tone. Although this may seem a poor stop-apportionment in its position, it must be borne in mind that it is not designed to form a foundational Subdivision, but rather an integral part of a complete accompanimental scheme. Even when used alone, the apportionment is capable of producing sixty-three different tonal effects and combinations, every one of which would be rich, refined, and valuable.

The Second Subdivision, rendered tonally flexible and expressive by being inclosed in Swell-box No. 1, comprises twelve complete stops, including the percussion CARILLON. Being under control, a considerable strength can be safely given to their voices. Pure Organ-tone is properly furnished by the DIAPASON, of full scale and intonation; the OCTAVE, suitably scaled and voiced; and the CORNET of IV. ranks, graduated and regulated in tone so as to form a correct harmonic structure with the preceding labial stops. This combination, in reality, forms the tonal foundation of the entire Manual Organ, and is greatly assisted by the addition of the ECHO DIAPASON of the First Subdivision. Free Organ-tone is furnished by the valuable and beautiful compound voice of the

KERAULOPHONE—valuable on account of its coloring properties in combination with Open and Covered Flute-tones, and its body-giving and enriching tonality when added to the voices of the softer lingual stops. Rich Covered Flute-tone is amply provided by the BOURDON and the highly efficient DOPPELFLÖTE. This Subdivision is singularly rich in lingual stops yielding Reed- and Brass-tones, of double, unison, and octave pitches; all of which are of great value by reason of their being under perfect control both as regards strength of tone and powers of expression. The wind-pressure for all the labial stops to be 3½ inches, and for the lingual stops 8 inches.

The Third Subdivision is stop-apportioned to contrast, to as marked a degree as is desirable, with the apportionments of the First and Second Subdivisions. Its chief tonal differences obtain in the introduction of Orchestral String and Flute tones, furnished by the CONTRABASSO, VIOLONCELLO, VIOLINO, and FLAUTO TRAVERSO. These are enriched by the exceptional voices of the GEMSHORN, and intensified by the Free Organ-tones of the DULCIANA and its attendant harmonic corroborating, five-rank CORNET, which, when artistically made and voiced, is, perhaps, the most beautiful and generally useful compound stop in the modern organ. The two lingual stops—the CONTRAFAGOTTO and HORN—yielding refined Reed-tone and Brass-tone, satisfactorily complete the series of lingual stops in the instrument. The HARP, such as is made of metal bars, having sympathetic resonators, by The Kohler-Liebich Co., of Chicago, is an invaluable addition to the Theater Organ, on account of the richness and purity of its tone and good blending qualities. The wind-pressure for the labial stops to be 3½ inches, and for the lingual stops 7 inches.

In the preceding three Specifications only three Percussion Stops have been introduced—CARILLON, HARP, and CELESTA—but there are others which deserve the consideration of the tone-specialist. Chief among these are the Xylophone, formed of wood bars, adjusted over resonators; and the Marimba Harp, formed of Nagaed wood bars, also fitted with resonators. This Harp has an agreeable tone, which is neither so resonant nor of so combining a quality as that of the Liberty Harp. When the stop is not inclosed in a Swell-box, it is, perhaps, desirable to select the Marimba Harp; the tones of which are neither very pronounced nor sustained, requiring no damper-action.

In many Theater Organs constructed in this country there have been introduced a number of noisy sound-producing accessories, under the impression, it would seem, that their peculiar effects add to the musical resources of the organ; and that, accordingly, their use heightens the realism attempted in the musical accompaniment. The percussion instruments of the orchestra—Drums, Cymbals, Triangle, etc.—have been added, under the idea, perhaps, that an artistic and effective use can be made of them in the organ as in the orchestra. Such might be attained were the instruments under the control of separate and skilled performers; but what artistic, or even seemly, use can an organist make of such accessories, with their penetrating voices, while both his hands and feet are fully engaged, and his mind intent on the hundred-and-one demands of the appropriate accompanimental music?

There are other discordant and very objectionable things being added to the Theater Organ, which have the effect of largely destroying its claim to be considered a Temple of Tone; degrading the music produced thereon; and, at the same time, lowering the dignity of the organist who may otherwise claim to be a musician. All such vulgar and claptrap devices have been studiously omitted in the Specifications.

ADDENDA*

THE POSITION AND ACCOMMODATION OF THE ORGAN

Although we have written, at considerable length, on this important matter in our essays on the Organ, it is desirable that it should not be passed over without some comment in this practical treatise. Of necessity, we shall have to repeat much that we have said on it elsewhere, which is little likely to be seen by those who scan these pages, but we shall do so as briefly and as directly to the point as possible.

Alluding first to the position and accommodation of the Organ in Churches, the question may be properly opened with a quotation from an Article on the subject by the late Rev. Sir Frederick A. Gore Ousley, an able authority on the Organ and matters ecclesiastical.

"It is evident that there are several various and often conflicting interests to be considered in the selection of a proper site for a Church Organ. There are first the interests of the Clergy, who regard the matter, perhaps, from an ecclesiological point of view. Then there are the interests of the singers in the choir, who will view the question on its vocal side. Next we have the interest of the organist, who regards the position of the Organ from a comparatively instrumental aspect. After him comes the architect, who chiefly looks at the appearance of the case, and too often hates the Organ entirely, and who would fain conceal as much of it as possible. Lastly, there is the organ-builder, who knows how much better his instrument will sound with free space around it than when boxed up in a small chamber, and who feels that his reputation is more or less dependent on the decision as to locality to which those who have the management of the affair shall finally come. Here is, then, a fruitful source of quarrels and differences, of contentions and recriminations, of jealousies and revilings, of grumbling and discontent. It is

* Found among the papers of the late Dr. Audsley. Since the manuscript was discovered too late to have made possible introducing the article where no doubt the author would have wished to have it, *i. e.*, included in Part First, the publishers assume full responsibility for placing it here. J. Fischer & Bro.

really a matter of wonder that such occasions as the discussion of the position for a new Organ so often pass off as amicably and peacefully as we find they do."

The writer of the truthful and trenchant remarks above, in enumerating the parties interested in the proper location of the Organ in a Church of any Denomination, strangely omitted to mention the people of the congregation, who have to listen to the instrument under all the conditions of its proper and legitimate use, and probably its illegitimate use also.

With regard to the proper position for the Organ in a Church, it may be dogmatically asserted that where the choir is, there the Organ should immediately adjoin; so that the desirable combination of the vocal and instrumental sounds may be firmly established. All musical authorities will agree on this matter. As a corollary to the quotation given above, we may add the remarks by the distinguished English Architect, Mr. Sommers Clarke, the only member of the profession known to us who possesses a thorough knowledge of, and a profound regard for, the Monarch of all Instruments. He asks:—

"What is a church built for? This I will try to answer, hoping that others will agree with me. It is built as a place in which divine worship is to be celebrated, and worship it must be remembered is not the same as prayer. A magnificent musical service, in a magnificent place, is the highest exemplification we can give of divine worship; and not only the clergy, but the people are interested in it, and assist in some way or other. . . In arranging a church the ability to render magnificent worship should not therefore be impeded.

"There was a time when Organs and singers had migrated to the west end. When the body and often the galleries of the church were full of square pews, it really did not matter where the singers were situated, they were sure to have some one looking at them in their pride of place, as people faced all ways. We can recall the gallery, with its brown front made as it seemed of gingerbread, and covered with shiny treacle, a pallid clock face in the middle, and over it a nice cosy red curtain to hide the organist, being a modest man. The select company of singers, not equally modest, did not require red curtains. The Organ rose behind, flanked by tiers of charity children. Magnificent worship was not got in this way. We seem to have agreed, notwithstanding many divisions of opinion on religious matters, that this was not nice; and on looking back it was found that it states in the prayer book: 'And the chancels shall remain as they have done in times past.' I cannot go into the whole question now, it is one of history; but I think you will find that in 'times past' the chancel was the place where the music was rendered, and if not intended for the purposes for which we once more use it, it is difficult to understand why this part of the church was planned as it was. The more the subject is considered the more clear does it seem to me that historical continuity fix us to the chancel.

"But let us now conceive ourselves to be members of the congregation. If we are to admit the propriety of ornate worship, why is not the eye as well as the ear to be studied? The very fact that we now aim—as did our forefathers—at building a dignified church, and also decorating it very considerably, shows that the old prejudices are dying out, and that people do not now think well to have splendid drawing-rooms but bare churches. And, happily, ornament in a church is no longer considered a party badge. I contend that—at least to me as a member of the congregation with, as I hope, artistic instincts—a fairly large chancel, the choristers in it, and the music they perform therein, are all more dignified and impressive because the whole scene is before me, and there is complete unity in it. Break this up and you lose a great deal. I must not dwell longer on this side of the question; but I have said enough to show why, as I contend, the chancel is the right place for the choristers, and will in ninety-nine cases out of a hundred continue to be used as such. If the choristers are in the chancel the Organ must be near them."

We may add that we are in perfect accord with the views expressed above; and it may be presumed that very few, who possess any knowledge of, and love for, a fine and impressive choral service, will question the desirability of placing the choir in a favorable position, in front of the congregation; and locating the Organ immediately adjoining, and, preferably, behind it. The rear position is greatly to be desired, especially if it is central. A lateral position is much less desirable, and a divided Organ, located on both sides of the choir space, is in all cases to be avoided.

As the plans of churches, required for different forms of worship, necessarily vary considerably both in disposition of parts and in dimensions, it is obviously impossible to formulate hard and fast rules respecting the location and accommodation for the Organ. In churches already built, the provision—good or bad—made by their architects practically settle the question in almost every case: and we are compelled to say that owing to the very general ignorance in the architectural profession on all matters pertaining to the Organ, very inadequate provisions are made and very unsuitable places are provided for the reception of the instrument in the great majority of modern churches. As we have said elsewhere: "The Organ can go anywhere; any sort of a place will do for the Organ!" are ideas which have been only too rife among church builders, and only too often acted upon when the slightest difficulty with regard to space has arisen, or when peculiarities of site have called for special ingenuity and care. We firmly believe some church architects have looked upon Organs as necessary evils—things with which they have nothing to do, except it be to take care that they are made as little of as possible, and kept well out of sight; unfortunately this may mean out of hearing also. As a rule, an Organ to be well *heard* must be well *seen*—every obstruction to sight will likewise be an obstruction to sound.

Owing to the ignorance or carelessness of church architects in organ matters, the very name *organ-chamber* has become an abomination to organ-builders and all interested in the artistic development of the Organ and organ music. Mistakes, without number, have been made, and in numerous instances where there were no difficulties to overcome, and where properly proportioned and constructed organ-chambers could have been furnished as easily as insufficient ones. If the following conditions are observed in the designing and construction of the organ-chamber no serious objections can be advanced against its introduction; provided, however, that an Organ of inordinate dimensions is not crammed into it.

Firstly—sufficient floor space must be provided to allow the Organ to stand, preferably on one level, without an undesirable crowding of its parts, and with sufficient space in all directions to give free egress to sound and an easy access to all parts.

Secondly—ample height must be given for the Organ to rise to the most favorable elevation, while standing on the floor level; and to accommodate the largest pipes of the Pedal Organ.

Thirdly—ample openings must be formed on all sides toward the interior of the church, for the free emission of sound from the inclosed pipe-work. And the openings must be as high as the chamber, to prevent the locking in of the sound above the pipe-work.

Fourthly—no obstruction beyond open case-work and the displayed pipes must be placed before the opening or openings of the organ-chamber; and the design of the case-work and pipe arrangement must not be of too close a nature as to be seriously obstructive. Undue obstruction means resort to objectionable high wind-pressures and consequently coarse and forced voicing.

Fifthly—every precaution must be taken to prevent damp, and to secure an equable temperature within the chamber. Any external wall should be built double, with an air cavity between. All the inclosing walls and the ceiling should be covered with grooved-and-tongued boarding, dressed, tightly jointed, securely nailed, and well varnished: or they may be wire-lathed and well plastered, and subsequently oil painted and varnished. The floor must be strongly constructed and covered with thick yellow pine boards, so as to enable the supports and other portions of the Organ to be securely attached to it.

The position of the claviers or console is almost of equal importance to that of the Organ. On this question Mr. Sommers Clarke has spoken so much to the point that we prefer to give his own words to a paraphrase of our own. He says:—

"We all know that the Organ must have plenty of space about it, height above it, and must not in itself be crowded; but there are other points on which the opinion of experts would be of great value. One of these is the position of the keyboards with regard to the Organ and the choir. Custom, ruled to a great extent by expense, makes it usual to place the Organ on one side of the chancel and the organist close to the Organ. The organist cannot hear his choir very clearly. The half of the choir nearest to him sings away from him, the other half that sings toward him has the first-mentioned half intervening. He is generally so near the Organ that he cannot hear how much or little noise he is making (and my experience is that to be on the safe side he generally makes too much); and lastly, having the Organ and the voices so close at hand, he knows but little what the congregation is about.

"As far as the choir is concerned the rules of ample space, height, and width are as essential for the voices as of the Organ.

"What then would be the conditions of an ideal position for the organist?

"1. That he should hear his choir well.
2. That he should hear the Organ well.
3. That he should be able to see the choir well and also see the clergy who may be serving at the altar.
4. That he may hear the congregation at least fairly well.
5. That he shall have a tolerable sight of the nave of the church and thus be able to keep his eye on processions or other functions taking place therein.
6. We might add, that he should be able to use the Organ in connection with a side chapel."

The writer who has been considering the arrangements of an Anglican church only, adds: "Where all these combinations are to be found I do not know. In a parish church of good size they would be difficult of accomplishment. They are not often approached in a church of the first magnitude."

In churches in which there is neither a ritual chancel nor an altar, all the really essential conditions stated above can be, and, indeed, have been satisfactorily met; especially so in cases where an organ expert has wisely been called in to direct the architect of the church in providing proper accommodation for the Organ.

We may conclude this portion of our treatise with a few remarks respecting the proper position of, and accommodation for, the Concert-room Organ: opening the subject with what we said in our address before The Musical Association of Great Britain, on February 4, 1889, when the late Sir John Frederick Bridge occupied the chair. After a somewhat lengthy dissertation on Church Organ matters, we added: There is certainly less difficulty and diversity of opinion anent the proper position for the Concert-room Organ, and under ordinary circumstances the architect has no excuse for a bad provision for its reception. Great mistakes have, however, been made by architects who have displayed much skill and judgment in other directions. The hall of the Liverpool Philharmonic Society is allowed to be one of the finest concert-rooms, acoustically and architecturally considered, in the world, yet the provision for its organ is simply ridiculous. The instrument has had to be crammed into a narrow, low, and deep chamber, from which the sound of the buried pipe-work can only reach the room through the narrow chinks between the front pipes which literally fill up the only opening of the chamber. The effect is that of a bee in a bottle.

Nothing in the shape of a confined chamber should ever be constructed for a Concert-room Organ, for as this instrument is required for solo performances, and, in conjunction with the orchestra, for the accompaniment of the most important choral works, its voice should be perfectly free; and every tonal effect and *nuance* it is capable of producing should be heard with distinctness and at their true values.

The ideal position for the Concert-room Organ is that occupied by the instruments in St. George's Hall, Liverpool, the Royal Albert Hall, London, and the Salle des Fêtes, Palais du Trocadéro, Paris—advanced and free from obstruction in front and on both sides; but exceptional conditions are necessary for the adoption of this disposition. A recessed treatment is much more likely to be favored by the designers of concert-rooms, a satisfactory example of which is furnished by the Albert Hall, Sheffield. Here the Organ, by Cavaillé-Coll, is exposed along its entire width; light case-work and displayed pipes forming a screen which offers little obstruction to the passage of sound. The recess provided by the Architect of the hall is central and of ample dimensions, measuring about 38 feet in width by 11 feet in depth, and carried up to the highest portion of the ceiling of the hall. The Organ is advanced into the hall, having a total depth of about 18 feet. The instrument has sixty-four speaking stops, including a 32-ft. Pedal Organ of twelve stops. The console is advanced and reversed; but it does not occupy the most desirable position.

As we have already written so largely regarding all organ matters, it is practically impossible to avoid repetition, and, indeed, we shall not attempt to do so here. The proper position for the Concert-room Organ is above and in a central position in the rear of the orchestra tiers or chorus seats; but, there, it must not be unduly elevated so as to place any of the more sensitive portions of its pipe-work in a high stratum of the heated air of the room. Of necessity, the upper ends of the larger pipes of the 32-ft. Pedal Organ stops may have to rise into a high stratum, but they will not be seriously affected; and it may be possible, and even convenient, to dispose such pipes horizontally. The desirable method is to dispose all the manual Divisions of the instrument as much as possible on the same level, and that as low as practicable; and to spread the instrument laterally, with the view of giving all the Divisions an equal chance of being properly heard, even at their softest. But this spreading must not be carried too far so as to approach that abomination—a divided Concert-room Organ; of which there are some regrettable examples in New York City and elsewhere in this country; largely due to the ignorance of architects and others connected with the planning of concert-rooms or auditoriums. An organ of moderate dimensions, properly centralized, is greatly to be preferred to a larger one, cut in two and located in widely divided chambers, the alternating sounds from which are distracting to the sensitive ear. Personally, we detest the Divided Organ.

Beyond the exterior or front screen, with its displayed pipe-work, the several tonal Divisions of the instrument should have no serious obstructions, to the free flow of sound, in front of them. The displayed pipes should, in all possible cases, be speaking ones; and the manual Diapasons of 16 ft. and 8 ft., and the Dulciana, 16 ft., and other suitable stops of the Pedal Organ, should certainly find salient positions so as to assert their unstrained voices without loss of grandeur or purity of tone.

In concert-rooms in which there is a level and unobstructed stage, the organ should be properly arranged immediately in the rear; not hidden behind destructive screen-work or heavy, sound-deadening curtains: but, on the contrary, artistically displayed as an organ ought always to be. Whatever instruments may be brought on the stage, the organ will ever be the monarch. Yet in how many cases has the Concert Organ been huddled, out of sight, in miserable lateral chambers, and where all that visibly indicates the existence of an organ is a movable console on the stage. This is not the way to treat The Temple of Tone, however poor its structure may be.

Photo by Maurice A. Audsley

George Ashdown Audsley, LL.D.
September 6th, 1838 — June 21st, 1925

George Ashdown Audsley, LL.D.

AN APPRECIATION

BY

T. Scott Buhrman

George Ashdown Audsley, LL.D.

AN APPRECIATION

BY

T. Scott Buhrman

"I HOPE to live to finish my 'Swan Song'—The Temple of Tone. Then my work will be done."

But "The Temple of Tone"—Swan Song of the grand old man of the organ world—is posthumously published. Its Author went to his well-earned rest at the summons of death, since he would take a rest at no other's bidding. One lovingly-contemplated chapter remains unwritten. In its place the indefatigable worker had already supplied his publishers with other and more valuable materials not specified in the original prospectus nor planned with the inception of the book.

Thus it happens that the chapter on The Gregorian Organ is in the hands of the reader, while the other chapter upon which the Author's views had already been published elsewhere remains unfinished and is unpublished here.

"He worked to the end and just laid down and went to sleep. A wonderful ending and one always wished for by him," wrote his son Mr. Berthold Audsley, with whom Dr. Audsley had spent the final and so happy years of his life on a beautiful hill overlooking the Orange Mountains, in the Metropolitan suburb of Bloomfield, New Jersey. Sunday, the twenty-first of June, in nineteen hundred and twenty-five, he rose, breakfasted, and had lunch as usual with his daughter-in-law and his two grand-daughters; his son Mr. Berthold Audsley was at the moment on the Pacific Coast. After lunch he went to his room, a combined work-room and rest-room, and laid down to rest. He went to sleep, peacefully, comfortably. And in an hour was translated into the great beyond.

Truly "a wonderful ending" for a noble life of service to his fellow men in causes which profited him nothing, but enriched every life with whom he came in contact.

Knowing his habits of work we are reasonably safe in assuming that the final pages of his manuscript for "The Temple of Tone" were written during the morning of the last day of his life. On these last pages he answers the question of how his interest in the organ began.

"Leaving the old City of Elgin, in the north of Scotland, at the age of eighteen, with only a very superficial knowledge of organ matters, gathered from a small instrument of one clavier and four or five speaking stops—the only organ in the city at the time—and arriving in Liverpool in the Autumn of 1856; I took an early opportunity of attending a Recital on the Grand Organ, which had been installed, only the year before, in St. George's Hall; and which was presided over by the distinguished organist, William T. Best. A remarkable combination—the greatest living organist; and the grandest organ that had ever been constructed.

"My feelings under the unique conditions, and as I listened, almost spell-bound, for the first time, to the floods of glorious tone that poured forth from the hundred stops of that majestic instrument, can, perhaps, be imagined by some organ-lovers who may have had a somewhat similar experience. The Recital was a revelation; and I left the Hall with a strange feeling of elation, knowing that so long as I resided in Liverpool there would be three Recitals every week on that matchless organ—any or all of which I could enjoy. I did not—could not—realize what that privilege meant then, and would mean to me in years to come. Bear with me, good reader. I was then a strangely interested lover of the organ—eighteen years of age: I am now a still greater devotee of the Temple of Tone, at eighty-seven. It has been one of the great—perhaps the greatest—Art Love's of my long life. In it I have trodden paths on which no one else has cared to venture. I have toiled at tasks, for the good of others all over the organ world, in which no one has lent a helping hand, and to which no rewards have been vouchsafed."

It were unfaithful to the reader to delete the touch of disappointment. Let us proceed:

"In Liverpool there was then, as there still is, an influential Musical Association, widely known as the Liverpool Philharmonic Society, possessing a Music Hall allowed to be perfect acoustically. In this a series of high class orchestral concerts was given every season. In addition, another, equally fine, series was given every Winter, each concert including a Beethoven Symphony as the *piéce de resistance*. My love for high-class music induced me to attend all these concerts; and they provided most favorable opportunities for the study of the tonal resources of the Grand Orchestra, with their powers of flexibility and expression while under the direction of the baton of the Conductor. Then, with a somewhat similar study of the tonal resources of the St. George's Hall Organ, under Best's remarkable knowledge and skill in their display, it was not long before my mind became deeply interested in the problems which presented themselves in the comparison of the tonal powers and musical characteristics of the two great fountains of beautiful sounds."

And now we reach the last paragraph, the last word written by Dr. Audsley on the organ. A never to be completed sentence gives it prophecy but not finality:

"In comparing the tonal attributes and resources of the organ and orchestra, there will be found much that is interesting and suggestive. These attributes and relative tonal resources may be briefly outlined here, because it was their impartial consideration that led me, step by step,"—

—and that sentence was never finished.

What interrupted the most important and prophetic paragraph ever written about the organ? Dare we say the beneficent destiny that rules the aspirations of men, stopped the pencil with a comma and stayed the period? Was it anything so unimportant as the call to luncheon? Or was it the Author's eternally active mind that caught a memoried glimpse of an experience that needed to be first searched out and there recorded? Or was it the hand of death, coming swiftly with an overpowering sense of fatigue, to take him from the drawing board at which he worked, to the couch upon which he rested?

Page 438 of his manuscript for "The Temple of Tone" is as clear and sharp as the indescribably beautiful copy his hands prepared forty years earlier. That page was completed, but page 439 carried only five words—

"led me, step by step,"—

—with that prophetic comma that calls so earnestly to the organ world to complete the work the grand old man himself had started.

Dr. Audsley was born September 6th, 1838, in Elgin, N.B., Scotland. He became interested in architecture and was a pupil of A. and W. Reid, architects, going to Liverpool in 1856, where he worked under Mr. John Weightman, borough surveyor, on plans for the local Library and Museum. After a partnership with Mr. John Cunningham, architect of the Liverpool Philharmonic Hall, he went into partnership with his brother Mr. W. J. Audsley, building various churches, the Welsh Church, St. Margaret's, Christ's Church, and the Jewish Synagogue, all of Liverpool, and many fine residences.

He was united in marriage to Mary McLellan, with a good Scotch name. With true Audsley reticence, his son, upon whom this Appreciation has had to depend for some of its biographical data, modestly declines to add historical details which we hoped to include. One of his sons, Mr. Maurice Ashdown Audsley, is a photographer in Philadelphia, to whom we are indebted for the beautiful portrait of his father; the other, with whom he made his home in Bloomfield, is the artist-modeller who originates and executes in carved cardboard architectural models which have been exhibited all over America, some of which have been insured in five figures.

Hall Caine, writing in 1881, said: "Mr. Audsley is an architect primarily and above all else" but "his broad claims upon public attention are those which come of his exercises in other, if kindred callings. . . . His earliest notable essay was made in conjunction with his brother in a folio work, issued in thirty parts, entitled 'Cottage, Lodge, and Villa Architecture'."

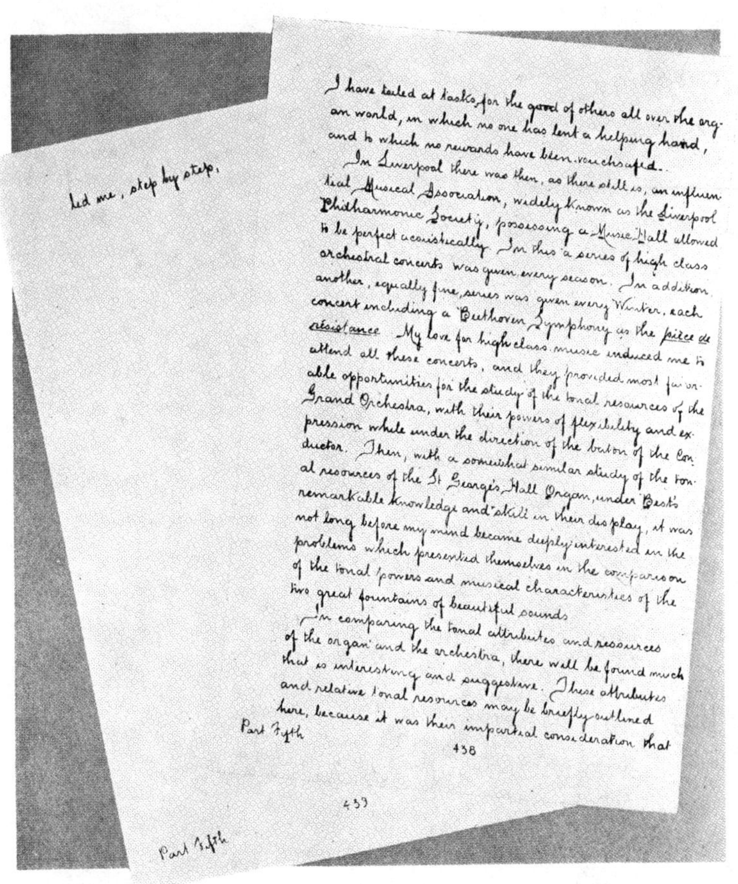

I have toiled at tasks, for the good of others all over the organ world, in which no one has lent a helping hand, and to which no rewards have been vouchsafed.

In Liverpool there was then, as there still is, an influential Musical Association, widely known as the Liverpool Philharmonic Society, possessing a Music Hall allowed to be perfect acoustically. In this a series of high class orchestral concerts was given every season. In addition another, equally fine, series was given every Winter, each concert including a Beethoven Symphony as the pièce de résistance. My love for high class music induced me to attend all these concerts, and they provided most favorable opportunities for the study of the tonal resources of the Grand Orchestra, with their powers of flexibility and expression while under the direction of the baton of the Conductor. Then, with a somewhat similar study of the tonal resources of the St George's Hall Organ, under Best's remarkable knowledge and skill in their display, it was not long before my mind became deeply interested in the problems which presented themselves in the comparison of the tonal powers and musical characteristics of the two great fountains of beautiful sounds.

In comparing the tonal attributes and resources of the organ and the orchestra, there will be found much that is interesting and suggestive. These attributes and relative tonal resources may be briefly outlined here, because it was their impartial consideration that

Part Fifth

438

led me, step by step,

439

Part Fifth

Facsimile of the chirography of Dr. George Ashdown Audsley.
His last written words, Pages 438 and 439, Part Fifth, The Chamber Organ, unfinished; intended for "The Temple of Tone."

His first writing on the organ was a series of thirty articles published in 1886 by the "English Mechanic and World of Science." Here was not the theory of organ building, but the practise of it; for in 1865 he had turned his gradually awakening interest in the organ away from problems of playing and to those of building an instrument for himself, which occupied his time for the next seven years, when the drawing room of his home was transformed into a work-shop from which gradually emerged a residence organ of such convincing merit that though containing only nineteen registers it sold as a used instrument for one thousand guineas at the same time the Regent Park organ of seventy-five registers brought only six hundred pounds. This original Audsley Organ, the only one ever built by Dr. Audsley's own hands, was sold when its owner moved from Ivy Villa, his London residence; at the present writing it is the property of Lord Dyzart, Ham House, near Richmond, Surrey, England.

The organ to Dr. Audsley was a perfected work of art. He could see it in no other light. Nor had he any sympathy with imperfection for any cause. This accounts for the marvelous mechanical perfection of his own organ, of his published books, of his written manuscripts, his drawings, his photographs, and even the packages which his own hands made to transport his manuscripts from Author to publisher. I had to buy a new pair of scissors of finest make, which I kept on my desk exclusively for his use in cutting string and adjusting paper for his manuscript packages, because the scissors I had used successfully for years caused him no end of annoyance in manipulation, good-humored annoyance to be sure, but annoyance none the less. I once chided him for the useless expenditure of priceless energy and time on details of unduly neat package-wrapping, for hand-printing long lists of specifications, and for similar evidences of that painstaking care that marked everything he ever did. Yes, he knew it was a waste of time; but, he sighed, "I can't seem to do it any other way."

There we have the whole biography of the man. He couldn't do anything that was not as near perfection as his marvelous hands and brain could make it.

In America he devoted himself to architecture as a profession. His Milwaukee Art Gallery, if my memory serves me rightly, was the architectural pride of his heart, though the Catholic Church of St. Edward the Confessor, in Philadelphia, was very dear to him, and the stalwart Bowling Green Offices at No. 9 Broadway, New York City, typified the solidity and nobility of his own character in a peculiar way. This Bowling Green office building remains one of the imposing buildings at the beginnings of Broadway, in spite of the towering structures of the new skyscraper world. Bowling Green Offices itself held the skyscraper record for a time, I am informed. The English Church in Grasse, southern France, is presumably his only architectural product on the Continent.

Dr. Audsley's greatest fame in the world of the organ came with the publication of his two volumes "The Art of Organ Building," published by Dodd, Mead & Co. in 1905. The perfection of drawing, the beautiful illustrations, the literary style—have never been matched in the realm of music literature. To one who has not examined these volumes, it would be impossible to describe them; to one who has never read them, it were useless to speak of their beautiful English.

His other organ books are "The Organ of the Twentieth Century," published by Dodd, Mead & Co. in 1919, in which the Author presents his advanced views on the artistic tonal structure of the organ of the future; "Organ Stops," published by the H. W. Gray Co. in 1921, devoted to a complete and masterful essay on virtually every register of the ancient and modern organ; and, finally, "The Temple of Tone," the very title of which came to him only in his maturest dreams.

"Mr. Fischer promises that 'The Temple of Tone' shall not be allowed to go out of print," he wrote in the last letter his pencil ever gave me; and around that statement there hovered the spirit of his greatest pride in his most cherished volume. Yet such was the caliber of the man that with him it was always his latest work that was his best, and in truth it always was; nothing of imperfection was ever done by George Ashdown Audsley.

Should "The Temple of Tone" have been "completed" by those closest to Dr. Audsley's heart and mind? The publishers decided against it.

The Prospectus included a "Glossary of all the Stops introduced in the Specifications of the different Organs" in the present book. It was never begun, and inasmuch as the Author's "Organ Stops" gives not only the subject material planned for inclusion here but also very much more, no attempt has been made to compile it from his manuscripts for repetition here.

Twenty-one manuscript pages were written on the Chamber Organ. The reader has already read the most important paragraphs from those pages, the others being introductory and largely repetitions of materials already published in other pages.

How could any other complete the plans of Dr. Audsley? Had such a step been taken, it would have been an emphatic violation of his spirit and wishes. It would be as easy to duplicate the "Sermon on the Mount" as to add anything of value to his unfinished "The Temple of Tone." Before we attempt to summarize the man or add one line to the books he has written we must know intimately every angle of his rare versatility. Once we stand in the presence of that versatility and have comprehended the consummate skill with which he wrought, we can but wonder and admire, not knowing which to the greater admire, his versatility or the artistic skill applied.

No words can adequately describe the beautiful coloring and tracery of the illuminated "Sermon on the Mount," which Dr. Audsley produced in collaboration with his brother. It is a very large book in page size, almost of newspaper size, with but half a hundred pages of wonderful coloring and line work, illuminating the full text of the "Sermon on the Mount." Then there are the four great volumes, "The Ornamental Arts of Japan," with one hundred plates, and "The Keramic Art of Japan," with forty-eight plates. Next come "The Practical Decorator," with one hundred and five color plates, "Polychromatic

Decoration as Applied to Buildings in the Mediæval Styles," in both English and French editions, with thirty-six color plates, and the Illuminated edition of "The Prisoner of Chillon," sixth in the Author's own valuation of the books he listed for me to examine first among his thirty or forty published works. One of his books sold for one thousand dollars a copy as the edition became exhausted.

Upon his "Art of Organ Building" he spent seven years; the drawings alone required the equivalent of two full years of a master draughtsman's time at eight hours a day; yet these colossal tasks were largely his way of spending leisure hours, and all of them had to be carried along with the strenuous architectural activities upon which he depended for his staff of life.

His most noted American organ was the St. Louis Exposition Organ of five manuals and one hundred and forty registers built at a cost of about ninety thousand dollars by the Los Angeles Art Organ Co. to the detailed specifications of Dr. Audsley, who alone was entirely responsible for the achievements this instrument represented apart from whatever superior workmanship the factory was able to evidence. That instrument was ultimately purchased by Mr. John Wanamaker for the Philadelphia store and has since been augmented to the world's largest organ.

Another important Audsley organ, built by Mr. Philip Wirsching, for the Catholic Church of Our Lady of Grace, Hoboken, N. J., represents the principle of compound expression in a way that made this instrument the object of many visits to the Church when Dr. Audsley sat on the bench with various of his friends, prominent in the organ playing fraternity, to whom he expounded in detail the aims and achievements of compound expression. This instrument also contains an example of a Compensating Mixture in the Pedal Organ; being unenclosed it is satisfactory only for full organ. For the residence of the late Mr. Eugene C. Clark, Yonkers, N. Y., Dr. Audsley designed both the music room and the organ, a duplexed instrument of twenty-two registers on each of the two manuals.

Dr. Audsley found the organ a stiff, unmusical, theoretical, impractical giant and immediately set himself to the giant's task of humanizing it in every conceivable artistic way. It meant nothing to him that organists claimed superiority for straight, flat pedal-claviers, or that builders claimed they couldn't build a fifty-thousand dollar organ for thirty. He was neither player nor builder, a neutrality he flung in the face of every opponent. He approached the organ from the single viewpoint of a love of the artistically beautiful; tradition meant nothing unless it contributed beauty.

When the American Guild of Organists made another attempt to bring uniformity out of the chaotic figures applied to console measurements, I observed Dr. Audsley for the first time at close range; we both were members of that committee. In the main, he was as silent as I; I had nothing to say but much to hope for; he had everything to say but nothing to hope for, for he was the world's greatest chronicler of the organ, its greatest authority, and what he could have contributed to console standardization would have been final—but he had nothing to hope for from the chaotic world of differences in which tradition-bound players and builders were then laboring and still labor. Not that the players or the builders do not long for better things, but that those better things cannot come, as Dr. Audsley never could understand, by the achievements of one man alone, but only by the long and tedious process of that evolution that marks time slowly and improvement equally slowly—but surely. Dr. Audsley was the soul of impatience when he was looking for the universal acceptance of principles he knew were incontrovertible; he was the soul of patience when writing a manuscript, searching his library, preparing a photograph, or penning one of his perfect drawings of an organ part.

Among the contributions which Dr. Audsley championed more than any other man, and for the present-day adoption of which we are indebted to him more than to any other, I declare the following and challenge history to deny him full and complete credit for every one of them:

I. Compound Expression—whereby pliability of crescendo is attained for the individual registers of any division, and by which, in its present trend of application, the organ is becoming more and more an instrument of musical expressiveness. Preceding Compound Expression came his use of more than one crescendo chamber in the organ; prior to Dr. Audsley's writings the organ had but one division under expression. Leeds Town Hall Organ of 1857 was the first organ in the world to have a second crescendo chamber, which housed a small Solo Organ of five registers.

II. String Tone Liberation—by which the organ world has in the past few years realized the importance of String Tone as the background upon which all the rest of the organ must play; the application in our Century of what much earlier generations had already experienced, learned, and applied to the orchestra. The culmination of the idea of String Tone importance leads to Dr. Audsley's Ancillary String Organ, with its multitude of ranks and stress on the off-unisons. The first String Organ in the world was specified by Dr. Audsley for the St. Louis Exposition organ.

III. Harmonic Corroborating Registers—whose importance is again being realized after a generation of neglect brought on by lack of artistic feeling in the use of these important coloring voices. The Harmonic Corroborating registers are at present undoubtedly the most discussed and accredited necessity for the true organ of the Twentieth Century—and the least accepted. The great barrier to their acceptance is that they add shadings but no independent solo voices to the organ, and until a very liberal appropriation is at hand the need is at present felt to be for more foundation and less superstructure. Dr. Audsley recognized this thoroughly; but he knew, as every man knows, that there were a dozen organs with more than a hundred registers, and not one distinctive feature in the entire specifications to make an artistic entity of any of them.

IV. Compensating Mixture—by which the laws of sound were harnessed to the task of artificially correcting the normal lack of balance between the high, medium, and low ranges of the gamut. Before he specified it for the St. Louis organ, the world had but one example, in Neu Ruppen, near Berlin, Germany; a crude affair after the pattern of the more or less screaming Mixture of a generation ago, which Dr. Audsley grandly loved to denounce—and did with a bitterness other men had learned to fear.

V. Timber Creating Mixtures—which used not the colorless Diapason family of pipes but adopted flutes and strings of marked color values, all carefully graded for pitch positions, for the production of Mixtures of distinctive tone qualities. The Timber Creating Mixture means the abandonment of black and white, and the use of the loveliness of colors.

VI. Individuality—that almost indefinable difference between two commonly like things, hardly applied to the organ before Dr. Audsley's time, and not even yet applied. It is a grave question if it can be applied literally, excepting by a brave man. As Dr. Audsley contended, the Swell of one organ is so much like the Swell of any other organ of the same gross size, that they can be interchanged with no consternation; and the Swell ensemble of any organ is so nearly a reflection of the Great, and the Choir a reflection of the Swell with a bright flute added, that individuality, personality, has not yet seriously entered the realm of organ building. This phase of Dr. Audsley's development was perhaps the last to receive his serious attention; certainly he has been able to convey to organ intelligence in general the least definite impression. Great pioneer that he invariably was, he in this particular merely points the way, but does not lead.

VII. Ancillary Organs—those wonderful creations of his imagination, those costly groups of massed tone that come to the instrument after it has already become a complete entity, to enrich it as by a distant choir, a secondary orchestra, a whole army of tones to be played at will from any manual, to be independent in crescendo control, merely to add a richness of artistic resource hardly comparable to any other division of the organ, and certainly not comparable to any other instrument or group of instruments. Among Ancillary Organs already experimented with by modern builders and players are the String Organ, the Flute Choir, and the Brass Choir, as found in West Point Cadet Chapel organ, Atlantic City High School organ, and, in the case of the String Organ, in various other instruments, all with more or less adequate resource—but every one in considerably less adequate perfection than advocated by the inimitable Dr. Audsley with his lavish disregard of costs. The great prophetic vision of Dr. Audsley had its most fertile employment because he, unlike builders and purchasers, was in no wise dominated by funds and appropriations.

VIII. The Audsley-Willis Pedal Clavier—unquestionably the most nearly perfected pedal clavier yet designed. Employing the epoch-making pattern of the Willis Clavier, he mollified its radiation, scaled its concavity to fit the swing of the average leg from knee to heel, slanted the keys to exactly conform to the thrust of the foot, altered the length and slope of the black-key surfaces, changed the length of white-keys from contact to pivot, and put the whole on a basis of that exact nicety of detail that marked everything he undertook.

Another achievement for which a rather careless organ world needs to honor his memory is the indefatigable research and compilation that resulted ultimately in his masterful book "Organ Stops," in which the technical is combined with the practical in a remarkable way, and where for the first time is available about all that can be known of the etymology of the names of organ registers, so flagrantly misused in to-day's practise.

But the chief error in judgment made by friends of the organ world in trying to rightly place George Ashdown Audsley in the realm of great men is that of considering him chiefly an organ architect, authority, and author. True, he was and is thus far the greatest and most productive the world has given; but to him it was—in spite of his burning zeal—only an avocation. How wonderfully he devoted himself to it.

Let us, in fear of misinterpreting him, consider his vocation and follow his other activities. Could any of us guess that the author of the Longman & Co. booklet on "Taste versus Fashionable Colours: A Manual for Ladies on Colour in Dress" was Dr. Audsley? Or that Dr. Audsley, great champion and master of debate, was the author of a book on color, of which the London *Times* said: "The glory of the book is the chromo-lithography for which, indeed, some new name ought to be invented, so unlike is it to anything which has been called chromo-lithography before; it can scarcely be surpassed by the most finished hand colouring"? For the production of this book, as also for the manufacture of many of his later engravings for books and articles published in the last decade of his eventful life, Dr. Audsley went personally to the manufacturer and stood by the workmen's benches as they executed the tasks assigned them at his bidding.

When the World War was threatening there was in the course of preparation the "Cyclopedia of English Pointed Architecture," in two volumes, profusely illustrated as only his pen could. The publishers, a British house, began work on the printing and manufacture of Volume I. while Dr. Audsley returned to America to complete the writings and drawings. But economic conditions in England demanded the conservation of every resource, material and human, and the book had to be abandoned by its publishers. It was never completed. The hundreds of photographic plates, taken by Dr. Audsley's own camera, were never printed. They are the heritage of another generation.

The amount of work his pen could undertake and successfully execute is astounding. But it is only he who knows the tireless research and preparation that preceded every literary effort who can estimate the unbelievable labors of this Trojan of authorship—and he can but wonder in amazement.

Dr. Audsley was bold in pen and mighty in championing his beloved art of organ building; but personally he was mild, retiring, kindly, and a true gentleman born. While he lived he avoided and even hated praise for himself, however much he relished it for the ideals for which he so mightily strove. A statement of his personal worth then would have been received with no gratitude. But George Ashdown Audsley was my great friend. To me he gave, when his life was closed and he could give nothing else, his entire collection of organ books and manuscripts. And to me and the work I represented he gave during the last decade of his life unstintingly of everything he thought he could give. There was no task he would not undertake, no token of friendship he was not ready and anxious to evidence on every occasion. In the surprising vigor of his early eighties, he visited me regularly; how delightful was his conversation, his wit, his sarcasm, his relish of the battle others dared give him; how earnest and self-sacrificing was his effort in behalf of the world of the organ. The grand old man had a sharp-cutting tongue that could and did flay his enemies. He thought they were his enemies because they challenged the progress of his beloved organ of the Twentieth Century, but secretly he held no enmity toward any man that I know of, and I knew his mind intimately. His arguments, in print, with the few brave men who undertook to debate his ideals, were sharp. But when he was commissioned to draw the specifications for and supervise the construction of an unusual organ, his confidence in the integrity of the organ builders was evidenced in every word of the long conference we had together on the possible and probable builder of the proposed organ. That builder would be a most surprised man were he to know the faith Dr. Audsley was evidencing in his sincerity as a builder of organs. Between written word and secret thought there was an unaccountable difference. He was of Scotch proclivities and his efforts were not to bestow praise but to incite to ever bigger and better achievement.

For two decades Dr. Audsley had sat regularly in his own particular corner of St. George's Hall, Liverpool, under the spell of the inimitable playing of the inimitable W. T. Best. Mr. Best and Dr. Audsley grew to be warmest friends, a friendship which carried Mr. Best's name and fame wherever Dr. Audsley found an open ear. Among the other close friendships formed by Dr. Audsley was that for Mr. Hilborne L. Roosevelt whom he considered one of the greatest of builders. He designed the title-page for the 1883 catalogue of Mr. Roosevelt and would have been insulted had his friend attempted to offer reward for such services—just as his masterful and intricate drawing for the front cover of "The American Organist" magazine was done solely as a matter of friendship and genuine personal interest. But when Dr. Audsley returned to his home, in which was then housed his marvelous residence organ, he was surprised by the arrival of a huge crate containing "the finest example of the Doppelflöte I ever heard," said he.

Mr. Roosevelt offered a specification for the famous Sydney organ which Dr. Audsley favored above all others, but the authorities decided it was better politics to purchase from a British house and the Roosevelt specification was rejected. One of the letters most prized by Dr. Audsley was that from his friend, the caustic Best. Mr. Best, himself equipped with a two-edged tongue, was on intimate terms with England's champion of the organ; perhaps Dr. Audsley acquired his "bitter tongue" from the example of his friend Best.

A few interpretations may be helpful to make Mr. Best's meaning clear at the distance of two-score years. First we have reference to Dr. Audsley's already blunt manner of saying things, which made him a scourge; the Megatherium was the accepted specification for the Australian organ, by Mr. Hill; the Royal College of Organists gets a reminder that banquets have been their chief successes; and finally the Unit Organ, ever the subject of Dr. Audsley's bitterest hatreds, gets a rap from Mr. Best.

4 Seymour Road, Broad Green,
Near Liverpool,
Septr. 27, 1887.

My dear Sir:

I duly received, and am obliged by your three Proclamations in the "Engineer" etc.; and hear that you are known as the "Scourge of the organ builders"—after the late Cambyses or Cyrus (father or son doesn't matter) named the Scourge of Gad.

I enclose food for your cat o' nine tails, being the Specification of the latest "Megatherium," destined for Kangaroo-land; if you already have a copy send this one back. I am afraid Tom Hill (who hatched the Frankenstein baby) has "gone wrong," and merely serves up 6 ordinary Church organs in the same Church House:—so blister him copiously. You ought, by the by, to get the "Musical Standard" of March 5th, 1881, in which there is a letter of mine on "Organ Construction" and in which I expound the word to the "College" of Boobies, I mean Organists, when they were busy with outside timber—belly-timber would have been more in their way?

In a week or two I expect to be in London (Langham Hotel) and should be glad to have a visit, as my time is too short to get out to Chiswick by Tubular or any other action.

Gt. haste,

Yours very truly,

W. T. Best.

P.S.—I also send you the latest in "Keeping down the expenses" in Church Organs. 31 stops spring out of the metal-tubs from 4! How about Birnam-Wood, Macduff? (many engravings required, nae doot.)

G. A. Audsley, Esq.

I have already included from Dr. Audsley's manuscript a statement of pessimism. It came from a man who had worked unceasingly all his life from ten to fourteen hours a day, and who at the time of writing was tormented with the realization that his days were numbered and his physical resistance gone. Yet the dream of his life for an organ built upon the Audsley System remained unrealized. It is a great pity that no purchaser could be found with sufficient wisdom to see the value of an Audsley Organ—and sufficient money to pay for it. Dr. Audsley had no such antagonism to the builder of organs as his published writings would indicate. We must remember that his birth and training were Scotch and English, and we need but to examine current British music magazines to see the manner in which men argue their theories in the British Isles. That manner transplanted into American journalism is out of its element and defeats its purpose. I could influence and persuade my eminent friend in other matters, but I was never able to convince him that the value of ninety-nine of his words was destroyed in the minds of thoughtless or careless readers—of whom the world will always have an abundance—by the one unintentionally bitter word that completed the hundred. It was easier to trust to the common sense and generosity of my own readers than to alter the life-long habit of expression of my distinguished friend.

"I am glad to know I am not hated by all organ builders, even if I am not loved. I would rather be respected than either," he wrote me. It was his incomprehensible earnestness. Can't we see it, and forget the rest?

He always wrote with pencil, though in 1922, I believe it was, he adopted the typewriter and turned out as fair a copy as an expert typist could do.

"I am writing this in pencil because it is likely to be of unusual length, and my skill with the typewriter is somewhat poor: the pencil has always been my right hand friend. Without it, my numerous books would never have been written."

I believe he almost loved his pencil. He was constantly referring to it.

"You must pardon pencil again; for ink somehow dirties my fingers, and steel pens have ways of their own; and the typewriter and I do not get along well together," which was more modest than truthful.

Dr. Audsley was a master of wit, but avoided it in his published writings, though in his personal correspondence he enjoyed the play of it. I had written him some encouraging news relative to his own writings:

"How you do pile it on when you are in a charming satirical mood. You call me a 'grand old corner-stone.' Old I am, and perhaps a stone of some kind; but as a 'corner-stone' I am rejected by the builders."

Again he answered a question with,

"You ask 'What on earth is an Oboe Gamba, and why?' I don't know, never heard of it. Where did you strike it? We shall be hearing of a String Flute next I suppose."

For the theater organ Dr. Audsley held high ideals and low hopes:

"I am quite prepared to be jeered at by the present school of self-opinionated and thoughtless theater organists; and shall be ready with more critical ammunition if they will openly dispute my contention. At present . . . they take all real enjoyment from any visit I make to Moving Picture Theaters. It is well I am not a professional musical critic; for it would be likely, if I were, that I should have a bad quarter of an hour at some street corner on a dark night."

The Audsley residence in London, adorned with its wonderful organ, was the scene of innumerable musicales; Dr. Audsley never tired of recounting those charming days. I want him to tell of just one:

"Dr. Pearce made his first acquaintance with Chamber Organ music, properly so called—solo and concerted—in my music-room in London; the only room in England, at that time, in which music of that nature and high class could be heard. On that occasion Hollins was at the Organ; Herr Schiever, leader of the Richter orchestra, held the Violin; and Herr Steudner-Wesling, of Vienna, was at the Steinway. That night Hollins played his remarkable improvisation of four movements, the finest work of the kind I have ever heard, not excepting Dupre's efforts."

After a life of service in the cause of organ building, Dr. Audsley wrote in one of his intimate letters:

"I have always enjoyed doing things for love rather than for money. Perhaps I have been foolish. I know wise people would call me so: anyway it is too late to mend."

About the time these quotations were written we were discussing a new series of articles for "The American Organist" magazine, for which the majority of his organ articles had been written.

"When you say that the series of articles ought to be done by me, you forget that I am eighty-five, and no longer the man I was a year ago, and I am far from well. No check you could send would dispose me to do what love would fail to command." Later he consented and wrote: "As you seem to have set your heart on my undertaking the Articles on organ-pipes, fully illustrated, I shall do my best to please you; perhaps I may be spared to do something in that line before I am called away." He undertook and finished the series.

In his letter dated September 5th, 1923, he wrote:

"To-morrow, when you receive this I shall be eighty-five, well on in my second childhood—going down hill! . . . Well, thank God, I have had a happy life, and, perhaps not an altogether useless one."

That was the last message he wrote in his eighty-fourth year. It is not the message of a disappointed man, nor of one in whose heart enmity existed for a fellow creature. He entered his eighties with confidence, happiness, and more vigor than even a young man should need. Then there was no talk of going down hill; it was still on the up-grade with him—his whole attitude reflected it. Only in the last two years did he make any reference to a vanishing vigor or an inactive memory, and even then the references were more the product of good humor than realization.

But as his eighty-sixth year came, there came with it a lessening energy that left its mark, and his happy but no longer weekly visits were tinged by the realization that the years, even if not the days, were numbered; plans then were conditional. Though that grand sweetness of genuine character never deserted him for a moment.

Would that we could live over again the last three years of our fellowship together!

Among his little-known activities and proposals were two of unusual note. He became Editor of a new music monthly under the title of "Musical Notes," which lasted for two issues and then passed out because of the financial burden connected with such a venture. It was strictly a journal with highest ideals. The second proposition was that he become an organ builder, and I have it on his own authority that shortly after he came to America to take permanent residence here, he was actively negotiating with others for the organization of a firm of organ builders, with western factory location, and himself at the head of the venture. For some reason or other, his plans never matured and he remained an architect.

Among the writings of the last decade of his life there must rank first his various articles and series of articles published in "The American Organist," New York; in addition he contributed a few articles and letters to "The Diapason," Chicago, and when the new quarterly, "The Organ," began publication in London he contributed a few articles to it.

Dr. George Ashdown Audsley was a genuine, a very charming, a great and gracious personality—one of those golden-hearted giants whose greatness passes almost unnoticed until the perspective of distance frames it in all its reality. Only the future can correctly estimate his contributions to the various fine arts for which he labored so silently but so earnestly.

His declining years were a Gibraltar of remarkable vitality. Never for a moment did he lose the mental vitality that distinguished him.

The resting place of his mortal self is Mount Hope Cemetery, at Yonkers, New York, to which he was lovingly escorted by his immediate family and a very few closest friends. His immortal spirit seeks not rest but the glory of continued achievement. It beckons us to-day as faithfully as it lead us yesterday.

May my readers bear with me in a final personal word of loving tribute to a very great and good man. He was my friend. I admired his lofty idealism, his great heart. He and I were associated, almost as father and son, in many a problem that was dear to his heart. If any act of mine in the editorial capacity in which I labored with him ever caused him any moment of regrets, I hope in the truer perspective of time that comes to all men, he has found it in his heart to forgive. And if any reader of these lines loves the organ as an instrument for the enrichment of human life, I summon him to a moment of beautiful reflection and gratitude to the mighty pencil, the untiring brain, the great heart of the father of us all in the world's noblest Temple of Tone, the Organ; to the man whose last letter to his friend and devotee, penned a fortnight to a day before his translation into the great beyond, closed thus, as it closes this tribute to his greatness:

"I have to express my appreciation of your kind wishes. I naturally wish to regain something approaching the health you have known me to enjoy; but it seems hopeless to be again what I was last year. I have been in the Doctor's hands, on and off, ever since last Christmas; and am now so weak and short-breathed that it is difficult for me to go up or down one flight of stairs. Thank God, throughout all I have been able to think clearly and write plainly. I hope to live to finish my 'Swan Song'—The Temple of Tone. Then my work will be done."

His Temple of Tone! First, last, always, his beloved Temple of Tone!

My reader, can such a man pass out of our lives without an inward sigh of personal loss, an outward and expressed token of affectionate esteem?

T. Scott Buhrman.

October 6th, 1925.